United Germany

United Germany

Debating Processes and Prospects

Edited by

Konrad H. Jarausch

berghahn
NEW YORK • OXFORD
www.berghahnbooks.com

Published in 2013 by

Berghahn Books

www.berghahnbooks.com

Library of Congress Cataloging-in-Publication Data

United Germany : debating processes and prospects / edited by Konrad H. Jarausch.
pages cm
Includes bibliographical references and index.
ISBN 978-0-85745-972-5 (hardback : alk. paper) —
ISBN 978-0-85745-973-2 (institutional ebook)
1. Germany—History—Unification, 1990. 2. Germany—Politics and government—1990– 3. Germany—Economic conditions—1990– 4. Germany—Social conditions—1990– I. Jarausch, Konrad Hugo.
DD290.25.U57 2013
943.087'8—dc23

2013005551

British Library Cataloguing in Publication Data

A catalogue record for this book is available from the British Library

Printed in the United States on acid-free paper

ISBN 978-0-85745-972-5 (hardback)
ISBN 978-0-85745-973-2 (institutional ebook)

Contents

Part III. Social Upheaval

Part IV. Cultural Conflict

Part V. International Normalization

Preface

A quarter century after the fall of the Wall, politicians, journalists, and scholars are still debating its chief consequence—German unification. On the one hand, during its twentieth anniversary the government led by the Christian Democratic Union (CDU) celebrated the restoration of the national state, the progress of inner unity, and the lifting of the Iron Curtain that reconnected Europe. In newspaper articles, television specials, and exhibitions, former dissidents also sought to recapture the courage of the opposition movement that overthrew the dictatorship of the Socialist Unity Party (SED) in order to memorialize "the peaceful revolution." On the other hand, opposition parties like Die Linke and the Greens denounced unification as a takeover of the East and decried the economic crisis that had produced mass unemployment, focusing on its negative consequences. At the same time, many displaced Eastern intellectuals continue to resent Western arrogance, cultivate a nostalgic image of the solidarity of the German Democratic Republic (GDR), and stress the lingering psychological divide.

In order to reflect these conflicting evaluations, this volume includes a diverse group of contributors who represent a wide range of experiential and analytical positions. Though there is some disagreement within each camp, the key difference between the optimists and the pessimists stems from each writer's role in the events, which tends to color his or her judgment. In spite of minor self-criticisms, Western commentators generally view unification positively, since they see it as a confirmation of the Federal Republic's democratic market economy. While appreciating many of the gains, Eastern observers tend to judge the result rather critically because they are more aware of the losses incurred in the process. Finally, American scholars have the luxury of viewing events from a transatlantic distance, which allows them to formulate a more dispassionate judgment. By discussing one theme from three different perspectives, this volume seeks to illustrate the diversity of experiences and analyses triggered by the end of the GDR.

Intended for an Anglo-American audience, this volume also seeks to provide reliable information and bibliography on German unification in order to help assess its progress. In contrast to other partial and impressionistic appraisals, this book is organized according to two additional principles. First, this is an interdisciplinary undertaking with chapters written by historians, social scientists, and cultural studies scholars in order to combine their distinct methodological insights. This diversity of analytical approaches and styles of presentation is intentional, as it represents the chief scholarly approaches to the problem. Second, this collection is more comprehensive than others because it addresses five important dimensions of the process: the transfer of political institutions, the economic crisis, the social impact on women, the cultural reflection of writers, and the foreign policy implications. Though far from being exhaustive, these issues ought to convey a sense of the multidimensional nature of the problems encountered during the transformation.

This book owes its existence to a suggestion by the publisher Marion Berghahn who wondered which of the competing claims about unification, the success story or the failure narrative, ought to be believed. Since the material is too vast for a single individual to cover, I recruited leading specialists in various fields in order to produce an interpretative mosaic. Though this is not a conference volume, David Barclay, Andrew Port, and the program committee of the German Studies Association selected four sessions on the topic for its Oakland meeting to discuss the initial versions of the essays. Dr. Thomas Goldstein provided translations of the essays by Gero Neugebauer, Heinrich Bortfeldt, and Rainer Land, while Dr. Eve Duffy translated the chapters by Ute Gerhard, Klaus Scherpe, and Frank Hörnigk. The Lurcy Foundation was kind enough to recompense them for their efforts. Finally, I want to thank all the contributors for revising their essays and patiently waiting for the production to take its course.

Since twenty-five years is too short a time span to complete a process as complicated as the unification of two unequal, ideologically hostile parts of a country, this volume does not pretend to pass ultimate judgment. Instead it seeks to present an intermediate balance sheet, based on essays that offer a mixture of personal experiences and analytical interpretations regarding the process and prospects of German unification. In contrast to the original focus of contemporary history on the Nazi dictatorship and the newer emphasis of the postwar period, this collection takes the caesura of 1989/90 as its starting point and ventures into what might be called the history of the present. By addressing the consequences of the overthrow of communism and the return of German unity, it seeks to open up the last two and a half decades to historical research. Since the record is not fully accessible nor the analytical distance sufficient, this book can merely make an initial effort to stimulate reflection and debate on how such a history might eventually be written.

Konrad H. Jarausch
Washington, January 2013

Introduction

Growing Together?

Processes and Problems of German Unification

Konrad H. Jarausch

In contrast to the accolades given to the "peaceful revolution" in 2009, the subsequent celebrations of the twentieth anniversary of German unification remained curiously muted. No doubt the political class was pleased with its achievement of reuniting the two hostile parts of the country in a peaceful fashion: "Never in its history has Germany been so democratic, law-abiding and social."[1] But in private conversations an introspective mood prevailed. Especially in the new-old capital of Berlin, colleagues were telling each other their complicated life stories in order to illustrate the gains or losses of the transformation after 1990. At the same time, political leaders pleaded for "sober patriotism" to be combined with tolerance, modesty, and solidarity. Rather than being obsessed with measuring the slow progress toward "inner unity," most public commentary treated unification as the new normalcy and mused about how to live with its consequences in the future.[2]

After four decades of Germany's division into ideologically opposed camps, it should not have been surprising that the process of coming together would be complicated. The accession of bankrupt postcommunist states to a successful Western-style country created additional difficulties. Since many Easterners were overwhelmed by the imposition of Western patterns, intellectuals like Hans-Joachim Maaz grumbled that their efforts to adapt were insufficiently appreciated. At the same time Western columnists like Arnulf Baring pointed to the ingratitude of former GDR citizens for the massive financial transfers, articulating a widespread resentment

---

Notes for this chapter begin on page 19.

against their sacrifices.[3] Academic opinion also remains split between pessimists who emphasize the noticeable gap in material indicators and the contrast in political attitudes, and optimists who stress the considerable progress in living standards and the basic agreement on democratic values.[4] Has the glass become half full or does it remain half empty?

One key issue in the debate about the problems of unification is the causal weight to be assigned to the disastrous GDR legacy versus the deficiencies of the parliamentary democracy of the Federal Republic of Germany (FRG). Of course, there is ample evidence pointing to the negative aftereffects of the SED, such as the ubiquity of Stasi corruption, the decrepitude of the planned economy, and the devastation of the environment, not to mention the psychological contortions caused by living under a dictatorship.[5] But one can find equal reasons to decry the depredations of casino capitalism, the excessiveness of the personnel purge, or the need to reform the FRG system, all of which are compounded by the frequent arrogance of Western advisors.[6] Hence, the complaints of both popular clichés of *Jammerossis* and *Besserwessis* seem to have a point. Moreover, their mutual misunderstanding is compounded by an underlying ideological polarization: while an anti-communist Right harps on the need to remove the noxious debris left by the GDR, an anti-fascist Left prefers to criticize the heartlessness of the competitive FRG.[7]

The scholarly literature is only moderately helpful in assessing the course and results of German unification, since it is itself part of the intellectual discussion. The well-funded social science effort to research the "post-communist transformation" in Eastern Europe that largely focused on the democratization of the political system seems to have fizzled out.[8] In the German context the transition was also overshadowed by the discussion of the progress of unification, which inhibited a comparative perspective. Due to the temporal proximity of the events and the lack of access to official documentation, few historians have so far dared to address the issue of unification. When they have written about the last two decades, as Andreas Wirsching has done, they have focused on social changes and the impact of globalization.[9] Interdisciplinary efforts to explore different facets of unification in essay collections have remained tentative because of the disagreement about how to turn their respective pieces into a larger mosaic.[10] Therefore a comprehensive assessment is still sorely needed.

Crucial for such an evaluation is the development of criteria that make the implicit assumptions about what constitutes unity explicit. To gain perspective it might be helpful to look at the precedent of the founding of the first national state in 1871, the degree of coherence in other federal systems like the United States, or the success of the transformation of other postcommunist states.[11] Such references suggest that the effort at "creating equivalent living conditions" (*Herstellung gleichwertiger Lebensverhältnisse*), mandated by the Basic Law, need not produce complete equality, but rather narrow the socio-economic differences. Similarly, joining disparate political cultures does not require agreement on every issue, but implies the need to respect other opinions as legitimate in debate. Crucial is the acceptance of a common constitutional framework for resolving conflict as well as the existence of a shared sense of cultural identity that allows a plurality of views. With these qualifications in mind, the following remarks will examine five policy areas in order to ascertain the successes and failures of the unification process during its first two decades.

Political Process

The chief political issue in the debate is the stability of democracy in the new states in the East. Even cautious Western commentators, like Gero Neugebauer, who concede differences in the approval of democracy, point to the establishment of a national party system, the realignment of conflict structures, and the push for more participation as indicators of a growing consensus. More skeptical Eastern observers like Heinrich Bortfeldt stress the asymmetrical character of unification, the disappointment of the civic movement in the "rule of law," the permanent minority position of the smaller third of the country, and the discrediting of the GDR through media scandalization, which makes Easterners "feel like strangers in their new home." Stressing a comparative perspective, American scholars like Helga Welsh challenge these simple dichotomies by pointing toward the important role of the unification discourse in the media as focused on the elusive concept of inner unity, which highlights the process' shortcomings rather than its accomplishments. Such divergent evaluations raise the question: how deeply rooted is democracy in the East and the West?

On a formal level the incorporation of East Germany into the expanded Federal Republic has been remarkably smooth, since it was already prepared by the peaceful revolution. Led by dissidents, the mobilization of the masses in large scale demonstrations produced pressure for a redemocratization of the GDR during the fall of 1989: the bloc parties began to emancipate themselves, the pseudo-parliament (Volkskammer) started to have contested votes, and the SED-led government transformed itself into a real coalition that even accepted opposition ministers without portfolio, thereby infusing the existing constitutional structures with real political life. The banners, slogans, assemblies, and discussions of the civic movement produced a moment of intoxicating politicization in which citizens vented their frustration and participated in decision making through the numerous roundtables. However, this popular movement did not create new institutions but rather culminated in the election campaign of March 1990 that restored the functioning of parliamentary democracy in the crumbling GDR.[12]

By eliminating the alternative of an all-German constitutional convention, accession according to paragraph 23 of the Basic Law mandated the transfer of existing FRG institutions to the East. The political parties that had cooperated in the first free elections began to merge during the summer of 1990, although their membership structure continued to differ. In preparation for incorporation, the de Maizière government also dissolved the administrative districts and restored the Länder that had existed up to 1952 in order to fit East Germany into the federal structure. At the same time, the cities, towns, and rural areas reclaimed their self-government, providing a local underpinning of democratic administration. Finally, independent interest groups and organizations such as trade unions and employers' associations also spread to the East, taking the place of the SED's "transmission belts" and reviving civil society. Both revolutionary experience and Western aid propelled this transformation process, quickly substituting Western structures during the self-dissolution of the GDR.[13]

For all of its speed, the results of this political import have been somewhat ambiguous because it has taken time for East Germans to grow into the new institutions. To begin with, in March 1990 the dissidents who had led the democratic awakening were relegated to the parliamentary margin due to their reluctance about unification and their amateurish campaign style. At the same time, the postcommunist Party of Democratic Socialism (PDS) succeeded in capitalizing on Eastern resentment against Western tutelage to establish itself as strong regional party with participation in some state governments. Moreover, the moderate Social Democratic Party (SPD) paid for its unwillingness to accept reform Communists with weaker representation in the new states than in the West. Even in the victorious CDU, East German members found themselves in a permanent minority position, muting their voices in decision making. Very few Easterners like Angela Merkel or Joachim Gauck therefore ascended to national prominence. Even the creation of an Eastern caucus in the Bundestag and Bundesrat could only partially counteract Western paternalism.[14]

The achievement of "inner unity" in political culture has also been lagging, since East Germans often feel like second-class citizens whose lives are insufficiently appreciated. The critique of the SED dictatorship and the scandalization of Stasi collaboration have created a widespread feeling of disparagement, because former GDR citizens see themselves as more closely identified with the political system than the privatized people in the FRG. As a result, representative surveys reveal more skepticism of democracy with only every third respondent satisfied with its current form. At the same time only every fourth East German favors the social market economy. Moreover, in comparing individual freedom with social solidarity, the new citizens choose the latter considerably more often than do West German respondents. While most East Germans consider their personal economic situation to be positive, they tend to be more pessimistic about the general outlook for the future. Though only one-eighth want the GDR back, this discrepancy reveals a considerably weaker attachment to parliamentary democracy in the East than in the West.[15]

In a formal sense the political transformation has been successful, as it avoided the conflict and turbulence usually associated with a fundamental change in systems. Within a relatively short period of time, East Germans could enjoy the fruits of a proven order—such as the rule of law and a competent administration—based on West German patterns transferred wholesale. But this regulated transition to a ready-made system also exacted a considerable price in foreclosing alternatives and blocking potential exceptions that would have preserved some presumed Eastern advantages. In the process, not only were discredited SED elites replaced, but the new citizens were relegated to the role of passive learners rather than active creators. Compared to the transition in other East Central European states, the fundamental asymmetry of a discredited system joining a successful concern left little room for newcomers to find their own way. While the subsequent metamorphosis of the PDS into the Left Party in the West signals the arrival of a five-party system on a national level, the embrace of democracy remains a work in progress.[16]

In psychological terms, the unification process has also left a series of scars which will take time to heal. In contrast to the self-determined transition of the East European neighbors, the transformation of the GDR has been largely managed by West Germans, fitting the five new federal states into the existing FRG pattern without sufficient attention to their experiences before and during the peaceful revolution. Hence many new citizens have felt overwhelmed and resent having exchanged their Communist masters for Western politicians, administrators, and journalists. Though some civil society groups sought to initiate an East-West dialogue, President Richard von Weizsäcker's advice to listen to each other's life stories has all too often been ignored. Even after realizing some of the advantages of the rule of law, many East Germans still feel like second-class citizens, because their struggles were not sufficiently appreciated.[17] Only by seizing the opportunities created by unification is the younger generation likely to overcome this difference, based on wounded pride.

Economic Problems

In the economic realm, the discussion continues to revolve around the reasons for the underperformance of the Eastern economy: was it the legacy of Communist mismanagement or the ruthlessness of the capitalist takeover? West German analysts like Wolfgang Seibel tend to stress the importance of Eastern wishes for currency parity as well as union demands for equality of wages, while arguing that the Trusteeship Agency (Treuhandanstalt), founded by the Modrow government, was a success since its privatization policy represented an institutional solution to an unprecedented problem of conversion. In contrast, East German intellectuals like Rainer Land still regret the failure of the potential alliance between SED reformers and civic activists that led to the Western domination of unification, which resulted in the collapse of many GDR companies and the creation of a fragmented economy that shows promise in some complementary areas. Ironically, the American historian Jonathan Zatlin is actually more critical of "putting the monetary cart before the economic horse" and of the lack of countercyclical spending. Will East Germany remain a Mezzogiorno or is it on the way to recovery at last?

The economics of unification proved surprisingly problematic, since the GDR factories were more decrepit than anyone realized. The key decisions about the form of the transition were already made with the offer of a currency, custom, and social union that recalled the nineteenth-century *Zollverein* as a step toward incorporation into a unified Germany. Critics often forget that it was pressure by the East German citizens, expressed by the slogan "if the DM does not come to us, we will go to it," that forced an excessive conversion rate of 1:1.5, though actual buying power was closer to 1:4.4. The impending state bankruptcy, continuing migration to the West, and limited window of diplomatic opportunity left decision makers little choice, even if many economists, like Bundesbank chief Karl Otto Pöhl, would have preferred a more gradual transition. Similarly, the Trusteeship Agency, first proposed by the civic movement and only then transformed into a privatization device, did not make a profit from disposing of publicly owned property but rather had to sell companies at an enormous loss.[18]

Instead of generating "flourishing landscapes," as promised by Chancellor Kohl, the introduction of the social market economy produced a veritable "unification crisis" in the new states.[19] The insufficiently understood reason for the adjustment shock was a double transition, from plan to market and from protection to global competition, that exposed the inherent weakness of Günter Mittag's *Kombinate*. Since labor productivity in the East was only about one-third of that in the West, most Eastern goods were suddenly priced out of the market. Moreover, the previous barter trade with the East European neighbors collapsed due to the conversion of the Council for Mutual Economic Assistance (COMECON) to convertibility, since these states could now buy cheaper and better products on the world market. At the same time, East German consumers contributed to the disaster by rejecting their own goods for the more attractively packaged Western wares that were only sometimes of superior quality. The result was a massive deindustrialization that shut down about two-thirds of East German factories within the first two years.[20]

The consequences of the unification shock for the Eastern standard of living were paradoxical, since they combined job losses with gains in consumption. The initial collapse of Fordist production and its replacement with less manpower-intensive industries led to a drop in the work force from 8.9 to 5.8 million. Since more Easterners than Westerners wanted to work, the result was structural unemployment at twice the Western rate that peaked in 1997 and again in 2004/05 at over 19 percent, two times the level in the old FRG. This figure did not even count people parked in retraining schemes (the infamous "ABM positions") or sent into early retirement, which affected women more than men. The Western social security systems cushioned these job losses with massive transfers to new clients who had never paid into them. Propelled by union pressure, Eastern wages quickly rose to about four-fifths of the Western rate, increasing buying power in the new states. Social protests were largely avoided, since Easterners were soon able to afford the same level of consumer goods as their Western cousins.[21]

Though initially dynamic, the subsequent catch-up process eventually stalled, creating the specter of a German Mezzogiorno permanently left behind. To jump-start the economy, the Kohl cabinet launched a German Unity Fund and a 7.5 percent surcharge on the income tax that financed the transfer of about 2 trillion Euros to the new states. These funds repaired infrastructure, renovated housing, and provided a safety net, triggering a rapid growth until the late 1990s. But after the IT bubble burst, East German production no longer expanded, freezing the gap in productivity at three-quarters and production levels at four-fifths of those of the old FRG. While agriculture was highly successful due to the larger unit size inherited from the collective farms (LPG), many newly created small businesses failed, and much of the modernized manufacturing remained under Western control. Deindustrialized towns like Hoyerswerda and many rural areas lost population when young women, especially, moved away. Yet around other cities like Leipzig, Dresden, Jena, and Berlin, growth continued, showing not just decline but also a new dynamism.[22]

The prospects for the East German economy therefore remain unsettled, pointing toward a fragmented pattern of contradictory developments.

Part of this disappointment must be attributed to the legacy of the GDR, which was much worse than the official claim of being the tenth leading industrial state suggested. But the severity of the adjustment was also a product of the triumph of politics over economics, since the desire of the East German people for instant access to Western prosperity produced decisions like implementing an excessive conversion rate and a rapid rise in wages that undercut their capacity to compete. While aggregate statistics show a perpetuation of the East-West gap, more differentiated regional data reveal a contradictory pattern of decline in some areas and actual growth in others. If the self-fulfilling prophecy of further contraction is to be stopped, it will be necessary to reverse the negative image perpetuated by the media and to tell more of the Eastern success stories. In terms of labor flexibility, the East is already ahead of the West in adjusting to global competition.[23]

The negative publicity in the national media about Eastern stagnation has exaggerated the difficulties of economic adjustment. Aggregate statistics that show a continuing gap in income and productivity mask the decline of some Eastern towns like Brandenburg that have lost key industries like steel and the rise of other neighboring cities like Potsdam that are already surpassing troubled areas in the West. While the East is still losing population, especially in outlying rural areas, its lower wage levels and more flexible labor contracts have retained some industries and favored other start-ups. No doubt, the collapse of the *Kombinate* and the rapid privatization have shifted ownership of large companies to the old FRG, but a new *Mittelstand* of smaller innovative firms is gradually emerging in the new states, not only supplying the big manufacturers, but also becoming more competitive in exporting products to the neighboring countries.[24] Only when such hopeful developments outweigh the continuing contraction in other areas will the East begin to prosper again as a whole.

Social Upheaval

More diffuse in its issues, the social debate turns on the impact of different experiences on East-West communication that have complicated the process of the East and West adapting to each other. Taking as an example women as potential losers of unification, Western feminists like Ute Gerhard still resent their exclusion from political decisions and ponder whether their own gender theory, which stressed that "the private is political," contributed to the misunderstandings with Eastern advocates of pragmatic equality. Eastern feminists like Ingrid Miethe point to the practical emancipation of GDR women, who are proud of reconciling work and family, which made them resent Western discursive dominance and produced recriminations rather than mutual understanding. American observers like Myra Marx Ferree take a comparative view instead, stressing that through global influences and European Union (EU) pressure some of the GDR solutions like public child care are coming back into the debate. The initial lack of understanding among feminists raises the more general question: how is the surprisingly difficult process of social convergence actually to succeed?

The social transformation yielded much frustration, since expectations of sameness at the time of the fall of 1989 quickly turned into realizations of difference due to decades of separate development. As the pictures of people dancing on the Wall show, the initial encounters were often joyful, with strangers embracing each other, because they allowed the resumption of personal ties that had been severed for so long. But the removal of the barrier also revealed how much Germans on both sides of the Iron Curtain had grown apart in their lifestyles and values due to their communist or democratic experiences. Moreover, the meeting was not of equals, since the Westerners were politically and economically dominant, relegating Easterners to the role of poor relations.[25] Even among groups like athletes or academics, who were engaged in similar pursuits, there were deep misunderstandings, since the different contexts had produced contrasting experiences that hampered communication and cooperation. Social responses to unification ranged from defensive withdrawal to eager exploration of difference.

Coping with the Westernization of Eastern society required a wrenching adjustment from collectivism to individualism in outlook and behavior. With the end of the GDR the vaunted *Kollektiv* of the tutelary state, mass organization membership, and institutions like polyclinics collapsed, removing a protective cocoon. Suddenly, the fresh FRG citizens were faced with new responsibilities, having to fill out tax returns or life insurance forms and needing to resist the blandishments of consumer credit, lest they bankrupt themselves. Much of their repertoire of coping mechanisms became worthless, since personal connections such as "vitamin B" (*Beziehungen*) which made negotiating the rules of a dictatorial system possible, were no longer useful. In contrast to the Eastern response of not wanting to stick out, post-1968 Western behavior put a premium on self-assertion and lifestyle dramatization—routines that seemed strange and irrelevant. Autobiographical accounts like Jana Hensel's or Ingo Schulze's stories describe the difficulties of negotiating this unknown terrain in which different rules applied.[26]

As in other historical upheavals, German unification turned social hierarchies upside down, creating both winners and losers in the process.

Predictably enough, the overthrow of the SED system cost the party *Nomenklatura,* officers in the People's Army and the State Security Service, and other regime-related personnel their privileges. Also displaced in the institutional transformation were many intellectuals, dismissed for political involvement, incompetence, or lack of funding, who then became spokespeople for Eastern victimization.[27] At the same time former regime opponents, active members of the churches, and surviving bourgeois professionals who had suffered from restrictions under the SED dictatorship now had a chance to advance into leadership positions previously denied to them. While the middle generation had the hardest time adjusting, people close to retirement age profited from the higher pensions and the young had new opportunities to learn and travel. A new elite of successful politicians, businessmen, and professionals therefore faced an older group of resentful victims of the transformation.[28]

The transfer of Western institutions was both necessary and problematic, because the Eastern arrangements had to be fit into the national pattern, yet some of the imports were themselves already in need of reform. For instance, the huge GDR Academy of Sciences was broken up in order to make its institutes compatible with the decentralized structure of the Max-Plank, Helmholtz, and Leibniz Societies of the FRG, setting free superfluous personnel. Similarly, the democratic restructuring of the universities that made them internationally competitive again was achieved at the cost of dismissing many Eastern faculty and hiring Western newcomers. During this housecleaning, too many SED-tainted institutions like youth centers or culture houses, which might have been worth preserving, were shut down. Only a few GDR legacies, such as the secular *Jugendweihe* that replaced a religious confirmation, survived. Ironically, a decade later some of the dissolved institutions like walk-in clinics or infant care centers returned in new guises as a result of overdue all-German or EU-inspired reforms.[29]

Has the enlarged Federal Republic therefore, as critics maintain, become "one state with two societies"? On the one hand, some social indicators point to a lingering difference: East Germans tend to be less well off; their poverty rate was 17 percent in contrast to the Western figure of 12 percent in 2005. Initially, Eastern women also engaged in a birth strike, dropping the reproduction rate even below that of their Western counterparts. Though 1.5 million Westerners have moved East since 1990, fifty thousand more Easterners migrate westward each year, depopulating entire areas. But on the other hand, life expectancy has increased by about a decade since unification, indicating that East Germans have become much healthier. Moreover, household income is approaching Western levels so that levels of ownership of consumer durables have become virtually identical. As a result, survey scores with regard to life satisfaction and other indicators are approximating each other in East and West. The evidence therefore points toward a narrowing of differences in a long-term process of halting integration.[30]

A case in point is the negative impact of the transformations unification has triggered for women. Western feminists found their agenda stopped in its tracks, because the task of helping the East trumped increasing gender equality. Many Eastern women, nine-tenths of whom worked, also found themselves unemployed, because the struggling companies shed the social services and white-collar jobs in which they concentrated. Moreover, the abortion controversy threatened what had been a practical right in the GDR since 1972. In contrast, gains such as freedom to travel, easier access to supplies, and better provision of fashionable consumer goods failed to outweigh the reduction of child-care services. Moreover, Western autonomous feminists, bent on an ideological agenda, and Eastern women's activists, intent on improving their daily lives, talked at cross-purposes. Only the realization that women in the old and the new states were equally affected by the new "risk society" and pressure from the EU improved communication so as to help develop a common response to these challenges.[31]

Cultural Conflict

The acrimonious cultural debates generally focus on the loyalty of prominent East German writers to the SED dictatorship and their criticism of the confusing pop culture of the Federal Republic. By looking at poems, short stories, and novels, Western scholars like Klaus R. Scherpe explain the demise of GDR literature as a result of the loss of the privileged role of its authors, the failure of their socialist ideology, and their lack of understanding of the rules of consumer culture. East German academics like Frank Hörnigk instead resent the Western discrediting of their own past and recount shocking experiences of displacement of Eastern intellectuals from their positions, rejecting the superficial condemnation of GDR literature which has created deep alienation between East and West. North American *Germanisten* like Frank Trommler offer a broader Cold War framework to account for the collapse of the Eastern "reading culture" due to the loss of its therapeutic function in the Western media landscape. These interventions raise the troubling question: does this cultural commentary merely reflect personal disappointments or does it offer a deeper understanding of the historic upheaval?

The cultural response to the democratic awakening was so ambivalent because intellectuals who had spearheaded the protests felt betrayed by the aroused citizens who rejected their dreams for a Third Way. The struggle against censorship led to an outpouring of wit in shouted slogans, funny placards, and critical statements—venting decades of frustration over the limitation of free speech by the SED. Rock musicians, actors, and writers were some of the first calling for the lifting of censorship and discrediting the ruling old men by satire. But with the dissolution of institutions like the Writers' League, which had guaranteed their income and other privileges, state support for culture vanished, so that authors now found themselves at the mercy of an unknown market for cultural production. Moreover, the revival of open debate robbed them of their special position within society where they served as a substitute channel of public expression and as conscience for the ruling party.[32] In the end, their project of democratizing socialism was overtaken by popular demands for the Western social market economy.

One ironic result of the transformation was the marginalization of Eastern intellectuals in the national German cultural institutions and media landscape. With readership plummeting, many party organs were forced to shut down since Easterners preferred the glossier presentation of *Bild* or *Super-Illu*. Western news corporations bought up Eastern papers and radio and TV stations and purged their leadership of Communist personnel, though in the ranks some Eastern journalists tended to survive. The newly formed regional conglomerates catered to a provincial Eastern media taste. While some GDR stars like Kurt Masur profited from the liberalization, other artists lost their safe positions in exchange for gaining more freedom of cultural expression. Since most Western readers were only mildly interested in what went on in the new states, the leading papers and media outlets hired few Easterners like Friedrich Dieckmann. Unused to market competition, many of the new foundations of 1989 like *Die Andere* went under, meaning that Easterners found their voices muffled in the national debates.[33]

Confronting the past of the SED dictatorship was also complicated by the resolve to do a better job with Communism than with National Socialism the second time around. Since prominent writers like Christa Wolf had defended Socialism while trying to reform it, Western literary critics fiercely attacked the failure of Eastern authors to distance themselves from the regime in a veritable writers' quarrel (*Literaturstreit*). The controversy escalated through the Stasi-scandalization of the media, when it was discovered that even such avant-garde poets and darlings of the Prenzlauer Berg scene like Sascha Anderson had worked for the ministry for state security.[34] Many former dissidents and regime victims who had suffered in prisons like Hohenschönhausen or Bautzen denounced the GDR as an *Unrechtsstaat*, an illegitimate state not respecting the rule of law. Moreover, a Bundestag Commission of Inquiry held two sets of widely publicized hearings to discredit the SED dictatorship. No wonder that with so much negative publicity many East Germans felt attacked, having their life histories disparaged retrospectively.[35]

Not surprisingly, disappointment with transition problems and resentment against wholesale condemnation inspired a nostalgic longing for an idealized GDR, called *(N-)Ostalgie*. The loss of familiar objects of material culture and difficulties in adapting to an unknown Western system made many East Germans recall their earlier life with fondness. In retrospect, the once-grey GDR looked comforting, making even the vexing standing in line remembered as "a community of solidarity." Businessmen quickly discovered that they could make money by catering to tastes for Eastern rock music, selling revived Eastern brands in special *Ostshops* and treating the GDR as a somewhat scary memory park.[36] Ironically, the commercialization of these longings created a posthumous East German identity that fed on hurt pride. Nonetheless, the claim that this *Ostalgie* amounted to a new East German ethnicity is an exaggeration, since most citizens of the new states have arrived in the FRG at least as members of their respective states like Saxony or Brandenburg.[37] Also, Westerners reacted to the disappearance of the old FRG with a sense of *Westalgie*.

Due to such contestation, the vanished GDR has become a lively site of cultural production, ranging from literary efforts to media representations and commemorations. Almost in ritualized fashion, critics of unification like Daniela Dahn decry East German discrimination while defenders like Richard Schroeder blame the SED for most current difficulties.[38] At the same time writers like Uwe Tellkamp communicate their ambivalent recollections of growing up in a dissolving GDR in ambitious novels like *Der Turm*.[39] Filmmakers present partly ironic, partly dramatic representations of East German realities in successful movies like *Goodbye Lenin* or *Lives of Others* that manage to convey some of the dreams and disenchantments under communism. By now the SED regime has even been turned into a family soap opera *Weissensee* on TV, indicating that the topic has become safe enough for entertainment.[40] Yet the memorialization of the GDR by the Federal Government and the Berlin Senate is likely to remain controversial since it conveys conflicting lessons of anti-totalitarianism or of participatory democracy.[41]

In the cultural response to unification writers lament about loss of their special position rather than welcome their new creative possibilities. Eugen Ruge's prizewinning novel *In Zeiten des abnehmenden Lichts* presents a swan song of the inevitable end of the GDR, but does not really suggest much hope for a better future. The book describes the failure of the antifascist grandparent generation to create a better socialism due to its proletarian illusions as well as the inability of the parent cohort to rebel against Stalinist repression. But the self-portrait of the children is also depressing, since the narrator fails to create a new life in the Federal Republic and is left to die in a provincial Mexican hotel overlooking a Pacific beach. The powerful descriptions conjure up the progressive erosion of the utopian faith in socialism and the subsequent disillusionment about the heartlessness of capitalist consumer society.[42] Whether with irony, nostalgia, or regret, much post-communist literature continues to be fixated on the grey GDR past rather than on a more colorful European future.

International Normalization

The emotional debate regarding foreign policy revolves around the implications of "normalization," searching for an appropriate role for the revived German national state in Europe and the world. Western commentators like Beate Neuss stress the partial revision of the paradigm of a "civilian power" toward accepting military missions abroad, necessitated by the Balkan Wars and legitimized by the Constitutional Court, which allowed *Bundeswehr* troops to participate in multilateral combat assignments beyond self-defense in the North Atlantic Treaty Organization (NATO) area. Eastern foreign policy specialists like Erhard Crome vehemently oppose this broadened reading of the Basic Law, claiming that the Two-Plus-Four Treaty forbids any use of military force in humanitarian interventions and betraying a deep suspicion of NATO as a Western alliance. Distanced U.S. observers like Andrew Port also criticize the unpredictability of German behavior, including the refusal to get involved in the second Iraq War or in the liberation of Libya, as irresponsible, since it did not follow Washington's lead. This dispute poses the question: what should be the correct role of the enlarged Federal Republic abroad?

In contrast to the difficulties with achieving "inner unity," the impact of unification on the course of German foreign policy has been more muted. Initially, the specter of an enlarged FRG revived historic fears of German expansionism among political elites and editorial writers in Israel, Britain, France, and Poland, just to name a few. But the joyful images of the fall of the wall kindled a sympathetic response among neighboring populations. Moreover, East European dissidents realized that their road to Europe led through a reunited Germany.[43] While U.S. President George Bush supported unification from the beginning, it took much persuasion to bring François Mitterrand on board through the promise of a common currency, and to persuade Soviet leader Mikhail Gorbachev with the offer of economic help to allow not just self-determination but also NATO membership. In the end the Two-Plus-Four negotiations seized the chance finally to solve the "German problem" through accepted frontiers, renunciation of ABC weapons and a considerable reduction in the size of the Bundeswehr.[44]

Even after unification the new Federal Republic preferred to behave as a "civilian power," avoiding unilateral acts of force and fostering international cooperation.[45] On the one hand, West Germans had been culturally demilitarized after the Second World War, leading many young men to reject military service even in a civilianized Bundeswehr that understood itself as "citizens in uniform." On the other hand, the East German peace movement had rejected the communist militarism of the National People's Army (NVA), while the SED peace propaganda against the West left a legacy of suspicion of NATO.[46] As long as it was a "semi-sovereign state," the old FRG had been able to hide under the American nuclear umbrella, preferring to pursue its interests through negotiation and, if necessary, through DM diplomacy. In contrast to the assertive Empire or aggressive Third Reich, the foreign policy culture of the Federal Republic was therefore characterized by multilateralism and consultation within NATO or the EU. Rejecting its domineering legacy, Germany had come to embrace the promotion of peace.

In response to international expectations, the FRG gradually reinterpreted these precepts, leading to a slow "normalization" in accepting more responsibility. Part of the problem was the prohibition of the Basic Law, formulated to prevent another world war, which allowed participation in collective security measures and use of force only in cases of self-defense (Articles 24 and 87a). Though Bonn refused to join in the first Gulf War, the Constitutional Court in 1994 ruled, in order to allow peacekeeping in the Balkans, that German soldiers could participate in actions of collective security as long as a Bundestag majority approved their deployment on a case-by-case basis, such as the Stabilization Force (SFOR) mission to pacify Bosnia. When the Kosovo crisis confronted the red-green cabinet with the request to authorize combat, Foreign Minister Fischer turned the "never again Auschwitz" slogan around to argue that Germans should not tolerate genocide at their doorstep. Yet sending troops to Afghanistan was initially justified as "reconstruction," and remained controversial when it looked more like war.[47]

Though returning to the center of Europe, united Germany continued to see itself as "a middle power," acting more regionally than globally. No doubt, Gerhard Schroeder embraced a more assertive style than Helmut Kohl, openly speaking of "national interest" and pursuing a permanent seat in the United Nations' Security Council. In negotiations about the EU budget, the red-green coalition was no longer content to offer more German money in order to facilitate compromise. Similarly, Berlin refused to go along with the preventive war against Iraq unleashed by President George W. Bush, because it considered the justification of "weapons of mass destruction" or al-Qaida flimsy, and instead preferred to create a coalition of the unwilling with France, Russia, and China. In the post–Cold War setting the German government also tried hard to mediate between Moscow and Washington in order to keep the Russian government involved in the international community.[48] While Chancellor Angela Merkel has been less assertive in appearance, she has also proven tenacious in advancing German views.

Will the Federal Republic eventually learn to play a leadership role in an integrating Europe? Several reasons speak against the resurgence of a "Fourth Reich," even in a more benign form.[49] The legacy of two failed attempts at domination has made neighbors wary of any efforts to lead; confronted with the consequences of unification and globalization, Germany does not have the resources to go it alone; and the limited size and lack of nuclear weapons of a volunteer Bundeswehr make it unsuited to serve as the core of a common defense. Yet there are also some factors that indicate that Germany is becoming a "regional hegemon" with a consensual approach that wields normative power: the FRG does have the largest economy in Europe and remains an industrial powerhouse; when Franco-German cooperation finds common ground, it pulls other EU members along, and the steadiness of the response to the Anglo-American financial meltdown commands respect. If it manages to articulate common European interests, Berlin's influence is likely to grow.[50]

The difficulties of German leadership in Europe have become evident through the sovereign debt crisis, in which Berlin has resisted international pressures to bail out its weaker neighbors with easy money. When Greek interest rates rose beyond the country's capacity to repay its debts due to internal corruption and irresponsible fiscal policy, domestic German opinion did not allow Chancellor Angela Merkel to rescue the country by writing a blank check. But since the Euro crisis threatened the future of the European Union and German exporters wanted to preserve their markets, the government had to respond. The result has been a controversial policy of creating a limited credit umbrella (European Stability Fund, etc.) while insisting on cut-backs to balance the budget and structural changes to restore competitiveness. Strongly criticized by financial interests and the *New York Times,* this stepwise approach has reassured markets with regard to Spain and Italy, much larger and healthier economies. Balancing domestic and international pressures, this cautious incrementalism in cooperation with France has calmed the hysteria of the financial markets due to the strength of the German export economy.[51]

Unification as Process

More than two decades after the peaceful revolution, the debate about German unification remains unresolved, since many hopes have been disappointed but most fears have also been belied. On the political level the transfer of democratic institutions appears to be working well enough, and in foreign policy the enlarged FRG still prefers to behave like a "civilian power." It is rather the collapse of most Eastern industry, the depopulation of stagnant regions, and the feeling of being a "second-class" citizen that gives reason for concern. To be sure, there are encouraging examples of civil society initiatives aimed at retying bonds across the former Iron Curtain, such as city partnerships, youth encounters, student contests, and the like. But there is no denying that united Germany is governed by Western elites, that the media slight Eastern topics, and that disparities in wealth continue between the old and new states. Moreover, divergent experiences also inform survey responses on issues like freedom and equality.[52] At this time it remains unclear whether these differences will decrease to the level of regional distinctions or whether the "Wall in the head" will remain, dividing the country internally rather than externally.

In the euphoria of the fall of the Wall, many Germans simply assumed, as in Willy Brandt's felicitous phrase, that "what belongs together, will grow together." By just removing the ugly concrete barrier, cutting many kilometers of barbed wire, and reopening roads, the divided parts of the country would reunite automatically. This widespread expectation was based on a somewhat naive hope for the reassertion of an underlying national unity rather than on a sober assessment of the impact of separate development during the preceding four decades in two hostile blocs. Chipping away at the Wall, opening new border crossing points, reconnecting rusty railroad tracks, reopening overgrown streets, rebuilding decayed bridges—in short, getting rid of the physical remnants of division—turned out to be the easier part.[53] But erasing the mental, institutional and social effects of living in two ideologically opposed systems proved to be much more complicated. Making the transition from a late communist dictatorship to a fledgling democracy with a market economy was an upheaval that would require several decades.

Unlike the struggles of neighbors, the German transformation was both privileged and problematic, because it took the form of national unification. In contrast to the expectation of many Easterners, the accession of the five new states to the Federal Republic meant that this was not a merger of equals, but the incorporation of a bankrupt state into a successful system that had prevailed in the Cold War competition. Transformation as unification meant that Western patterns, institutions, and even elites would be transferred to the East rather than Easterners being allowed to find a Third Way or to contribute much of their own legacy to the new mix.[54] No doubt, joining the FRG offered an attractive shortcut to material prosperity and political liberty—but this option, which neighboring countries did not possess, has exacted a steep price in deindustrialization and Western tutelage. East Germans were more quickly able to obtain consumer goods, gain human rights, and participate in politics, but also found themselves in a dependent role, living on transfers from the West.

Though critics preferred a slower transition through a deliberate merger between equals, the Kohl government and East German voters decisively rejected this alternative. No doubt, unification via paragraph 146 of the Basic Law would have permitted an all-German debate about a new constitution that could have picked up innovative ideas of the Round Table. Also holding off the introduction of the DM, choosing a lower currency conversion rate, or pursuing an industrial policy might have preserved more Eastern industry and safeguarded more jobs.[55] But the reasons for moving quickly seemed ultimately compelling: on the one hand, the instability in the Soviet Union meant that there was only a limited window of diplomatic opportunity that might slam shut at any moment if Gorbachev were overthrown. On the other hand, the East German citizens who had been deprived for decades did not want to wait any longer for a Western standard of living. Rapid unification offered them a once-in-a-lifetime chance to move to a new country without actually leaving home.[56]

Reversing the effects of decades of division and forging a new kind of unity among Germans has therefore turned out to be a lengthy process full of mistakes and unanticipated difficulties. The fall of the Wall was only the first step along a road that would take an entire generation or more to traverse. Also, the cost of Western financial support to the East has amounted to a staggering 2 trillion Euros, much more than Chancellor Kohl was willing to admit. Only after the transfer of Western institutions had been completed could overdue reforms for the entire country like the modernization of universities be begun and some Eastern institutions like child care centers be revived.... But in the meantime a generation has grown up without personal recollections of division, in a society in which Easterners and Westerners mingle with a sense of shared identity, evident during the last soccer World Cups of men and women.[57] Since only a small minority wants the Wall back, unification has become the new normalcy. Germany therefore can now build on its regained unity in order to meet new globalization challenges like economic competitiveness, integration of immigrants, and the Euro crisis.

Notes

1. 20 Jahre Einheit, *Tagesspiegel*, 2 October 2010, plus the series of life stories in the same paper. Cf. "Geheimakte Deutschland," *Der Spiegel*, 27 September 2010.
2. Raj Kollmorgen, "Diskurse der deutschen Einheit," *APuZ* 30–31 (2010), 6–13.
3. Compare Hans-Joachim Maaz, *Der Gefühlsstau. Psychogramm einer Gesellschaft*, 2nd ed. (Munich, 2010) to Arnulf Baring, *Deutschland gehört nicht nur den Deutschen* (Stuttgart, 2007).
4. Klaus Schroeder, *Die veränderte Republik. Deutschland nach der Wiedervereinigung* (Munich, 2006).
5. Richard Schröder, *Die wichtigsten Irrtümer über die deutsche Einheit* (Freiburg, 2007).
6. Daniela Dahn, *Wehe dem Sieger! Ohne den Osten kein Westen* (Reinbeck, 2009).
7. Konrad H. Jarausch, "The Federal Republic at Sixty: Popular Myths, Actual Accomplishments and Competing Interpretations," *German Politics and Society* 28 (2010), 10–29.
8. Wolfgang Merkl, *Systemtransformation. Eine Einführung in die Theorie und Empirie der Transformationsforschung*, 2nd ed. (Wiesbaden, 2010).
9. Manfred Görtemaker, *Die Berliner Republik. Wiedervereinigung und Neuorientierung* (Berlin, 2009); Andreas Wirsching, *Preis der Freiheit. Geshchte Europas in unserer Zeit* (Munich, 2011).
10. Wolfgang Schluchter and Peter E. Quint, eds., *Der Vereinigungsschock. Vergleichende Betrachtungen zehn Jahre danach* (Weilerwist, 2001); Peter C. Caldwell and Robert R. Shandley, eds., *German Unification: Expectations and Outcomes* (New York, 2011).
11. Otto Pflanze, *Bismarck and the Development of Germany: The Period of Unification, 1815–1871* (Princeton, 1963). Cf. Ronald Speirs and John Breuilly, eds., *Germany's Two Unifications: Anticipations, Experiences, Responses* (New York, 2005).
12. Ilko-Sascha Kowalczuk, *Endspiel. Die Revolution von 1989 in der DDR* (Munich, 2009).
13. Lothar de Maiziere, "Ich will, dass meine Kinder nicht mehr lügen müssen," *Meine Geschichte der deutschen Einheit* (Freiburg, 2010). That aspect of unification is often taken for granted.
14. Russel Dalton and Willy Jou, "Is there a Single German Party System?" in *From the Bonn to the Berlin Republic: Germany at the Twentieth Anniversary of Unification*, ed. Jeffrey J. Anderson and Eric Langenbacher (New York, 2010), 251–269.
15. Klaus Schroeder, "Deutschland nach der Wiedervereinigung," *APuZ* 30/31 (2010), 13–19.
16. Rolf Reissig, "Von der privilegierten und blockierten zur zukunftsorientierten Transformation," APuZ 30/31 (2010), 20–25.
17. See the essays in Angelika Timm, ed., *20 Jahre deutsche Einheit: Ein Staat—zwei Identitäten?* (Tel Aviv, 2011).
18. Wolfgang Seibel, *Verwaltete Illusionen. Die Privatisierung der DDR-Wirtschaft durch die Treuhandanstalt und ihre Nachfolger 1990–2000* (Frankfurt, 2005).
19. Jürgen Kocka, *Die Vereinigungskrise. Zur Geschichte der Gegenwart* (Göttingen, 1995).
20. Holger Wolf, "German Economic Unification Twenty Years Later" and Stephen J. Silvia, "The Elusive Quest for Normalcy: The German Economy Since Unification," in Anderson and Langenbacher, *From the Bonn to the Berlin Republic*, 321–330; 331–349.
21. Michael C. Burda, "Wirtschaft in Ostdeutschland im 21. Jahrhundert," *APuZ*, 30/31 (2010), 26–33.
22. Felix Ringel, "Hoyotopia allerorten? Von der Freiheit zu bleiben," *APuZ*, 30/31 (2010), 40–46.
23. Ulrich Busch and Rainer Land, "Ostdeutschland. Vom staatssozialistischen Fordismus in die Entwicklungsfalle einer Transferökonomie," in *Berichterstattung zur sozioökonomischen Entwicklung in Deutschland. Teilhabe im Umbruch. Zweiter Bericht*, ed. Forschungs-

verbund Sozioökonomische Berichterstattung (Wiesbaden 2012). Cf. also Joyce M. Mushaben, "Be Careful What You Pray For: Employment Profiles among East and West Germans," *German Studies Review* 33 (2010), 565–578.

24. See the targeted economic development policy of the state of Brandenburg: http://www.brandenburg.de/de/wirtschaft.
25. On an ironic level, Peter Timm's movies *Go Trabi Go* from 1991 and 1992 dramatized these difficulties.
26. Jana Hensel, *Zonenkinder* (Reinbek, 2002); Ingo Schulze, *Simple Storys. Ein Roman aus der ostdeutschen Provinz* (Berlin, 1998).
27. Daniela Dahn, *Westwärts und nicht vergessen. Vom Unbehagen in der Einheit* (Berlin, 1996).
28. Martin Diewald, Anne Goedicke, and Karl Ulrich Mayer, eds., *After the Fall of the Wall: Life Courses in the Transformation of East Germany* (Stanford, 2006). Cf. the dissertation in progress by Volker Benkert on different types of transition (Potsdam, 2013).
29. Peer Pasternack, "Erneuerung durch Anschluss? Der ostdeutsche Fall ab 1990" and Konrad H. Jarausch, "Säuberung oder Erneuerung? Zur Transformation der Humboldt-Universität 1985-2000," in *Gebrochene Wissenschaftskulturen. Universität und Politik im 20. Jahrhundert,* ed. Michael Grüttner, Rüdiger Hachtmann, Konrad H. Jarausch, Jürgen John, and Matthias Middell (Göttingen, 2010), 309–326, 327–351. Cf. Helga A. Welsh, "Policy Transfer in the Unified Germany: From Imitation to Feedback Loops," *German Studies Review* 33 (2010), 531–548.
30. Hilary Silver, "The Social Integration of Germany since Unification," in Anderson and Langenbacher, *From the Bonn to the Berlin Republic,* 183–206. See also the data in Statistische Ämter der Länder, eds., *Von der Bevölkerung bis Wahlen—20 Jahre Deutsche Einheit in der Statistik* (Bad Ems, 2010).
31. Donna Harsch, *Revenge of the Domestic: Women, the Family, and Communism in the German Democratic Republic* (Princeton, 2007) and the dissertation by Sarah Summers on "Reconciling Family and Work" in the Federal Republic (Ph.D. diss., University of North Carolina, Chapel Hill 2012).
32. Dissertation: Thomas Goldstein, "Writing in Red: The East German Writers Union and the Role of Literary Intellectuals in the German Democratic Republic, 1971–90," (Ph.D. diss., University of North Carolina, Chapel Hill, 2010).
33. Lecture of Dr. Lutz Mükke on the underrepresentation of East Germans in the media at the media dialogue in Cotonou/Westafrica, September 2010.
34. Bernd Wittek, *Der Literaturstreit im sich vereinigenden Deutschland. Eine Analyse des Streits um Christa Wolf und die deutsch-deutsche Gegenwartsliteratur in Zeitungen und Zeitschriften von Juni 1990 bis Ende 1992* (Marburg, 1997). Cf. Christa Wolf, *Stadt der Engel oder The Overcoat of Dr. Freud* (Frankfurt, 2010).
35. Andrew Beattie, *Playing Politics with History: The Bundestag Inquiries into East Germany* (New York, 2008); Konrad H. Jarausch, "Memory Wars: German Debates about the Legacy of Dictatorship," in *Berlin since the Wall's End: Shaping Society and Memory in the German Metropolis since 1989,* ed. John Alexander Williams (Newcastle, 2008).
36. Dominic Boyer, "Ostalgie and the Politics of the Future in Eastern Germany," *Public Culture* 18 (2006), 361–380. Cf. also Dietrich Mühlberg's postscript in Evemarie Badstübner, ed., *Befremdlich anders. Leben in der DDR* (Berlin, 2000).
37. Marc Howard, "An East German Ethnicity? Understanding the New Division of United Germany," *German Politics and Society* 13 (1995), 49–70. Cf. Joyce M. Mushaben, "Unification and the Law of Unanticipated Consequences," *German Studies Review* 33 (2010), 483–488.
38. See Dahn, *Wehe dem Sieger!* and Schroeder, *Die wichtigsten Irrtümer über die deutsche Einheit.*
39. Uwe Tellkamp, *Der Turm. Geschichte aus einem versunkenen Land* (Frankfurt, 2008); Ingo Schulze, *Neue Leben. Die Jugend Enrico Türmers in Briefen und Prosa* (Berlin, 2005).

40. Bradley Prager, "Passing Time since the Wende: Recent German Film on Unification," in Anderson and Langenbacher, *From the Bonn to the Berlin Republic,* 115–130.
41. Martin Sabrow und Irmgard Zündorf, eds., *Wohin treibt die DDR Erinnerung? Der Streit um eine Debatte* (Göttingen, 2007); Klaus-Dietmar Henke, ed., *Die Mauer. Errichtung, Überwindung, Erinnerung* (München, 2011).
42. Eugen Ruge, *In Zeiten des abnehmenden Lichts* (Reinbeck, 2011). See also "Das Beste an Lenin ist sein Bart," *Tagesspiegel,* 28 January 2012.
43. Harold James and Marla Stone, eds., *When the Wall Came Down: Reactions to German Unification* (New York, 1992); Renata Fritsch-Bournazel, *Europe and German Unification* (New York, 1992).
44. The grand game literature, like Alexander von Plato, *Die Vereinigung Deutschlands—ein weltpolitisches Machtspiel. Bush, Kohl Gorbatschow und die geheimen Moskauer Protokolle* (Berlin, 2002), is somewhat misleading.
45. Hanns Maull, *Germany as a Civilian Power? The Foreign Policy of the Berlin Republic* (Manchester, 2001).
46. Dissertation: Kathleen Nawyn, "Striking at the Roots of German Militarism: Efforts to Demilitarize German Society and Culture in American-occupied Württemberg-Baden, 1945–1949," (Ph.D. diss., University of North Carolina, Chapel Hill, 2008). Cf. James Sheehan, *Where Have all the Soldiers Gone? The Transformation of Modern Europe* (Boston, 2008).
47. Helga Haftendorn, *Coming of Age: German Foreign Policy since 1945* (Lanham, MD, 2006).
48. Joschka Fischer, *Die rot-grünen Jahre. Deutsche Außenpolitik vom Kosovo bis zum Irak* (Cologne, 2007); Max Otte, *A Rising Middle Power? German Foreign Policy in Transformation, 1989–1999* (New York, 2000)
49. Compare Edwin Hartrich, *The Fourth and Richest Reich* (New York, 1980) and Jorge Semprun, *Blick auf Deutschland* (Frankfurt, 2003) to Beverly Crawford, "The Normative Power of a Normal State: Power and Revolutionary Vision in Germany's Post-Wall Foreign Policy," in Anderson and Langenbacher, *From the Bonn to the Berlin Republic,* 287–305.
50. Christiane Lemke, "Germany's EU Policy: The Domestic Discourse," *German Studies Review* 33 (2010): 503–516.
51. Jack Ewing and Liz Alderman, "German Chancellor, Citing Europe's Progress, Asks for Patience," *New York Times,* 26 January 2012. Cf. Carsten Volkery, "Legal Loopholes: Critics Question Merkel's Fiscal Pact Proposal," *Spiegel-online,* 27 January 2012.
52. Hans-Hermann Hertle, *Die Berliner Mauer. Monument des Kalten Krieges* (Bonn, 2007); Leo Schmidt, ed., *Die Berliner Mauer. Vom Sperrwall zum Denkmal* (Bonn, 2009).
53. Michael Richter, *Die friedliche Revolution. Aufbruch zur Demokratie in Sachsen 1989-1990,* 2 vols. (Göttingen, 2009) is the most detailed regional study.
54. This charge of missed opportunities, raised by unification critics, still influences a good deal of scholarship. But see Eric Langenbacher, "The Germans Must Have Done Something Right," in Anderson and Langenbacher, *From the Bonn to the Berlin Republic,* 397–413.
55. Andreas Rödder, *Deutschland, einig Vaterland. Die Geschichte der Wiedervereinigung* (Munich, 2009).
56. Jennifer Yoder, "The Integration of Eastern German Political Elites since 1989," *German Studies Review* 33 (2010), 549–564.
57. Beatrice von Weizsäcker, *Die Unvollendete. Deutschland zwischen Einheit und Zweiheit* (Cologne, 2010).

Part I

Political Processes

Chapter One

Two Decades of Unity

Continuity and Change in Political Institutions

Gero Neugebauer

The historical and political conditions that governed the transformation of the GDR into a democracy differ on essential points from those generally involved in the collapse of the socialist camp in Europe. Most of the former Warsaw Pact states embedded the transformation of their political and economic systems into a concept of reconstructing their nation. In contrast, the conditions in Germany were determined by the situation of a divided country on whose soil two states existed. The one, the Federal Republic of Germany (FRG), belonged to the Western Alliance under the leadership of the United States, and the other, the German Democratic Republic (GDR), to the Soviet-led alliance. The collapse of the GDR, beginning in 1989, led not to a new state but rather, after a brief orientation phase in October 1990, to unification with the other German state.[1] Therefore, the case of the GDR indeed constitutes a system transformation, but it did not result in a state with a new political and economic system. Rather, after the rapid transformation of the GDR to a democracy, the division of the country ended in the fall of 1990 with the unification of both states, through which the new East German states joined the Federal Republic on the basis of Article 23 of the Basic Law. With that, the GDR ceased to exist.

This unification cannot be seen as a simple reunification. For roughly forty-five years, two German states existed with different political, economic, social, legal, and cultural systems, and ultimately, societies, on a territory smaller than that of previous state, the German Reich. The one

Notes for this chapter begin on page 42.

failed, while the other succeeded in the confrontation of systems. The institutions of the FRG along with its different subsystems determined the integration of East German society. This process was facilitated by the commonalities which had remained, such as the same language, common history before 1945, cultural and academic traditions, and familial ties. In this respect, on 3 October 1990 "two patterns of socialization"[2] were brought together. In the end, however, the result was a new "Berlin Republic," i.e., the new Federal Republic of Germany.

The illusion of independent GDR development lasted only for a few weeks after the beginning of the peaceful revolution. When West German Chancellor Helmut Kohl decided on the strategy of unifying Germany and received the approval of President George Bush and General Secretary Gorbachev, hopes of an independent existence for the GDR in Europe ended. The course of the transformation led quickly to the radical change of structure and of political institutions.[3] An attempt by East German politicians to negotiate the terms of unification on the basis of their own draft constitution failed, as did other later initiatives.[4] A majority of politicians and the East German populace accepted unification on the basis of the provisions of the Federal Republic's constitution. With that, the West German political system and its constitutional order determined the direction and content of development. The negotiations between both German governments, most importantly with the state treaty of 18 May 1990 and the unification treaty of 20 August 1990, as well as between them and the victorious powers of the Second World War (the "Two-Plus-Four negotiations"), created further preconditions for unification. The prerequisite for unity was the contractually agreed-upon economic and currency union.

Unification led to an enlargement of the Bundestag—instead of 497 seats as in 1987, there were now 692 delegates—and of the Bundesrat: to the previous eleven states five new ones were added. Theoretically, the latter expansion meant more difficulties for the federal government in certain legislative procedures, while the enlargement of the Bundestag offered a wider range of political careers. East Germans' expectations that some of their own institutions could survive in an altered environment were not fulfilled. The Round Table, at which the representatives of the old GDR and the citizens' movements and opposition parties had negotiated arrangements for the transformation of their system, was preserved merely as a symbol. Only two institutions outlived the GDR. One preserved the secret documents of the Ministry for State Security for later analysis; it exists today as the Federal Authority for the Documents of the Former Ministry for State Security (BStU).[5] The second was the Trusteeship Agency (Treuhandanstalt). It had already been established in connection with the privatization of the GDR economy by a decision of the government on

1 March 1990; after 3 October 1990 it was subordinated to the Federal Ministry of Finance and ceased its operation four years later. The Trusteeship Agency had the task of reorganizing and privatizing GDR state assets according to the principles of the social market economy. Critics reproached the institution for continuing centralistic structures as well as for dismantling industry in the East German states and squandering formerly public property in the interest of individual, mainly West German, actors.

The Political Systems of the GDR and FRG

Since their founding in 1949, the Federal Republic of Germany and the GDR opposed one another as political, economic, and social competitors—and from1955/56 on as military opponents through their membership in military alliances. Furthermore, the Federal Republic insisted that there was but one German nation and that it alone represented Germany. For a long time it therefore refused to recognize the GDR as an independent state. After the commencement of intergovernmental relations in 1974, it declared that special relations would prevail between both German states. The GDR leadership disagreed with this view, yet tolerated it in order to achieve its goal of gaining de facto diplomatic recognition. It could then claim that its population constituted an independent "socialist nation."

The organizations of the states were based on different political concepts. The political system of the GDR corresponded in its essential features to the Soviet model, but with a noncompetitive multiparty system in which the socialist party held the key position. The state was structured in a centralistic manner and had territorial-administrative subdivisions with fewer decision-making powers. The system called itself a socialist democracy. In fact, it was an authoritarian regime at whose top the highest decision-making unit of the ruling socialist party, the Politbüro, concentrated political power. From 1946 until the fall of the Berlin Wall in November 1989, this system nonetheless retained several parties and nominal parliamentary institutions. The party structure was a so-called bloc system and consisted of the Socialist Unity Party (SED), the Christian Democratic Union (CDU), and the Liberal Democratic Party (LDP), as well as the National Democratic Party (NDP) and the Democratic Farmers' Party of Germany (DBD). Parliamentary institutions existed on the national (People's Chamber) as well as regional (District Council) and local (County Council) levels. The SED dominated all levels of the system and all its institutions, determined the number of seats in the parliaments, and decided, with the help of a nomenclature, appointments to positions in the state apparatus, economic management, and the educational and cultural institutions.

The other parties recognized, formally and practically, the leading role of the SED and acted under its supervision and guidance as organizations for particular societal groups (Christians, craftspeople, private entrepreneurs, etc.). Despite formal elections, there was neither a democratic contest among parties nor a programmatic competition, much less a political opposition or social movement outside of the established system of the "National Front"[6] under the leadership of the SED. Possibilities for the population to influence politics were strictly regulated and highly formalized. Basic political rights were not guaranteed; criticism of politics was either instrumentalized for party-political purposes or practiced through West German media. The system avoided revolts and internal unrest, with one exception in 1953. Beyond the Stasi, its stability was based, among other things, on the fact that the discontented could leave the country illegally until the construction of the Berlin Wall in 1961, and thereafter, the population was promised social benefits in order to keep them quiet.

The Federal Republic of Germany was a federal state with a parliamentary democratic system. Created after the end of the Second World War in part by the policies of the Western allies, it was also based in part on experiences of the first German democracy from 1919 until 1932 and on the tradition of German federalism. Unlike in the Weimar Republic, the role of parties was strengthened and they were granted quasi-constitutional status in the Basic Law. Administration, like parliament, functioned practically as party-state institutions and the parties dominated the allocation of positions in the government sector.

The party system was geared toward competition. In 1949 ten parties and voters' associations were represented in the Bundestag. In 1980 there were just three—the Christian Democratic Union (CDU)[7] and its Bavarian sister, the Christian Social Union (CSU), the Social Democratic Party of Germany (SPD), and the Free Democratic Party (FDP). None of the other parties gained more than 5 percent, the share of votes necessary to send delegates to the parliament. In 1983 four parties were represented in the Bundestag when the Greens arrived as a new party. This party had emerged at the end of the 1970s from various new social movements, especially the anti-nuclear power movement, the women's movement, and the peace movement, as well as environmental initiatives.

For the first quarter century, the Center-Right camp dominated the West German party competition, because the CDU and CSU as well as the FDP were supported by a bourgeois majority in the electorate. But thereafter, the polarization in the party system declined, because in 1959 the SPD had undertaken a programmatic change of course away from a socialist and toward a social democratic party on the basis of a pluralistic understanding of democratic socialism. This shift opened it up to new voting blocs and thereby contributed to the gradual decline in the sharpness of the disputes as well as differences among the parties.[8] The reforms paid off when the SPD became the governing party in a coalition with the FDP from 1969 until 1982; the CDU started its modernization of party politics and organization only in the late 1970s.

In the party system after 1983 the Social Democrats and the Greens on the one side and the Union on the other reflected opposing poles in the various policy fields. Until 1953, there was a decidedly leftist party in the form of the Communist Party. It had been banned in 1956, and in 1968 a refounded German Communist Party achieved no political or electoral success. Although in 1969 a right-extremist party, the National Democratic Party of Germany (NPD) which had formed from small nationalist parties five years earlier, profited from an economic crisis, it succeeded neither then nor at any point thereafter in gaining entry into the Bundestag.

The Development of Democracy in United Germany

During the transformation, the GDR had created the legal preconditions for democratic elections with the passage of an electoral law and a political party law. The three elections that took place in GDR territory in 1990—the People's Chamber election in March, local elections in May, state elections in October—followed to a large degree the standard of the electoral system of the Federal Republic. The sole exception was the omission of the 5-percent hurdle in the People's Chamber election, designed to exclude splinter parties. In December 1990, the fourth election was at the same time the first all-German election. With this, there was an unusual feature. Two election areas were created: the Western area encompassed the "old" West German states and the Eastern election area the "new" East German states. In order to avoid diminishing the chances of the small parties from the East, a 5-percent hurdle was established for each election area. A party whose percentage of second votes amounted to just above 5 percent could thereby send delegates to the Bundestag even if this proportion, projected onto the national level, would have amounted to less than 5 percent. The East German Party of Democratic Socialism (PDS), as the successor party of the former governing SED, profited from this rule. Its nominal West German branch clearly failed, while the PDS received roughly 11 percent of the vote. The West German Greens also fell short of the 5-percent hurdle in the Western election area with the result of 4.9 percent, while the East German Party Bündnis 90, with which they arranged a political alliance, entered the Bundestag. West German delegates dominated the composition of the Bundestag, since except for the PDS and initially the

FDP, the number of East German members in a party never outweighed those of West Germany. In all other parties there were far more West German than East German members. Thus Western perspectives determined the response to the unification problems in the East German states. This helped the PDS to claim that it would be the true political representative of so-called specific Eastern interest.

The desire for free elections had strongly motivated the actors in the peaceful revolution, since the GDR's electoral system only allowed the formal act of voting by approving a prearranged list that permitted no choice among parties, programs, or people. To be able to choose freely was regarded as the basic prerequisite for the development of democracy. Already in the GDR part of the population had developed into virtual supporters of West German parties through observing elections in the Federal Republic. Thus it was generally assumed that approval of democracy would be demonstrated through electoral behavior, especially through voter turnout. In this regard, the development of voter turnout since 1990 is not reassuring.

In the first all-German elections the voter turnout amounted to 77.8 percent. At the time it was already lower in all East German states (except Berlin) and only in Baden-Württemberg in the West. In 1994, 79 percent of voters participated. It was lower in two West German states—Bavaria and Bremen—as well as in all East German states. In 1998 participation climbed to 82.2 percent because of the polarization of the election campaign. As usual, voting was below average in all East German states and in Bavaria. In 2002, when the Union candidate, Bavarian Minister-President Stoiber wanted to make sure that the East Germans did not decide the outcome of the entire election, voter turnout amounted to 79.1 percent on average. This level was not reached in Bremen or in any East German state. These states and Hamburg once again achieved this result in 2005 when the average was 77.7 percent. And in 2009 all East German states as well as Bremen were below the already low average voter turnout at the national level of 70.8 percent; this was most apparent in the East German state Saxony-Anhalt with only a 60.5 percent turnout.[9]

In fact, Bundestag elections cannot be won in the East, due to the smaller size of its electorate, but they can be lost there when the difference in percentages among the parties is small. Poorly organized parties in the East might not gain sufficient votes to secure a better result overall. The SPD, which for several years has occupied third place in East Germany behind the CDU and the PDS, must finally learn this. In this regard it could not console itself with the fact that in every election since 1990 the PDS has only once, in 1998, jumped over the 5-percent hurdle at the national level with a percentage of second votes slightly over 1 percent in the West, but a good 25 percent in the East. That has become the most important reason for its merger with a small new party in the West, the WASG (Wahlalternative Arbeit und Soziale Gerechtigkeit), now called Die Linke, in 2005/07.

In 1990, it became apparent that the East Germans who were critical to hostile toward the former GDR considered the political order of the FRG positive. However, in the first ten years after unification the assessments of democracy continue to differ between East and West Germany:

Table 1.1. Support for Democracy in Germany as the Best Form of Government (in percent).

	2000*	2006/07*	2000ˣ	2006/07ˣ
"Democracy in Germany is the best form of government"	80	89	49	63
"There are other forms of government that are better."	9	3	27	12

* West Germany, ˣ East Germany

Notes: The "other form of government" does not in every case mean support for the "socialist democracy of the GDR."

Source: Datenreport 2008, p. 397.

However, it becomes apparent in the East that the attitude toward socialism as an idea—"Socialism is a good idea in principle that was badly carried out"—was still predominantly positive in East Germany in 1991, but in the West predominantly negative (76 percent and 40 percent agreement, respectively). In the period from 1991 to 2006, this statement was positively assessed in East Germany by an average of 76 percent; in the West, by only 45 percent.

After 2006, data compiled regarding the attitude toward democracy showed disappointing results. Thus in 2006 roughly 71 percent of those questioned (74.8 percent in the West and 57.2 percent in the East) approved of democracy as the form of government in accordance with the principles of the Basic Law. In 2010 it was 73.6 percent (the West was 78.4 percent; the East, 55.3 percent), i.e., in the West slightly higher and in the East slightly lower.[10]

Approval of the democratic system does not necessarily mean satisfaction with the performance and functioning of democracy, i.e., with the change between government and opposition, the guarantee of social security, the choice of policies or their results. In 1990 it became apparent in East Germany that scarcely 40 percent of those questioned were satisfied; in 2006 it was roughly 38 percent. In West Germany at this time, the figure of just below 70 percent had fallen to roughly 62 percent.[11] According to another source, in 2006 it was exactly 46 percent (in the East 27.3 percent and in the West 50.8 percent). In 2010 the figure improved slightly to 46.1 percent due to higher approval in the East (32.1 percent compared to 49.8 percent).[12] When the question was whether one believed he or she had influence over politics, in 2010 exactly 94 percent of West Germans answered "no" and in the East 94.4 percent answered "no," which was 2.1 percent lower than in 2006.[13]

The difference also becomes apparent in the different attitudes toward democracy.

Table 1.2. Typology of Democratic Attitudes. (in percent).

Attitude	All of Germany	West	East
Anti-democratic*	4	3	6
Critical of the system	17	15	26
Critical of policy	30	31	29
Satisfied	39	42	28

* Are satisfied neither with the system nor the functioning of democracy and disapprove of the idea.

Source: Berlin-Brandenburg-Bus 2008, interviewees from 14-years-old on; percentages add up to 100 when missing results (I don't know/no answer/not classifiable) are included.

Confidence in democratic institutions is influenced by trust in the parties and above all in the East by the attitudes toward the performance of the political system. Well over a decade after the start of the German unification process, this differed to some extent between the East and the West. Fifty-six percent of West Germans and 44 percent of East Germans had confidence in the institutions of the Bundestag and federal government.[14] Skepticism prevailed over the statements of politicians before elections. In April 2009, 38 percent of those questioned explained that they would only partially believe such statements; 59 percent did not believe them at all.[15] Distrust vis-à-vis political elites, which was justified because they lacked the ability and will to place themselves into people's everyday concerns, fears, and hardships, grew especially dramatically among East Germans.[16]

The existing differences between East and West show different levels of support for democracy. This is connected to the fact that both parts of the country had varying expectations of democracy. Indeed, since 1990 an increasing majority of East Germans did not want the GDR back, nor do they today. In early 2009, just 10 percent of former GDR citizens declared that they would want the GDR back.[17] It is clear that the overwhelming majority have no longing for the prior political regime. Several had demands for social rights in unified Germany—the GDR regime promised them improvements, but then failed to deliver them, which contributed substantially to the frustration with the system. These demands then became the criteria that determined expectations of and approval for democracy in East Germany. After all, the East Germans were promised "greener landscapes." West Germans, who remembered that the West German "economic miracle" had contributed substantially to the acceptance of democratic institutions and thereby democracy, believed that this would happen again. Yet the economic development from 1990 on, as well as its impact on the effectiveness of the welfare state, has adversely affected the fulfillment of many demands. The problems brought about through the dismantling of industry, rising unemployment, and other economic problems triggered an inter-German migration from East to West, confirming among those remaining the opinion that they would become second-class citizens.

Such an attitude adversely affected the formation of national identity. The process of German unity was supposed to involve forming a new nation, leading to a community of citizens with a national identity beyond their regional one. Here clear differences also became apparent. Between 1991 and 2006 roughly 72 percent of West Germans felt attached to Germany; in the East it was, in contrast, roughly 8 percent less. In April 2009 only about half of East German citizens felt strongly connected with the Federal Republic. At the same time, those under age 30 clearly showed stronger ties to the Federal Republic (53 percent) than older people. That only 38 percent of the age group of 50-to-60-year-olds were attached obviously reflected their social situation and individual experience since 1989. Similarly, only 32 percent of the unemployed stated that they felt at home in the Federal Republic.[18]

Altogether, much indicates that it could still be too early to speak of a democratic consensus supported by a large majority across East and West Germany, not only regarding the functioning of democracy, but also concerning the sense of belonging to a single nation. Yet the tendency toward consensus is increasing.

The Establishment of a National Party System

The preconditions for the establishment of a party system were created during the first stage of the upheaval in the GDR in the autumn of 1989. The national bloc slowly dissolved itself, while the political initiatives and groupings founded after 1989 organized outside of it. Yet only one of these groups, the Social Democratic Party (SDP) in the GDR, understood itself from its foundation as a political party that wanted to compete with the SED; others soon followed it.

The second stage of this process, starting in 1990, was characterized by an attempt to establish a new system of competing parties in the GDR. This forced the old and the new East German parties to develop platforms and to look for a social base whose interests they could represent. Under the pressure of free and democratic elections for the GDR People's Chamber in March 1990, quite diverse parties and political associations were founded, most of which did not survive the initial phase. Their independent development effectively ended even before this election when the West German parties began to look for partners in the East with whom they wanted to campaign in the national elections at the end of 1990. In the run-up to the People's Chamber balloting this led to alliances with East German parties, the support for individual parties by West German partners; otherwise, parties like the post-communist PDS or those of the citizens' movement–derived Bündnis 90 had to go it alone because like the PDS, they found no partners, or like Bündnis 90, they did not want them.

The elections for the People's Chamber in March 1990, in which twenty-four parties and political associations competed, proved to be a catalyst for the East German party system. Since there was no exclusion clause, 0.2 percent of second votes sufficed for representation in the parliament. The "Alliance for Germany" of the CDU, the Democratic Awakening (DA), and the German Social Union (DSU) achieved victory, far ahead of the SPD and the PDS. All other parties and electoral alliances, including those of the civil rights movements, gained only meager results.[19] The bourgeois alliance led by the CDU together with the SPD formed a grand coalition after the election, which initiated the process of unification of the GDR with the Federal Republic on the basis of treaties that had yet to be negotiated.

In the following stage, during local elections in May 1990 and state elections in October, the structure of the East German party system further adapted to the West German pattern. The most important precondition for this was the merger of the East German party organizations of the CDU, the SPD, and the FDP with their West German partner parties in the summer and fall of 1990. Lasting remnants of the East German system were preserved for the time being in the form of the electoral union Bündnis 90 and the PDS.[20]

The transformation was completed through the Bundestag elections in December 1990, which led to the formation of a coherent party system with five parties—the CDU/CSU, the SPD, the FDP, the PDS, and Bündnis 90—but still featured two clearly distinguishable outcomes in the East and West. The distinctions consisted on the one hand of the different strengths of the parties. Thus the small parties of the Greens and the FDP obtained only slight or no approval in East German state parliaments and effectively remained West German parties until the beginning of 2000. The different starting conditions in the East German states also had an effect. While the PDS, the CDU, and the Liberals could draw upon the infrastructure of their East German predecessors, both the SPD and the Bündnis/Grüne were forced, as new parties, to establish new structures. The expectation of a second party system beside the traditional West German pattern was defeated. Since the system developed on a coherent institutional basis and voting rights and party rights remained unchanged, there could be only one party system despite various differences in terms of competitiveness and anchoring in society. Within the parties, it was striking that initially the left wings of the CDU, but not particularly those of the FDP, were strengthened, and East-West conflicts were dealt with not across but within the parties. And in contrast to the West, the ideological poles in the East were occupied on the one side by the PDS and on the other by the CDU. The SPD found itself in a position between the fronts. It could be open for cooperation with one or the other party, but after 1998 it was mainly so with regard to the CDU.

The results of the Bundestag elections of 1990 and 1994[21] did not, despite both East German newcomers, lead to a basic change in the structural asymmetry of the party system, as the predominance of the bourgeois camp of the Union and the FDP was preserved. However, the results of the 1994 Bundestag elections already showed that the progressive dissolution of the large social-moral milieus, above all of the trade unions but also of the bourgeois Protestants, had a negative impact on the SPD. Nevertheless, it was clear that the social democratic camp's mathematical chances for a change of government could only be realized if the SPD and Bündnis/Grüne would accept the PDS as a potential coalition partner. While the PDS tolerated the SPD in Saxony-Anhalt between 1994 and 2002, it refused to even contemplate cooperation or a coalition at the federal level. It thereby founded a tradition whose essential features continue to have an effect today. Two new coalition governments between the SPD and the PDS, formed after 1998 in East German states (1998/2002 in Mecklenburg-Western Pomerania, 2001/11 in Berlin), altered nothing in this regard. The reasons for this are lingering anti-communist attitudes in the SPD, the refusal of certain PDS leaders who were once members of the SPD, and the fear that the CDU would gain campaign advantages from the accusation that the SPD was collaborating with the PDS.

The PDS, whose parliamentary survival after 1990 was regarded by most as uncertain, stabilized itself in 1994 along a new line of conflict—the inter-German East-West tension. It overcame initial difficulties, stabilized itself as the party that purported to represent East German interests,[22] and occupied the third position in the East German party system; the FDP and Bündnis/Grüne did not, with very few exceptions, succeed in state parliaments after 1994 and therefore remained substantially weaker in the East than in the West. The PDS, whose meager results in 1994—it remained under the 5-percent hurdle, yet won four direct mandates and could therefore form a caucus in the Bundestag—did not meet expectations, refrained, with very few exceptions, from participation in state parliamentary elections in West Germany, a necessary strategy in view of its internal problems and slight chances.[23] Right-wing extremist parties, which after 1990 failed to attract voters in the East German states, only resurfaced in noticeable size there in 1998.

In 1998 there was an upheaval in the German party system. This was correlated less with the achievement of the PDS, which barely cleared the 5-percent hurdle, and more with the change of the strength among the large parties.[24] While the SPD was convincing with a reform-oriented program and the commitment to link innovation and social justice, the CDU/CSU failed because it had been led for too long by the same chancellor, could no longer mobilize several of its supporters, and lost some of its East German support. With its victory, the SPD could return to power and form a coalition with the Bündnis 90/Greens. Indeed, while this red-green coalition often suffered defeats in the subsequent state elections, it was able to very narrowly repeat the success of 1998 in the 2002 Bundestag election.[25] It was notable that in 1998 as well as in 2002 the SPD could form a coalition with the Greens without the PDS. This strengthened the SPD in its belief that it could continue to dispense with the PDS, which in the 2002 election completely collapsed and won only two direct mandates. This result made clear that the approval for the representation of East German interests in the electorate had waned, without the SPD being able to improve its position in the West at the same time. This threatened substantial dangers for the party in the following Bundestag election, although as a leftist party it should have profited from the movement of other parties toward the center. While the differences between the East and West electoral areas had further weakened—the FDP, like the Bündnis/Grüne, found approval in several Eastern state elections—the PDS retained its status as an important regional party.

The SPD foundered in the early Bundestag election of 2005[26] and thereafter entered into a CDU-led grand coalition. Through these election results the situation in the whole system changed when an all-German Left Party was formed out of the East German PDS and the West German WASG. The merger process was completed in June 2007. It ended the status of the PDS as an Eastern party and made the party a force on the federal level.[27] The results of the election alliance including both parties—8.7 percent in the 2005 vote—meant the beginning of the re-establishment of the five-party system, first formed in 1990. This was confirmed through successes of the Left Party in four West German state parliamentary elections in 2008 and 2009. At the same time the FDP and Bündnis/Grüne regressed in most but not all East German states.

The outcome of the 2009 Bundestag election definitively confirmed the five-party system,[28] because the Left Party afterward entered further West German state parliaments. The election results accomplished a change of government to a black-yellow coalition of the CDU and the FDP, which had already been evident for some time. The SPD found itself in the opposition on the side of the Left Party and the Greens. The SPD's loss of more than 6 million votes vis-à-vis 2005 reflected its declining significance. The Left Party, prompted by the improvement of its results by 3.2 percent, claimed to be the only genuinely left social democracy, but underestimated the difficulties that would emerge alongside the SPD in the opposition. The Greens began to consider more seriously how they could improve their options, even through a rapprochement with the CDU if necessary. After 2008 they did this in a state coalition in Hamburg, although the coalition ended prematurely in 2010. After state elections in March 2011 in Baden-Württemberg and Rhineland-Palatinate the Bündnis/Grüne entered coalitions with the SPD. On the other hand, the SPD did not make a pact with the Left Party in Saxony-Anhalt because it did not want to serve as its junior partner instead of with the CDU.

The national CDU must begin to look around for a new coalition partner in preparation for the Bundestag elections in 2013 because the FDP has crashed. Therefore it has been courting the Greens, but does not exclude the SPD. But the Greens know that they must have the courage to pursue new themes and strengthen their identity as a party of social justice. Their only option for wielding power is through cooperating with the SPD in dissolving the "black-yellow" coalition. The Left Party, whose internal splits result from divergent leftist traditions and contrary interests of leading actors, did not expand on its electoral success of 2009. It failed in three state elections in West Germany. That extremist right-wing parties in East Germany have become stronger since 1998 could be connected to the diminishing integration of East German protest voters through the PDS. Though the German People's Union (DVU) succeeded in the state parliamentary election of Saxony-Anhalt and later in Brandenburg, it has vanished in the meantime. In 2004, as in 2009, the National Democratic Party (NPD) succeeded in Saxony and in 2006 and again in 2011 in Mecklenburg-Western Pomerania. In the West German state parliamentary election it found no success, save one exception: the DVU/NPD has one mandate in Bremen.

This contradictory process of differentiation and adjustment is also reflected in the dwindling significance of the "GDR factor" in the selection of political leaders. Already before the Bundestag elections of 2009 the impact of the GDR legacy had declined. Since 2005 it is no longer represented in the party system by just the PDS and the Left Party, respectively, but also by the West German parties FDP and the Bündnis/Grüne, which have become more successful in the East German election area—and furthermore by the CDU and the SPD. However, within the party elites the proportion of those who had been politically socialized in East German states has hardly grown. Admittedly, the Hamburg-born, and since 2005, reigning Federal Chancellor Angela Merkel was raised in the GDR, but in the election campaigns she has refrained from touting the fact. None of the ministers of the coalition ruling since 2009 came from an East German state. In the Bundestag two of the six vice presidents are of East German background.

It took a long time for the situation to improve at the highest level. In the 1994 federal presidential election the Bündnis/Grüne nominated a prominent civil rights activist; he received no support from other "Western parties." In 1999 the CDU/CSU fielded—unsuccessfully—an East German politician for the office of federal president; the East German PDS nominated a West German theologian. In 2010 the SPD and Bündnis/Grüne nominated the East German politician Joachim Gauck, who was regarded as a symbolic figure of the German unification process. The Left Party nominated a Western-born woman who in the past had sympathized with the PDS. Christian Wulff, the former CDU Minister-President of Lower Saxony, was successful, but then had to leave his office earlier than expected. In 2012 Joachim Gauck succeeded him due to an agreement of all parties—except the Left and the NPD. The situation of representation was no longer regarded as a lingering East-West conflict, but remnants of it still exist within the parties. In the policy of the Left Party the so-called Eastern interests play only a minor role. They do not determine the identity of this party, which is no longer a party of and for East Germans, although they have a majority among the membership. This is perhaps due to the shift of political issues as well as to the emphasis by more radical politicians.

Changes in Conflict Structures and Party Competition

These political shifts express the changes of interest that arise from the impact of societal developments and their effects on political institutions. The transformation in society is leading to alterations of attitudes and value orientations, which ultimately have nothing to do with the immediate effects of German unification but rather are attributable to the pressure of global developments on the one hand and the differentiation and dissolution of nation-states on the other.[29] The lasting weakness of representation and integration in the large parties shows that they are no longer capable of granting their supporters the promised welfare-state benefits and services that secured differing levels of prosperity and participation in political, social, and cultural affairs. At the same time the consequences of social and value changes increased the competition for party affiliations and electoral choices.[30]

The social change and the change in values it triggered altered the conflict structures in society and thereby also in the party system. After 1960, the old class conflict between capital and labor no longer found political representation in the SPD. The cessation of serious conflicts between church and state altered the situation for the CDU. The modernization of society improved the position of the FDP. The collapse of the Soviet bloc ended the East-West conflict and reduced the significance of anti-communism for the mobilization campaigns of the CDU/CSU through ideological polarization. Moreover, the PDS strategy of posing as representative of East German interests has clearly diminished since 2005. This is also true for the position within the Left that wants to resuscitate the old conflict between capitalism and socialism as the basis of party competition. Above all, the effects of globalization and further European integration are still unclear.

The conflict structure of the party system, which has been changing for quite some time now, determines the competition among parties. The economic-social confrontation, which has long marked party competition, has been replaced by the social justice–market freedom pair of opposites as a line of conflict. Moreover, this is complemented by a second line of conflict "on the contrast of libertarian and authoritarian values."[31] Representatives of the extreme positions on the socioeconomic spectrum are the Left versus the FDP, on the political-cultural dimension the Bündnis/Grüne versus the NPD. The parties currently compete between two political poles: a neoliberal-authoritarian stance on one side and a social-libertarian attitude on the other side. Parties at the edges have greater difficulties with being invited by competitors into government coalitions. At the same time, voting behavior and electoral results have lead to development of a "fluid" party system. A coalition between a bigger and a smaller party may become less predictable than in the past. Smaller parties may become stronger—and may fail again. New parties like the "Pirate Party" appear briefly like shooting stars. They benefit from different factors like criticisms of politics or new issues. Old issues take a backseat or vanish, forcing parties to think about their opportunities to represent relevant social interests. Thus at present the political parties and even other political institutions have to face future challenges beyond German unification, which is losing the relevance it once had in the near past.

Outlook on the Future

The transfer of political institutions from West to East and the alignment carried out in the process of German unification has not proceeded without problems. These ranged from a lack of understanding of East German living conditions on the part of West German bureaucrats and politicians to the consequences of the transfer of institutional structures. For instance, some federal state or territorial administrative patterns, which were already considered in need of reform in the West, were nonetheless transplanted to the East with all their problems and deficiencies.[32]

The development of an all-German party system occurred primarily according to established procedures, and party unifications led to innovations only in a few cases. Until the present day the various organizations and membership strengths of the parties and their presence in the state parliaments as well as the distribution of their voters can be clearly distinguished in East and West.[33] Since in the Bündnis/Grüne are represented in every East German state parliament, and the FDP in three, their claims to act as national parties cannot be disputed. The right-extremist party NPD cannot say the same for itself. Moreover, the merger of the PDS and the WASG signaled the end of the effort to establish an East German–based party in the German party system. Beyond the social tensions of the electorate and the competitive situation, the remaining differences between East and West are possible options for creating coalitions.

Differences can also be perceived with regard to the results of the transformation of elites in political institutions. The persistence of old and the ascent of new indigenous elites in the parties as well as in the parliaments and administrations has led to a juxtaposition of East German old and new elites with West German ones.[34] The effects of extensive exclusion of East German scientific, cultural, and also technical elites from the process of transformation no longer benefit Die Linke as much as they did before. A pervasive willingness to end the marginal role of East German elites at higher political levels can now be seen. Four out of five minister-presidents of East German states are natives. The federal president and federal chancellor have East German backgrounds. This shows a considerable improvement over the previous lack of integration in and impact on Western-dominated structures.[35]

In the year 25 of the new calendar, democracy has achieved a stable, yet in no way crisis-proof, position in Germany. The quantitative dimension of the approval of democracy as a system and of its functioning still illustrates a perceptible difference between West and East Germany. But East German assertions of feeling like "second-class citizens" are gradually losing importance. The latter underscores that there exists both consensus and difference between West and East in Germany regarding the acceptance of democracy and the sense of belonging to a common nation. For anti-democratic behavior and criticism of the system are found in both East and West, yet more strongly in the East.[36] Insufficient consideration of different political and private socializations as well as institutional experiences in the old regime and the expectations of the new one have contributed to this divergence. Many decisions in individual policy fields likewise have their share in it, beginning with the privatization of the East German economy and the integration of the police and judiciary into new structures, and ending with the selection of elites in culture, science, and politics. The differences may vanish into German history as soon as witnesses of the unification process disappear.

East and West Germans and international authors regret to different degrees that the dynamics of the peaceful revolution were not utilized in the creation of German unity in order to address and restore the legitimacy of various structural reforms for the system of political institutions.[37] Recent events prove the growing readiness of citizens to oppose the institutional and political lethargy that had spread in the Federal Republic and threatened to lead democracy into a crisis. In this respect, unification delayed the development of democracy in Germany, although it is correctly assessed as a victory of the parliamentary democracy system over the Soviet system.

Despite the fact that some shout "We are the people," the peaceful revolution in the GDR cannot be compared with the protest movements that have emerged since 1990 in Germany, such as the anti-Hartz IV campaign or protests against the renovation of the train station in Stuttgart ("Stuttgart 21") and then against the "withdrawal from the withdrawal" from nuclear power.[38] The initial policy reactions to this criticism attributed the crisis to the traditional political institutions. They strengthened the wish, raised for years by civil society, to reform democracy, but there is no demand for a systemic change. The new protest movement, anchored in all layers of society, was and is, moreover, neither a revival nor a renaissance of the peaceful revolution of the GDR. The protests have to be understood as a signal that the political institutions of the system of the Federal Republic must open themselves to greater participation of citizens in order to reduce the resentment of institutions and authoritarian decisions and in turn strengthen the viability of the parliamentary system in times of crisis. Whether this could occur through more deliberative democracy or through participation in decision-making processes by introducing plebiscites and referenda on the national level should be discussed just as much as the strengthening of civil society vis-à-vis the state. The memory of the fate of the GDR's political regime and its inability to learn could, twenty years after its end, help to launch such a process.

Notes

1. For the overall process see Konrad H. Jarausch, *The Rush to German Unity* (New York, 1994).
2. Wilfriede Otto, "Die politischen Systeme," in C. Burrichter, D. Nakath, and G.-R. Stephan, eds., *Deutsche Zeitgeschichte von 1945 bis 2000. Gesellschaft—Staat—Politik. Ein Handbuch* (Berlin, 2006), 270–326, 319.
3. Gero Neugebauer, "Change and the Transition of the East German Political System: A Chronicle," in F.D. Weil, ed., *Democratization in Eastern and Western Europe: Research on Democracy and Society*, vol. 1 (Greenwich, 1993), 299–326.
4. Cf. Erich Fischer, ed., *Verfassungsdiskussion und Verfassungsgebung 1990 bis 1994 in Deutschland* (Schkeuditz, 2005).
5. The first three leaders of this agency were active members of the East German civil rights movement.
6. The National Front was an alliance of all of the parties and mass organizations existing within the Party, which was responsible for the organization of elections among other things. It was under the leadership of the SED.
7. The CDU's organizational area does not include the state of Bavaria; in Bavaria the only Christian party is the CSU.
8. Gerard Braunthal, *Parties and Politics in Modern Germany* (Boulder, 1996), 71f.
9. http://www.bundeswahlleiter.de/de/bundestagswahlen/downloads/bundestagswahlergebnisse/btw_ab49_wahlbeteiligung.pdf.
10. Oliver Decker et al., *Die Mitte in der Krise. Rechtsextreme Einstellungen in Deutschland 2010, Studie im Auftrag der Friedrich-Ebert-Stiftung* (Berlin, 2010), 98.
11. Bundeszentrale für politische Bildung, *Datenreport 2008, Ein Sozialbericht für die Bundesrepublik Deutschland* (Bonn, 2008), 397.
12. Ibid.
13. Ibid.
14. Oskar Niedermayer, *Bürger und Politik. Politische Orientierungen und Verhaltensweisen der Deutschen. Eine Einführung* (Wiesbaden, 2001), 66.
15. Gunnar Winkler, *20 Jahre friedliche Revolution 1989 bis 2009. Die Sicht der Bürger der neuen Bundesländer. Auf Grundlage der empirischen Erhebungen*, Sozialwissenschaftliches Forschungszentrum Berlin-Brandenburg e.V. June 2009 (*Beiträge zur sozialen Transformation der neuen Bundesländer*, vol. 24), 42.
16. Winkler, *20 Jahre*, 42f.
17. Ibid, 47 (Table 8).
18. Winkler, *20 Jahre*, 46. In the West, the supporters of the Greens and in the East those of the former Left Party/PDS were the ones who expressed the weakest ties to Germany.
19. The alliance consisted of the CDU (40.5 percent), the DSU (6.3 percent), and the DA (0.9 percent). The SPD won 21.8 percent, the PDS 16.3 percent, and the Bündnis 90 2.9 percent; the rest was distributed among five additional parties and associations. Cf. http://www.parties-and-elections.de/germany2.html, 14 April 2009.
20. The Bündnis 90 united with the Greens at the beginning of 1993. The PDS merged with the West German WASG in the summer of 2007 to become the Left Party.
21. In 1990, CDU/CSU won 43.8 percent of the vote, the SPD 33.5 percent, the FDP 11 percent, the Bündnis 90/Greens 5 percent (3.8 percent in the West and 1.2 percent in the East), and the PDS 2.4 percent. In 1994, the CDU/CSU won 41.4 percent of the vote, the SPD 36.4 percent, the FDP 6.9 percent, the Bündnis 90/Greens 7.3 percent, and the PDS 4.4 percent. See http://www.wahlrecht.de/ergebnisse/bundestag.htm, 14 March 2009.
22. In specific areas (pension rights and property rights, among others) the consequences of regulations in the unification treaty have been felt as unjust by those affected. Hence a pension was derided as a "punishment pension," since income components that had

been paid while someone was a member of the Ministry for State Security or the institutions of the SED were not credited to the recipient, lowering the amount. The judiciary softened or removed quite a few of these regulations. The PDS has understood itself as the representative of "hurt feelings" as well as alleged or actual loss of socioeconomic status.

23. Gero Neugebauer and Richard Stöss, *Die PDS. Geschichte Organisation Wähler Konkurrenten* (Opladen, 1996).
24. The CDU/CSU garnered 35.1 percent of the vote, the SPD 40.9 percent, the FDP 6.2 percent, the Bündnis 90/Greens 6.7 percent, and the PDS 5.1 percent.
25. The CDU/CSU garnered 38.5 percent of the vote, the SPD 38.5 percent, the FDP 7.4 percent, the Bündnis 90/Greens 8.6 percent, and the PDS 4.0 percent.
26. The CDU/CSU won 35.2 percent of the vote, the SPD 34.2 percent, the FDP 9.8 percent, the Bündnis 90/Greens 8.1 percent, and the Left Party/PDS 8.7 percent. http://www.wahlrecht.de/ergebnisse/bundestag.htm, 14 April 2009.
27. The PDS, as well as the WASG, saw in the merger the only possibility for overcoming the 5 percent hurdle in the early new election of 2005. The admission of the former SPD chair Oskar Lafontaine provided the electoral alliance with additional media attention and attracted voters who had not accepted the PDS as a left alternative to the SPD or to the Bündnis/Grüne.
28. The Union obtained 33.8 percent, the SPD 23 percent, the FDP 14.9 percent, the Left 11.9 percent, and Bündnis 90/Greens 10.7 percent of the second vote.
29. Richard Stöss, "Mehr Kontinuität als Wandel. Das Parteiensystem vor und nach der deutschen Vereinigung," in R. Czada, H. Wollmann, eds., "Von der Bonner zur Berliner Republik. 10 Jahre deutsche Einheit," special issue of *Leviathan* 19 (1999), 308–327, 323.
30. Elmar Wiesendahl, "Am Volk vorbei. Die Volksparteien nach dem Wegfall ihrer Voraussetzungen," in *Vorgänge. Zeitschrift für Bürgerrechte und Gesellschaftspolitik* 180, no. 46, (2007), 4–14.
31. Neugebauer and Stöss, *Die PDS,* 274.
32. Gert Joachim Glaeßner, *Demokratie und Politik in Deutschland* (Opladen, 1999), 573.
33. The ratio of East German to West German voters is approximately 50/50 for the Left Party; for all other parties it is 20/80.
34. Helga Welsh, "Parliamentary Elites in Times of Political Transition: The Case of Eastern Germany," *West European Politics* 19 (1996), 507–524.
35. Jennifer A. Yoder, *From East Germans to Germans? The New Postcommunist Elites* (Durham, 1999).
36. Johannes Kuppe, "Das vereinigte Deutschland nach der Überwindung der Zweistaatlichkeit," in Burrichter et al., eds., *Deutsche Zeitgeschichte von 1945 bis 2000,* 161–180.
37. Those that argue like this include E. Fischer, G.J. Glaeßner, J. A. Yoder, and G. Winkler.
38. At the end of 2010, the Merkel government decided to rescind the 2002 phaseout of nuclear energy of the previous government implemented by the SPD and Bündnis 90/Greens. But after accidents at the Japanese nuclear power plant in Fukushima, the decision was reversed in response to large protests. Yet the CDU/FDP coalition still did poorly in subsequent state parliamentary elections and internal crises erupted in these parties.

Chapter Two

United, Yet Separate

A View from the East

Heinrich Bortfeldt

At the last meeting of the People's Chamber on 2 October 1990, its vice-president, Reinhard Höppner (SPD), expressed his anticipation of the coming day of German unification in the following words: "Tomorrow we celebrate a wedding. Everyone knows it will only become a good marriage if both sides change, grow together, and regarding joint property, do not constantly discuss thereafter who brought what into the marriage."[1] Two decades later, for the twentieth anniversary of the first free election of the GDR People's Chamber on 18 March 2010, Parliament President Norbert Lammert complained that the public television stations had refused, despite numerous requests, to broadcast the celebration in the German Bundestag. Instead, at that time the ZDF channel aired reports on *Drehscheibe Deutschland* about fears of genetically modified potatoes, about clients swindled by homebuilders, and about a cow-milking competition in Lower Saxony.[2]

Similarly, for the 2010 anniversary year, the newsmagazine *Focus* carried the headline, "And who now helps those from the West? How the reconstruction of the East ruined the old Federal Republic."[3] "Flourishing landscapes" of the East, like Dresden and Leipzig, were compared with problematic municipalities of the Ruhr, such as Duisburg, Oberhausen, and Gelsenkirchen. The central art exhibition for the sixtieth anniversary of the founding of the Federal Republic, "60 Years, 60 Works," in the Martin Gropius Building in Berlin ignored GDR art completely. The Rhenish curator Walter Smerling justified his purely West German view of an en-

Notes for this chapter begin on page 61.

tirely West German art with the words: "I think the problem of the GDR will, over time, evaporate as an ugly raindrop of history. The GDR actually plays no role in the development of art."[4]

All these remarks illustrate the problems of reunification. They testify to the difficult heritage of the GDR and the confusion about the appropriate way to deal with it. They reduce reunification to a cost-benefit calculation. They mention losses but not gains. Yet they also describe the incomprehension, ignorance, and arrogance—just like a last, confused hurrah of the defunct Bonn Republic.

So what remains of the wedding twenty years ago, of the "growing together," of mutual changing, as Höppner hoped for and envisioned? What has become of the hopes and dreams? The East Germans appreciated their newly gained freedom with entirely new life opportunities in a world without walls. They "dreamt of paradise—and woke up in North Rhine-Westphalia," as Joachim Gauck vividly put it. This was certainly not *the* paradise of East Germans had dreamt about. But after the euphoria, the exceptional circumstance par excellence, the excessive expectations, the auspicious promises, the unbelievable surplus of hope, the only result could be a harsh arrival at reality.

The Starting Point of 1989/90

The basic conditions seemed to be extremely simple and favorable: the number one country from the West merged with the number one country from the East. Though they were artificially divided, there were common cultural traditions, family relations, cross-border media, the "we are one people" call in the East and the "brothers and sisters" declarations in the West. According to Willy Brandt, now that which belonged together could finally grow together. In reality, though, reunification turned out to be an "asymmetrical process." Both sides quickly ascertained that in spite of everything, they had developed apart from each other for forty years. The East Germans had drawn themselves a false, one-sided picture of the rich and prosperous Federal Republic—they could hardly have a realistic perception. It was an "image of longing." In the GDR under Honecker, the FRG was declared to be a foreign land according to a policy called "demarcation" (*Abgrenzung*).

While the Federal Republic's reunification mandate of the Basic Law was still in force, in day-to-day practice it had faded more and more into the background. For many West German intellectuals, German division was the punishment for Auschwitz; for a younger political generation, Tuscany and Provence were closer than Leipzig or Dresden. On the June 17 holiday, many preferred to go swimming in the Wannsee instead of commemorating the 1953 uprising in East Berlin. During the Cold War, the two German states stood on different sides of the competition between the two systems and were more likely to define themselves by their differences than their commonalities. Thus in 1989 two completely different worldviews encountered each other with completely different ideas about the political order in areas such as markets, freedom, democracy, money, and property.

As in the GDR, state socialism in Europe was worn out: politically, economically, and morally. It quickly became apparent that the GDR didn't really rank among the ten leading industrial countries of the world. The economy was exhausted, having already deteriorated for years. A people, walled in since 1961, was henceforth confronted with the reality of the Free World. "Germany" was always synonymous with the successful West Germany; despite international recognition and relative prosperity, the GDR was and remained until the end always the "second" German state, smaller and poorer, and, as the "state behind the Wall," constantly competing for recognition.

In 1989, world history quite unexpectedly knocked on the German door. No one was prepared; there was no historical model, no master plan. There was indeed a "Ministry for Inter-German Questions," but no ministry for "All-German Answers." From almost standing still, under extreme time pressure, facing a brief, once-in-a-lifetime international window, the unification process had to be initiated. Time horizons shrank from five-to-ten years to eleven months. The people on the streets pushed the politicians forward. In mid-December 1989, there were still 73 percent of East Germans who pleaded for a sovereign GDR. Less than two months later, at the beginning of February 1990, there was a complete reversal, with 76 percent now in favor of unification.[5]

Gorbachev and Shevardnadze fought for their political survival in the crisis-ridden Soviet Union, and no one knew if and when the military would topple them. During this time, German policy in East Berlin and in Bonn faced its greatest challenge in the postwar period. The first freely elected minister-president of the GDR, Lothar de Maizière, attempted to have a reformed, now democratic GDR play a dignified part in the unification process. The brief but intense process of democratization after a peaceful resolution formed part of the East German dowry.[6]

Yet given these different starting conditions, a marriage on equal footing was not possible. The accession of the new states was the legally correct procedure according to Article 23 of the Basic Law . This was the simplest and quickest solution. That is, the loser of the Cold War joined the victor, the soft East Mark to the hard D-Mark, the petitioner to the club of the well-to-do, a minority of 16 million to an overwhelming majority of 62 million. For the East Germans it was a complete change of system; it meant adaptation as a survival strategy through learning by doing. Wolfgang Schäuble, former minister of the interior and leader of the West German team negotiating the unification treaty, clearly indicated to the GDR negotiators who had the final say and where he placed his priorities: "Dear people, it is about an accession of the GDR to the Federal Republic, not a reciprocal event. You are warmly welcomed.... However, this unification does not take place between two equal states. We will not start all over again from equal positions."[7]

The marginalization of East Germans was not inevitable due to this inequality, but it had to be expected. Thus the Federal Republic naturally gained strategic sovereignty over the collapsing GDR. East Germans were granted participation in the West German welfare state; in return, however, they ceded control over this process to West German elites. Unified Germany should become, essentially, an enlarged, old Federal Republic, somewhat more Eastern, somewhat more Protestant. Continuity and stability took priority over any experiments, e.g., no new constitution or any type of confederation model, to say nothing of a third way. A majority wanted this, not just in the West but in the still-existing GDR as well. At the time, most East Germans in their unification euphoria wished everything to become for them as it was in West Germany. They wanted to participate in the West German success story, meaning that it should be applied to East Germany as well. The reconstruction of the East meant, in essence, the replication of the West. There was an almost limitless faith in West German solidarity, in its resources, and in the West German elites.[8]

Under these circumstances one could not and would not want to learn from those who had lost. The East Germans, however, had made the experience of the stormy autumn of 1989, in which they took their destiny into their own hands, the subject of history, and swept away the system in a revolution. It was a high point of political engagement, actual grassroots democracy—and full of dreams. On the other hand, the East German chances of participation diminished by delegating control of this process to Bonn. The East Germans were relegated to the school desk in order to learn the West German system, which often resulted in disregard for their experiences and devaluation of their lifeworlds.

Yet this was necessary, because to completely reconstruct the administration, judiciary, economy, and thus a political system, and to make it functional in only a short time, required West German help. The Federal Republic undertook the redevelopment of East Germany with considerable resources. This was not entirely altruistic: the transfer of elites with and without "hazard zone pay" from West to East was an enormous job-creation measure for the West. The new sales market in the East and the subsidies, which in large part flowed back into West German companies, worked like a stimulus plan for the West. In addition, East Germany was "adjusted to the market."[9]

Many East Germans wanted to quickly leave the past behind them and become like West Germans. Initially, it was even embarrassing for some to be recognized as East German in language, attitude, and clothing, even if soon after the currency union of 1 July 1990 the economic consequences became noticeable. Already by the end of August, 361,286 people were registered as unemployed, which corresponded to an unemployment rate of 4.1 percent. In fact, 1.5 million employees, more than twice as many as in July, had to work less than full time. In September 1990, 86 percent of GDR citizens were worried about their jobs, according to a survey of the election research group. On the other hand, 3,180 students from the GDR had already enrolled for the summer semester at West German universities, and 4.7 billion D-Marks were already allocated in the second half of 1990 for the renovation of the GDR transportation system.[10]

Foreign countries also did not want any German experiments. Forty-five years after the Second World War, the Federal Republic had matured into an economic and political anchor of stability and a dependable partner and ally in Europe. Other nations preferred for that to remain the case. The breathtaking internal dynamic, coupled with the international risks, led all of Germany to renounce any reform efforts to modernize the already overextended West German welfare state along with its bureaucracy and regulatory frenzy, as well as to prepare it for globalization.[11] While that would have been timely, it likely asked too much of all sides. In this exceptional situation, Helmut Kohl was the ideal symbolic figure. He appeared as solid as a rock, exuding confidence, courage, and certainty. More than a few West Germans longed to return to the security and comfort of when the world was still neatly arranged—and the pensions secured.[12] One could certainly call that *Westalgie* (nostalgia for West Germany).

By ignoring the reform gridlock, Chancellor Kohl postponed its solution to the twenty-first century, and German unity was all-too-one-sidedly blamed for causing this prior problem. Yet at the time, everything appeared to be relatively simple: with a catch-up modernization, everything ought to change in the East but absolutely nothing in the West. This was a doubly privileged special case of the transformation, since the GDR automatically became a member of the European Union—which its Eastern European neighbors envied. Helmut Kohl promised his West German compatriots that they could pay for unity with petty cash, and promised the East Germans flourishing landscapes after a brief period of hard times.

Although this was completely unrealistic, both sides wanted to believe it as part of the euphoria of unity.

German unity occurred during a phase of radical change worldwide, the "disappearance of boundaries" and the increasing dissolution of traditional economic and social models. New conditions of global competition, the end of traditional industries, the advent of completely new branches of industry, and structural change in entire regions had already led by the end of the 1980s to an unfamiliar complexity in the Federal Republic as well. Even without German unity, the West German economic and social model would have had to have been reorganized. The fatal flaw of unification was that this model, which in principle was no longer appropriate, was transferred to the East.[13] In summary, one can say that in 1989/90 the GDR was at an end while the Federal Republic was successful, but needed reform.

Successful System Transfer

The transfer of the political system and integration into the Western model proceeded most rapidly and with the least friction on the political-administrative-legal level. In contrast, the economic-social realm shows no self-sustaining growth after twenty years as the East still has to be drip-fed from West Germany; the gap between East and West has not closed and grows even wider. Apart from a few exceptions, East Germany will remain a region left behind. And in the mental-cultural area, mutual misperceptions, subcultural divisions, and feelings of being a stranger in one's own country abound, reactions that will surely disappear in time but are lasting far longer than originally thought.

The GDR citizens had experienced the power of democracy and freedom themselves in the autumn of 1989. At numerous demonstrations, roundtables, and dialogue forums, they participated in the process of democratization from below. They made history—a grandiose experience, which was, on occasion, later romanticized to some extent. Nevertheless, this is an essential difference from the West German attitude toward democracy. The relationship of the East Germans to democracy derives not only from comparison to their experience with dictatorship and with socialism in the defunct GDR, but also from their own experience with achieving democratization in 1989/90. Both allow many East Germans to react more sensitively to societal problems and also explain a certain skepticism vis-à-vis the federal German, capitalist societal system. This is often overlooked by the West German side.[14] These are experiences with a failed system, or at least socializations, that West Germans do not possess.

At least after the first free election of 18 March 1990, the GDR was a "society in transition" with only a limited future. The stated goal of the de Maizière government was to lead a democratized GDR to unity on the basis of Article 23 of the Basic Law. For that, a process of preparation and adaptation was necessary, so that the GDR could, without major friction, dock at the Federal Republic, the country of destination. Next, local self-government had to be restored and the states reconstituted to make it compatible with the federal structure of the Basic Law. The first state treaty of the economic, currency, and social union, and the subsequent unification treaty took important steps regarding the market economy, privatization, the introduction of the D-Mark, and social security legislation; altogether, it was a process of legal harmonization and the creation of the rule of law in East Germany. Ultimately this meant the transfer of the Basic Law along with its corresponding institutions to the area of the GDR.[15]

The rapid effort at adaptation by de Maizière government succeeded in a very short time at integrating the new federal states into the institutional order of the Federal Republic. In particular, the rapid construction of a functioning administration in accordance with the rule of law sped up the process of administrative adjustment and consolidation, thus preventing inefficiencies and tensions. The quick political-institutional transfer from West to East proved to be a successful model, a privileged German exception when compared with the rather halting and contradictory transformation processes in the Eastern European states. The success of the political regime change is all the more astonishing given the background of the two former states with completely opposed societal systems.

Yet these advantages and benefits were also accompanied by disadvantages, which can explain the lower level of acceptance of the system in the East. The harmonization of institutions was imposed on East Germans from "outside." Since it did not correspond to Eastern life experiences, it has been weakly anchored in minds and culture. East German deficits in competence and political actors produced a comprehensive transfer of elites, which was experienced by many Easterners as incapacitation and heteronomy. Therefore the basic approval of and identification with the political order and its institutions is much less pronounced than in the West. It should be added that after forty years of dictatorship and a complicated phase of societal upheaval and adjustment, civil society could not grow quickly enough. Even twenty years after the creation of a functioning institutional framework, a conflict between political structure and political culture can still be observed.[16]

When the political parties in the still-existing GDR, be it the old bloc parties or the newly founded SPD, merged with their West German sisters, they were increasingly dominated by the latter. The only party no one wanted anything to do with was the successor to the old SED state party, the PDS. It was the political street urchin, with whom all coalitions were forbidden. The SPD was not prepared to integrate even the reform-oriented part of the PDS. Thus the PDS remained a regional party of the East with unique characteristics. Since its Western expansion was unsuccessful, it, nonetheless mutated into representing the interests of the East. Against the backdrop of declining euphoria about unity and increasing frustration with unification problems, defiance against being overwhelmed by Western dominance, the PDS, anchored in the municipalities, could rise from a marginal group to a people's party garnering more than 20 percent of the vote. Since it had voted against the unification treaty and criticized the unification process, the PDS now saw itself validated in its warnings about its dire consequences.

Rather fickle voting behavior, low rates of voter participation, and less pronounced party ties clearly distinguish the East from the West. In the East, the FDP and Greens are comparatively underrepresented. In contrast, the PDS long remained a fringe party in the West. In the East, an orientation toward strong personalities, not necessarily toward parties, is obviously more pronounced. The longtime minister-presidents of Saxony and Brandenburg, Kurt Biedenkopf and Manfred Stolpe, respectively, were regarded as beloved fathers of the people.

For GDR citizens, free elections and a diverse party landscape were new phenomena. In four decades they had no experience of the sort. In the GDR one "voted for" the single ticket of the National Front. There were no campaigns, no campaign rhetoric, no free parliament, no search for a majority, no alternating coalitions. East Germans had not experienced representative democracy—with both its advantages and its deficits. Many were, per "Western television," enthusiastic about the culture of open debate in the Bundestag and wanted such a thing in the East as well. Given the unanimity and lack of public debate in the East, this was hardly surprising. Forty years of state socialism had also left behind a certain distrust of new commitments as well as of parties. Four decades of living under different societal systems had also created distinctive sociopolitical value systems. Thus GDR citizens consider "democracy" a positive value, but stress the values of equality and justice along with the state's comprehensive responsibility for the welfare of its citizens much more strongly than do their West German compatriots.[17]

Having been weaned from personal responsibility and having experienced the egalitarian claims of the GDR's welfare dictatorship, many East Germans preferred state redistribution to individual initiative. Moreover, they were confronted with a gap between rich and poor, which they did not know in the GDR and thus perceived as unjust. Twenty years after the fall of the Wall, two-thirds of all East Germans had the feeling that things in their society were "not fair"; in the West it was 59 percent. Thus it is unsurprising that 67 percent of East Germans but also 53 percent of West Germans are dissatisfied with the functioning of the political system. However, over 90 percent of all Germans are satisfied with the "idea of democracy."[18]

Due to the conflict-ridden adjustment to the market economy, and the unexpectedly twice as high unemployment in the East, doubts about democracy emerged. It had not been possible to experience democracy in the GDR. There were no tough struggles to find majorities in a time-consuming discussion process without predetermined outcome. One was confronted with decisions one had to accept. Even today many East Germans react with incomprehension to overly long decision making and press for greater effectiveness. Among older functionaries, the Bundestag and government are often misunderstood and defamed as merely "puppets" of capital. There were also misconceptions regarding the function and task of the state under the rule of law. The rule of law was confused with fairness; there was an illusion that rule of law and morality were identical. The civil rights advocate Bärbel Bohley herself indulged in this wishful thinking when, after the fall of the Wall, she disappointedly confessed: "We desired justice and received the rule of law instead." This quote already expressed contempt for the state governed by the rule of law.

In postwar West Germany, acceptance of democracy was accompanied by steady economic growth, personal advancement, growing prosperity, great satisfaction, and a lack of crises or disruptions. Under these conditions, democracy could grow strong and successful. These favorable circumstances were simply not present in the East in the exceptional situation after 1989. This fact has occasionally eroded their faith in (West) German democracy. As necessary as West German external control was, it rendered it unnecessary for East Germans to act creatively and made it easier to assign blame to the West German side. GDR citizens had been brought up under conditions of tutelage; the SED state thus left behind wards. The new life in democracy, freedom, and rule of law first had to be learned. Yet at the same time, the rapid transfer of the West German political system to the acceding territory made the learning process and identification more difficult. This "deficit of subjectivity" also frequently led to a retreat into the private sphere. Since it had not evolved naturally, the system was perceived as something foreign. Facing a comprehensive top-down logic, the diminished willingness to adapt, and a defensiveness vis-à-vis West German dominance triggered some reversion to distinct East German traditions.[19]

In the East one could hear more and more often the sentence: "What good is democracy and freedom if I can't buy anything and I can't travel!" Anxiety about employment, a completely new phenomenon for East Germans, often overshadowed the gain in liberty. Due to the economic and financial crisis of 2009, the blatant greed of financial managers, the amoral enrichment at the expense of the "little people," and unchecked financial capitalism in a global world that has become confusing, the call for greater state regulation, for more fairness, has become louder, combined with growing doubts about the functioning of democracy. According to "Social Report 2010" of the People's Solidarity Organization, only 25 percent of East Germans felt like "proper German citizens" after twenty years of unity. Yet in contrast, among the younger generation and higher-income East Germans there is a "stable, increasing identification with the Federal Republic."

Concerning attitudes toward democracy, there are still differences between East and West. While in the old states, 82 percent of citizens consider democracy very important, the proportion in the East is only 69 percent. The study concludes that the lower acceptance in the East can be attributed less to political convictions than to personal living circumstances. Thus, for instance, two-thirds of those interviewed between eighteen- and sixty-five-years-old had to find an occupation that had nothing to do with their original training. In both parts of the country, the number of people without social insurance as well as anxiety about the future was increasing. In this regard, East and West had grown somewhat closer.[20]

Disputes about GDR History

The GDR has become a "battlefield of memories," as Martin Sabrow correctly concludes.[21] The best example is the fifth volume of Hans-Ulrich Wehler's *Deutsche Gesellschaftsgeschichte, Bundesrepublik und DDR, 1949–1990.* One of the best-known historians of the Federal Republic, Wehler writes in his foreword that he describes the GDR merely as a negative foil to "the historically superior state, namely the FRG," and thus cannot grant it "equivalent treatment." He continues: "All of the wrong decisions that were made in East Germany had to be corrected in a cumbersome process according to the West German model. This is the burden which the new Federal Republic [has had to bear] since 1990."[22]

The contest revolves around which interpretation will dominate. An undifferentiated condemnation of GDR history has triggered as an act of defiance an equally undifferentiated idealization of the GDR. Both go hand in hand. What is missing are the nuances; instead black-and-white images proliferate. Public memory is dominated by both extremes: villainous stories about the "Stasi" and heroic stories about the "miracle of the peaceful revolution." The memory of the dictatorship is focused on the victim-perpetrator conflict. According to Lothar de Maizière, in the GDR there were "perhaps two percent victims and perhaps three percent perpetrators. But 95 percent were ordinary people. They did not want to be anything else, tried to make the best out of their lives for themselves and their family. Yet in hindsight, the GDR population is divided into perpetrators and victims. Now all must see how they can get to the victims' side, because otherwise they will be counted as perpetrator. They have to tell their opposition stories and how often they clenched their fist in their pants pocket. But they were neither the one, nor the other."[23] The people were overwhelmingly conformist and had come to terms with the system in their own way. In 1989, *the* people were also not in the streets of Leipzig, as only 13 percent of the city's population participated in the demonstrations.[24]

Similarly, the renowned British historian and expert on Germany Mary Fulbrook, who has given detailed attention to memory culture in Germany, argues that the presentation of GDR history in Berlin is "too strongly fixated on the Stasi and the Wall." This focus on the instruments of repression makes "all GDR citizens victims." Eighty percent of the population is left out of these representations. They demand "greater courage to differentiate."[25]

With the official memorial institutions concentrating on power and repression, there remains little space for private recollection within families and circles of friends. Why, as historian Thomas Großbölting asks, "was everyday life in the GDR supposed to have been drab? And if so, is it more colorful today?" The generalized depreciation of life in the GDR with the "intent of delegitimizing it" is not only detrimental to a complex understanding. It ultimately leads to a division of memory into a private version and an official version that is communicated through the media. Furthermore, it is counterproductive as it directly promotes a nostalgia for East Germany, "which in most cases stems less from the political justification for the old system, than, above all…[from the wish] to defend and justify one's own life or that of parents or grandparents when faced with accusations perceived as unfair."[26] The nostalgia of many East Germans has perhaps less to do with the GDR than with the dream of a West that has not been fulfilled.[27]

The civil rights activist Wolfgang Templin also disagrees with Wehler and concludes that "the trilogy of Wall, shooting order, and barbed wire" does not suffice to explain a complex forty-year history. Above all, he misses "the fascination with the idea of the century—communism—and the mobilizing and integrative powers of the grand experiment connected with it."[28] The well-known civil rights activist Jens Reich also harshly criticized Wehler's fifth volume: the East German people are presented only as a "suffering object," as a "thoroughly ruled flock of sheep," yet never as "active subjects." Furthermore, the interaction with West Germany is left out. In such an account, the reviewer cannot recognize himself, but remains a stranger. In this reaction, he is not alone.[29]

To interpret the GDR only through its failure leads to an imbalance. The GDR must be seen in its rise and fall. There were reasons for its emergence and there were reasons for its failure. Yet this was not really the intention of official memorialization. The GDR was not supposed to be remembered in its entirety, but rather as the "SED dictatorship," as a relevant foundation calls it. The scandalization of the Stasi, together with the "obtrusive one-sidedness" in the depiction of the GDR have, according to Peter Bender, played a decisive role in alienating West and East Germans from one another.[30] "For Wehler (and the vast majority of the younger generation) the Federal Republic became the benchmark; mine remained Germany. The GDR was presented as so dark and inadequate, one couldn't think of it as part of Germany." Wehler describes two societies, but not how they related to each another. Bender recollects that since 1990 *Germany* has once again become the benchmark.[31]

With the unification in 1990 the GDR came to an end, but the old Federal Republic also took its leave. Yet hardly anyone in West Germany wanted to believe the latter. Those, like Wehler, who think exclusively in the categories of the old Federal Republic, appear not yet to have properly arrived in the now twenty-year-old unified Germany. It obviously does not occur to Wehler to recognize this other part of Germany as part of his own history.

Conversely, one hears the accusation again and again that some/many East Germans have still not arrived. But what does "arrived" mean? Arrived where? Should they have come at all? Should East Germans become 100 percent West German? Is that even desirable? In fact, a majority of East Germans feel East German and not German; in terms of ethnicity, many more likely see themselves as Saxons, Thuringians, or Brandenburgers. According to an Emnid Institute poll, 49 percent of the East Germans questioned approved of the statement: "The GDR had more good sides than bad. There were a few problems, but one could live well there."[32] All of this raises the question: how much GDR still remains in the East Germans twenty years after its end? This varies by age group: how much of what persists is repression, idealization, nostalgia, actual life experience, and memory that should be preserved?

It is certain that those who idealize the GDR are no longer just the old elites, former functionaries, and diehards. No, even young people who barely experienced the GDR glorify it, historian Stefan Wolle concedes. This idealization has actually reached "the heart of society." Many East Germans perceive any criticism of the system as a personal attack on themselves. The actual tragedy consists of the fact that downplaying the dictatorship has been accepted in order to preserve their self-esteem. "People defend their own life," the Berlin political scientist Klaus Schroeder declares.[33] Also typical of a certain defiance is the opinion: "I am doing better today than before, but I am not more satisfied." For above all the "false picture of the East that the West disseminates" makes people dissatisfied.[34]

To the question, "What will remain from the GDR in the long run?" Lothar de Maizière answered: "That the great majority of East Germans, in the situation in which they had to live, kept their dignity—to the extent which the system allowed them."[35] And that is precisely the crucial point: many East Germans feel their dignity is violated if the GDR (themselves included) is reduced to a "Stasiland," "illegitimate state," "doping nation," or the "second German dictatorship." In terms of political consequences, this resentment made the PDS/Left Party strong in the East. Recent surveys and analyses attest that for most East Germans, the symbolic recognition as "social equals" is much more important than the achievement of equality in material living conditions.[36]

On the opposite side, the assessment of the West—after an initial "test the West" phase—comes off as quite disenchanted. Disillusionment with capitalist reality and its financial and economic crises, with the uncertainty of the job market, and with a democracy, which, to invoke Churchill, is the worst form of government, except for all others, has contributed to a rethinking. The conditions in united Germany have been called into question more strongly than ever before. Now East Germans experience that in the party bribery scandal a word of honor can be more highly regarded than the law, that large companies, like Deutsche Bahn, Deutsche Bank, Telekom, the grocery discounter Lidl, and the clothing discounter Kik spied on their workers systematically, and that there is doping in professional sports. Moreover the presidential election of Christian Wulff was a "sham vote" which was "riddled with party politics." The issue was not about "who is most suitable for this position. It was about power, about revenge…The delegates[were] robbed of their dignity." This statement refers to an obligation to vote along party lines, which frequently makes party membership more important for one's career than an examination certificate.[37]

Thus many East Germans believe they are experiencing déjà-vu. They have seen this once before, even if in another form. Where on earth have we landed over there? Or, to quote Monsignor Ducke, moderator of the Round Table, who said in an exaggerated and facetious manner: We made preparations to break out of our prison cells, tediously chiseled and hammered—and where have we landed? In the neighboring cell! All of this led Klaus Wowereit, the SPD mayor of Berlin, to the remarkable insight: "Not all that glitters in the West is gold, and not all that existed in the GDR was bad."[38]

The former interior minister, Thomas de Maizière, conceded correctly on the twentieth anniversary of the unification treaty that it would have been more intelligent "to have retained a little more than the 'little men' and green arrows" from East German traffic signs.[39] After twenty years of unity, one has the exact impression that without labeling it as GDR heritage, what is worth preserving from the GDR is once more sneaking in through the back door: new medical centers, which were previously called outpatient clinics, comprehensive kindergarten care, promotion of talent, compatibility of job and family, educational structures such as all-day schools, independent and self-confident working wives, new understandings of roles in the family,[40] equality of men and women, equal pay for equal work—various things that were normal in the GDR but are only now, twenty years later, discussed in the Federal Republic.

Lingering Estrangement

A majority of East Germans still feel like strangers in their new home. That surely also has to do with the fact that twenty years after unification the East is barely represented in the political, economic, intellectual, and media elite of Germany: none of the thirty DAX companies are headed by East Germans, none of the sixteen judges on the Federal Constitutional Court come from the East, 95 percent of chairs in the Humanities and Social Sciences—including at East German universities—are occupied by West Germans. No public broadcast companies have East German directors, no supraregional newspapers, even those that are most read in the East, have East German editors-in-chief. Johanna Wanka from Brandenburg was appointed, in April 2010, as the first East German in the cabinet of a West German federal state. At the same time, the first woman with an immigrant background, the German-Turk Aygül Özkan, was selected for a ministerial post at the state level. East Germans obviously have just as much difficulty as immigrants in advancing to top levels of leadership. Of the 200 generals in the German armed forces, one comes from East Germany. East Germans are absent wherever power is concerned. However, they are disproportionately overrepresented where death is involved: 60 percent of the lower ranks of German soldiers deployed abroad come from East Germany. Michael Wolffsohn, well-known historian of the German armed forces, says laconically: "'It is thus so: Whoever is poor, must be more likely to die in Afghanistan.'" East Germans are more likely affected by unemployment and poverty, and therefore to go into the military.

The replacement of elites was complete. Yet this exchange had not taken place among East Germans and had not opened up new chances for the opposition after the removal of old SED cadres. For the most part, they were marginalized. The West-East transfer had long-term consequences, for example, through lifetime positions in public service, the creation of new networks, and the corresponding immigration. Moreover, the capital-rich West has effectively bought into the Eastern lands, from the most beautiful locations along the Baltic coast or Berlin's Prenzlauer Berg district to land purchases in the fertile Börde district near Magdeburg. The capital-poor East Germans, who in any event lacked the necessary know-how, had hardly any chance in the division of the "GDR pie." Thus it is unsurprising that many East Germans tend not to see the giant transfer payments from the West, but instead perceive this process as a "takeover." Significantly, Condoleezza Rice in her most recent book finds, with a view toward 3 October 1990, that it had been about an "acquisition," not a merger.[41]

Thus at the beginning of the 1990s, structures were created that have since hardened and that over decades have excluded the East Germans from power, property, and influence. It is no wonder that 64 percent of East Germans still feel like second-class citizens. The fatal problem is not only that the East Germans assess themselves in such a manner, but that every fourth West German, according to Wilhelm Heitmeyer, views the East as a land of second-class citizens. The Bielefeld sociologist speaks of "social division," of lingering "foreignness," of the East German "feeling of disintegration and disadvantage."[42] The sociologist Raj Kollmorgen calls it outright discrimination.[43]

The converse question must likewise be examined: how much of the old FRG can still be found in West Germans twenty years after the end of the Bonn Republic in the now unified Germany? After all, the period of united Germany amounts to a third of the total existence of the Federal Republic. And how much of unified Germany is actually contained in the West already? The answer corresponds with the result of a long-term study of the Allensbach Institute for Public Opinion Research, whereby, given concerns about the future, many West Germans considered Germany's best time to have been the 1970s. Only 2 percent perceive the last decade as a good time.[44] In contrast, in the East a majority assesses the time since 1989 positively.

According to political scientist Klaus Schroeder, "The degree of 'nostalgia for the West,' exceeds—largely unnoticed by the public—in this respect, that of 'nostalgia for the East.'"[45] Thus there is not just in the East, but obviously also in the West a form of nostalgia that glorifies the (seemingly) good, predictable old days full of prosperity and tranquility. On closer inspection, this, too, was a fallacy. So have the Westerners also arrived in the reunified, modern Germany of the twenty-first century?

Because the difference of Easterners is not accepted, East Germans must always be measured by the West German norm and constantly justify themselves if they deviate from it. They live under a constant pressure to conform and explain themselves if they are not in accordance with Western ideas of society, life, and the future.[46] Yet in the meantime they have gotten "a kind of head start in terms of experience at coping with transformations," as the former Federal President Köhler claimed.[47] Sociologist Wolfgang Engler even goes as far as to attribute to East Germans a kind of avant-garde function in terms of coping with crises, since their experiences might be significant for the development of all of Germany.[48] East Germany could be understood as a laboratory for a necessary all-German modernization.

The East Germans know from their own experiences what reform gridlock and refusal to modernize mean. They have an entirely different tale of woe. Already in the autumn of 1990, industrial production was halved from 1989 before it fell to a low point of only 30 percent a half-year later. Since 1990 every second family has been affected by unemployment. "Change," "flexibility," "adaptation," and "retraining" are constant companions for East Germans. They come from a shortage society, not an affluent society. They have long since lost their sense of entitlement, unlike their West German compatriots. "Protection of vested rights" was a foreign word in the East. Because of this, they manage better in difficult times and they are actually better prepared for the problems of globalization. They do not complain and they work longer for less money than their West German compatriots.

In addition to contraction and structural change, there have emerged projects at the local and regional levels, which show much creativity—including local mass transit, renewable energy, more efficient forms of administration, removal of prefabricated housing, new forms of medical provision, numerous cultural projects, many German-Polish initiatives in the Oder region, and finally projects against rightist extremism. In spite of all these problems a new diversity is also being created here, a diversity which could play a pioneering role for other regions in West Germany that have to struggle with similar challenges.[49]

Nevertheless, East Germans are primarily seen as a burden for the united German society, as well as for its prosperity. "Nothing has unified the West Germans so much as the accession of the East Germans," writes the Leipzig cultural sociologist Thomas Ahbe.[50] In turn, nothing has unified the East Germans so much as the perceived withdrawal of affection by the closed West German society.

A Balance Sheet

Although much has been accomplished in the twenty years since unification, it is justifiable still to speak of two partial societies within unified Germany. Drawing up a balance sheet, Thomas de Maizière, who participated in the reunification process from start to finish, observes: reunification was a "precipitous political birth" under enormous time pressure. "There was a paternalistic attitude in the West vis-à-vis the East, along the lines of the motto: We know what the right thing is for our sisters and brothers in the East.… In truth, however, we didn't know it."[51] One can also label this an admission of Western arrogance. Similarly, the economist and former finance minister of Saxony-Anhalt, Karl-Heinz Paqué, observes that what was achieved isn't disappointing, but the expectations were simply too high.[52]

Twenty years after the unification, what we need is less a reckoning with the past than an all-German unity project for the future. Achieving unity is more and more overshadowed by other problems like migration, the aging of the population, excessive budget deficits, federalism, internationalization, and technological change. These challenges affect all of Germany.[53]

The Germany of 2010/11 is no longer comparable to that of twenty years ago. One can see how much it has changed, for instance, by the facts that it is governed by an *East* German chancellor, German soldiers are aware of their international responsibility, there is a leftist party within the five-party spectrum, the German economy sells more cars in China than in the United States, the CDU quarrels over what, if anything, is still conservative, and a German foreign minister takes his partner along on international trips. None of this was conceivable in 1990.

In historical and international perspective and apart from understandable everyday worries, frustrations, disappointed hopes, and also injuries, and in spite of justifiable criticism of its implementation, one can and should ultimately be happy about the removal of the Wall and barbed wire, about the end of the Cold War and German reunification.

If one considers that in the worst-case scenario both sides of this heavily armed border would possibly have marched to war against each other, the "Ossi-Wessi" squabble seems quite negligible. The fraternal strife has indeed continued, but both sides are coming together. West Germans were spectators at the self-liberation of the East Germans and felt like paymasters who were treated ungratefully. East Germans for their part felt robbed of their identity and found themselves in a permanent situation of facing excessive demands. Yet the Germans, after their first successful revolution—and a peaceful one at that—had valiantly seized the opportunity. With the peaceful unification in accordance with their European neighbors, the Germans received an unexpected new chance. To seize it is the task of all Germans. The end of division and the end of the Cold War, Konrad Jarausch writes, was a "double stroke of luck" that could "become crystallization points of a democratic memory."[54] Especially the GDR but also the Federal Republic and the new Germany still seek suitable and appropriate *lieux de memoire*.[55] We should simply accept our different historical memories.

In order to take up the opening image of the wedding once more: Höppner's hopes of a loving marriage have not been fulfilled. Indeed, if anything, it has become a marriage of convenience. Now all Germans are in the same boat with a common future. They will certainly not go before the divorce judge. Their silver anniversary is about to take place. By then, perhaps they will have achieved a bit of wisdom that can only come with age.

Notes

1. www.bundestag/Volkskammer/Dokumente/Protokolle.
2. Dr. Norbert Lammert, "Mit dem 18. März 1990 gingen die Deutschen den Weg zur Einheit," in *Das Parlament. Dokumentation*, 22 March, 2010, 17.
3. *Focus*, 1 February, 2010.
4. Sebastian Preuss, "Die DDR, ein ästhetischer Zoo?" *Berliner Zeitung*, 17 March, 2009.
5. Hannes Bahrmann and Christoph Links, eds., *Am Ziel vorbei. Die deutsche Einheit—eine Zwischenbilanz* (Berlin, 2005), 334f.
6. Michael Richter, "Doppelte Demokratisierung und deutsche Einheit," *APuZ*, 15 March, 2010, 20ff.
7. Wolfgang Schäuble, *Der Vertrag. Wie ich über die deutsche Einheit verhandelte* (Stuttgart, 1991), 31. A similar account is found in Helmut Kohl, *Vom Mauerfall zur Wiedervereinigung. Meine Erinnerungen* (Munich, 2009), 360.
8. Rolf Reißig, "Anspruch und Realität der deutschen Einheit. Das Transformations- und Vereinigungsmodell und seine Ergebnisse," in Bahrmann and Links, *Am Ziel vorbei*, 293ff.; idem, *Gesellschaftstransformation im 21. Jahrhundert. Ein neues Konzept sozialen Wandels* (Wiesbaden, 2009).
9. Olaf Baale, *Abbau Ost* (Munich, 2008). See also "Beutezug Ost—Die Treuhand und die Abwicklung der DDR," *ZDF-Dokumentation*, 14 September, 2010.
10. *Neue Chronik DDR*, 7th/8th series, (Berlin, 1991), 21, 1ff.

11. Paul Nolte, *Riskante Moderne. Die Deutschen und der neue Kapitalismus* (Munich, 2006).
12. Markus Feldenkirchen, "Wir Kohl-Kinder," *Der Spiegel* (2010), no. 13, 39f.
13. Rainer Land and Andreas Willisch, "Ostdeutschland—ein Umbruchszenario. Warum der Aufbau Ost als Nachbau West nicht gelingen konnte," in *Am Ziel vorbei,* 11ff.
14. Michael Richter, "Doppelte Demokratisierung und deutsche Einheit," *APuZ,* 15 March 2010, 20ff.
15. Lothar de Maiziere, "Die Übernahme des Rechtssystems," in *Am Ziel vorbei,* 48ff ; idem, *Ich will, dass meine Kinder nicht mehr lügen müssen. Meine Geschichte der deutschen Einheit* (Freiburg, 2010).
16. Rolf Reißig, "Von der privilegierten und blockierten zur zukunftsorientierten Transformation," *APuZ,* 26 July 2010, 20ff. and idem, "Anspruch und Realität der deutschen Einheit," in *Am Ziel vorbei,* 293ff.
17. Siehe Kai Arzheimer, "Das Wahlverhalten. Besonderheiten in Ostdeutschland als Modell künftiger gesamtdeutscher Entwicklungen," in *Am Ziel vorbei,* 60ff.
18. "Umfrage der Berliner Zeitung zum 20. Jahr des Mauerfalls," *Berliner Zeitung,* 2 January 2009.
19. Raj Kollmorgen, *Ostdeutschland. Beobachtungen einer Übergangs- und Teilgesellschaft* (Wiesbaden, 2005), 59ff.
20. "Sozialreport. Ostdeutsche fremdeln mit der Bundesrepublik," *SpiegelOnline,* 31 August 2010.
21. Martin Sabrow, "Die DDR erinnern," in *Erinnerungsorte der DDR,* ed. idem (Munich, 2009), 16.
22. Hans-Ulrich Wehler, *Deutsche Gesellschaftsgeschichte,* vol. V (Munich, 2008), xv.
23. "Es entsteht immer dieses Schwarz-Weiß. Lothar de Maiziere im Interview," *Tagesspiegel,* 3 August 2008.
24. Dirk Pilz, "Das war eben so," *Berliner Zeitung,* 12 November 12, 2010.
25. Quoted in Markus Hesselmann, "Erinnerungskultur. Eine schräge Geschichte," *Tagesspiegel,* 18 July 2007.
26. Thomas Großbölting, "Die DDR im vereinten Deutschland," *APuZ,* 21 July 2010, 35–41.
27. See Daniela Dahn, *Westwärts und nicht vergessen. Vom Unbehagen in der Einheit* (Reinbek, 1997).
28. Wolfgang Templin, "Das unselige Ende der DDR," *APuZ,* 25 March 2010, 4f.
29. Jens Reich, "Wir Ostler waren nicht nur Untertanen," *Tagesspiegel,* 2 October 2008.
30. Peter Bender, "Erinnern und vergessen. Deutsche Geschichte 1945 und 1989," in *Zweimal Deutschland. Eine ungeteilte Nachkriegsgeschichte 1945–1990,* ed. idem. (Stuttgart, 2009), 296f.
31. Peter Bender, "Bundesrepublik oder Deutschland?" *FAZ,* 24 September 2008. Cf. Patrick Bahners and Alexander Cammann, *Bundesrepublik und DDR. Die Debatte um Hans-Ulrich Wehlers "Deutsche Gesellschaftsgeschichte"* (Munich, 2009), 315ff.
32. *Berliner Zeitung,* 26 June 2009.
33. Quoted in Julia Bonstein, "Heimweh nach der Diktatur," *SpiegelOnline,* 29 June 2010.
34. Ibid.
35. "Es entsteht immer dieses Schwarz-Weiß."
36. See Ray Kollmorgen, "Diskurse der deutschen Einheit," in *APuZ,* 26 July 2010, 13.
37. *Der Spiegel,* 28 June 2010.
38. "Klaus Wowereit im Interview mit der Berliner Zeitung," *Berliner Zeitung* (Magazine), 14/15 August 2010.
39. See Holger Schmale, "West-Sekt in Ost-Gläsern," *Berliner Zeitung,* 1 September 2010.
40. Donna Harsch, "Footnote or Footprint? The German Democratic Republic in History," *Bulletin of the German Historical Institute* 46 (Spring 2010), 9ff.
41. Condoleezza Rice, *Extraordinary, Ordinary People* (New York, 2010), 265.

42. Wilhelm Heitmeyer, ed., *Deutsch-deutsche Zustände. 20 Jahre nach dem Mauerfall* (Bonn, 2009), 13ff.
43. Christoph Cadenbach and Bastian Obermayer, "Geschlossene Gesellschaft," *SZ Magazin* 30 (2010). For details of the transformation process, see Kollmorgen, *Ostdeutschland.*
44. *Berliner Zeitung,* 4 March 2010.
45. Klaus Schroeder, *Deutschland nach der Wiedervereinigung, APuZ,* 30–31 (2010), 19.
46. Jana Hensel, "Wir sind anders," *Die Zeit,* 23 September 2010.
47. "'Die Devise muss lauten: Die Demokratie—das sind wir!' Grußwort von Bundespräsident Horst Köhler zum Thema 'Wandel durch Bürgerengagement,'" East-West Forum, Gut Gödelitz, Saxony, 11 May 2010. www.bundespräsident.de/Reden-und-Interviews/.
48. Wolfgang Engler, *Die Ostdeutschen als Avantgarde* (Berlin, 2002).
49. Rolf Woderich, ed., *Im Osten nichts Neues? Struktureller Wandel in peripheren Räumen* (Berlin, 2007).
50. Thomas Ahbe, "Der Osten aus der Sicht des Westens. Die Bilder von den Ostdeutschen und ihre Konstrukteure," in *Am Ziel vorbei,* 276.
51. See Alexander Neubacher and Michael Sauga, "Abbau Ost," *Der Spiegel,* 26 (2010).
52. Karl-Heinz Paqué, *Die Bilanz—eine wirtschaftliche Analyse der deutschen Einheit* (Munich, 2009).
53. Rolf Reißig, "Deutsche Einheit: Weiter- und Neu-Denken," in *20 Jahre deutsche Einheit—Facetten einer geteilten Wirklichkeit,* in ed., Elmar Brähler and Irina Mohr (Gießen, 2010), 195ff.
54. Konrad H. Jarausch, "Der Umbruch 1989/90," in Sabrow, *Erinnerungsorte,* 526ff.
55. Martin Sabrow, ed., *Erinnerungsorte der DDR.*

Chapter Three

Debates and Perceptions about German Unification

The Centrality of Discourse

Helga A. Welsh

Nation-building efforts are crucial when hitherto disparate entities merge or territories secede to establish independent statehood. The last two centuries have been rife with such processes. In Europe, the end of the Cold War triggered secessions in the name of self-determination, often accompanied by conflict. Heated and at times violent struggles led to the dissolution of the Soviet Union and Yugoslavia, while the two parts of Czechoslovakia, the Czech Republic and the Slovak Republic, divorced amicably. Germany countered the trend: self-determination by peaceful means led the two states to merge after a forty-year division. The fall of communism provided new impetus to democratization studies, which is now a recognized subfield of political science.

Broadly defined, unification studies analyze the history of the GDR, the background and conditions under which the two Germanies merged in 1989/90, the transformation of the Eastern part of the country, similarities and differences between East and West, and the consequences of the merger for both parts as well as the whole. Often supported by research grants, it was a growth industry in the German academy for a short time. German-language publications on the subject between 1990 and 2007 comprise the majority of entries in the 45,000-record database at the Technical University of Dresden.[1] During this time, research on unification shifted from structural-institutional and economic aspects to culture and history,

Notes for this chapter begin on page 77.

only to be overtaken by topics affecting the nation as a whole.[2] Juxtaposing the work of East and West German social scientists, Raj Kollmorgen identifies two opposing narratives: "unification as a grandiose flop" and "unification as full success." He concludes, "*alas — also on the issue of the German-German unification process — no 'objective truth' or* [*evaluative*] *'objective' correctness*" exists.[3]

The current book also relies on the premise that origins will matter when developing a balance sheet on unification. I write this essay as a political scientist, socialized and educated in West Germany, who has written on East Germany and lived and worked in the United States for more than two decades. Thus, the text combines an insider's and an outsider's perspective; physical distance from German scholarly debates may lower the political and emotional stakes, but, confirming Kollmorgen, does not promise objectivity. Nor is my view purely political, as transitions from dictatorship to democracy and command to market economy involve lengthy, multifaceted transition processes, intermingling political, economic, social, and psychological variables.

The two preceding chapters by Heinrich Bortfeldt and Gero Neugebauer provide a wealth of data and analytical perspectives on German unity twenty years after its formal conclusion in October 1990, ranging from institutional transfer, attitudes, and perceptions, to some of its consequences for the country as a whole. This chapter complements their approaches by drawing attention to the discourse surrounding debates related to unification. I limit the term discourse to *communication*, putting aside its impact on policy formation and implementation. The goal is not to distinguish the agents of the discourse in detail; I challenge simple East-West dichotomies but also employ them as a shortcut in explaining divergent points of view.

Discourse analysis relates to the study of a set of ideas and asks when, how, and why they were expressed and by whom.[4] It is about spoken or written words that often rest on implicit assumptions, two of which will be the focus of my essay. I take as my point of departure embedded but mostly tacit tensions that accompanied the merger of East and West from the beginning. First, the German variant of federalism builds on diversity but highlights unity, exposing dilemmas that unification intensified. Second, East-West evaluations have been afflicted by different, yet only vaguely defined expectations regarding the outcome of "inner unity." Taken together, these unresolved tensions have had lasting consequences for debates and perspectives on the success and shortcomings of unification. Before turning to these two dichotomies, I ask to what extent German unification can be framed as part of a broader dialogue about system transformation and integration. I then review the major stages of unification discourse, highlighting both continuity and change, using national elections and the writing of GDR history as examples.

Unique or Typical?

Undoubtedly, the merging of two countries, divided for a time and then united, is rare. The Cold War divided four—Germany, Vietnam, Yemen, and Korea. Germany, Vietnam, and Yemen have since regained single statehood although in Yemen regional conflict persists; Korean unity remains elusive. In drawing attention to the unification of Germany, the only reference point in scholarly literature has been Vietnam, yet there are more differences than resemblances between them. Germany is democratic; Vietnam still clings to communist ideology. In Germany, unification evolved from a peaceful revolution; Vietnam suffered civil war and international intervention. Geography also matters: the implosion of the German Democratic Republic (GDR) was closely interwoven with the third wave of democratization and the collapse of communism in Central and Eastern Europe. No similar diffusion processes account for the Vietnamese experience. Nonetheless, such joint challenges as nation building invite comparison.[5]

Most accounts treat German unification as a singular case, introducing only within-system comparisons: how have the two parts of the country been affected by unification, and to what extent has the role of unified Germany been altered? This analysis can and should be complemented by attention to comparative cross-national perspectives. Three aspects of comparison come to mind: regions, system transformations, and integration processes.

Regionalism

All states, whether federal or unitary, are marked by regional differences. Maps of Germany, broken down according to wealth distribution, unemployment, or demographic trends, expose regional variations, but the territory of the former GDR stands out: in most areas, an observer, ignorant of the contours of the five Länder in the East, can still identify them relatively easily, despite pockets of difference. However, looking at regional disparities from an international perspective shows Germany in a slightly different light. For example, using the ratio of GDP per capita in the poorest and richest regions relative to the national average, Germany has the lowest income inequality compared to the United States, Britain, France, and Japan; even the most recent economic recession (2008/09) did not halt the trend toward convergence.[6] European Union policy aims to bridge regional differences in income and opportunities within its member states. Unification has increased Germany's demand for, and share of, regional funds, but its regional disparities do not set it apart from other member states.

System Transformation

Differences among them notwithstanding, most transitions exhibit common features, such as high levels of uncertainty, a changing set of political actors, pressing time constraints, and the need to contest the past and to raise visions of the future.[7] Julio María Sanguinetti, President of Uruguay from 1985 to 1990, highlights the sense of urgency after the fall of the dictatorial regime, referring to this psychological phenomenon as "now-ism" (*ya-ismo*).[8] While this alone does not explain the speed with which unification was negotiated and implemented, it is important to remember when assessing opportunities grasped and missed.

Other aspects of German unification benefit from the cross-border view. In all postcommunist countries, the social shock of the transition invited perceptions of winners and losers, referring to ruptured careers, psychological adjustments, tangible measures of consumption and wealth, and other personal assets or calamities.[9] Polish scholar Aleksander Smolar asked why, only ten years after the revolutions in Central and Eastern Europe, hardly anyone celebrated.[10] The dramatic regime change in the former GDR is also receding into the past. Germans remember more and more vaguely the initial sense of disbelief, accompanied by joy, when the Berlin Wall was first breached. Elation has been supplanted by concern. The drama, exhilaration, and anxieties cannot be preserved; they were extraordinary and short-lived. Dealing with the communist past in terms of lustration, criminal prosecution and restitution, and revising history constitutes another set of commonalities among postcommunist countries.

Similarly, expressions of nostalgia for communist-era specialty shops, TV shows, foods, and discos are common in all postcommunist societies. They evoke personal memories and can function as outlets for disappointment. They also work selectively: the pleasant may be highlighted over the painful. In East Germany, as in most other settings, nostalgia has not threatened democracy,[11] yet it helps to explain persistent feelings between East and West.

Integration

A comparison between unification on the one hand and European integration on the other can also be useful. When Germany was struggling with unification, the European Union and NATO extended eastward to encompass Central and Eastern European countries and the Baltic States. To explain this extension, constructivist approaches supplemented rationalist perspectives. Rationalists list tangible costs and benefits of enlargement; constructivists highlight moral imperatives.[12] Ten years after the fall of communism, Aleksander Smolar remarked that both Eastern and Western Europeans are ambivalent toward each other. When the East joined the West, the people did "experience not the reunification of Europe but the very different process (probably the only realistic one) of the enlargement of the European Union."[13] Some similarities to the German case are striking. Just as the "return to Europe" turned out differently from what East Europeans expected, so did unification. Unification was also never a decision based on gains and losses; it was always based on historical responsibility. The costs are measured in different categories. For some, unification subsidizes the East; for others, it is associated with feelings of second-class citizenry and loss of identity. East Germans and East Europeans value their newfound freedom of choice in consumer goods, travel, and political preference; such benefits are taken for granted, while costs are lamented.

Arguments against such comparisons are manifold. For the communist leadership in the former GDR, the existence of the democratic and capitalist West Germany made consolidation and regime legitimacy difficult. For its citizens, the Federal Republic of Germany, not neighboring socialist countries, was the reference point. Not surprisingly, the comparison with the West only intensified after unification. Most see East Germany's transitions from communism to democracy and a market economy as unique due to the availability of a "ready-made state" as part of its accession to the Federal Republic and the financial and manpower transfer from West to East. When almost everything changes for one part of the country, and for the other, life is largely untouched, their communication is hampered. Critics are quick to point out that successful outcomes in Germany, in comparison to other countries, do not transform the perceptions of, or instill pride in, East Germans.[14] Others refer to the Western blueprint for institutional transfer and Western financial and labor resources as significant intervening variables that reduce the value of comparisons. The democratic and economic yardstick of Western models was a feature of regime transitions in Europe, but the implications were not as immediate or as constantly referenced in the media.

Therefore, East Germany and unification tend to be omitted or only mentioned in passing in the substantial literature on transitions; they are rarely measured against the yardstick of other postcommunist countries.[15] This bird's-eye view relegates challenges associated with the "crisis" or "shock" of unification—among them, in no particular order, the dominance of political considerations in the merging of the two economies; the emphasis on restitution instead of compensation as part of the privatization process; the lack of attention to the shared nation-building enterprise, including but not limited to the unification process itself in 1990—to failed or missed policy decisions and miscommunication. Yet, it is important to remember that some of the woes of German unification are symptomatic of larger transition and integration processes, yet are accentuated and shaped by the specific German situation. In equal fashion, regional inequality and diversity are issues of wider significance beyond Germany. Highlighting the particulars of a specific country, even using the terminology of exceptionalism, is not an isolated phenomenon, even in comparative research. Furthermore, the treatment of Germany as a special case has a long history—from the debate about the *special path* in its historical development to its role as a model of a conservative welfare state or of a coordinated market economy. They coexist with the more recent claim that Germany, with unification, has become a normal nation-state, more like its neighbors.[16]

From the Front to the Back Burner

For years following the opening of the Berlin Wall in November 1989, no other topic engaged German politics and media more than the process and consequences of unification. Critics on the political left in East and West Germany argued about the pace, with some even questioning the desirability of unity. They were silenced not so much in debates but through swift political action and grassroots pressure. Controversies over whether and under what parameters unification should take place were fleeting, whereas debate about its consequences has been lasting.

Taking national elections as the first barometer of change, in 1990 and 1994 they were dominated by unification-related questions. The term "unification crisis" captured a variety of sometimes contradictory feelings; it framed the discourse and identified its codes. The East became associated with deindustrialization, unemployment, and Stasi involvement. East-West dichotomies intensified; institutional transfer was viewed as either colonization or as swift democratization and financial transfer as reparation for past injustice or as burden on the West. Most of all, it juxtaposed Western dominance and arrogance against Eastern ingratitude. Debates cut short due to real and perceived time pressures in 1990 were now played out with fierce intensity. Should the capital move from Bonn to Berlin? To what extent should the Basic Law be amended?

By mid decade, a saturation effect set in; when the 1998 election campaign heated up, the crisis of the East had become a German crisis. Newly elected Chancellor Gerhard Schröder (SPD) promised to make rebuilding the East (*Aufbau Ost*) the chancellor's prerogative, but challenges associated with Europeanization and globalization took precedence, leading to "a new post-unification landscape."[17] Unification had delayed long overdue domestic reforms in (West) Germany but ultimately acted as a stressor. Overhauling the pension, healthcare, labor market, and education systems—to name some of the most important—was pressing and no longer restricted to the East. The following years were consumed with discussions about the need for policy changes and the problems inherent in bursting the logjam of reforms. By the time the 2002 elections were fought, those concerns, not East-West questions, framed the debate.

In spite of occasional flare-ups, such as the Hartz IV debate in 2003/04, when unemployment and social welfare benefits were combined at the lower welfare level, "event orientation" has set in, focusing on the commemoration of dates associated with the fall of communism and unification.[18] At other times, the legacies of unification seem to be accepted as facts; they are no longer elaborated in detail, maybe because of their potential as dynamite: exposing frustration with the financial costs of unification, the lagging economic recovery of the East, and the continued perception of separation. Today, most East and Western Germans no longer want to read or talk about them. The fading unification discourse suggests a degree of normal relations between East and West, yet, for some, the downplaying of differences implies resignation.[19] Out of sight is not out of mind; rather, these questions bubble below the surface.

The history of the GDR has also been largely removed from public scrutiny. Initially, learning about it was important in view of the magnitude of what had to be accomplished and to move the unification process along. While East Germans were relatively well informed about some aspects of life in the West, the opposite held true for most West Germans. The longer the nation's separation continued, the more the communist-governed East was seen as a tabula rasa, but a sober, factual analysis of its history pre-1989 was "in the short run, not a realistic prospect."[20]

In fact, analysis of German history and politics is routinely based on the continuous development of the West, the Federal Republic, using approaches—neocorporatism, social market economy, coalition government, and multilevel governance—established in the West. Yet, whether the GDR is just a "footnote in world history," as expressed with some melancholy by East German writer Stefan Heym when its end was imminent, remains a matter of controversy.[21] According to James McAdams, forgetting about the GDR is the norm today, and occurs not through conscious neglect but habit; GDR history in today's Germany is "barely a whisper."[22] But "history is never dead," William Faulkner once remarked, and the legacy of GDR history persists. Debating the past, including its role in unified Germany, is one aspect; vilifying negative facets is another.

In particular, the immediate postunification years saw the use and misuse of history for political purposes; stark contrasts between dictatorship and democracy prevailed in the public discourse, which excoriated the activities of the state security services, the infamous Stasi, and overlooked the complexities of life under communism in the GDR. Many East Germans countered by emphasizing features they had cherished and felt they also had a right to be proud of their lives.[23] Germany's treatment of the communist past can be praised as model, significantly influencing other postcommunist countries, or condemned for inhibiting reconciliation among East Germans and between East and West Germans.[24]

Despite recurring discursive tropes, some "irritants of the past" have largely dissipated. The 2007 merger of the communist successor party, the Party of Democratic Socialism (PDS), with a Western splinter group of disgruntled SPD members and trade unionists signified the party's arrival in the West. The newly created Left Party is still marginalized by the political establishment but no longer just a regional (Eastern) party. Preoccupation with the PDS, disparagingly referred to in some Western circles as the "red socks," has turned to a sober, and at times still emotional, evaluation of the consequences of a five-party system on coalition arithmetic and policy making. Shocking allegations against the Stasi have disappeared from the headlines; recent controversies surrounding the work of the agency dealing with Stasi files were mostly a manifestation of insider political power struggles, not a focus of public discourse. Chancellor Helmut Kohl's promise of "blooming landscapes" is no longer used to ridicule unification's lack of economic progress but to highlight some of its accomplishments; not all parts of East Germany are "blooming," but some undoubtedly are.[25] Indicative of another discursive change, Federal President Christian Wulff, commemorating twenty years of unity, invited Germans to interpret the iconic demonstration chants in the autumn of 1989, "We are the people," to apply to all people who live in Germany, turning it into a call for tolerance of, and respect for, diversity.[26]

The twentieth anniversary of the opening of the Berlin Wall in November 1989 and, less than one year later, the official merger between East and West Germany in October 1990, prompted a flurry of unification accounts and attempts to draw a balance sheet on unity.[27] Demonstrating the return to greater normalcy in East-West relations, book titles no longer proclaim *The Shock of Unification, Problem Case: German Unity,* or *Target Missed.*[28]

German Federalism: Unity vs. Diversity

International comparisons notwithstanding, regional differentiation strikes a sensitive chord in Germany. To silence actual and anticipated critics immediately following unification, politicians reinforced existing hopes that the East would become the West, and the West could remain the West. Terms such as "blooming landscapes" and "inner unity" were soon interjected into debates and later catapulted to symbolic significance as measures of progress or lack thereof. On 1 July 1990, on the occasion of the economic, social, and monetary union between the two states, Chancellor Kohl proclaimed, "No one will be worse off than before—and many will be better off," and inserted the promise of "blooming landscapes" in the former GDR. He cautioned that the transition would not be simple for East Germans and would require sacrifices on the part of West Germans, but the overall tone was reassuring.[29]

These promises fell on fertile ground, while cautions fell by the wayside. West Germans had started to feel comfortable in the "old" Federal Republic and saw little reason to change. East Germans, long deprived of many consumer commodities and the freedom of the West, were impatient to catch up without realizing the drastic changes it would involve; their lives were turned upside down. In 1994, the word *equality* was changed to "uniformity of living conditions" in the Constitution without affecting expectations. One decade later, Federal President Köhler's admission that different standards of living were a fact and that eliminating them would unjustly burden future generations ignited immediate rebuttal on the part of Eastern politicians.[30] In such an environment, convergence, the "tendency of societies to grow more alike, to develop similarities in structures, processes, and performances,"[31] still fell short of public expectations.

To understand the preoccupation with leveling living conditions, one must understand German federalism. According to some, it is in a class of its own, particularly since its many cooperative features function in an environment of intense party competition.[32] By definition, federal systems are geared to preserve regional differences, and they are found in a variety of political settings; they all define power-sharing principles, yet their institutional designs and functions often stress different priorities. In contexts characterized by categorical inequality between groups, territorial stability and conflict management are of primary importance.[33] In the United States, separation of powers and regional autonomy carry significant weight, but the German federal system has always favored centralization and equality. It balances joint decision-making structures and a high degree of interdependence with substantial intrusion by the federal government into subnational politics. A centralized system of revenue extraction and distribution across the Länder ensures that funds move from the richer to the poorer regions.

Until unification, centralizing policy tendencies seemed to reflect public preferences. After 1990, the merging of East and West exposed asymmetries in size and wealth among states. Greater economic and social diversity produced a "growing 'territorialization' of political discourse and party competition."[34] Reforms followed a trend seen in other federal states: concurrent disentanglement of competencies in favor of subnational units.[35] As a general rule, states with greater financial clout, such as Bavaria and Baden-Württemberg, advocate greater decentralization, while "poorer" states, such as those in the former East Germany, tend to favor greater federal involvement. Cooperative federalism, with its emphasis on "solidarity, consensus and the desirability of common standards across the federation," has encountered "a rival set [of ideas] focused on self-reliance, autonomy, and differentiation of standards."[36] While elites struggle over power competencies, citizens favor a high degree of standardization, if not uniformity, in policies across the nation; those expectations are reinforced by the federal government's setting of "frameworks and standards to avoid negative external effects between competing regions."[37] Competitive federalism, with its emphasis on diversification, autonomy, and performance, routinely runs into mental and institutional roadblocks, while interregional competition has increased.

What is Inner Unity?

Public opinion data consistently show that Germans, East and West, overwhelmingly supported unification in October 1990 but agree that their differences outweigh their similarities; indeed, after a slight dip around 2004/05, this perception has edged up.[38] Such sentiments are reinforced by empirical evidence: in many areas economic, political, and social, Germany as a whole is the unit of reference, but East-West differences matter.[39] How to interpret convergence and persistent divergence twenty years after unification is no longer a politically urgent question, but it still has significance.

Unions of two or more distinct parts require recognition as well as acceptance of differences, even when the major goal remains their elimination. This strategy is difficult to implement in any setting. East Germans expected their different lives and the aspects they considered worth preserving to be accepted but desired equal status, representation, and living circumstances. Westerners were prone to accept differences in wealth, income, and opportunities, but expected East Germans to assimilate Western political preferences, behavior and mentality, and institutions.[40]

In discourse the expression "inner unity" has become a widely accepted shortcut to refer to the end goal of unification.[41] Yet, the terminology is elusive as standards regarding unity as opposed to diversity are often assumed and expectations differ. Inner unity refers mostly to aspects of political culture—that is, to what extent orientations toward the political system are shared in Eastern and Western Germany—but it has also been extended to encompass living conditions. Questions include: how different can the two parts be without jeopardizing a common future? Should the result be respecting and building on mutual differences or converging toward a common political culture and living conditions?

Inner unity, or lack thereof, is related to identity, and East-West dichotomies occupy a prominent place. During the country's division from 1945 to 1989, they solidified, and new ones arose after its end. They have acquired a degree of homogeneity normally associated with ethnic groups with venerable religious, linguistic, cultural, and historical traits, but they are actually amorphous cognitive constructs, a kaleidoscope of perceptions and affiliations. There is no uniform explanatory scheme for East-West differences and commonalities, and there are cross-cutting cleavages at macro and micro levels. Furthermore, research on local and regional identities in the Eastern part of the country—their expressions under communism and persistence and reinvention after its fall—draws a more differentiated view of Eastern Germans than is commonly assumed.[42] For example, writing GDR history cannot be reduced to plain East-West dichotomies; rather, it exposes anti- and pro-communist views shared by groups in both sectors. In an environment of intense party competition, alliances are routinely formed across the federal states.

Political culture studies have drawn on a variety of theories to explain or to dismiss persistent differences in East and West German perceptions, attitudes, and behavior.[43] However, surveys differ, and their interpretation matters. For example, when respondents were asked in 2009 whether they were proud of the German constitution and being German, practically no differences were found between East and West.[44] Yet plenty of data confirm continued disunity. A gap persists between East and West on whether democracy is the best form of government, with stronger affirmation in the West, but those who think that a different form might be better remain few overall (in 2008, 11 percent in the East and 3 percent in the West). Many analysts conclude that Eastern Germans approve of democracy in general but differ in normative values, with the greatest difference in the opinion about social justice, here defined as absence of poverty and moderate income differentials (in 2009, 53 percent in the East, versus 38 percent in the West).[45] Tereza Novotna asserts that Central and Eastern Europeans "(with the possible exception of Hungary) are much happier with developments after 1989 than their Eastern German counterparts."[46] Leaving aside the definition of "happiness," this claim seems inflated measured against other survey results. According to 2009 data from the Pew Research Center, for example, more East Germans approve of the change to democracy and to capitalism than do their Central and Eastern European neighbors. In addition, "Czechs, Poles, Slovaks and East Germans reported the most satisfaction with their lives and posted the greatest gains over the past two decades."[47] In comparing egalitarian norms in postcommunist countries, data indicate that East German expectations are on par with those of Poles and Hungarians but differ from those of West Germans, although some convergence has occurred since 1990.[48]

The persistence of East-West differences points to shortcomings in prevailing socialization experiences and in the perception of political, economic, and social performance. To explain them, Novotna cites the West's dominance of the unification process, whereas Detlef Pollack sees deficiencies in economic performance, with many Eastern Germans perceiving unjust wealth distribution and themselves as second-class citizens.[49] Both authors highlight unequal power distribution as an obstacle to inner unity. Institutional transfer has largely been a one-way street from West to East, although, in the long view, it encompasses more differentiated patterns of adaptation and innovation, and feedback loops that transcend straightforward imitation and did not leave Western institutions unscathed.[50] Elements in reforming day care and secondary and vocational education and the introduction of integrated medical care centers came from East to West. Those stimuli are rarely acknowledged, exposing continued blind spots: "nobody dares to say," comments one East German, "that this [all-day schools and child care places] might be inspired by the East … They say it's inspired by Scandinavia and France."[51]

Could problems in nation building have been amended by greater attention to symbolic politics? The priority of this task during regime transitions is undisputed.[52] The Western part of Germany always insisted on the unity of the nation, even when it was two states. Such an attitude may explain why, as Michael Naumann, German minister of culture from 1998 to 2001, remarked, "In the years since unification, we failed to create new symbols for the future, a new constitution, a large-scale project apart from the former chancellor's 'flourishing landscapes.'"[53] In contrast, throughout the former communist bloc, new national anthems, flags, and national holidays, the naming and renaming of political parties and streets, the creation and/or destruction of statues, even the design of postage stamps and bank notes were used to gain legitimacy and (re)create collective identities.

Since unification amounted to an enlargement of West Germany, nation building has been a lopsided enterprise, favoring the West. East German symbols were destroyed, and West German ones adopted. The renaming of streets or destruction of statues aroused controversies in all postcommunist societies, but in Germany, they were often portrayed as East-West conflicts, although the discourse was more differentiated and involved cleavages on both sides.[54] Undeniably, the Monday demonstrations in major GDR cities, meetings at the Nikolai Church in Leipzig, and, above all, the opening of the Berlin Wall have come to embody the peaceful East German revolution, serving an important symbolic function in the unification narrative. Nevertheless, the dearth of emblems associated with unification itself—leaving aside German Unity Day, which lacks the emotional resonance of national holidays in other countries, on 3 October—is striking. Reflecting the convoluted nature of decision making as well as the sensitivity of the topic, it took more than two decades to agree on a monument to commemorate German unity, and its design was immediately criticized.[55]

Looking Back and Moving Ahead

After the fall of the Berlin Wall, Chancellor Willy Brandt exclaimed that now the two parts of Germany, which belonged together, could grow together. But crafting the two highly unequal parts into a whole turned out to be more difficult than anticipated, particularly because the parameters of the process or end product were inadequately understood. According to Peter Bender, astute commentator on the history of the two Germanies, unification relegated major elements that had shaped their relations after World War II—the division into two states, the separation of the people, and, with few exceptions, animosity—to the dustbin of history. What remained were alienation and imbalance.[56] These elements proved to be lasting, feeding on each other.

This essay has emphasized the centrality of discourse, which often clusters around real and perceived dichotomies between East and West. Unification accounts, I suggest, have exposed tensions and contradictions that elude simple answers to a seemingly simple question: what is the state of German unity twenty years after the formal merger of East and West? To this day, in recollecting the past two decades, Eastern views tend to emphasize the pressure to conform, battles over memory, hardship, and anguish, while many Western voices highlight change, institutional transfer, and progress toward convergence. All acknowledge the ambivalence of the outcomes.

Independent of approach, all accounts include qualifiers. Yes, opportunities were grasped and others missed; success in one policy area has been tempered by problems in another. What constitutes inner unity remains a matter for debate. The framework of comparison also matters. Without glossing over differences, analyzing similarities in system transformation, integration, and nation building allow comparative perspectives that can enrich the German debate.

Unification completed the attainment of full sovereignty that was halted after World War II and the onset of the Cold War. Secure in its border, with a stable democracy, Germany has once again climbed toward a major role in Europe. The most important concern in many other postcommunist countries—the consolidation of democracy—is not a problem in Germany.[57] Unification has been difficult, but most outcomes give reason for reassurance.

Notes

1. Due to the financial costs of updating the database, new entries are now sporadic. I am grateful to Hendrik Berth of the Technical University of Dresden for information about the database. See http://www.wiedervereinigung.de; see also his article "DDR und Wiedervereinigung—bald kein Thema mehr für die Wissenschaft?" *Deutsche Studien,* 143/144 (2000), 340–350.
2. Alexander Thumfart, "Bilanz der Einigungsbilanzen—Forschungs- und Meinungskonjunktur der letzten 15 Jahre," *Politische Vierteljahresschrift,* 48 (2007), 564–584.
3. *Ostdeutschland: Beobachtungen einer Übergangs- und Teilgesellschaft* (Wiesbaden, 2005), 218 [italics in original].
4. The literature on discourse analysis has grown substantially in recent years. For a prominent example, see Vivien A. Schmidt, "Discursive Institutionalism: The Explanatory Power of Ideas and Discourse," *Annual Review of Political Science,* 11 (2008), 303–326. For a more detailed view of the German discourse, see Kollmorgen et al., eds., *Diskurse der deutschen Einheit. Kritik und Alternativen* (Wiesbaden, 2011).
5. Claire Sutherland, *Soldered States: Nation-building in Germany and Vietnam* (Manchester, 2010). The author compares nation-building efforts in Germany and Vietnam, countries that share the experience of division, communism, and subsequent reunification. In both cases, she finds, "the official ideology in the defunct states has been variously vilified, undermined or forgotten."
6. "Internal Affairs," *The Economist,* 12 March 2011, 83–84.
7. The list of publications on this topic is long. The following examples are illustrative and refer to a range of transitions. Paul Christopher Manuel, *Uncertain Outcome. The*

Politics of the Portuguese Transition to Democracy (Lanham, 1995); Guillermo O'Donnell and Philippe C. Schmitter, eds., *Transitions from Authoritarian Rule: Tentative Conclusions about Uncertain Democracies,* 2nd ed. (Baltimore, 1991); Valerie Bunce and Mária Csanádi, "Uncertainty in the Transition: Post-Communism in Hungary," *East European Politics and Societies,* 7 (1993), 240–275.

8. "Present at the Transition," in Larry Diamond and Marc F. Plattner, eds., *The Global Resurgence of Democracy* (Baltimore, 1993), 56.
9. For a critical assessment, see Andrej Rychard, "Beyond Gains and Losses: In Search of 'Winning Losers,'" *Social Research,* 63 (1996), 465–484.
10. "History and Memory: The Revolutions of 1989–91," *Journal of Democracy,* 12 (2001), 5–19.
11. Joakim Ekman and Jonas Linde, "Communist Nostalgia and the Consolidation of Democracy in Central and Eastern Europe," *Journal of Communist Studies and Transition Politics,* 21 (2005), 354–374.
12. See, in particular, the work of Frank Schimmelfenning, "The Community Trap: Liberal Norms, Rhetorical Action, and the Eastern Enlargement of the European Union," *International Organization,* 55 (2001), 47–80.
13. "History and Memory," 13.
14. See, for example, the critique of Richard Schröder's *Die wichtigsten Irrtümer über die deutsche Einheit* (Freiburg, 2007) by Warnfried Dettling, "Die deutsche Einheit—eine Erfolgsgeschichte?" *Die Zeit,* 26 March 2007, http://www.zeit.de/2007/13/P-Schroeder.
15. "'A Very Orderly Retreat': Democratic Transition in East Germany 1989–90," *Debatte,* 14 (April 2006), 7–35; Tereza Novotna, "The Transplantation and Adaptation Types of Political Integration: The Case of German Unification in Parallel with the Eastern Enlargement of the EU," *Perspectives,* 16 (2008), 77–102.
16. Konrad A. Jarausch, "The Federal Republic at Sixty: Popular Myths, Actual Accomplishments and Competing Interpretations," *German Politics and Society,* 28 (Spring 2010), 25. "A Muted Normalcy," in "Older and Wiser. A Special Report on Germany," *The Economist,* 13 March 2010, 15–16.
17. Perry Anderson, "A New Germany?" *New Left Review,* 57 (May/June 2009), 5.
18. Kollmorgen, "Diskurse der deutschen Einheit," *Aus Politik und Zeitgeschichte,* 30–31 (2010), 7.
19. Thomas Kralinski, "Warum der Westen den Osten braucht," *Berliner Republik,* 3 (2003), 10.
20. Helmut Wiesenthal, "Post-Unification Dissatisfaction, or Why Are So Many East Germans Unhappy with the New Political System?" *German Politics,* 7 (1998), 27.
21. Donna Harsch, "Footnote or Footprint? The German Democratic Republic in History," *Bulletin of the German Historical Institute,* 46 (Spring 2010), 925. See also Thomas Lindenberger, "What's in a Footnote? World History!" ibid., 27–31.
22. A. James McAdams, "The Last East German and the Memory of the German Democratic Republic," *German Politics and Society,* 28 (Spring 2010), 39.
23. "Stolz aufs eigene Leben" is the widely-cited article in *Der Spiegel,* 3 July 1995, which appeared at the height of the unification crisis.
24. See, for example, the contributions in Katrin Hammerstein et al., eds., *Aufarbeitung der Diktatur—Diktat der Aufarbeitung? Normierungsprozesse beim Umgang mit diktatorischer Vergangenheit* (Göttingen, 2009).
25. "Allensbach Umfrage zur Deutschen Einheit: Blühende Landschaften," *Frankfurter Allgemeine Zeitung,* 22 September 2010.
26. The speech was excerpted in http://www.sueddeutsche.de/politik/2.220/jahre-deutsche-einheit-dokumente.
27. See, for example, special issues of *German Politics and Society* 28 (Spring and Summer 2010); *German Politics* 19, and *German Studies Review* 33 (October 2010).

28. The complete citations are: Wolfgang Schluchter and Peter E. Quint, eds., *Der Vereinigungsschock. Vergleichende Betrachtungen zehn Jahre danach* (Weilerswist, 2001); Rainer Hufnagel and Titus Simon, eds., *Problemfall Deutsche Einheit. Interdisciplinary Betrachtungen zu gesamtdeutschen Fragen* (Wiesbaden, 2004); Hannes Bahrmann and Christoph Links, eds., *Am Ziel vorbei. Die deutsche Einheit—Eine Zwischenbilanz* (Berlin, 2005). Recent publications include: "20 Jahre Einheit in Uneinigkeit," special issue of *Vorgänge. Zeitschrift für Bürgerrechte und Gesellschaftspolitik*, 48 (September 2009); Heike Tuchscheerer, *20 Jahre Vereinigtes Deutschland. Eine 'neue' oder 'erweiterte Bundesrepublik'?* (Baden-Baden, 2010).
29. "Kohl's Celebration of the Currency Union, July 1, 1990," in Konrad Jarausch and Volker Gransow, eds., *Uniting Germany: Documents and Debates, 1944–1993* (Providence, 1994), 172–174.
30. "Ostdeutsche Politiker kritisieren Köhler," 13 September 2004, http://www.faz.net/-01tvv1.
31. C. Kerr, cited in Christoph Knill, "Introduction: Cross-national policy convergence: Concepts, approaches and explanatory factors," *Journal of European Public Policy*, 12 (October 2005), 764–774.
32. Fritz W. Scharpf, *Föderalismusreform. Kein Ausweg aus der Verflechtungsfalle?* (Frankfurt, 2009), 8; Arthur Benz, "From Unitary to Asymmetric Federalism in Germany: Taking Stock after 50 Years," *Publius: The Journal of Federalism*, 29 (Fall 1999), 5.
33. Richard Simeon, "Constitutional Design and Change in Federal Systems: Issues and Questions," *Publius: The Journal of Federalism*, 39 (2009), 242–244.
34. Charlie Jeffery, "Federalism: The New Territorialism," in *Governance in Contemporary Germany: The Semisovereign State Revisited*, ed. Simon Green and William E. Paterson (Cambridge, 2005), 84; Klaus Detterbeck and Wolfgang Renzsch, "Multi-level Electoral Competition: The Case of Germany," *European Urban and Regional Studies*, 10 (2003), 257–269.
35. Dietmar Braun, "Making Federalism More Efficient: A Comparative Assessment," *Acta Politica*, 43 (April 2008), 21.
36. Jeffery, "Federalism," 86.
37. Arthur Benz, "Inter-Regional Competition in Co-operative Federalism: New Modes of Multi-Level Governance in Germany," *Regional and Federal Studies*, 17 (2007), 422; Thieβ Petersen et al., "Public Attitudes towards German Federalism: A Point of Departure for a Reform of German (Fiscal) Federalism: Differences between Public Opinion and the Political Debate," *German Politics*, 17 (2008), 559–586; Bertelsmann Foundation, ed., *Bürger und Föderalismus. Eine Umfrage zur Rolle der Bundesländer*, http://ww.bertelsmannstiftung.de/bst/de/media/xcsm_bst_dms_23798_2.pdf.
38. Cf. Forschungsgruppe Wahlen, *Politbarometer Extra* 09/2004, 09/2007, and 09/2009 (Mannheim).
39. See *Von der Bevölkerung bis Wahlen—20 Jahre Deutsche Einheit in der Statistik*, ed. Statistische Ämter der Länder, www.statistikportal.de/Statistik-Portal/20JahreDeutscheEinheit.pdf.
40. Helga A. Welsh, "East-West Encounters in Unified Germany," in David P. Conradt et al., eds., *Power Shift in Germany: The 1998 Election and the End of the Kohl Era* (New York, 2010), 196.
41. See the entry "Innere Einheit" in Werner Weidenfeld and Karl-Rudolf Korte, eds., *Handbuch zur deutschen Einheit, 1949–1989–1999* (Frankfurt, 1999), 454–466.
42. Lindsay M. Pettingill, "Towards an Appreciation of German Disunity," *German Politics and Society in the GDR*, 28 (Winter 2010), 69–77.
43. For a synthesis of the different approaches and a new one, see Tereza Novotna, "Hastily Arranged Marriage: Political Attitudes and Perceptions in Germany Twenty Years after Unification," *German Politics and Society*, 28 (Winter 2010), 19–40. See also Detlef

Pollack, "Wie ist es um die innere Einheit Deutschlands bestellt?" and Oscar W. Gabriel and Sonja Zmerli, "Politisches Vertrauen: Deutschland in Europa," in *Aus Politik und Zeitgeschichte,* 30–31 (2006), 3–7, 8–15. For a more "sanguine view," see Russell J. Dalton and Steven Weldon, "Germans Divided? Political Culture in Unified Germany," *German Politics,* 19 (March 2010), 9–23.

44. Gary S. Schaal et al., *60 Jahre Grundgesetz. Deutsche Identität im Spannungsfeld von Europäisierung und Regionalisierung. Ergebnisse einer repräsentativen Bevölkerungsbefragung* (Dresden, n.d.), tu-dresden.de/die_tu_dresden/fakultaeten/philosophische_fakultaet/ifpw/poltheo/zvd/news/Bericht_60 percent20Jahre percent20Grundgesetz.pdf.
45. Edeltraud Roller, "Einstellungen zur Demokratie im vereinigten Deutschland. Gibt es Anzeichen für eine abnehmende Differenz?" in Peter Krause and Ilona Ostner, eds., *Leben in Ost- und Westdeutschland. Eine sozialwissenschaftliche Bilanz der deutschen Einheit 1990–2010* (Frankfurt, 2010), 597–614.
46. Novotna, "Hastily Arranged Marriage," 30.
47. *Two Decades after the Wall's Fall. End of Communism Cheered but Now with More Reservations* (Washington, DC: Pew Global Attitudes Project, 2 November 2009), 4.
48. Ursula Dallinger, "Erwartungen an den Wohlfahrtsstaat. Besteht eine 'innere Mauer' zwischen Ost und Westdeutschen?" in Krause und Ostner, *Leben,* 573–596.
49. "Wie ist es um die innere Einheit bestellt?" *Aus Politik und Zeitgeschichte,* 30–31 (2006), 3–7.
50. Welsh, "Policy Transfer in the Unified Germany: From Imitation to Feedback Loop," *German Studies Review,* 33 (October 2010), 531–548.
51. Katrin Bennhold, "20 Years After Fall of Wall, Women of Former East Germany Thrive," *New York Times,* 5 October 2010.
52. Victor W. Turner, *The Ritual Process: Structure and Anti-Structure* (Chicago, 1969). Ann Swidler distinguishes between the impact of culture on "settled lives" and "unsettled lives." See her article, "Culture in Action: Symbols and Strategies," *American Sociological Review,* 51 (1986), 273–286.
53. "Toward the Berlin Republic—Past, Present, and Future," in Dieter Dettke, ed., *The Spirit of the Berlin Republic* (New York, 2003), 336–367.
54. See, for example, Maoz Azaryahu, "German Reunification and the Politics of Street Names: The Case of East Berlin," *Political Geography,* 16 (1997), 479–494; Julie Mostov, "The Use and Abuse of History in Eastern Europe: A Challenge for the 90s," *Constellations,* 4 (1998), 376–386.
55. "Berliner Einheits-Denkmal. Ehrlich verschaukelt," *Spiegel Online Kultur,* 14 April 2011, http://www.spiegel.de/kultur/gesellschaft/berliner-einheits-denkmal-ehrlich-verschaukelt-a-756941.html; Kia Vahland, "Einheitsdenkmal in Berlin. Demokratie zum Schaukeln," Süddeutsche Zeitung, 14 April 2011, http://www.sueddeutsche.de/kultur/zum-entwurf-des-einheitsdenkmals-demokratie-zum-schaukeln-1.1084869.
56. Peter Bender, *Deutschlands Wiederkehr. Eine ungeteilte Nachkriegsgeschichte 1945–1990* (Stuttgart, 2007), 269.
57. In 2010, the British magazine *The Economist* ranked Germany in the select group of twenty-seven full democracies; the only postcommunist country included is the Czech Republic.

Part II

Economic Problems

Chapter Four

Institutional Coping

The Treuhandanstalt and the Collapse of the East German Economy, 1989–1990

Wolfgang Seibel

The brief economic history of the final phase of the GDR was characterized by dramatic decay and the quest for institutional stability. One part of the remedies that emerged out of the various attempts to restabilize both the economic and the political situation was the so-called Treuhandanstalt. Founded on 1 March 1990, it was designed to be the institutional backbone of state ownership of industrial assets. Its purpose was to prevent the people-owned assets from being sold out in what was then a gold-rush atmosphere for Western investors. At the same time, keeping the "public property" (*Volkseigenes Vermögen*) under preliminary state control was, in the eyes of a solid majority of the relevant political forces in a self-democratizing GDR, the crucial prerequisite of the gradual economic reform whose indispensability was virtually uncontested across the political spectrum.

In a matter of months, however, the Treuhandanstalt dramatically changed its character. By the end of the dramatic year of 1990, it had become a federal authority in charge of privatizing the state-owned industrial assets as quickly as possible. This paradoxical convergence of structural stability under the condition of a total change of purpose, however, only reflected the double collapse of GDR statehood and the East German economy. Even in the early stages of its existence, the Treuhandanstalt proved to be the institutional anchor to which the political stability of a

Notes for this chapter begin on page 101.

vanishing state and its integration into the West German political and economic system was linked.

This essay analyzes the nature of this institutional paradox. Its general argument is that the early phase of the Treuhandanstalt represents an example of institutional stability as a political problem and a dynamic political outcome in a sense outlined in the recent literature on gradual institutional change.[1] The stability of the Treuhandanstalt, despite substantive change of purpose and dramatic turbulences that turned the political and economic environment upside down, may be interpreted as resulting from a good fit between environmental challenges and institutional properties.[2] Moreover, it is an example of what Mahoney and Thelen call institutional stability as a political problem and a dynamic political outcome.[3] The very same societal and political forces that shaped the turbulent political and economic environment of the Treuhandanstalt also influenced the latter's institutional properties, including a substantially altered purpose. How to cope with the political and economic situation in a GDR in demise and with the Treuhandanstalt as an institution were just two aspects of one and the same politico-economic process. In what follows, the crucial characteristics of that process and the emergence of the Treuhandanstalt as an institutional coping mechanism are analyzed.[4]

From Gradual to Abrupt Transition

Two key decisions were overwhelmingly influential in shaping the integration of the GDR into the political and economic system of Federal Republic: the announcement of the West German government on 7 February 1990 that proposed formal negotiations with the GDR government on an inter-German currency union, and the fixing of the related conversion rate for wages and savings to 1:1, laid down in the intergovernmental treaty of 18 May 1990. These two decisions initiated a shock-like transition from a planned economy to a market economy that characterized the trajectory of economic transformation in post-1990 East Germany in a path-dependent way.

An early currency union was the opposite of what the Bundesbank and the independent and nonpartisan government board empowered to analyze economic developments had recommended. Until late January 1990 the West German Federal Government had treated an inter-German currency union as the capstone of economic transition within the GDR, rather than its starting point. The 1:1 conversion rate for wages and a certain amount of savings was chosen against the advice of the Bundesbank and also of the Council of Economic Experts (Sachverständigenrat). Both institutions had emphasized the disastrous consequences of a 1:1 conversion rate that would force East German firms to pay wages in hard currency at a level that could not be covered by the profits made under the conditions of low productivity and a largely obsolete capital stock. However, the early currency union at disastrous conversion rates not only defied West German preferences for gradual transition from a socialist economy to capitalism, but also East German reform options that had emerged since the autumn of 1989.

When Prime Minister Hans Modrow took office on 17 November 1989, a reformist intellectual elite became temporarily influential—loyal communists who nonetheless had repeatedly criticized the actual practice of economic planning and production, and who therefore had been neutralized by the regime. Typical representatives of this group were Christa Luft, minister for the economy and deputy prime minister, and Wolfram Krause, previously deputy chairman of the Commission for Economic Planning (Staatliche Plankommission). Krause had been ousted from the Berlin district administration of the communist SED in 1978. Luft had been president of the Hochschule für Ökonomie "Bruno-Leuschner" in Karlshorst. Modrow and Luft convened a Task Force for Economic Reform reporting to the Council of Ministers of the GDR and appointed Wolfram Krause as its director. These politicians and functionaries represented the reformist wing of the SED and, consequently, those hoping for renewal of socialism and the resilience of the GDR as a sovereign state. They also sought to maintain the system of collective ownership of industrial assets in the form of "people's property."

The idea of modernizing the socialist economy, however, was soon eclipsed by the idea of a "Third Way" that was widespread among those forming the Round Table on 7 December 1989. This body was composed of representatives of the political parties and societal groups within the official National Front and the representatives of the civil movement that formed the core of the political opposition.

Among those promulgating a Third Way beyond capitalism and socialism, the group Democracy Now (DJ) came up with the most elaborate ideas in the field of economic policy. Wolfgang Ullmann, a trained theologian, together with Matthias Artzt, an engineer, and the physicist Gerd Gebhardt, had drafted a paper entitled Future Through Self-Organization in early November 1989. It advocated the legalization of private ownership of firms and industrial assets under the condition of "social responsibility" of the owners.[5] Moreover, the paper stated that the "strategic goal" was to "transfer as much as possible of the property of the people directly to the citizens of the GDR."[6] Ullman, Artzt, and Gebhardt constituted themselves as the Free Research Group for Self-organization.

On 6 December 1989, Ullmann took his seat at the Round Table as its representative.

The goal of a "socially committed" market economy combined with a far-reaching transfer of "people's property" to the people of the GDR resulted in preliminary considerations concerning the institutionalization of a certain trusteeship function with the main purpose of transforming the people's assets into a legal form that could persist in case the GDR became part of the Federal Republic. These considerations were, then, laid out in a paper drafted by Ullmann and others and submitted to the Round Table, where the paper was put on the agenda on 12 February, 1990.[7] The core of the document was a proposal for the immediate creation of a trust corporation in the form of a holding company for safeguarding the shareholder rights of GDR citizens to the people's property of the GDR.

A couple of weeks earlier, on 28 January 1990, Prime Minister Modrow had met the chairmen of the parties of the political opposition and the previous "bloc parties."[8] As a result of that meeting, the date of the first free elections of the GDR parliament was moved up from 6 May to 18 March 1990, while the date for general municipal elections remained 6 May 1990. Most importantly, however, participants in the meeting formed a "government of national responsibility" that included the opposition parties and representatives of the civic movement that had initiated the decisive protests in the autumn of 1989. The new interim government was confirmed by the Volkskammer on 5 February 1990.[9]

It was during the parliamentary session of 29 January 1990 that the minister for mechanical engineering, Karl Grünhold, mentioned in a report on the overall economic situation that in the fourth quarter of 1989 alone, 350,000 citizens, the equivalent of 2 percent of the population, had left the GDR—amounting to a rate of 1.4 million citizens per year. During the same Volkskammer session, Prime Minister Modrow intimated that the state budget deficit had risen to 17 billion Marks. The economic situation was deeply "disturbing."[10]

When the West German government declared its readiness on 7 February 1990 to negotiate with the government of the GDR about an inter-German currency union, this was primarily meant as a political signal to the people of the GDR. The wording of the offer was significant. According to the press release, the Federal Government was ready "immediately to start negotiations about a currency union with economic reform."[11] The reference to "economic reforms" was, at this point, probably just a rhetorical formula designed to conceal the abrupt change of course to which the federal government had meanwhile committed itself.[12]

The declaration of 7 February 1990 in favor of "immediate" negotiations about a currency union was the result of political necessity that was at least as international as it was domestic in nature. The German Federal Government was exposed to tremendous pressure from both inside and outside Germany, resulting from the expectation that only the government in Bonn was in the position to restabilize, at least temporarily, the situation in the GDR—which found itself at the brink of demise. The key to restabilization was the reduction of the wave of immigrants that, at a rate of 3,000 to 5,000 people per day, threatened to undermine both the economic viability and the absorption capacity of the Federal Republic.

However, the implications of what was required inside versus outside Germany were divergent. While the obvious destabilization of the GDR required decisive steps toward an inter-German integration far beyond the "federative structures" mentioned in Chancellor Helmut Kohl's "ten points plan," the key players outside Germany—the governments of the United States, the United Kingdom, and France—insisted on decelerating the pace of inter-German rapprochement. Their main motive was the fear of negative repercussions to the cooperative and prudent government of the Soviet Union under Gorbachev.[13]

The preparation of an economic and currency union uniting the two German states and the decision to move the Volkskammer elections up to 18 March 1990 paid tribute to the delicate dilemma the West German government found itself in. Intensifying economic cooperation in general and the announcement of a currency union in particular were credible signals sent to the GDR populace, indicating that the West German government was irrevocably determined to assume political responsibility for Germany as a whole. By way of initiating a currency union, the West German D-Mark, the symbol of the "economic miracle," became the token of the inter-German merger. These prospects would not only contain the wave of inter-German migration, but the measure would also bring the GDR state budget and currency system under the control of the West German government and the Bundesbank. At the same time, it remained below the level of a regular unification of the two German states, which would have spectacular international implications and represent a fundamental change of the geopolitical order after World War II.

There was yet another implication: any kind of "economic reform" such as the one envisaged in the reform-minded SED circles around Wolfram Krause and Christa Luft and around Wolfgang Ullmann became totally illusory as early as February 1990. Not that the respective ideas of economic reforms were unrealistic from the very outset; presumably, they would have been appraised in the West as "revolutionary" if they would have been presented a year earlier. However, the very state order that was the indispensable framework for the implementation of any kind of reform was dissolving irreversibly.

The civic support, necessary for any meaningful reform, had begun to evaporate completely. This was the price to be paid for forty years of dictatorship. And it was the existence of a real alternative, the West German Federal Republic and its political and economic order which made the sustainable restabilization of GDR statehood fundamentally illusory. After all, hundreds of thousands of GDR citizens had "voted with their feet" for it just a couple of months after the fall of the Berlin Wall. It was not just the political system but the actual state of the GDR that lacked a minimum degree of civic loyalty. So, political and economic reforms under the condition of a maintained GDR statehood obviously had no basis either.

In January 1990, the Arbeitsgruppe Wirtschaftsreform, chaired by Wolfram Krause, had drafted a paper that was published as supplement to the journal *Die Wirtschaft* on 1 February 1990. The authors wrote: "The regulatory influence of the state has to be reduced to a scale that shapes the conditions for economic growth, stability and proportionality as well as the social and ecological direction of economic development." Governmental regulation of the economy should focus on making "economic methods" more effective. It should, therefore, initiate a reform of the price system, a tax reform, a "performance-based payment principle," a "policy of scarce money on the basis of a performance- and efficiency-oriented loan policy," the development of the "state-bank of the GDR ... [in]to an institution independent from governmental interference," and the erection of a system of "independent commercial banks."[14] From today's perspective, these ideas may even appear to be neoliberal. They were presented, however, by loyal SED/PDS cadres.

The Treuhandanstalt and the Currency Union

The paper drafted by the research group "Selbstorganisation" that reached the agenda of the Round Table on 12 February 1990 contained the proposal to create a "trusteeship corporation" in order to protect the property rights of GDR citizens. The formal purpose of the suggestion was to close a legal lacuna that could be foreseen in the case of an "affiliation of the GDR to the Federal Republic" since the collective ownership of industrial assets did not exist in the West German legal system. The basic idea was, accordingly, to guarantee the "public property" (*Volkseigentum*) not only nominally but literally in the form of individual entitlement.

Similar ideas were developed within the Arbeitsgruppe Wirtschaftsreform around Wolfram Krause and his SED/PDS comrades. Here, the initiatives were even more pragmatic. The reform-minded postcommunists suggested simply transforming the so-called "people owned firms and factories" (*Volkseigene Betriebe* and *Kombinate*) into limited liability corporations and joint stock companies in accordance with West German corporate law. The irony was that the Limited Liability Corporation Law of 1892 and the Stock Corporation Law of 1937 had never been suspended in the GDR and, consequently, could serve as the basis of the transformation even in the framework of the GDR legal system. The shares of the capital stock of those newly created corporations, however, should have been held by a Treasury office. This was where the proposals of both groups converged. The Treasury Office (proposed by the Arbeitsgruppe Wirtschaftsreform) and the Treuhandgesellschaft (proposed by the Freies Forschungskollegium Selbstorganisation) were very similar form and function. Both were designed to keep the collective ownership of industrial assets in public hands. The main difference between the two proposals was that the research group Selbstorganisation insisted on transforming the collective ownership of the "people" into individual legal entitlements of the citizens of the GDR.

Regardless of those differences, on 1 March 1990, the Council of Ministers of the GDR decided to create an "authority for the trusteeship administration" of the *Volkseigentum,* designated as the Treuhandanstalt.[15] On the same day, the Volkskammer passed an ordinance regulating the transformation of state-owned firms into private companies.[16] This was the birth of the Treuhandanstalt.

The Volkskammer elections of 18 March 1990 resulted in a surprising victory of Helmut Kohl's Christian Democrats, a quasi-plebiscitarian decision in favor of a swift reunification of the two German states. The Christian Democrats not only benefited from Kohl's charisma but also from the organizational infrastructure that the East German CDU had at its disposal as a member of the national bloc. Lothar de Mazière became the first and last prime minister of the GDR to emerge from free elections acting as the head of a grand coalition comprising all major political forces with the exception of the SED/PDS. The coalition agreement of 12 April 1990 expressed the political will to achieve national reunification through the accession of the GDR to the Federal Republic on the basis of a currency and economic union. Of pivotal importance, also in the perception of contemporary observers, was the commitment to a currency conversion rate of 1:1. It was beyond any doubt that the East German government had not the slightest leeway to deviate from this self-binding pledge. It is only with the benefit of hindsight, however, that the decision of 12 April 1990 turned out to be the critical junction at which the breakdown of the East German economy under conditions of unrestricted market forces became unavoidable.

The coalition agreement of 12 April 1990 had been prepared under the massive pressure of East German public opinion. Two weeks earlier, on 29 March 1990, West German newspapers reported on a confidential memo submitted to the central board of the Bundesbank for a meeting held in the presence of the federal minister of finance, Theo Waigel, advocating a general conversion rate of 2:1 (i.e., two GDR-marks to be converted to one D-Mark). According to that scheme, only individual savings up to an amount of 2,000 GDR-Marks per person should have been converted at a rate of 1:1. The paper was leaked to the press and what followed was a public outcry in the GDR. For the first time since the dramatic autumn of 1989, massive rallies were organized, expressing the disappointment of East Germans who, just a couple of days earlier, had voted for what they thought would be a prosperous future.[17] These protests suddenly jeopardized the recent gains in political stability that had been realized through the formation of a democratic government constituted by a grand coalition.

The intergovernmental treaty (*Staatsvertrag*) of 18 May 1990[18] finally stipulated a conversion rate of 1:1 for salaries and wages, stipends, pensions, housing rents, and "further permanent payments." Savings were to be converted at a rate of 1:1 up to limits starting at 2,000 GDR-Marks for children and juveniles and ranging to 4,000 GDR-Marks for adults and 6,000 for the retired.

The agreement of 18 May 1990 was the formal watershed that resulted in a bizarre combination of risk escalation and risk mitigation. The risk of triggering the final breakdown of the GDR economy grew inevitably with any step closer to conversion parity between the two currencies. The reason was that East German firms were forced to pay salaries and wages in hard currency at a level that could never be matched by the proceeds they were able to realize through the sale of their outmoded products on a competitive market. The fate of the GDR economy was virtually sealed when the conversion rate of 1:1 for salaries and wages took effect on 1 July 1990.

By the same token, however, any conversion rate below parity would have been fundamentally incompatible with the goal of political stabilization in both East *and* West Germany. When facing not only political disappointment but also a substantial reduction of available income and a standard of living that was decreasing instead of increasing, hundreds of thousands of East Germans would have chosen the obvious alternative, which was to leave their own disadvantaged currency zone and to settle in West Germany, where welfare payments alone would have been provided for a standard of living they never would achieve on the basis of the meager salaries paid in West German currency but based on East German labor productivity (which is estimated to have reached only 30 percent of West German productivity).

Even if East Germans would have decided to stay and benefit from the welfare system that was expected to be transferred from West, the dilemma remained the same. Hundreds of thousands of East Germans whose salaries would fell below a certain minimum would have been entitled to receive welfare payments. Pensions in particular would not suffice to make a living. This was spelled out to Helmut Kohl by his minister for labor and social affairs, Norbert Blüm, in a letter of 27 March 1990.[19] Blüm, consequently, strongly advocated for a 1:1 conversion rate for wages and pension payments because otherwise, as he wrote, the West German government could not keep the promise to transfer the West German welfare system to East Germany. It became crystal clear that no politically viable alternative existed to a conversion rate that would necessarily push the East German economy over the brink of collapse.

The Changing Role of the Treuhandanstalt

The currency union based on a 1:1 conversion rate totally changed the role of the *Volkseigenes Vermögen* and of the Treuhandanstalt that had been founded by the Modrow government. With the West German government in charge of the GDR budget and fiscal system, the people's property was designed to function as a deposit for the huge governmental investments necessary for the modernization of the East German economy and public infrastructure. As an influential comment *on* the *Staatsvertrag* put it: "The Treuhandanstalt, assuming the ownership function for state owned firms in the GDR, has the task to mobilize the public property whose industrial assets alone represent an estimated value of several hundreds of billion Deutsch-Marks. Considerable resources are to be mobilized through an active privatization policy in order to ensure focused but broad measures of restructuring."[20]

In the perception of contemporary observers, this arrangement could easily appear to be a fair deal. On the one hand, the Federal Republic would bear all the major risks connected to the heavily indebted state budget of the GDR and the huge investments necessary for economic modernization in East Germany. On the other hand, the government of the GDR conceded that the *Volkseigenes Vermögen* would be used to cover the budget deficit and the costs of economic reform and reconstruction rather than to have the East German people participating in what, technically at least, used to be *their* property.

The bitter irony was that whatever the use of the public property would be, the currency conversion rate of 1:1 made it null and void. The excessive conversion rate for salaries and wages not only made the state-owned firms held by the Treuhandanstalt unprofitable, it also made them impossible to sell, making the lion's share of the *Volkseigenes Vermögen* worthless. Whether the taxpayer and the Federal Government would have the staying power necessary for a credit-financed restructuring of the East German economy under the vague prospects of an ultimate redemption through the sale of restructured and newly profitable firms was more than questionable. As would soon be clear, the Federal Government was not willing to take that risk.

Accordingly, the *Staatsvertrag*, effective 1 July 1990, defined an extremely narrow path for how to use what was left from the *Volkseigenes Vermögen* and, consequently, for the policy of the Treuhandanstalt. It was also a logical consequence not only that the West German government became responsible for the GDR budget and fiscal system but also that West German managers and bureaucrats took charge of the Treuhandanstalt as an institution. Step by step, the board of the Treuhandanstalt was "Westernized." The last East German left the board in June 1992. It happened to be the very same Wolfram Krause, the former SED dissident, who was reactivated by Prime Minister Modrow in the fall of 1989 as the intellectual mastermind of economic reform in a socialist framework.

The speed of privatization, however, was soon dictated by the consequences of the currency union. The deep economic depression of the East German economy that followed the introduction of the D-Mark on 1 July 1990 translated itself into a dramatic devaluation of the Treuhandanstalt assets. This, in turn, intensified the privatization efforts, which again accelerated the drop-off in prices in the market for firms. Soon, many Treuhand companies could only be sold at "negative prices," i.e., with the help of government subsidies. This was obviously the opposite of the official purpose of the Treuhandanstalt's assets, which the *Staatsvertrag* treated as the collateral of the budget deficit caused by the state-financed modernization of the East German economy. Basically, the *Staatsvertrag* suspended itself.

On the night of 17 June 1990, the Volkskammer passed the Treuhand-Gesetz, or the Law Pertaining to the Privatization and Reorganization of the People's Assets. This happened, according to the minutes of the respective Volkskammer session, with a "great majority."[21] The new law became effective 1 July 1990, together with the *Staatsvertrag* that regulated the currency union and the transfer of the West German social security system in particular. The new law stipulated the privatization of the state-owned assets as its primary task.[22]

The Treuhand law was designed to adapt the policy and the organizational structure of the already existing Treuhandanstalt to comply with the new requirements established by the *Staatsvertrag*. While the law itself remained relatively vague and abstract, a new charter issued by the

Council of Ministers of the GDR on 22 July 1990 defined the essentials. The charter gave the Treuhandanstalt the right to refinance itself on the capital market by issuing government bonds. This meant in practice that the Treuhandanstalt and its budget was separated from the regular federal budget and, thus, from normal parliamentary control.

This was not the only deviation from the regular model of democratic control and West German constitutionalism. The Treuhandanstalt reorganized itself as a tightly centralized authority in charge of privatizing state-owned industrial assets of unprecedented size and scale. This institution neither had anything in common with the initial trusteeship founded by the Modrow government nor anything in common with the federal structure of the West German polity. Nonetheless, the new Treuhandanstalt was not an institutional neophyte. Ironically, it very much resembled the centralized economic governance structure of the very GDR and the corresponding planned economy it was supposed to dismantle.

Even more bizarre was the fact that, from late summer 1990 on, an organizational reform initiated by the newly appointed President Detlef Rohwedder suppressed what was left in terms of decentralized structures. This affected the huge holding companies under the name Treuhand-Aktiengesellschaften that, according to the law, were designed to function as the operational units in charge of privatization and restructuring.[23] In the perception of Rohwedder and others, however, the Treuhand stock companies could easily emerge into uncontrollable industrial conglomerates and thus undermine the core purpose of the Treuhandanstalt, which was swift privatization.

Rohwedder, instead, reanimated the Councils of Economic Administration in the previous fourteen districts of the GDR and rebaptized them Treuhandanstalt branch offices. These units were as dependent on Treuhandanstalt headquarters in Berlin as the Wirtschaftsverwaltungsräte had been on the central branch ministries during the communist era. Also internally, the Treuhand headquarters in Berlin was reorganized in accordance with the logic of those branch directorates, each of them in charge of a specific segment of the GDR economy and in most of the cases employing the very same rank-and-file personnel that already had served under a state-controlled economy. The tactical rationale of tight administrative control remained the same as under communist rule. An experienced troubleshooter of the crisis-ridden West German steel industry, Rohwedder had realized the necessity of exerting strict managerial control over an industrial empire that produced gigantic losses of taxpayers' money day by day. Even the physical location of the Treuhandanstalt headquarters was a replica of the communist past. In March 1991, the headquarters moved from the vast complex of the former "House of the Ministries" that, indeed, had accommodated the branch ministries of the GDR and was located at the corner of Leipziger Straße. The ultimate irony was that the GDR branch ministries themselves had been the beneficiaries of the Nazi past. Their building had been erected as Hermann Göring's Reichsluftfahrtministerium in 1935. The Treuhandanstalt had to cope with all sorts of legacies, indeed.

Patterns of Institutional Stabilization

The economic depression that followed the currency union of 1 July 1990 implied the necessity to accelerate the privatization of the state-owned industrial assets at all costs. By the same token, however, the Treuhandanstalt had to serve as an institutional buffer and absorb the social and political costs caused by its own privatization policy. Economic depression meant that the Treuhandanstalt, as the owner of several thousand firms, had to lay off hundreds of thousands of employees. It thus contributed considerably to the unemployment rate in East Germany that quickly rose to more than 20 percent in 1991. It was the very same institution, however, that successfully served as a political shock absorber, which was desperately needed by the Federal Government in Bonn. The institutional stability of the Treuhandanstalt became a key factor ensuring the smooth implementation of the Federal Government's privatization policy for East Germany. The main component on which this achievement was based was the combination of a rigid organizational core, GDR style, and a flexible organizational periphery in accordance with West German federalism and neocorporatism.

The key period for these institutional components to emerge was the first half of 1991. In that period, political pressure on the Treuhandanstalt increased massively because the results of privatization remained modest while layoffs, corporate debts, and open unrest among East German workers grew steadily. At the end of the first quarter of 1991, 85 percent of the initial 8,000 firms were still in the trusteeship portfolio. East German industrial output had sunk to 45 percent of its 1990 level. The unemployment rate had risen to 11.7 percent, but unemployment in an artificial second labor market, largely funded through government contributions, accounted for an additional 13 percent. Thus a quarter of the active population had no regular job or no job at all.[24]

In February 1991, a wave of wildcat strikes triggered by layoffs and actual or anticipated shutdowns swept across Treuhand firms. This affected not only the agency itself but also the weak state governments that meanwhile had been established according to the West German pattern. State politicians became increasingly nervous and turned to the Federal Government, asking for support in what they perceived as a struggle against the federal Treuhandanstalt and its privatization policy. In a similar vein, the unions asked for a decelerated pace of privatization and for either the dissolution of the Treuhandanstalt or its transformation into a federal agency for economic reconstruction.[25]

The Treuhandanstalt could fulfill its political main task—shielding against the political pressure targeted at the Federal Government in Bonn—only under the condition that the powerful challenging actors were integrated or neutralized. The potential strength of those actors was defined by the political system of the Federal Republic and the characteristic state-economy relationship within it. The crucial challengers were the East German Länder and the unions. It is remarkable that the Treuhandanstalt indeed managed to integrate the states and the unions and to neutralize their political pressure. Unlike prominent forerunners such as the Tennessee Valley Authority, it managed to integrate those challenging actors without changing course. Instead, it continued its rigid privatization policy and that policy was de facto tolerated by both the Länder and the unions.

Union leaders and the East German prime ministers were coopted into the board of the Treuhandanstalt as early as autumn of 1990. This classic pattern of cooptation[26] turned out to be the backbone of the Treuhandanstalt's stability. However, mere representation of potential challenging actors in the decision-making bodies of the Treuhandanstalt was not enough. The decisive question was whether the mechanism of cooptation would lead to effective cooperation.

The wave of strikes and unrest in early 1991 triggered a cascade of arrangements between the Federal Government, the Treuhandanstalt, the governments of the East German Länder and the unions. On 8 March 1991, the Federal Government announced a program called Gemeinschaftswerk Aufschwung Ost, consisting of a whole bundle of financial and infrastructural support initiatives benefitting the East German Länder.[27] On 14 March 1991, an agreement was reached between Chancellor Helmut Kohl and the prime ministers of the East German Länder on "Principles of Cooperation between the Federal Government, the State Governments and the Treuhandanstalt for the Recovery of the East."[28]

Part of the agreement was the establishment of Treuhand-Wirtschaftskabinette, a slightly pretentious designation for regular meetings of board members and relevant ministers of the respective Land. On 20 March 1991, the economics ministers of the East German Länder issued a joint statement requiring the Treuhandanstalt to coordinate regionally important decisions with the respective Länder and establishing a catalogue of standard operations procedures.[29] These procedural stipulations were adopted by Birgit Breuel, the board member in charge, in a letter of 25 March 1991, to her fellow board members, heads of divisions, and heads of the branch offices.[30] On 13 April 1991, a common declaration was issued by the DGB, the umbrella organization of the unions, the white collar union, and the Treuhandanstalt, containing a "guideline for social plans," covering support for laid-off workers.[31] On 17 July 1991, a guideline for the formation of associations for labor support, employment and structural development was agreed upon.[32]

The Federal Government and the leading officials of the Treuhandanstalt were determined to integrate the East German state governments as well as the unions into core components of strategic decision making. The resulting arrangement proved to be remarkably effective in stabilizing the weak political side of the Treuhandanstalt. This was demonstrated by, among other things, the fact that even leading Social Democrats and influential union leaders were outspoken in their support of the Treuhandanstalt when the agency was challenged by protests and opposition. When the Social Democratic opposition used its parliamentary minority right to create a committee to investigate the practice of the Treuhandanstalt in 1993, two prominent Social Democratic members of the board reacted in open protest. One was the prime minister of the state of Brandenburg, Manfred Stolpe, the other one the union chairman for the chemical industry, Hans-Hermann Rappe.[33]

The unions in particular had their own incentives to support the grand design of the Treuhandanstalt policy behind closed doors while endorsing, in selected cases, the public protest against it. Toward their East German clientele, the unions needed to demonstrate their ability to influence strategic decision making, which they did through a series of basic guidelines agreed upon in the first half of 1991. Vis-à-vis their West German clientele, by contrast, the unions had to demonstrate that they would not allow low-wage competitors to emerge in East Germany. The unions were successful in achieving both requirements—at the expense of East German jobs.

On 1 March 1991, the East German employers' association and the unions in the metal industry reached an agreement according to which wages would be raised in incremental steps up to the West German level by 1995. What might appear in hindsight to have been a reckless imposition of competitive disadvantages to the detriment of East German firms was the result of convergent interests among employers, union representatives, the Federal Government, and the immediate beneficiaries among East Germans in the metal industry who were happy enough to keep their jobs.

Both employers' associations and organized labor were still weak in East Germany in 1991. There were neither experienced nor politically uncontaminated union leaders, nor were the union functionaries at the plant level as established and accepted as their West German counterparts. This implied that both the representatives of the employers and the representatives of the employees who were negotiating about wages and labor arrangements in East Germany were actually West Germans. The Federal Government, represented by the Treuhandanstalt, was still the by far largest and most important employer in East Germany. When an area was facing a severe regional depression, the Treuhandanstalt was dependent on both the neutralization of the unions as a pressure group and their mobilization as an integrative factor at the plant level. Being committed to the protection of the interests of the large majority of West German unionized labor and West German industry, the representatives of the employers and those of the unions had a common interest: to keep the emergence of wage-based competition in East Germany under control.

Against this cartel of interests, the Treuhandanstalt stood no chance in the attempt to assume the classic role of an employer interested in containing wage costs. In a subtle way, this demonstrates that the institution was far from pursuing a reckless (or "neoliberal") entrepreneurial policy. It was a highly politicized agency that fulfilled its political function with a remarkable degree of flexibility. The core of that political function was formed by the need to make the consequences of the currency union of 1 July 1990 compatible with the requirements of political support and integration in accordance with dominant West German institutional patterns and power structures.

As powerless as the East Germans were once they had abandoned their own sovereign state, the main burden of adaptation was put on their shoulders. This was being done, however, by changing coalitions under the cover of various ideologies and interests. Nothing could be more aberrant than the notion of East Germany falling prey to a political and economic *Anschluss* in a quasi-colonial and neoliberal vein. Not only was the revolution of 1989 initiated and performed entirely by the East Germans, but they also had the decisive say on the trajectory of economic change. It was they who made the key decisions of 1990 that paved the way to reunification and its economic consequences: the Volkskammer election of 18 March 1990 was chiefly a plebiscite in favor of a swift accession of the GDR to the Federal Republic *and* a currency union at a conversion rate of 1:1. It was the East Germans who reinforced that pressure when the first freely elected GDR government was formed under Prime Minister Lothar de Mazière in early April 1990. It was they who rendered obsolete the projects of reforms and gradual transition to a capitalist market economy that had been developed by reform-minded communists and the advocates of a Third Way.

Between the fall of the Berlin Wall and the signing of the currency union treaty, the East Germans had achieved almost everything they has asked for through protests, flight, and voting at the ballot boxes: the removal of dictatorship; the prospect of dissolving their own state; the promise of an early currency union at attractive conversion rates for wages, savings, and pensions; and the transfer of one of the most elaborate welfare systems as a "safety net" in case all the other provisions would not reduce the remaining risks to zero. Finally, East Germans through their own protests managed to achieve a continual increase in wages independent of labor productivity in 1991.

The East Germans, however, lacked the human, structural, and ideational means to keep what they had initiated under control. The new democratic elites were inexperienced and without any regional professional support by experts or bureaucrats. No relevant institutional structures emerged from the revolution of 1989 except for the Round Table—and the Treuhandanstalt. Both were ephemeral bodies that either disappeared with the election of 18 March 1990 or completely changed their character with the currency union of 1 July 1990.

Finally, no compelling narrative has put the events of 1989 through 1991 in the historical context they emerged from: the linkages among dictatorship, war, geopolitics, postwar reconstruction, economic governance, and the conditions of political stability. While it was plausible to revive the myth of the West German economic miracle when the currency union was prepared in early 1990 in an attempt to connect what had begun as a movement for freedom with the prospect of economic recovery, this narrative was a first step to make West German standards the measure of all things.

There were, moreover, also international pressures that influenced crucial decisions within Germany. As we know from documents that have become accessible in the meantime,[34] there was a strong consensus that the "German uncertainties" should not cause serious trouble for a third time in the twentieth century. This was what dictated the American, the British, and the French efforts to persuade Helmut Kohl to restabilize, even if only temporarily, the GDR at all costs. The currency union was just the most effective means to achieve that goal. It was a political measure form the very outset. However, it could not be "sold" to the public as such.

As a consequence, the economic transformation of the GDR economy not only started with illusions, but also neglected to explain the geopolitical contexts and the historical conditions of German reunification. The fact that the international community finally tolerated a reunited Germany was interpreted as a matter of course rather than a political miracle. By the same token, the economic consequences of the currency union at a disastrous conversion rate continue to be debated as a matter of Eastern versus Western economic performance and prosperity rather than as part of the price to be paid for Germany's second chance.

Institutional Coping

The Treuhandanstalt, the largest privatization agency ever, originated at the convergence of various political attempts to regain control over a political system and an entire economy at the brink of collapse. It was the common purpose of both reform-minded intellectuals within the communist SED/PDS on the one hand and the representatives of the civil movement that formed the political opposition on the other hand to maintain state ownership of the *Volkseigenes Vermögen* at least for the foreseeable future. There was also consensus among these groups, however, that state ownership was not an end in itself but the institutional basis of economic reform as a prerequisite of a political and economic revitalization of the GDR.

When the prospects of keeping GDR statehood intact evaporated with the elections of 18 March 1990, both the economic and the political environment changed dramatically. The elections were a plebiscite approving of a swift integration of the GDR into the Federal Republic. It was also common sense that the first step in that direction had to be an inter-German currency union which itself was designed to serve a double purpose. One was to underline the commitment of the West German Federal Government to assume full responsibility for the political and economic fate of the GDR. The other purpose was to secure tight fiscal control over what was left from the GDR's state budget and monetary system. It was a logic of give and take: the intergovernmental treaty of 18 May 1990 stipulated that the people's property should serve as collateral for the fiscal risks to be borne by the West Germany. This was what warped the purpose of the Treuhandanstalt. When the inter-German currency union was realized on the basis of a 1:1 conversion rate for salaries and wages—an unavoidable measure for maintaining social peace and containing inter-German migration—it automatically destroyed the already severely damaged profitability of East German firms. As part of the Treuhand portfolio, these firms where eating up taxpayers' money day by day. Not only did this trigger a wave of massive layoffs, once the heydays of reunification euphoria were over, it also forced the Federal Government to sell the assets at a dramatically accelerated pace.

The irony was that the Treuhandanstalt, originally created to safeguard state ownership of the *Volkseigenes Vermögen*, now became the indispensable tool of massive privatization. Maintaining stability while reversing course was the resulting challenge. The stability of the Treuhandanstalt, in turn, was the prerequisite of stable political and economic change in a reunited Germany in general. By virtue of a remarkable structural elasticity, the Treuhandanstalt performed the role of an institutional coping mechanism that absorbed the shock waves triggered by its own privatization activity. It was a particular combination of instrumental, political, and symbolic functions that formed the basis of that mechanism.[35] The result was institutional change that, paradoxically enough, was gradual and revolutionary at the same time.

In the initial phase the Treuhandanstalt successfully kept the state-owned assets of the *Volkseigenes Vermögen,* but eventually it was successfully transformed into a rigid tool of large-scale privatization. Ironically, the new elite of West German managers who joined the board of the Treuhandanstalt in the summer of 1990 recentralized the organizational structure in a way that made it quite similar to the prior structure of the GDR economy—a pattern that it was designed to overcome. The very logic of control akin to that of a state-planned economy was an inevitable ingredient of the managerial grip required for governmental control over an industrial empire of more than 8,000 firms earmarked for privatization. It was with substantial bitterness that the reform-minded GDR elites who had invested considerable hope into the prospects of gradual economic transformation by way of decentralization and a "socially responsible" market economy realized that West German administrative and corporate elites re-established a rigid and centralized governance for the purpose of accelerated privatization involving considerable social costs in terms of massive unemployment.

The political function of the Treuhandanstalt was connected to its integrative role vis-à-vis potentially challenging actors such as the unions and the emerging East German Länder governments. It was in accordance with the classic pattern of cooptation and cooperation that the Treuhandanstalt integrated or neutralized these actors. Although the unions and the Länder governments were still weak in 1990/91, it took a series of accords to mitigate the tensions between the representatives of East German labor and regional interests and a federal authority responsible for tens of thousands of layoffs each month. Skillful maneuvering and active political networking of top-ranking Treuhand officials contributed to solid political support as a complement to internal managerial and organizational rigidity.

Last but not least, the contribution of the Treuhandanstalt to political stabilization was paradoxically connected to its symbolic function. For most East Germans, it became the institutional incarnation of the dark side of reunification. *Die Treuhand* became a synonym of a combination of Western hegemony and crude capitalism. None of these sentiments were grounded in reality. After all, the Treuhandanstalt was just coping with the consequences of the currency union that had been requested by the East Germans themselves. But the psychological projections onto the Treuhandanstalt reduced considerably the immediate risk of delegitimization at the expense of the Federal Government itself. The Treuhandanstalt, which was located in Berlin when the Federal Government still resided in the city of Bonn, served as an institutional scapegoat, absorbing much of the negative emotions, if not hatred, that otherwise could have seriously threatened the support for the Federal Government. When the coalition of the Christian Democrats and the Free Democrats won the federal elections of 1994 by a narrow margin, part of that success was due to the fact that the dramatic economic frictions that accompanied the East German transformation had been successfully buffered by both the structural elasticity and the symbolic usefulness of the Treuhandanstalt.

Notes

1. Avner Greif and David D. Laitin, "A Theory of Endogenous Institutional Change," *American Political Science Review* 98 (2004), 633–652; Wolfgang Streeck and Kathleen Thelen, eds., *Beyond Continuity: Institutional Change in Advanced Political Economies* (Oxford, 2005); James Mahoney and Kathleen Thelen, eds., *Explaining Institutional Change: Ambiguity, Agency, and Power* (New York, 2010). I am indebted to Marius Busemeyer for pointing out several aspects of the literature on gradual institutional change relevant to the subsequent interpretation.
2. James Mahoney and Kathleen Thelen, "A Theory of Gradual Institutional Change," in *Explaining Institutional Change*, 1–37.
3. Mahoney and Thelen, "A Theory of Gradual Institutional Change," 7–10.
4. For an earlier version see Wolfgang Seibel, "The Quest for Freedom and Stability: Political Choices and the Economic Transformation of East Germany 1989–1991," in Peter C. Caldwell and Robert R. Shandley, eds., *German Unification: Expectations and Outcomes* (New York, 2011), 99–120.
5. Wolfram Fischer and Harm Schröter, "Die Entstehung der Treuhandanstalt," in Wolfram Fischer, Herbert Hax, and Hanskarl Schneider, eds., *Treuhandanstalt. Das Unmögliche wagen. Forschungsberichte* (Berlin, 1993), 17–40.
6. Ibid.
7. Runder Tisch, 12 February 1990, Vorlage Nr. 12/29, reprinted in *Treuhandanstalt Dokumentation 1990–1994*, vol. 1 (Berlin, 1994), 24–26. Cf. Marc Kemmler, *Die Entstehung der Treuhandanstalt. Von der Wahrung zur Privatisierung des DDR-Volkseigentums* (Frankfurt, 1994), 69–82.
8. "Blockparteien" was the unofficial designation of the parties LDPD, CDU, NDPD, and DPD, which, collectively, constituted the Democratic Bloc, which in turn was a partially

successful attempt to mobilize the loyalty of noncommunist and nonsocialist political forces to communist rule.

9. Walter Romberg (SPD), Rainer Eppelmann (Demokratischer Aufbruch), Sebastian Pflugbeil (Neues Forum), Wolfgang Ullmann (Demokratie Jetzt), Tatjanja Öhm (Unabhängiger Frauenverband), Gerd Poppe (Initiative Frieden und Menschenrechte), Klaus Schlüter (Grüne Liga), and Matthias Platzeck (Grüne Partei) became members of the cabinet as ministers without portfolio.
10. Volkskammer der Deutschen Demokratischen Republik, 9. Wahlperiode, 15. Tagung, 29 January 1990, *Stenographische Niederschrift*, 423.
11. *Bulletin des Presse- und Informationsamtes der Bundesregierung*, 8 February 1990.
12. The *Münchner Merkur* of 20 January 1990 quoted minister of finance Theo Waigel as saying, "A sustainable monetary union must be created by the market. The preconditions for this must be created by reforms in the GDR."
13. In a lengthy discussion with Kohl on 4 January 1990, French President Mitterand warned of the effects of reunification on the Soviet Union: "The Germans must understand that Eastern Germany is a member of the Warsaw Pact and Western Germany a member of NATO, that the economic systems and many other things are different and that any unwise step will require Gorbachev to react or to disappear. For him, the President, the only true problem would be to harmonize this contradiction. The unification of Germany must not happen in such a way that the Russians harden and react with sabre-rattling. We are on the verge of such a development." Bundesministerium des Innern, *Sonderedition aus den Akten des Bundeskanzleramtes 1989/90* (Munich, 1998), 682–690.
14. Arbeitsgruppe Wirtschaftsreform, "Zielstellungen, Grundrichtungen, Etappen und unmittelbare Maßnahmen der Wirtschaftsreform in weiterer Verwirklichung der Regierungserklärung vom 17.11.1989," reprinted in *Treuhandanstalt Dokumentation 1990–1994*, vol. 1, 7–14.
15. *Gesetzblatt der DDR* 1990, Teil I, 107–108.
16. "Verordnung zur Umwandlung von Volkseigenen Kombinaten, Betrieben und Einrichtungen in Kapitalgesellschaften oder Umwandlungsverordnung," *Gesetzblatt der DDR* 1990, Teil I, 332.
17. "Beim Geld hört die Freundschaft auf. Der vom Zentralbankrat vorgeschlagene Umtausch 2 : 1 löst in der DDR Empörung und Enttäuschung aus," *taz*, 3 April 1990; "'Bei 2 : 1 gehen wir eben wieder auf die Straße'. Auch in den Leitartikeln der DDR-Zeitungen wird der genannte Umtauschkurs einhellig abgelehnt," *Stuttgarter Zeitung*, 3 April 1990; "'Der Wahlspeck wird wieder eingesammelt'. Die Bonner Geldumtausch-Pläne für die DDR stiften Ärger quer durch die ganze Republik," *FR*, 4 April 1990; "2 : 1 und die Nerven. Die Empfehlungen des Zentralbankrats zur Umstellung der DDR-Mark treffen den bloßgelegten Nerv einer Bevölkerung in Existenzangst," *Die Welt*, 4 April 1990; "Empörung in der DDR, Streit in Bonn: Welcher Umstellungskurs für die Währungsunion ist der richtige?, 2 : 1—eine Illusion," *Die Zeit*, 6 April 1990.
18. The treaty's complete title was "Staatsvertrag zur Wirtschafts-,Währung- und Sozialunion," *Gesetzblatt der DDR* 1990, Teil I, 332 and *Bundesgesetzblatt* 1990 Teil II, 537.
19. Blüm to Kohl, 27 March 1990, in *Sonderedition aus den Akten des Bundeskanzleramtes*, 979–980.
20. Klaus Stern and Bruno Schmidt-Bleibtreu, *Kommentar zum Staatsvertrag zur Wirtschafts-, Währungs- und Sozialunion* (Munich, 1990), 63.
21. Volkskammer der Deutschen Demokratischen Republik, 10. Wahlperiode, 15. Tagung, 17 June 1990, *Stenografische Niederschrift*, 561.
22. "Gesetz zur Privatisierung und Reorganisation des volkseigenen Vermögens (Treuhandgesetz)," *Gesetzblatt der DDR* 1990 Teil I, 300–304.
23. *Gesetzblatt der DDR* 1990 Teil I, 300–304.

24. Deutsches Institut für Wirtschaftsforschung, "Gesamtwirtschaftliche und unternehmerische Anpassungsfortschritte in Ostdeutschland," 3. Bericht, *DIW-Wochenbericht* 39–40 (1991), 553–574.
25. *FAZ,* 8 November 1991, 17–18; *Handelsblatt,* 7 November 1991, and 28 November 1991, 5.
26. Philip Selznick, *TVA and the Grassroots: A Study in the Sociology of Formal Organization* (Berkeley, 1949).
27. *Bulletin des Bundespresse- und Informationsamtes,* 12 March 1991.
28. "Grundsätze zur Zusammenarbeit von Bund, neuen Ländern und Treuhandanstalt über den Aufschwung Ost," *Bulletin des Bundespresse- und Informationsamtes,* 15. März 1991.
29. "Beschluss der Wirtschaftsministerkonferenz vom 20. März 1991," reprinted in *Treuhandanstalt Dokumentation 1990–1994,* vol. 2, 371–374.
30. Reprinted in *Treuhandanstalt Dokumentation 1990–1994,* vol. 2, 369–370.
31. Reprinted in *Treuhandanstalt Dokumentation 1990–1994,* vol. 9, 712–716. *Sozialplan* is the common term for an agreement between employers and unions about social benefits to mitigate layoffs.
32. "Rahmenvereinbarung zur Bildung von Gesellschaften zur Arbeitsförderung, Beschäftigung und Strukturentwicklung (ABS)," reprinted in *Treuhandanstalt, Dokumentation 1990–1994,* vol. 9, 546–552.
33. "Arbeit der Treuhand wird überprüft," *Die Welt,* September 1993; "Treuhand unter der Lupe," *Berliner Zeitung,* 30 September 1993.
34. Bundesministerium des Innern, *Sonderedition aus den Akten des Bundeskanzleramtes*; Foreign and Commonwealth Office, *Documents on British Policy Overseas,* series III, vol. VII: *German Unification, 1989–1990* (London, 2010).
35. Mahoney and Thelen, "A Theory of Gradual Institutional Change," in *Explaining Institutional Change,* 1–37.

Chapter Five

East Germany 1989–2010

A Fragmented Development

Rainer Land

According to Wolfgang Seibel, the East Germans were not victims of a colonization or an *Anschluss,* but rather they have gotten what they themselves chose between the autumn of 1989 and early 1990: removal of the SED dictatorship, introduction of the D-Mark, economic and currency union, conversion of wages and salaries as well as a substantial part of the savings deposits at an exchange rate of 1:1, the social security system of the Federal Republic, and national unification with West Germany. The course was set in principle through the decision to enact a rapid currency and economic union, the 1:1 exchange rate, the accession according to Article 23 of the West German constitution, and the further choices stemming from it. From an economic standpoint this path to unification was irrational because the ensuing unification crisis, the deindustrialization, and the subsequent slow development between catching up, stagnation, and setbacks were, in principle, unavoidable consequences of these initial decisions. However, they were desired politically, to wit, primarily by the majority of the GDR population. On this, I essentially agree with Wolfgang Seibel. Since the pressure of mass migration made it necessary to find a convincing solution, the rapid economic and political unification seemed to be the logical answer. There would have been other alternatives, but these lacked the required support.[1]

When in February 1990 I pointed out to a meeting of the East Berlin SPD the consequences of an almost seamless integration of GDR companies into the West German and European market economies and thereby the world market, and predicted an unemployment rate of more than 15

Notes for this chapter begin on page 117.

percent (an unbelievable notion for the GDR), I was received with boos and hisses. Naturally there were people at the time who said that a confederative development with gradual economic integration over roughly ten years would be economically sensible. For this period, there still would have been separate currencies, but they would be coupled in a common confederative bank, which would have enabled citizens and businesses to exchange currencies under certain conditions. I had spoken about this in December 1989 with the then–chief economist of Deutsche Bank, Norbert Walter. He had said in turn: "You must pull the cart out of the mud yourself; we can only help. But it would be quite wrong if the West German economy would primarily focus on the GDR in the coming years. For us, it's about Western Europe and above all about the competition with Japan [this was before the collapse of the Japanese financial system], Asia, and the United States. An orientation toward the GDR and Eastern Europe would set back structural changes and necessary reforms."[2]

At a larger meeting of managers and economic experts at the Arthur D. Little management consulting firm in February 1990 in Wiesbaden, there was a peculiar constellation. Western bankers and Eastern academics were *against* rapid currency union, while Eastern managers and Western politicians were *for* it. The managers from the East, including heavyweight directors of large companies who, "at home in the GDR," would previously not have lent an ear to a rebellious little assistant professor like myself, were vehemently in favor of adopting the D-Mark, preferably immediately. The person who screamed the loudest had his job only a few more months before his Kombinat Steine und Erden, a large corporation that produced construction materials, was dissolved.

Thus there were people in the FRG and in the GDR who wanted another path and were trying to conceptualize it. But Wolfgang Seibel is correct; the decision was, essentially, made by the political will of the GDR population in the demonstrations of December 1989, by the immense emigration, which had persisted since early 1989, and by the elections for the Volkskammer in the spring of 1990. The decision was not simply imposed upon the population. Admittedly, Wolfgang Seibel also alludes to the interest of and pressure from the Western allies, who wanted to avoid instability in the core of Central Europe, and Helmut Kohl more or less gave the "order" to stabilize the GDR through the merger with the FRG, "cost what it may." That is likely to have been the case.

The Failed Alternative

Yet I cannot stop myself from adding something else: it was also the firm self-interest of a part of the West German political class that contributed to the acceleration of the unification process. This is because Kohl's power was at a low point in the summer of 1989 and the prognoses said that the CDU would lose the upcoming Bundestag elections during the following year. When Helmut Kohl encountered the jubilant GDR population in Dresden, the idea came to him and his advisers that this movement could be used to change the trend of the voter support once again so that he could continue to serve as the great "Chancellor of German Unity" with the help of the East German voters. Naturally, Kohl and his people were familiar with the arguments that this was economically unsound, but these scruples were subordinated to concern for political power, which quite obviously was also fully in line with the will of the Allies and of the GDR population. The resistance, which existed in the West German political elite as well, was shoved aside by this historically unique alliance among the government of the West, the people of the East, and the Allies.

It should be noted that at that time the West German economy was not yet on the path toward uniting with the East; it began very hesitantly and neither precipitated the unification process nor expedited it, initially. It is wrong to explain the deindustrialization of East Germany primarily as a result of the *subjective* self-interest of West German companies in acquiring East German businesses, markets, and real estate, or rather in removing Eastern competition. All of this also played a role in the subsequent course of events—although competition for resources is a natural part of a market economy. If several thousand businesses go up for sale in the short term—with excellent properties, high hopes, and false expectations—then a fierce battle begins, a battle that might not always go smoothly. In this respect, I do not, in principle, want to reject the widespread allegations that there were many bad decisions, corruption, and stupidity during the Treuhandanstalt privatization. I only assert that this is not an explanation for the deindustrialization of the 1990s and the problems in subsequent years. The Trusteeship Agency had to process the consequences of a decision that it had not brought about, with which it did not have much leeway, and, above all, to which it had no basic alternatives. So far I agree with Wolfgang Seibel.

More redevelopment, less liquidation, less corruption, and more autonomy of the businesses in the search for their own path would perhaps have been desirable. Though it might have been more expensive, on balance it might have turned out to be more favorable, but whether it would have been better—and how much better—no one can say for certain. Theoretically, there would have been the possibility of gradually integrating both economic systems and in the meantime living in a confederation with separate yet flexibly linked currencies. Poland, the Czech Republic, Croatia, and other former Eastern Bloc states that in no way could have had the option of accession to a West European state show that a gradual transformation could have been successful and have had advantages as well. For instance, economic development in Poland since 1990 has been more dynamic than that in East Germany.

I briefly want to suggest a second thought. Clearly it was the political will of the GDR population, expressed in the emigration, the demonstrations of December 1989, and the general election of early 1990 that brought about the decision to implement the quickest possible unification. And it was also the people's movement that repeatedly accelerated this process; further, the newly elected Volkskammer of the GDR allowed no deviations from this path. Still, in October 1989, the main strand of the debate had turned toward a reformed socialism, toward a Third Way.[3] Where did the subsequent change of opinion come from? Were these actually only the illusions of an economic miracle, self-deception fueled by the fully stocked supermarkets and department stores in the West?

In our book *Fremde Welten,* Ralf Possekel and I have developed an alternative thesis about the relationship between the citizens' movement and the younger SED reformers in the 1980s.[4] Our opinion is that the majority of the GDR population in December 1989 and January 1990 oriented itself toward leadership by the political elite of West Germany and decided definitively against its own elites—not only the old SED power elites, but the citizens' movements and the SED reformers of the Perestroika faction as well. This orientation was more likely a rational calculation and less an expression of feelings of national unity. The reason for this choice by the people standing on the streets and demonstrating was that in November 1989 the power vacuum created by the fall of SED rule was not promptly filled by any legitimate political leadership within the GDR. In their own country there was no political organization or coalition that wanted to assume power and could legitimately and credibly have exercised it. Thus the majority of GDR citizens decided in favor of leadership by the political elite of the FRG and abandoned its own.

The power of the SED effectively imploded in two months (mid October through mid December). It would only have been able to survive if it had very quickly established a new political leadership and filled the vacuum. Yet where would this have come from? The citizens' movement defined itself by its distance from power and was not prepared to assume it; perhaps it was not capable of it conceptually either. The younger SED reformers wanted power, but lacked legitimacy given their closeness to the SED. Only through a radical and unambiguous break, through a clear separation from "their party" could they again gain political leeway. Yet the avant-gardism in communist tradition, the *conspiratorially oriented avant-gardism* of this intellectual and political generation of the 1980s, was an obstacle for them. The citizens' movement and SED reformers would need to have jumped over a long shadow in order to seize power in the fall of 1989—on the one hand over the shadow of its symbolically charged distance from power, and on the other over its avant-gardism, which prevented it from separating from a party that maneuvered itself onto the ash heap of history. Yet neither faction was capable by itself of assuming leadership.[5]

The entire development would have been different if in December 1989 a politically pragmatic alliance of relevant actors among the SED reformers and the citizens' movement had come together, if they then had toppled the Modrow government, proclaimed a provisional government (instead of allowing the old SED government to remain in power and to control it merely through a Round Table and ministers without portfolio) and above all organized immediate elections for a constitutional assembly. Societal reform through constitutional debate[6] appeared to be the order of the day. A discussion about the constitution—not calm and contemplative, but rather struggling for clarity amidst the rush of events instead of chasing illusions—might have brought self-discovery and legitimacy. At the time and for this reason in a few weeks there emerged the draft constitution of the Round Table, a truly great success in the history of liberal German constitutions. It stood in the tradition of the Weimar constitution, which emerged from the events of the November revolution of 1918, and the Basic Law, which drew lessons from the disaster of National Socialism. In addition to this, the Round Table's draft constitution learned from the faulty development of the GDR under state socialism and the experiences of the autumn of 1989.

It would have been possible in early 1990 to decide on this constitution, to constitute a new GDR, and to set out on a path toward unification via confederative structures. A newly constituted statehood would also have provided legitimacy for negotiating on equal footing—even if not on the same level of power—about the conditions of German unity according to Article 146 and about the manner of economic unification. The GDR population would probably have wanted this solution, if it had quickly put an end to the implosion of power and a viable perspective had become visible. Naturally, acute problems, like access to the D-Mark, would also have to be sorted out quickly. For all of these questions there were talks, concepts, and even initial negotiations; I was sometimes there when it happened. It failed because of the *new* GDR elites, not the old ones, who were already powerless. The citizens' movements didn't want to dirty themselves with power, and to the younger SED reformers around leaders Gysi and Bisky, the salvation of the party, the preservation of the SED, and its transformation into a "normal" party fit for parliament were more important than the country and its population. Thus, from the standpoint of the GDR population, the legitimacy of power passed over to the political class of West Germany, from whom they now expected solutions and leadership. Their own people had played their hand, but they had played themselves out. In short: it is wrong to attribute the consequences of unification to the Trusteeship Agency.

Economic Consequences

And how has this history proceeded up to now? The development is well known and needs only to be outlined here: after unification came the economic shock and the so-called deindustrialization. Industrial production declined more than 60 percent in two years, and the overall economic performance around 30 percent during the same time. The number of people in the workforce decreased by 1993 from 8.9 to 5.8 million, a downturn of 35 percent; moreover, it should be added that almost 15 percent of those accounting for the difference were unemployed. Almost half of the jobs were lost, at least in the short term.[7]

After overcoming the shock of transformation came stabilization. In 1994, for instance, the production level of 1989 was regained, and indeed at a clearly higher productivity level. Yet because of this, the number of people in the workforce was approximately a third lower than in 1989, while unemployment remained high and even increased further. In 1997 East Germany reached approximately 76 percent of the West German gross domestic product per inhabitant. Since the mid 1990s, however, the catch-up development after the economic slump of 1990/91—which took place from 1992 through 1996 with high annual GDP growth rates of around 8 percent—has come to a halt. In important macroeconomic indicators, the level of East Germany has remained around 30 percent lower than that of West Germany since that time period. The growth of the East German economy was no higher than that of the West German economy and was even below it in most years since 1997; East Germany could not make up the difference in the respective levels with the old states. Accordingly, East German unemployment up to now has been almost twice as high as in West Germany and in 2005 reached a high point at more than 20 percent. In 2009, in the twentieth year of unity, GDP per capita, at 70.5 percent of the West German value, was still almost a third below the level in the old Federal Republic.[8]

The immense emigration (up to 35 percent in some areas), the substantial regional disparities, the wage disparity, and the still-high support payments constitute transfer traps, well known in development economics.

These factors are—quite plausibly—considered to be the reasons for a lag that will continue into the future. The Halle Institute for Economic Research predicts a second deindustrialization because of the shortage of skilled workers, which is attributed to their selective emigration. Several regions have lost more than 30 percent of their population, including as much as 80 percent of the younger generation, especially young women and men with good grades, a high level of motivation, flexibility, and mobility. High unemployment among thirty-five- to sixty-year-olds and the simultaneous shortage of skilled workers form an extremely volatile political constellation, which promotes not only radicalism, xenophobia, and far-right ideologies, but also political populism.

East Germany would seem to have become the German Mezzogiorno—if this were the whole story. Yet there is another side that is often overlooked by those who only perceive the downside, and likewise by those who would rather make the situation seem better than it is. This development can best be described as *fragmentation*—and it had already begun in 1990.

The GDR had a Fordist industry oriented toward the goal of mass production with a strong component in engineering and plant manufacturing, and thus toward the production of the capital equipment for mass production, which was at least partially geared toward export to the COMECON countries or to the global market. The GDR economy could compensate for the lag in the economic productivity of this branch thanks to an exchange rate of around 1:4 for the D-Mark and a wage level below that of the FRG. However, as early as in the 1980s this state socialist system of export-oriented production of capital equipment for mass production no longer functioned well, above all because of the altered terms of trade and the disproportionately rising costs of energy and raw materials, as well as because of the inability of the planned economy to react with innovations and systematic increases in productivity.[9]

The currency and economic union of 1990 now completely removed the context for this variant of a Fordist production model. There were no longer importers from the COMECON, because they would now have to pay in hard currencies. Export to Western countries, as a rule, could no longer be profitable because of the inappropriate exchange rate. The foreign markets effectively collapsed within just a few weeks.[10]

One can say the same for the domestic markets even if it was not quite as extreme. Manufacturers of qualitatively better consumer goods from the West quickly captured a substantial part of the East German domestic market as the people no longer wanted the old GDR goods to begin with. As we now know about West German products, especially foods, sometimes they were only better packaged and jazzed up with flavor enhancers, but they were often in fact also dramatically better and more innovative. Consequently, West German production also broke into the domestic market.

At the same time, however, there began a *selective* process of restructuring in which the activities of the businesses themselves, but also the strategy of the respective Trusteeship Agency division, the wishes of the potential investors from the West or from abroad (and only rarely from East Germany), the demands of the unions and work councils, and naturally also the decisions of the communal actors all played a role. They attempted, from the perspective of their respective interests in each individual case, to find a path of survival for the companies concerned. With several it was soon clear how it could work; with others it was rather quickly clear that it would not work at all. And many more others, by experiments, bankruptcies, mishaps, and new beginnings, found themselves a more or less viable place and a new development path in a new environment.

I want to state clearly that there is some probability that rational decisions emerged in this process, but certainly not always. In many cases it was the correct decision to close this business and to preserve others, and in many cases the chosen path was viable in the medium term. Yet it has often been observed that businesses were closed even though they might have been saved in a different combination of circumstances. This probably also includes the fact that many competitors were bought and then closed, out of a desire to remove competition from the market, even though it would have been possible to restructure the company to make it competitive. And in several cases businesses were preserved that actually should have been closed.

This *selective* reorganization took place in the context of the *preexisting* economic structures of the Federal Republic, and the criterion for the ability of a company to restructure was not its condition in itself, nor its function or its competitiveness in the no-longer-existing economic structures of the deceased GDR, but rather the fit and potential competitiveness in the new context. Reorganization meant adaption to these new structures—and indeed, under extensive reduction of direct export market influences, since the GDR businesses had of course just dropped out of them.

The "value" of a company, especially its earning power, is not a substantive quality of its properties, machines, assets, and buildings; it depends on the network of economic connections that the company cultivates. Therefore it was entirely logical that businesses that in the context of the GDR economy and the COMECON market operated quite profitably and had a corresponding net worth all of a sudden had no or a much lower value in the new economic context of Germany and the EU. The "devaluation" of the nationally owned tangible assets connected with the economic union and the selectivity of the industrial reorganization are the results of the objective constellations of a societal process and not the consequence of arbitrary decisions by the Trusteeship Agency or investors.

This reorganization in the context of the West German economy meant, for example, that businesses that produced products *similar* to those of West German companies (concerning exportable goods or services) were dealt a comparatively worse hand, particularly in markets with excess capacities, which in 1990 was often the case. In many but not all cases the assumed lag in productivity and the generally excessive size of personnel made the odds still worse for such businesses. In the course of the market adjustment, such East German companies often closed and their West German competitors took over the market, improved their capacity utilization, and expanded production where appropriate. In general, no one would have been able to imagine the reverse scenario.

Only a disproportionately low portion of East German businesses with parallel product ranges and production capabilities were utilized to increase capacities. Because global markets for Fordist mass production and its capital equipment were barely expanding while global competition for these markets increased, this was a more or less automatic consequence of the starting conditions, which logically had to result in the disappearance of substantial parts of East German industry, as the reorganization was simply not adopted gradually or followed by the simultaneous building of new and different industrial capabilities.[11]

What was necessarily preserved with this selective reorganization were businesses for local and regional markets: handicrafts, the construction industry, small-scale production, and services. The numbers account for the fact that their productivity in the mid 1990s lagged roughly 30 percent behind their West German equivalents. Nevertheless, they didn't go under, because they predominantly produced locally marketable products that foreign competition could not really affect. The lag in productivity had mostly simple causes: lower product prices (in Putlitz I can still go to the barber for five Euro and the hourly rate of the heating repairman may be roughly half what it is in Bavaria) and less capacity utilization rather than worse work or inferior products. Since the population declined continually and income, after the first strong increase, has barely grown since 1994, and even declined partially, this regional economy oriented toward local markets as a rule could not improve its capacity utilization, to say nothing at all of growth. It has plodded along for the last fifteen years, aside from a few prosperous regions, Jena, Dresden, Leipzig, Potsdam, and parts of Berlin. Stagnation dominates the picture of these industries.

This dimension of fragmentation appears to fit entirely into the outlined macroeconomic Mezzogiorno scenario: the more transregionally oriented parts of GDR industry, which boasted parallel capacities to West German industry, shrank and disappeared, and their functions were taken over by West German companies. Or they became extended workbenches. Those companies acting locally plodded along at a stagnating level. The construction industry at first had a tremendous boom and then shrank again slowly over many long years.[12]

Positive Signs

Yet this image is incorrect. Already by the end of the 1990s one could, if one wasn't ideologically inflexible, observe genuine success stories, including, above all, export-oriented industrial companies. Today this includes, for example, a network for optical professionals in Thuringia, tool and textile engineering in Chemnitz, the specialized vehicle manufacturer Multicar, the Plauen lace network, a manufacturer of special operating tables in Saxony, a manufacturer of ship propellers in Waren, as well as some electronics businesses in Dresden, to name several of the by-now many businesses that often arose via spin-offs from former GDR businesses in the course of the Trusteeship Agency privatization.

There are also newly founded businesses like "Biocon Valley," which arose from research institutions in Mecklenburg-Pomerania, a biomedical technical school with several firms in Teterow, or the Q-Cells plant established in the open countryside at the chemical site in Bitterfeld-Wolfen, which developed and manufactures solar cells. Incidentally, this also includes several manufacturers of wind turbines and many small solar energy firms that do not produce solar cells but rather design, mount, and maintain modules or equipment. Selective restructuring in this regard means that businesses that had *complementary* and compatible (and thus not simply the same and therefore superfluous) structures or products that could be developed from the available or new resources, were dealt a fairly good hand because they fit the needs of the world market or the West German economy well, filled holes, took over unoccupied niches, or even created new ones. Curiously, this also applies to the large agricultural businesses of the GDR, which were a perfect match for the mass producers in the Western European and global food industry and which therefore as a rule do very well.

Such *complementary* development naturally only worked if an array of favorable conditions, by all means also including accidental ones, allowed this potential to be released or even first developed if the right people convened and the critical mass was there. The Trusteeship Agency, however, could hardly have had such an innovative view; it could not utilize and support a possibly emerging new complementary industrial structure as a measure of redevelopment, privatization, liquidation, or selection, because they of course weren't psychics. The conception was reconstruction of the East as the replica of the West (and this was the crux of the matter), not rebuilding of the new all-German industry.[13] Therefore several companies disappeared, firms that perhaps would have stood a chance in view of complementary new development paths, and many remain that would have better been closed because they will soon be superfluous—for example, brown coal mining, coal power stations, and the large energy providers and network operators, which from the present view would have been better left outside because they constrain structural changes with a policy of oligopolistic self-interest. A conception of experimental reorganization would have perhaps been more expensive in the short-term, but perhaps would have been more promising in the long run.[14] This is an argument that applies not only to East Germany but also to other old industrial regions that must seek out new paths within structural changes.

In any event: the result of selective reorganization was not only a reduction of industrial potential and not only a more or less languishing and slowly shrinking regional economy, but also a small but excellent and, more importantly, growing and potent new industry oriented toward the world market, which it is often claimed to be more capable than the comparable segment of West German industry. Yet fragmentation also means that these businesses are usually integrated strongly into transregional networks—through their West German parent companies, through worldwide connections, through global clusters of suppliers, through research and development cooperation, and through tapping new markets. They are part of globally organized R&D and production clusters and are scarcely linked to the local economy where they are based. This is a phenomenon that differentiates the East German fragmentation from the traditional structure of Fordist production clusters. My report of a visit to a biomedical technical school records the following: "Question—How deeply connected is the business with local companies, component suppliers, etc.? Answer: If equipment is broken, the technician comes from the US. If the bathroom light won't turn on, the electrician comes from Teterow."[15]

Consequences of Fragmentation

The term "fragmentation" does not only mean "parallel development," but also emphasizes the fact of divergent development directions and innovation speeds. We also have fragmentation between different regions, some of which are prospering, while others are declining.

This divergent development is obvious because the public budgets in the East have to be supported through financial transfers from the West, whereas in private business East Germany has become a net capital exporter—meaning more money flows from East to West than vice versa—since 2001. In 1995 the production gap between production and expenditure (including consumption plus investments) in East Germany was roughly one-third of East German GDP. The difference had to be made up through goods and commodities delivered from West Germany or from abroad and financed through monetary transfers from the West to the East. For a long time, it appeared as if this production gap would remain constant; that is, the performance gap (GDP per inhabitant and per employed person, respectively) did not decrease. Since then, however, the production gap is no longer 30 percent, but instead only 10 percent of East German GDP. This decrease is very likely explained mainly through the widening and deepening of these successful complementary developments. In a few years East Germany has thus attained on average the level of West German industry and will also soon attain that of the West German economy—but fragmentation will remain. This is also the reason why East Germany will continue to be an economy dependent on transfers, which it can't sustain on its own—in doubly paradoxical ways. Fragmentation and transfers are therefore interdependent.

Currently, public transfers are still around 80 billion Euros annually, a total that is decreasing only very slowly, although the production gap has declined to around 30 billion Euros annually. Where is the difference of 50 billion? It must be in a net cash flow from East to West, which we calculate by account balances, but cannot be located statistically in this way without further details. I repeat: East Germany must, according to account balances, be a net capital exporter to West Germany! A truly curious notion—but it is true.[16]

Obviously, it is therefore a matter of return flows and profits from investments of private investors, which go back into the West. In net terms, since 2000 the return flows from old investments have been larger than the inflows of new investments; before 2000, private investment inflows were larger in the East than the return flows. In doing so, it may be a matter of return flows and profits from property and land, of rentals and leases, of investment revenues from businesses and, last but not least, of the tremendous investments in wind turbines and increasingly in solar power systems, many of which in East Germany are above average and can make good money at present.

As correct as it is that investors, after a certain time period, receive their money back and, if it has gone well, with profit, such a transfer constellation, with more investment resources flowing out of a region still in need of development than flowing into it, is precarious. The reason is precisely this fragmentation. Large parts of the economy plod along, producing only meager revenue. The regions with small revenue, high unemployment, and a high proportion of pension and transfer payment recipients must be financed through external means—especially from the pockets of Western and also Eastern taxpayers. Public transfers are needed here. On the other hand, a different part of the economy generates high income, repays credit and interest, and pays out profits, which, however, on balance do not flow once more into investments for overcoming fragmentation, nor are they brought in to finance the required transfers, but rather they flow out of the region. In the best case, they arrive again in the East via the circuitous path of tax payments in the West, whereby the larger portion of the taxes received in West Germany probably comes from the middle class and not the income of well-financed investors.

In short: East Germany is neither a uniformly thriving country, nor is it a wasteland or a new Mezzogiorno; rather it is a fragmented society with a fragmented economy, a double transfer society, publicly dependent on the West, yet in the meantime privately a good investment for the wealthy. And all of this makes for the great social, demographic, and political problems, social segregation, and the apparent lack of perspective for many resulting from it. The fifteen or twenty year old age cohorts who graduated school from roughly 1990 to 2007 are especially unfortunate, as only one-third could find a job and an acceptable income at home, while one-third permanently migrated and one-third landed in precarious and permanent dependence on transfer payments. These times are over; the low birthrate age groups and the growing demand for workers are creating an urgent demand for skilled employees so that today all East German youths, if they are not irreversibly discouraged because of living circumstances in their parents' house, at school, or in the villages and cities, have a great chance for training and higher employment prospects. It will only be a few years until word of this spreads, wages increase once more, the treatment of the workforce by companies and schoolteachers improves again, and the negative atmosphere that blocked a whole young generation and drove them from the country vanishes. Almost as bad as the fate of their older siblings, who for fifteen years have rotated between hopeless temporary employment situations, is that today's young generation between sixteen and twenty-six still believes that they have no future in East Germany, that there will never be a future there, and that they need to leave—although soon, perhaps even now and in the foreseeable future, this will no longer be the case.

Notes

1. Rainer Land and Ralf Possekel, *Fremde Welten. Die gegensätzliche Deutung der DDR durch SED-Reformer und Bürgerbewegung in den 80er Jahren* (Berlin, 1998), 204ff.
2. Rainer Land, notes of a conversation with Norbert Walter, Berlin, December 1989.
3. Rainer Land, "Die sozialökonomische Seite der Konzeption der entwickelten sozialistischen Gesellschaft und ihre Weiterentwicklung," in *Philosophische Grundlagen der Erarbeitung einer Konzeption des modernen Fremde Welten. Sozialismus. Materialen der Eröffnungsberatung November 1988,* ed. Andrè Brie, Michael Brie, Rainer Land, and Dieter Segert (Berlin, 1989), 57–74.
4. Rainer Land et al., *Fremde Welten. Die gegensätzliche Deutung der DDR durch SED-Reformer und Bürgerbewegung in den 80er Jahren.*
5. Rainer Land, "Staatssozialismus und Stalinismus" in *Die PDS—Herkunft und Selbstverständnis,* eds., Lothar Bisky, Jochen Czerny, Herbert Mayer, and Michael Schumann (Berlin, 1996).
6. Rosemarie Will, Ulrich Busch, Rainer Land, and Gerhard Quilitzsch, "Gesellschaftsgestaltung durch Verfassungsdiskussion," in Humboldt-Universität zu Berlin, *Beiträge zur Sozialismusdiskussion in Theorie/Aktuelle Politik/Strategiediskussion,* November 1989 through January 1990. Also found in condensed form in *Neues Deutschland,* 20–21 January 1990 and in *Der SED-Reformdiskurs der achtziger Jahre. Dokumentation. Bestand Forschungsprojekt Moderner Sozialismus* (Berlin), vol. 5.
7. Ulrich Busch and Rainer Land, "Ostdeutschland: Vom staatssozialistischen Fordismus in die Entwicklungsfalle einer Transferökonomie," in *Berichterstattung zur sozioökonomischen Entwicklung in Deutschland. Teilhabe im Umbruch. Zweiter Bericht,* ed., Forschungsverbund Sozioökonomische Berichterstattung (Wiesbaden, 2012).
8. Rainer Land, "Zur Lage in Ostdeutschland. Bericht des Netzwerkes und Innovationsverbundes Ostdeutschlandforschung," *Berliner Debatte INITIAL,* 5 (2005).
9. Rainer Land, "Fordismus und Planwirtschaft," in *Russland wieder im Dunkeln,* ed. Michael Brie and Ewald Böhlke (Berlin, 1992); Rainer Land, "Staatssozialistische Planwirtschaft und wirtschaftliche Entwicklung—Warum Planwirtschaft nicht innovativ sein kann," www.rainer-land-online.de (2010).
10. Ulrich Busch and Rainer Land, "Der Fordistische Teilhabekapitalismus als Regime sozioökonomischer Entwicklung und der Umbruch. Deutschland 1950 bis 2009," in *Berichterstattung.*
11. Rainer Land, "Es gibt keine einfache Lösung. Die Umgestaltung der ostdeutschen Industrie im Kontext der globalen Krise moderner Wirtschafts- und Lebensweise," in Werner Schulz and Ludger Volmer, eds., *Entwickeln statt abwickeln. Wirtschaftspolitische und ökologische Konzepte für die fünf neuen Länder* (Berlin, 1992). Katharina Bluhm, Horst Kern, Rainer Land, Ulrich Voskamp, and Volker Wittke, *Die Bedeutung des DDR-Produktionsmodells für Pfade der industriellen Reorganisation: Vergleichende Fallstudien in zwei Kabelwerken. Projektbericht des von der VW-Stiftung geförderten Forschungsprojekts* (Göttingen, 1991).

12. Rainer Land and Andreas Willisch, "Ostdeutschland—ein Umbruchsszenario. Warum der 'Aufbau Ost' als 'Nachbau West' nicht gelingen konnte," in *Am Ziel vorbei. Die deutsche Einheit—Eine Zwischenbilanz,* eds. Hannes Bahrmann and Christoph Links (Berlin, 2005).
13. Rainer Land, "Der Herbst 1989 und die Modernisierung der Moderne," *Berliner Debatte INITIAL* 2 (2000).
14. This would have been asking too much intellectually of most politicians and business managers and also would not have been popularly accepted. "No experiments" was the frequently used watchword in this period, which itself was in fact a single grand experiment, unfortunately without alternatives.
15. Rainer Land, notes of a visit to a technical school.
16. Ulrich Busch and Rainer Land, "Ostdeutschland: Vom staatssozialistischen Fordismus in die Entwicklungsfalle einer Transferökonomie," in *Berichterstattung,* 175f.

Chapter Six

Getting Even

East German Economic Underperformance after Unification

Jonathan R. Zatlin

In 1970, communist party leader Walter Ulbricht promised that East Germany would overtake West Germany without catching up to it (*überholen ohne einzuholen*). More than twenty years after it gave up on communism and adopted capitalism, however, East Germany has yet to catch up with, much less overtake, West Germany. Although many believed that rapid unification with West Germany would lead to "flourishing landscapes," in the infamous words of West German Chancellor Helmut Kohl, economic growth in the regions comprising the former GDR has been mired in stagnation since 1996.[1] In fact, the region continues to struggle with high levels of unemployment, widespread dependency on West German handouts, and little prospect of self-financing growth. As a result, the post-1945 economic gap between East and West remains, mitigated only by welfare benefits. It is no wonder that the stubborn underperformance of the East German economy has been the source of the greatest frustration to Germans on both sides of the formerly divided country.

Even the most pessimistic critics of what Konrad Jarausch aptly termed "the rush to unity" did not anticipate the difficulties that attended East Germany's transition to a market economy, much less the region's persistent imperviousness to countercyclical policy measures.[2] Indeed, despite the massive transfer of wealth from West Germany and investment programs underwritten by the European Union, aggregate growth in Eastern Germany has remained anemic at best. Except for a brief boom from 1993

Notes for this chapter begin on page 128.

to 1996, East German gross domestic product (GDP) has fallen well short of growth rates necessary to overcome the gap between the two regions. Instead, per capita GDP has stagnated at roughly 80–85 percent of the West German levels.[3]

The main reason for the failure of economic convergence between the two German regions is the size and shape of the East German industrial base, which remains significantly smaller than its West German counterpart. In 2008, for example, 6.4 percent of Easterners were employed in the manufacturing sector, compared to 10 percent of Westerners. Despite the region's modern infrastructure, moreover, East German businesses enjoy no significant competitive advantages over their neighbors and are generally less efficient than West German firms. Contrary to Rainer Land's portrait, moreover, the success of East German firms in research-oriented sectors remains exceptional. As a result, labor productivity in the new German states has recovered from its low in 1989/90, but the gap in productivity persists: in 2008 labor productivity in Eastern Germany was still only 77 percent of Western levels.[4]

The most serious consequence of low productivity and a lack of innovation has been stubbornly high unemployment. Despite the ability of West German industry to export the country out of the Great Recession (and the concomitant demand-pull from West German firms), some 11 percent of East German workers remained unemployed as of July 2011, nearly double the West German rate of 5.9 percent.[5] Another 15.9 percent of the East German workforce was "partially employed" (those defined by the International Labor Organization as underemployed minus part-time workers) as of April 2011, nearly double the 8.7 percent in West Germany.[6] If we add to these figures hidden unemployment resulting from forced early retirements, involuntary part-time work, make-work and training programs, East German unemployment remains at levels not seen since the Great Depression.[7] Nor do the aggregate figures conceal regional success stories. Even Saxony, despite its reputation as a comparatively dynamic region, has seen lackluster job creation. In December 2010, for example, 11.1 percent of the Saxon workforce, slightly more than the regional average, was officially unemployed.[8]

In addition to the social dislocation and psychological burden that attend joblessness in a society that prizes industriousness, unemployment at such high rates represents a fiscal strain on united Germany's large public debt. In a European context that is increasingly allergic to high levels of sovereign debt, propping up East German living standards via government spending has been a source of constant tension, whether articulated in bestselling books like Gabor Steingart's *Germany, the Decline of a Superstar* or the debate over the Hartz IV welfare reform.[9] In addition to fueling a more general debate over the relative efficacy of Keynesian and neoliberal approaches to economic growth, moreover, the failure of convergence continues to influence electoral politics, greatly benefiting the SED's successors, the Party of Democratic Socialism (now reorganized as the Linkspartei). The disparity in job creation has also lent longstanding xenophobic resentments in Eastern Germany a certain acceptability, leading to racially motivated violence and the increased popularity of far-right groups such as the National Democratic Party.[10]

The Foundations of Economic Divergence

The roots of East German economic underperformance lie in Marxist-Leninist economic theory and practice. As it did throughout the Soviet Bloc, economic planning in East Germany encouraged all sorts of inefficiency and waste while discouraging technological and organizational innovation. In the GDR, moreover, the losses in productivity resulting from the SED's attempt to suppress market forces and allocate resources according to political directives were compounded by the poor quality of East German leadership. In particular, communist party leader Erich Honecker's feckless strategy of assuaging popular discontent by improving living standards nearly bankrupted the country. Because East German industry was unable to manufacture the necessary consumer goods, Honecker financed higher levels of consumption by borrowing from the capitalist West, thereby encouraging East Germans to live beyond their means and mortgaging the GDR's future to its political enemies.[11]

Honecker's attempt to postpone the day of fiscal reckoning, however, was doomed by a series of exogenous shocks during the 1970s. The jumps in commodities prices from coffee and sugar to oil and gas shook the entire industrialized world, including the GDR. In the West, higher prices for natural resources led to inflation without growth, or "stagflation," which was finally resolved by implementing a punishingly tight monetary policy. In the East, Soviet subsidies for oil and key metals dampened the inflationary effects of higher prices somewhat. But the GDR was nevertheless forced to trade more of its wealth for the same amount of natural resources. Fearful that passing on price increases to East German consumers would trigger a popular insurrection as it had in Poland in 1980, Honecker reacted by reducing investment in East German production instead of cutting back consumption.[12] Years of neglect, however, had made replenishing East Germany's capital stock imperative. According to the SED's own calculations, 53.8 percent of all capital equipment in the GDR was obsolete or worn-out by 1988.[13] The stock of moribund and defective machines and equipment weighed on East German productivity, which had fallen by 1989 to about 30 percent of West German rates.[14] As a result, East German industry was increasingly incapable of delivering basic goods and services, much less exporting enough to pay down the country's debts.[15]

Institutionalizing the Economic Gap

By the late 1980s, neither Western loans nor communist propaganda could conceal the tangible deterioration in East German living standards. But the combination of the Berlin Wall, which restricted the circulation of people and information, and the East German mark, which functioned more like scrip than money, prevented a proper assessment of the country's economic decline. Within eight months, popular anger had demolished both East German institutions, and with them the GDR's economic and political sovereignty. East Germans often recall the courage and West Germans the daring that made unification possible. Yet both sides are inclined to forget that the fall of the Wall and rapid monetary union also integrated the two economies on terms unfavorable to East Germany.

The decision to opt for a rapid rather than a gradual monetary union had more to do with labor markets than monetary regimes. When East German demonstrators tore down the Wall on 9 November 1989, they swept aside the basis of communist rule, and with it the main barrier to East German labor mobility. Suddenly free to move about, East Germans responded to the push of a precarious economic future in the GDR and the pull of prosperity in the Federal Republic by migrating westward in droves. During the final months of 1989, some 343,854, or 2.5 percent of the GDR's workforce, fled the country, leaving some key sectors, such as medicine and transportation, dangerously understaffed. By January 1990, East German outmigration exceeded 2,000 people a day. The sheer size of the exodus constituted as much an economic as a political crisis for both German states. The continuing depletion of its workforce threatened to bring the GDR to an economic standstill, further disrupting the already halting delivery of goods and services. Nor was the Federal Republic prepared for the task of integrating the influx of refugees. The threat of an East German collapse, which would only stimulate more outmigration, demanded resolution.[16]

By the end of January, however, no one seemed to have a viable plan that might stop the labor exodus. As Wolfgang Seibel reminds us, neither the new group of communist leaders led by Hans Modrow nor the various opposition groups were able to devise a coherent response to the GDR's changed economic circumstances. In contrast, ordinary East Germans understood very well the meaning of their newly won labor mobility and the political leverage it represented. At demonstrations throughout the country, they laid out the next logical step in the economic integration of the two German states: rapid monetary union. Chanting "If the D-Mark doesn't come to us, we'll go to it," millions of demonstrators linked labor markets to monetary regimes, in effect arguing that their freedom to travel could only be constrained by monetary policy.

To West German policymakers, economists, and business leaders, however, the connection between monetary and labor market policy seemed tenuous at best.[17] In fact, most economic observers regarded extending the West German monetary umbrella to the GDR as dangerously premature. Their opposition to an immediate currency union with the GDR was shaped in part by European efforts to bring about a monetary union. For some thirty years, successive West German governments had argued that monetary coordination across divergent economic regions could only work if preceded by sufficient economic and political integration. Europe, they pointed out, did not qualify as an optimal currency area. Not only was it economically diverse, but it also possessed none of the adjustment mechanisms that might compensate regions with lower productivity rates for their loss of an independent monetary policy. In what became known as the "coronation theory," West German financial experts and politicians insisted that monetary union should crown rather than inaugurate political and economic integration.[18]

In the East German case, West German economic experts objected that surrendering the East German mark would eliminate the GDR's most effective mechanism for making djustments to the productivity gap between the two regions. Once the GDR adopted the West German mark, which was one of the world's most valuable currencies, East German goods and labor would be priced out of international markets overnight. In addition, they warned that integrating the two monetary regimes would stimulate wage demands, as East German workers, supported by West German trade unions concerned about protecting their bargaining power, sought wage increases in excess of East German productivity. Without a more gradual transition to the ruthless efficiencies of international competition, East Germany faced a brutal process of furious deindustrialization and mass unemployment.[19]

The one exception to this view was the West German chancellor, who understood very well the entanglement of politics with money represented by East German labor mobility. On 6 February 1990, Kohl surprised even his closest advisors by offering East Germans the West German mark.[20] Kohl insisted that integrating the two monetary regimes would give East

Germans "a signal to stay" because it symbolized a West German political commitment to their future.[21] In addition, Kohl and his aides contended that introducing a stable currency like the West German mark would unleash dramatic productivity increases, thus sparing East Germans from the austerity measures lower growth would require. To lend their claim historical legitimacy, conservative politicians invoked the 1948 introduction of the D-Mark, which was intertwined in popular imagination with the West German "economic miracle."[22] It turned out that Kohl was wrong on both counts: monetary policy was no substitute for labor market regulation or real productivity increases.[23] But the economic flaws associated with surrendering the East German mark mattered less than its political promise. Monetary union offered a clear path to a political union, which was what the vast majority of Germans desired. Accordingly, hitching East Germany to West Germany's monetary fortunes completely changed the balance of political power in both German states, generating electoral victories for Kohl's conservative allies in the East German parliamentary elections of 18 March 1990 and in the all-German elections of 2 December 1990.

As politically brilliant as it was, however, Kohl's offer of the D-Mark was not merely an attempt to buy off East Germans with West German money. Thanks to Kohl's political daring, rapid monetary union turned out to be the very foundation of German unification. Extending the West German monetary umbrella to the GDR launched the institutional transformation of East German society. Even before the D-Mark replaced the *Ostmark* in July, the reorganization of the banking system had begun apace, followed by the privatization of East German industry described by Seibel and the preemptive adoption of West German commercial standards by East German firms. Furthermore, monetary union entailed the surrender of the GDR's monetary, fiscal, and by extension political, sovereignty well before the GDR's formal dissolution on 3 October 1990. Having transferred its budgetary power to the West German central bank, the last and democratically elected East German government enjoyed increasingly little decision-making autonomy. Finally, German monetary union enabled Kohl to portray unification as inevitable even to Germany's most skeptical neighbors. With Kohl's help, monetary policy drove politics before it.[24]

Despite Kohl's unquestionably historical achievement, however, placing the monetary cart before the economic horse institutionalized the economic gap between the two regions. As its detractors had warned, introducing the West German mark drastically raised variable costs for East German firms. Now denominated in one of the world's most valuable currencies, East German goods and labor were priced out of international markets. Even though they rose to a mere 50 percent of the West German level at the end of 1990, real wages exceeded the productivity levels they warranted and kept rising.[25] In addition, producers were saddled with crushing debts right out of the starting gate, as West German technocrats unfamiliar with economic planning transformed the accounting fictions forced onto East German firms by central planners into real and expensive liabilities.[26] Unable to compete with sleeker, more efficient Western corporations, East German firms suffered a severe price-cost squeeze that quickly put them out of business.

Some of this creative destruction was salutary. Many of the "dinosaurs" of East German production, as the West German neoliberal economist Hans Willgerodt described them, were too slow to escape extinction no matter how gradual the transformation process.[27] The GDR's much vaunted vertically integrated state corporations (Kombinate) operated without regard to cost or competition.[28] Given that demand for East German goods was inelastic in the short run because of their poor quality and lack of conformity with Western standards, moreover, these industrial behemoths had no future. To give but one example, the Trabant automobile was in great demand before 1989, when the choice facing East German consumers was to drive it or not drive at all. But the Trabant was also notoriously unfashionable, unreliable, unsafe, and, because it was also outmoded and completely overpriced, unable to compete with the more modern, safe, efficient, powerful, and comfortable Western cars, once the barriers to trade fell. Unable to find customers at home or abroad, the once-mighty IFA-Personenkraftwagen Kombinat, which in early 1990 still employed 61,419 workers in thirty-five factories, went bankrupt.[29]

But even producers of saleable goods were unable to offer them at market-clearing prices. Nor did the shock therapy unleashed by the introduction of the D-Mark reduce costs sufficiently to unlock entrepreneurial solutions to East Germany's changed circumstances. No leaner, more agile automobile producers took IFA's place, despite the large pool of knowledgeable and disciplined East German automotive workers. Instead, Volkswagen bought up the Skoda Works in Czechoslovakia, where the currency and the labor were comparatively cheap—and this despite the offer of substantial subsidies to build in Saxony.[30] Rather than emerging from rapid monetary union as one of the most efficient and modern regions in Europe, East Germany quickly divested itself of its production facilities, as some 80 percent of East German firms were forced into bankruptcy by the price-cost squeeze.[31]

Kohl's offer of the West German mark only interrupted the labor exodus for a brief moment. In response to wage differentials, but also for fear of becoming unemployed, East Germans resumed their westward migration. From mid 1990 to the end of 1992, an estimated 1 million people permanently left Eastern Germany, at a rate of about 1,000 a day. Between 1992 and 2002, another 521,000 East Germans left for West Germany.[32] Only in the last few years has East German migration slowed, as mobility, wage rates, and demographic factors such as age and gender found a tenuous equilibrium across German labor markets.[33] Precisely because the circulation of West German money institutionalized the productivity gap between the two economically divergent regions, the effects of rapid monetary union have yet to subside. In addition, the lack of convergence has been reinforced by a uniform monetary policy that is often out of step with the East German business cycle.[34]

Policy Failures after Monetary Union

Rapid monetary union is not the only cause of the Eastern Mezzogiorno. Although much went well afterward, including the privatization of East German industry, the poor design of economic policy contributed to the East German slump. A shift in the European Union's attitude toward state subsidies for East Germany beginning in 1996, for example, scared off private investors. As Irwin L. Collier has shown, the European Commission disallowed 241 million of the 781 million DM in subsidies offered to Volkswagen to build new plants in Chemnitz and Mosel as anticompetitive. According to Collier, the case spread uncertainty about the costs of investment, reducing the flow of private investment into East Germany.[35]

But one could also criticize the Federal Republic's decision to rely on subsidies through tax breaks rather than direct investment during the initial period of reconstruction.[36] After all, the drastic reduction in the size of state intervention contributed to the dramatic collapse in demand for East German goods and the failure of East German businesses. There was no way to prevent the loss of sales for regional producers, since initially both companies and consumers, now free to choose their suppliers, preferred West German goods. In the transition from the planned to a market economy, moreover, reducing the presence of the state in the price-formation process was absolutely necessary. But the deep budget cuts, especially by local authorities, translated into a drop in demand, spelling the end for many East German producers that might have otherwise survived. Together, the lack of direct investment in infrastructure and the sharp decline in government expenditure served to reinforce the cyclical contraction.[37]

In the absence of substantial and immediate participation of the state in the work of reconstruction, sustaining demand became more costly later on. As a result, the economic boom from 1992 to 1995/96 was more shallow and short-lived than necessary, while the countercyclical measures later required to stimulate demand were larger than might have otherwise been necessary. Between 1991 and 2003, West Germany transferred a whopping 1.25 trillion Euros to East Germany.[38] As a result, "every third deutschmark spent in East Germany came from the West" in the first decade after unification.[39] But because most of the funds transferred have been spent on consumption rather than investment, and the goods purchased have for the most part not been of East German provenance, the transfer of West German wealth to East Germany did not facilitate economic convergence. More than half of the redistributed funds were disbursed as welfare payments. The welfare handouts spared East Germans the material privations of their Eastern European neighbors and reduced the attractions of political extremism. But only 12 percent of the transfers were devoted to improving infrastructure. Ironically, the artificial increase in living standards recalls Honecker's irresponsible emphasis on consumption at the expense of investment. Similarly, the subsidies provided to East German producers have created conditions that recall economic planning. The massive transfer payments have rendered the cost of capital negative, shielding many firms from hard budget constraints and promoting indifference to transaction costs.[40]

The legacy of communist economic mismanagement, coupled with the victory of political expediency over economic expertise during the process of unification, and the insufficient countercyclical spending during reconstruction have all weighed on East German economic growth. After a short takeoff, GDP in the new Bundesländer returned to anemic growth rates between 1997 and 2005.[41] In the five years since 2006, East German economic activity has stabilized at higher levels, more or less matching West German growth rates.[42] In other words, the East German pattern of growth has finally converged with West Germany, but at a much lower level of per capita GDP. Without an obvious source of innovation to accelerate East German productivity, the economic gap seems frozen, and with it the need to continue massive transfers of wealth and the distributional conflicts that attend it. Land is right to argue that some regional sectors, from dairy production to plumbing, continue to thrive. The indirect integration of East German commerce into global markets via West German partners—their "fragmentation"—may promote the region's specialization as suppliers of nonfinished goods and services. Regional and sectoral integration may even act to cushion East Germany from future systemic shocks, the way that rapid monetary union did not. But it will do so only by preserving the continued economic divergence and dependence that slowed East German growth after 1989.

To misuse the poet Hölderlin, it is possible that in the dangers of the European sovereign debt crisis there is hope. The threat to the Euro has underscored the disadvantages of a one-size-fits-all monetary policy. Not only are low productivity areas hit harder by economic downturns and policy failures, but the lack of monetary autonomy also encourages a resort to fiscal priming. In other words, West German policy before 1989 was correct: economic convergence alongside strong supranational institutions is essential to the creation of a stable single currency. This is not to argue that culture and history are irrelevant. On the contrary, they are often decisive, since they operate in a feedback loop in which cultural attitudes shaped by material reality and historical memory find their way back into decisions about economic policy. Thus, West Germans argue in the terms of their own monetary culture that the debt crisis is the fault of profligate and fiscally undisciplined southern Europeans who must be shown tough love by their more responsible northern neighbors. But West Germans make this argument, which is no more than economic perception of the taxpayer who sees no benefit in the institutions he or she supports, only at the expense of their Eastern cousins. Perhaps once East Germans apply the lessons of their own monetary experience to the European experiment, they will add something useful to this oddly uneconomical debate, and in doing so, overtake their neighbors.

Notes

1. Manfred Görtemaker, *Unifying Germany 1989–1990* (New York, 1994), 124. Kohl first used the phrase in a speech on 20 February 1990.
2. Irwin L. Collier, "A Splendid Failure? Reflections on Two Decades of East German Economic Reconstruction," in Peter C. Caldwell and Robert Shandley, eds., *German Unification: Expectations and Outcomes* (New York, 2011), 179–104; Jonathan Zatlin, "Rethinking Reunification: German Monetary Union and European Integration," in ibid., 85–133.
3. According to Collier, "A Splendid Failure," 180, a continuous price-adjusted GDP growth rate of 9 percent in the new Bundesländer would have led to convergence with the old Bundesländer by 2002, while a continuous 3 percent rate would lead to convergence by 2028. Real East German growth rates have been less than 3 percent, however.
4. According to the German Institute for Economics (DIW), a major reason for the region's low productivity rates is the large number of small businesses: 63 percent of East Germans employed by industry work in firms with fewer than 250 employees, as compared to 41 percent in West Germany. In addition, these small East German businesses are mainly local suppliers rather than end producers. They are also less likely to be found in research-oriented sectors, such as pharmaceuticals or high-tech, less involved in exporting their goods, and more involved in assembling rather than manufacturing products. *Wochenbericht des DIW Berlin* 51–52 (2010), 3, 5.
5. Under the impact of the recession, unemployment rose to a high of 8.6 percent for all of Germany in January 2010, or 13.5 percent in the East and 7.3 percent in the West,

but had fallen to a low of 6.9 percent, or 10.9 and 5.8 percent respectively, in June 2011. Obviously, official figures do not include those who are no longer looking for work or who did not register with the government. Economists have estimated the number of nonregistered unemployed in the East variously, but often at around 15 percent. Bundesagentur für Arbeit, ed., *Der Arbeits- und_Ausbildungsmarkt in Deutschland—Monatsbericht Juli 2011* (Nuremberg, 2011), 15, 59–61.

6. Ibid., 69–70.
7. In 2001, Michael C. Burda and Jennifer Hunt estimated hidden unemployment in the East at 12 percent, a figure that has surely diminished somewhat since then. Michael C. Burda and Jennifer Hunt, "From Reunification to Economic Integration: Productivity and the Labor Market in Eastern Germany," *Brookings Papers on Economic Activity* 2 (2001), 2.
8. Even during the recovery Eastern labor markets failed to grow faster than their Western counterparts. *Der Arbeits- und Ausbildungsmarkt,* 15, 59–61; Stefan Arent, Alexander Eck, Michael Kloß, and Robert Lehmann, "Konjunkturprognose Ostdeutschland und Sachsen 2010/2011: Normalisierung der Konjunktur," *ifo Dresden berichtet* 1 (2011), 21.
9. Gabor Steingart, *Deutschland, der Abstieg eines Superstars* (Munich, 2004). Anxieties over the failure of countercyclical policies and the drag represented by East Germans on German growth hit a peak around 2004. See, for example, the cover of *Der Spiegel* 15 (2004), "1.25 Trillion Euros for What?"
10. Jonathan R. Zatlin, "Scarcity and Resentment. Economic Sources of Xenophobia in the GDR, 1971–1989," *Central European History* 40 (2007), 1–38.
11. Jonathan R. Zatlin, *The Currency of Socialism: Money and Political Culture in East Germany* (Cambridge, 2007).
12. Under Honecker, investment in production was greatly surpassed by investment in consumption. Investment in consumer goods and services rose by a stunning 200 percent between 1970 and 1989 compared to a mere 22 percent rise in investment in manufacturing. Stiftung-Archiv Parteien und Massenorganisationen der DDR (SAPMO-BA), DY30, JIV 2/2A/3252, Schürer, "Analyse der ökonomischen Lage," 30 October 1989, 5.
13. Bundesarchiv Berlin (BArchB), DE1, 55384, Klopfer, "Persönliche Notizen über ein Gespräch beim Mitglied des Politbüros und Sekretär des ZK der SED, Genossen Dr. Mittag," 23 November 1988, 6; Bundesbeauftragter für die Staatssicherheitsunterlagen (BStU), Arbeitsbereich Mittig, Nr. 58, "Zu den ausgewählten Problemen," 12–13. In 1989, only 27 percent of all East German machines were five years old or fewer, compared to 35 percent in West Germany. BStU, Arbeitsbereich Mittig, Nr. 58, "Zu den ausgewählten Problemen," 16–17, and Anlage 6, 42; *Neues Deutschland,* 11 November 1990.
14. George Akerlof, Andrew K. Rose, Janet L. Yellen, Helga Hessenius, Rudiger Dornbusch, and Manuel Guitian, "East Germany in from the Cold: The Economic Aftermath of Currency Union," *Brookings Papers on Economic Activity* 1 (1991), 5–6; Rüdiger Dornbusch, Holger Wolf, and Lewis Alexander, "Economic Transition in Eastern Germany," ibid. 1 (1992), 245; A. J. Hughes Hallett, and Yue Ma, "East Germany, West Germany, and Their Mezzogiorno Problem: A Parable for European Economic Integration," *The Economic Journal* 103 (1993), 417; Joachim Ragnitz, "Lagging Productivity in the East German Economy: Obstacles to Fast Convergence," in Michael Dauderstädt and Lothar Witte, eds., *Cohesive Growth in the Enlarging Euroland* (Bonn, 2001), 94. At the time, most Western analysts believed East German productivity and living standards came to about half of West German levels. Deutsche Bundesbank, "Die Wirtschaftslage in der Bundesrepublik Deutschland im Herbst 1989," *Monatsbericht der Deutschen Bundesbank* (Frankfurt, December 1989), 15; "Reform der Wirtschaftsordnung in der DDR und die Aufgaben der Bundesrepublik," *Wochenbericht der DIW* 6 (1990); *Das Handelsblatt,* 14 January and 8 February 1990; interview, Thilo Sarrazin, Mainz, 13 June 1996; Phillip J.

Bryson and and Manfred Melzer, *The End of the East German Economy: From Honecker to Reunification* (New York, 1991), 99.

15. For more on the GDR's liquidity crisis and its declining terms of trade during the 1980s, see Zatlin, *The Currency of Socialism,* chapters 3 and 4.
16. A total of 72,729 left the GDR in January 1990. Hartmut Wendt, "Die deutsch-deutschen Wanderungen. Bilanz einer 40jährigen Geschichte von Flucht und Ausreise," *Deutschland Archiv* 34 (1991), 393. See Akerlof, "East Germany in from the Cold," 45. Because the Federal Republic had never recognized the GDR diplomatically, East Germans were regarded automatically as West German citizens—or more correctly, as refugees who were entitled to government assistance to ease their integration into the FRG. "Rethinking Reunification," 85–133.
17. Michael Kreile maintains that support for Kohl's initiative was broader than commentators have suggested, but does not offer enough evidence to substantiate his point. Michael Kreile, "The Political Economy of the New Germany," in Paul B. Stares, ed., *The New Germany and the New Europe* (Washington, 1992), 55–92. Many of the country's most influential economists, financial experts, and commercial leaders loudly voiced their resistance to rapid monetary union, while most of Kohl's supporters argued on political rather than economic lines.
18. For more on the ways in which the coronation theory and the theory of optimal currency areas shaped reactions to rapid monetary union, see Zatlin, "Rethinking Reunification."
19. In contrast to the European case, a unified but asymmetrical monetary policy would be mitigated by labor mobility and supraregional institutions strong enough to transfer enough wealth to smooth over the lack of economic convergence. The point, however, is that despite a large migration of workers and massive transfer payments, a large productivity gap continues to characterize the new German polity.
20. Whether his politically astute assessment of the political landscape imbued the decidedly bland Kohl with the charisma Seibel attributes to him is questionable. Nevertheless, Kohl's political daring and diplomatic farsightedness certainly warrant greater praise than his contemporaries were willing to concede. Compare Wolfgang Seibel, "The Quest for Freedom and Stability: Political Choices and the Economic Transformation of East Germany 1989–1991," in *German Unification,* 99–120 with Zatlin, "Rethinking Reunification."
21. Ironically, the idea was first made public by Ingrid Matthäus-Maier, an economics expert who had changed her party affiliation from the Free Democrats (FDP) to the Social Democrats (SPD). Ingrid Matthäus-Maier, "Signal zum Bleiben," in *Die Zeit,* 19 January 1990.
22. Despite popular memory, the DM's relation to the "economic miracle" was indirect, not least because the currency's strength reflected the very real story of productivity increases. More importantly, the GDR's starting point in 1989 was worse than the FRG's in 1948. Geoff Pugh, "Economic Reform in Germany: The 1948 Currency and Economic Reforms in Comparison with the 1990 Economic and Monetary Union," in Thomas Lange and J.R. Shackleton, *The Political Economy of German Unification* (Providence, 1998), 120–138; Manfred E. Streit, "German Monetary Union," in Deutsche Bundesbank, ed., *Fifty Years of the Deutsche Mark,* 640–643.
23. This is not to argue that a rapid currency union had enjoyed no economic advantages over a more gradual solution. Perhaps most importantly, postponing monetary union would have required the Bundesbank to intervene in currency markets to protect the East German mark from traders testing the central bank's resolve, which would have been expensive and risked its credibility. To preserve the D-Mark's stability, the Bundesbank raised interest rates to levels not seen since the Great Depression, creating a more harsh business environment for East German companies by tightening credit condi-

tions at home and exacerbating the economic contraction of Germany's main trading partners.

24. Akerlof, "East Germany in from the Cold"; Dieter Grosser, *Das Wagnis der Währungs-, Wirtschafts- und Sozialunion. Politische Zwänge im Konflikt mit ökonomischen Regeln* (Stuttgart, 1998); Kreile, "The Political Economy of the New Germany"; Seibel, "The Quest for Freedom and Stability"; Otto Singer, "Constructing the Economic Spectacle: The Role of Currency Union in the German Unification Process," *Journal of Economic Issues* 4 (1992), 1105–1106; Jonathan R. Zatlin, "Hard Marks and Soft Revolutionaries: the Economics of Entitlement and the Debate over German Unification, November 9, 1989–March 18, 1990," *German Politics and Society* 33 (1994), 57–84.
25. Akerlof, "East Germany in from the Cold," 42–43.
26. On this point, see Zatlin, *The Currency of Socialism*, epilogue.
27. Hans Willgerodt, *Vorteile der wirtschaftlichen Einheit Deutschlands. Gutachten* (Cologne, 1990).
28. To argue, as Rainer Land and others do, that East German industry was somehow Fordist is empirically incorrect. Although organization around the assembly line and the one-product strategy of East German production superficially resembled the Fordist model, it lacked the integration of production with consumption. East German producers never sought to reduce costs or stimulate demand by raising domestic consumption. Since GDR manufacturing failed because it was inefficient, wasteful, and completely ignored consumer preferences, it would be more accurate to imagine its organization as Taylorist in inspiration, not in execution.
29. BArchB, DE1, 56350, Wirtschaftskomitee, Abteilung Finanzen und Preise, "Expertise zur Rentabilitätslage von Wirtschaftsbereichen der DDR unter den Bedingungen der Einführung der D-Mark als einheitliche Währung," 2 March 1990, Anlage 2; Akerlof, "East Germany in from the Cold," 14. For more on the Trabant and the IFA combined, see Zatlin, *The Currency of Socialism*, chapter 5.
30. As discussed below, the EU disallowed a portion of those subsidies, which created some uncertainty about investment conditions. But since Volkswagen could have nevertheless counted on 540 million DM, its decision to forgo German and European support for building an East German plant and move production to Czechoslovakia underscores that currency and wage considerations were more important than subsidies.
31. Irwin L. Collier, "The Twin Curse of the Goddess Europa and the Economic Reconstruction of Eastern Germany," *German Studies Review* 20 (1997), 411–417; Akerlof, "East Germany in from the Cold," 14, 28, 36–37.
32. Ibid., 42–55; *Der Spiegel* 3 (1993), 52; Jan Priewe, "Zwischen Abkoppelung und Aufholen—das schwache ostdeutsche Wachstumspotential," *WSI Mitteilungen* 12 (2002), 706.
33. Hans-Werner Sinn, "Germany's Economic Unification. An Assessment after Ten Years," *National Bureau of Economic Research Working Paper 7586*, 9–10; Lothar Kettenacker, *Germany 1989: In the Aftermath of the Cold War* (Harlow, 2009), 198–199.
34. The Bundesbank's reaction to monetary union illustrates how tight money policies necessitated by aggregate economic indicators stifled the asynchronous growth that East Germany required to catch up to West Germany. Reacting to inflationary pressures emanating from monetary union as well as to the need to reassert an independence on which the Kohl government had infringed, the Bundesbank aggressively tightened credit conditions. By 1992, German interest rates had reached their highest levels since the 1931 Banking Crisis. The central bank's disinflationary policies dampened growth rates and cut short the economic boom that took place in the new Bundesländer between 1992 and 1996. See Collier, "A Splendid Failure"; David Marsh, *The Euro: The Politics of the New Global Currency* (New Haven, 2009); Arbeitskreis "Volkswirtschaftliche Gesamtrechnungen der Länder" im Auftrag der Statistischen Ämter der 16 Bundesländer, des Statistischen Bundesamtes und des Bürgeramtes, Statistik und Wahlen,

ed., *Bruttoinlandsprodukt, Bruttowertschöpfung in den Ländern und Ost-West-Großraumregionen Deutschlands 1991 bis 2010,* Reihe 1, Band 1 (Stuttgart, 2011), section 1, 1–3, www.statistikportal.de/Statistik-Portal/publ.asp#Gesamtrechnungen.

35. Collier, "A Splendid Failure," 194–199. Collier argues that the attempt to harmonize Europe's economies in preparation for the Euro is to blame for East Germany's situation.
36. Between a third to half of private investment costs were initially subsidized through tax breaks, then allowed to lapse. Karl Heinz Paqué, *Die Bilanz: Eine wirtschaftliche Analyse der Deutschen Einheit* (Munich, 2009), 3.
37. Akerlof, "East Germany in from the Cold," 37–41. A similar process took place during the Great Recession in the U.S., when individual states used federal stimulus packages to balance their books rather than to modernize infrastructure, which only reinforced recessionary impulses.
38. Burda and Hunt, "From Reunification to Economic Integration," 11; Sinn, "Germany's Economic Unification," 9–10; *Berliner Zeitung,* 7 April 2004; *Der Spiegel* 15 (2004), 25.
39. Sinn, "Germany's Economic Unification," 6.
40. Ibid., 14–16.
41. The old Bundesländer also grew at a slower average annual rate of about 2.2 percent, although this level of growth was more in keeping with developments in the Federal Republic before 1989. Calculations based on ibid.
42. From 1992 to 1995, the new Bundesländer grew at rates that far outstripped the old Bundesländer. In 1992, for example, the GDP of the new Bundesländer grew at the torrid pace of 26.8 percent compared to 5.6 percent in the old Bundesländer—which was itself an impressive rate for an industrial economy. In 1993, growth slowed somewhat in the East to 21.9 percent, versus 0.9 percent in the West, diminishing further in 1994 to 16.6 percent while picking up in the West to 3.9 percent. By 1995, growth continued at the slower pace of 8.2 percent and 3.3 percent respectively, and fell further to 3.9 percent and 1.3 percent respectively. In contrast, during the next ten years, East German growth remained anemic, often less than the 2 percent required to create jobs and in 2005 even falling well below the performance of the West at 0.8 versus 1.5 percent. Ibid.

Part III

Social Upheaval

Chapter Seven

1989 and the Crisis of Feminist Politics

Ute Gerhard

In summarizing the consequences of unification for feminist politics and the women's movement based on West German experiences, I cannot help but make a few personal preliminary observations. In his 1967 essay "On the Difficulties of Being An Insider," Hans Magnus Enzensberger reflects on the problems of accepting a German national identity. He lists the wearisome prejudices, the outrage, and the everyday skeptical expectations (often unspoken) that Germans generally experience from those of other nations and describes how helpless and how incapable of finding an adequate reaction he feels.[1] Precisely because the members of the 1968 generation struggled so openly with both the German past and their own personal heritage and attempted to come to terms with that history, it was difficult for them to develop a sense of German national identity. Overall, Germans came rather late to developing a united German national consciousness, as the nation-state did not gain its legal foundation until 1871 and in the ensuing years was faced with disasters and defeats. The result was a plurality of affiliations, distancings, and demarcations—most recently the division of Germany after 1945.

Speaking on behalf of my generation, I can attest to the fact that the idea of a West German "national" identity was utterly foreign to us, and in fact was, given Germany's division, entirely absurd. It was clear to us that we could neither "master" the past nor forget it, and we therefore gratefully accepted the offer of a kind of "constitutional patriotism," one which defined citizenship and identity not according to ethnic or cultural commonalties, but instead according to constitutional principles of democratic participation and common liberties.[2] The democracy bestowed upon the

Notes for this chapter begin on page 150.

Germans by the victors took on new life with the new social movements of the 1970s—foremost among these was the women's movement—and was substantiated by civic practices, including civil disobedience. For the same reasons, during the process of European integration, many West Germans enthusiastically embraced a European identity. It may not make sense to draw an analogy to the situation of a "West German" today, but I believe that in a critical sense I could find a parallel to Enzenberger's reflections in the unification process that I could contrast to Ingrid Miethe's essay, "On the Difficulties of Being a West German."

With the end of the provisional status of the Federal Republic and the creation of a newly unified Germany, the question of nationality arose anew. At the beginning of the 1990s, in the face of xenophobic violence in the new Germany and ethnically charged wars in Europe, the goal was to avoid the rise of revisionist nationalism. With the fall of the Soviet Union and its member states and the onset of a new influx of immigrants—refugees from the former Yugoslavia, or ethnic Germans from Eastern Europe—the issue of belonging became complicated, and identities multiplied. In the reunited Germany there were, according to one's provenance, age, gender, class, or wealth, new inequalities and injustices. These were compounded by the fact that it seemed that West Germans could continue to live just as they had been, while East Germans had lost everything known to them: their social safety net, their East German identity, and often even their very means of existence. New sensitivities, injuries, and misunderstandings arose that reverberate to this day.

East Germans can rightly claim for themselves alone the responsibility for having carried out this revolution with peaceful means in the face of great risk. Joy at the fall of the Wall and the end of a dictatorial regime united us all and continues to unite us. Nonetheless, the debate still centers on the extent to which East Germans (and as in earlier revolutions, this means specifically women) were robbed of the fruits of the revolution, while the West Germans could count themselves among the winners, even coming out ahead in the bargain. It is against this backdrop that I will attempt to bring my view, as a West German, leftist, second-wave feminist, to the debate.

1989 as a Feminist Turning Point

The world political events of the year of 1989 and the resulting unification of two separate German states represent a remarkable historical turning point for women, for feminism, and for feminist politics in Germany, because they fundamentally altered political priorities and discourses. Previously, the women's movement in West Germany had made great strides up until the end of the 1980s. After the feminist awakening and the stormy battles at the beginning of the 1970s, in which fiercely contested debates extended beyond calls for equality to include principles of autonomy and the ability to realize oneself in private and political spheres, a new cultural movement and counterculture arose that was divided and divisive within itself.[3] This movement, along with other new social movements within an altered civil society, permanently influenced and changed the Federal Republic.

The "new" women's movement, so named to differentiate it from the "old" movement that took place at the turn of the century, drew on a broad network of women's groups, with activities in the areas of education, counseling, and social work and including a varied media landscape spanning journals, books, campaigns, and congresses. At the beginning of the 1980s, the success of this mobilization resulted in the formation of new groups. For instance, the women's movement gained momentum from the peace movement, from a new orientation toward women's questions within the unions, and from feminist theology. This theology, so troubling to church authorities, resulted in an ecumenical meeting of women in Vancouver in 1983 and the first demands for gender mainstreaming. Simultaneously, women began speaking up in unions, parties, and institutions, and in some instances alliances were formed between activists within the movement and members of the established elite. Even the press organ of the German Women's Council, the umbrella organization of the state-sponsored established women's groups (from which the "new" women's movement had sought to distance itself and vice versa) could not avoid taking up feminist themes like the problem of violence against women. In this manner, traditional political organizations, parties, and institutions were increasingly reacting to the demands of the autonomous women's movement, realizing them in a specific way that robbed them of their more radical, utopian vision. One example is the family policy initiated after the so-called conservative turn of the Kohl government at the beginning of the 1980s. This policy addressed women's work and family issues with calls for "Motherhood in a New Guise," so that the introduction of a child benefit allowance would secure the gender-specific division of labor within the family.[4]

The Green Party, which was first represented in the Bundestag in 1983, marked the beginning a period when self-declared feminists occupied positions of political power. This reinvigorated discussions about women and politics in a number of ways, for instance with a new debate about quotas and the drafting of an anti-discrimination act, which, however, did not win a majority in the Bundestag in 1986.[5] Finally, the establishment of equal rights officers at the state level and in the municipalities created an entirely new field of political administration, which, based on personal and political factors, served as an interface among administration, politics, traditional women's groups, and initiatives within the women's movement.[6] Concurrently, women's history and gender studies began to make institutional gains with the establishment of professorships for women at the end of the 1980s: new curricula, graduate schools, and research centers were founded; the analysis of gender roles began to appear in lesson plans and on the agendas of university research centers. Inspired by the women's movement, this research resulted in new analyses and information, but also in criticism, as such research refused to serve as the movement's handmaiden.

This phase of professionalization and consolidation, which resulted in a differentiation and a pluralism of interests and ideas, overlapped with the so-called silent revolution—the collapse of the real existing socialist state system. This highly dramatic, unforeseen political upheaval also revealed the weaknesses of a social movement that was based on democratic principles and had done without a strict organization or hierarchies and had instead relied on a decentralized network of groups, projects, and facilities, drawing from these a wealth of ideas and personnel. Even at the end of the 1980s, alliances between the West German women's movement and political parties were met with great skepticism from both sides; on the one hand there was a radical core group within the autonomous women's movement that refused to be taken in by the patriarchal state and its representatives; on the other, a more participatory wing that sought to resolve the contradiction between autonomy and participation in the ruling system using a strategy of intervention and involvement.[7] These various approaches, along with the fact that, due to its fluidity, the women's movement did not possess an organizational structure or speaker within the political sphere who might have been able to represent its interests vis-à-vis politics, would prove to be a distinct disadvantage during the process of reunification of the two German states.[8]

In any case, when the unification treaty was concluded on 20 September 1990, hastily and under political pressure, leaders of the women's movement and representatives of established women's organizations were not included in the negotiations and were excluded from any decision making. The speed and scope of the unification process, which was hurried along by the collapse of not only the GDR's economy but all of its political institutions and could no longer be constrained, will not be considered here in detail.[9] From a feminist perspective, the circumstances of unification were perceived as an unparalleled orchestration of the West German patriarchy and a "triumph of the Fatherland."[10]

The political and economic committees responsible for evaluating and "winding down" East German universities were almost exclusively filled with men, especially as women's history and gender studies were still in the early stages of institutionalization. "No one can deny," the then–Bundestag president and CDU politician Rita Süßmuth noted cautiously, "that the politics of unification are associated with the names of men, and not women…"[11] The new insignificance of women's issues became apparent when the "Academic Advisory Committee for Women's Issues," convened in 1989 before the *Wende*, was stopped from publishing a study on women's pensions carried out in the fall of 1990 that contained obviously inopportune results for social policy.[12] After completing its report, the committee was dismissed without further ado by the then–minister for women's issues, Angela Merkel.[13]

Without a doubt, women's issues and feminism were on the defensive after the historical events of 1989, and not only in Germany. Beginning in the 1990s, other Western countries began to experience a "backlash" and such questions, now correctly identified as issues of gender politics, were removed from the political agenda.[14] Practically, this meant that many projects for women in West Germany were denied state funds that had previously supported a wide range of social and pedagogical initiatives—supporting mother's groups, medical counseling, and cultural activities for women by women. At the very least one could not deny the need for shelters to protect women from violence, which is why the former GDR also saw the surprisingly sudden spread of women's shelters. With the end of "real existing socialism" and the disappearance of two competing state systems, it was apparently not only the competitive state marked by Western capitalism that emerged as a winner. In the face of increased global connections and economic interests that had imposed upon politics the rules of the marketplace, the transformation was also accompanied by a remasculinization of politics and the re-emergence of neoliberal principles, with an emphasis on privatization, deregulation, the retreat of the state, and cuts in social services. Women's issues and gender policies neither carried any weight nor had any advocates within this setting. Therefore West German politicians and opinion leaders, in their overestimation of their own abilities and in their self-importance, truly believed at the beginning of the 1990s that the high employment rates of East German women would "normalize" as they adapted to West German circumstances.[15]

Contrasting Different Experiences

In fact, the West German women's movement came to a historical impasse with the unification of the two German states, because it had previously only represented West German women's experiences and goals. The movement could only live on if it united with the East German women's movement and continued as a united German movement. If at first West German feminists were all too confident that they would receive support from East German women, who had experience in the areas of equal rights and citizens' movements (in the expectation that East German women would follow their example, somewhat akin to the West German policy of accession), differences and unexpected misunderstandings quickly came to the forefront. West German feminists, who had been and still remained wedded to the idea of maintaining a critical distance from institutionalized politics and who were used to defeat and marginalization, were astonished at how quickly their East German sisters were prepared to use their newly won "freedom from the state" to gain direct "participation in the state" as an interest group organized around a political party in a partnership between the Independent Women's Association and the Greens.[16]

The anti-institutional skepticism of the West German women's movement regarding the state and party politics, which was characteristic of other "new" social movements, was not merely a sign of radicalism, but rather a reaction to the structural anchoring of traditional gender roles within West German social policy. This had become clear at the latest in the 1990s during the process of European integration. In comparison to other EU countries, West Germany's "modernization deficit" was due to low birth rates[17] and a low number of mothers in the workplace.[18] Since the 1990s, political scientists and international observers comparing social welfare policy have determined that the West German welfare state—with its social security system based on work and its family policy centered on male breadwinners—is the prototype of a conservative corporative welfare-state regime. In this system, the main actors, work and capital, made a class compromise with representatives of the state that they would uphold and defend the ideology of a gender-specific division of labor.[19]

Developments in the GDR occurred in an almost inverse parallel fashion. According to the socialist emancipation theory in the tradition of Marx and Engels as well as August Bebel and Clara Zetkin, "the emancipation of the woman"[20] would happen via integration into the workforce. This was encouraged and even enforced with a practically seamless offering of state institutions designed to provide "collective" childcare and education.[21] In contrast, West German family policy trumpeted the model of the traditional bourgeois nuclear family with relatively large social transfers, even though much had been done to achieve equal rights within family law and alternative models had challenged the ascendancy of the traditional family. A combination of labor policy, social welfare policy, and tax codes strengthened the model of the male breadwinner and the role of women within the family was at the heart of West German policy up to the

1990s. In the GDR, however, starting in the 1970s, women (and especially mothers) were integrated into the workforce with the help of a range of social services (the so-called "mommy policy"). This realization of equal rights was celebrated as "the greatest achievement of the GDR"; for those involved it was "proof of socialism's superiority over capitalism."[22]

At unification, the effects of these opposite social views on women from both East and West were especially apparent in the structuring of women's work. Women's employment rates in the GDR had been over 80 percent since the 1970s, which was high compared to other nations. In 1989, when 90 percent of the women worked, the rate was almost equal that among men. In West Germany, women's employment rates rose slowly starting in the 1970s and stood at 55 percent in 1989.[23] The differences were even greater and longer lasting with regard to working mothers. The GDR was remarkable in that not only were most women employed, but over 90 percent of women had borne at least one child.[24] In comparison, in West Germany 35 percent of married working women between twenty-five and fifty-five years old had no children.[25] At the same time, the percentage of working women with small children (younger than six) was and remains lower in West Germany than in the East. In 2004, only one in three West German women with children were active in the workforce, while in East Germany, almost every other mother (44 percent) was working, although women's employment had declined in the East since reunification.[26]

Particularly since the competition between East and West was carried out in the area of women's politics and family policy, it is not surprising to note that the forty-year-long parallel histories left their mark on women's lives and everyday practices, as reflected in differing perspectives, interests, and experiences, not to mention differences in circumstances and opportunities. One can only explain the attitude of West German women, who were accused of being "know-it-alls" (because they insisted on including feminine endings on proper nouns), with the fact that these feminists based their self-perceptions and their political efforts on their observation that the only way to bring about social and cultural changes in gender relations was to radically oppose the patriarchal state and its norms. They were keenly aware of how fragile and at-risk their hard-won gains were. Even a shared language has not made communication any easier, as the political concepts at stake can take on very different meanings in different contexts. This applies to such fundamental terms as "equality" and "emancipation"—terms that were discredited in the GDR because they were associated with state-mandated women's policies and were seen as already having been accomplished. This is linked to the experience of family life, which many women living under the socialist dictatorship saw as a occurring in a private sphere, a niche or "space of freedom." "Family and friends filled the space where civil society could not exist; the private sphere was the only space for the development of individual initiative and autonomy ... the locus of anti-politics, in opposition to the over-politicized and didactic, exhortatory nature of the public sphere."[27] In the face of this experience of gender neutrality within the private sphere, the insistence of West German feminists that even within this private sphere (secured within the legal and political liberal framework as a place of equality) violence and misdeeds occur, is likely to have been seen as a political luxury of an affluent society.

The experiences of the Western women's movement can be aptly summarized with the motto "the private is political," which encompasses not only the relationships between citizens and the state but those among citizens themselves, relationships which should be democratic in a gendered sense—free and equal. The public versus private dichotomy served as the starting point for feminist critique and social analysis. According to this critique, gender hierarchies and the gendered division of labor within the family and the workplace (and with this the associated norms, rights, and social policy) were kept in place as private patriarchy and served as the reason for exclusion from or discrimination within the public sphere. Beyond economic independence, feminists fought for the right to self-determination within the most intimate spheres of sexuality and to self-determination over one's own body. The recurring political contests regarding abortion serve here as the symbolic representation of a traditional gender hierarchy.

A further concrete piece of evidence for the opposing trajectories of women's rights in East and West is the right to carry out an abortion within the first three months of pregnancy, affirmed in a law passed in the GDR in 1972, at the height of West German feminist mobilization around this reproductive issue. In the GDR, this was not the result of any sort of mobilization (which would have not been possible in any case); rather, the law was passed in parliament with the justification that it served in the fight against class in the tradition of the workers' movement.[28] Within the larger social gains of the 1970s and 1980s, especially for working mothers, the "women's question" was considered solved in the eyes of the state, and the majority of working women in East Germany viewed equal rights in terms of economic independence and qualified work. The "Uprising of Women to Begin their 'Happy Revolution'" in November 1989 (which led to the founding of the Independent Women's Association [UFV]) was accompanied by public protests and declarations regarding "the bankruptcy of socialism's patriarchal patterns of life and structures."[29] But according to the declaration of 3 December 1989 and the "Manifesto for an Autonomous Women's Movement," the main goal was first and foremost "to acknowledge and represent the interests of women" and to offer "a socialist alternative" to reunification policies. It was clear—so it seemed to East German feminists—"that reunification would mean three steps backward for women's rights." Instead, women like Ina Merkel demanded "a modern socialism on German soil," "an ecological reorganization of society," "democracy, self-governance, and transparency," "a multicultural society," and a "sense of solidarity among all social groups."[30]

What this reveals is that even in this period of mobilization and unique political opportunity, when exchanges between feminists in both Germanies could result in agreement about an "Eastern Patriarchy, Western Patriarchy," the goals and aims of women from East and West were quite different; it was extremely difficult to weigh the cultural achievements and freedom of self-expression and understanding against material losses and social standing. At this moment, two very "different sisters" came together.[31]

East German women had to pay a very high price for their newly won freedoms in the face of the new demands of a free capitalist market system with a massive loss of jobs, and the associated social insecurities. When the UFV failed to win seats in the first free elections to the Volkskammer in March 1990 in an alliance with the Greens, East German feminists had to concede that they failed to mobilize the "average woman." They were unable "with their demands and their criticisms to find any resonance with the daily experiences of most women."[32] East German women authors have confirmed that the "myth of accomplished equality" had apparently taken firm root, as strongly as the idea of historical "proletarian anti-feminism," which was not only celebrated in the East, but enjoyed a long theoretical tradition among the left in the West as well.[33] Annette Simon, a GDR psychoanalyst and the daughter of Christa Wolf, notes in her attempt "to know myself after the fact," that there was also a '68 generation in the GDR, whose traumatic experience was the repression of the Prague Spring. Indeed "the members of this generation, who helped constitute the citizens' movement and without whom it would not have been possible … had no public outlets, no media … [and were] unable to articulate their stance towards life in a politically coherent fashion."[34] While "democratic culture had a more profound influence on the '68 generation in the FRG than its members are willing to admit … there was no similar cultural revolution in the GDR, because it was repressed with every means available."[35]

To explain the difficulties East and West German women had in communicating with each other, we must also consider controversies within the feminist movement. At the *Wende,* Western feminist theorists were occupied with epistemological debates about women's ability to act, identity politics, and the discursive dimensions of power. The so-called "cultural" or "linguistic turn" in the humanities and social sciences resulted in a radical epistemological shift that turned its back on "grand narratives" of emancipation to focus instead on the deconstruction of prior categories and meanings. This self-reflective epistemological approach meant that feminist theory was seen as a type of critical social theory. It also meant that the category of "woman" as an object of united politics was itself deconstructed. Feminist theorists today have admitted self-critically that these epistemological debates and discourse analyses focusing on language, meaning, and knowledge have overshadowed historical and sociological analyses of social issues and deeper structural transformations, especially in regard to gender roles since 1989.[36] The "cultural turn" in feminist theory is not only linked to the rise of a new generation of gender researchers, but is also linked to the theoretical brilliance of poststructuralist, postmodern, and postfeminist gender theory (especially as it draws on the work of Judith Butler).[37] This work won for gender studies the acclamation of leading philosophers and real academic credentials, something that is essential as the theorists' relationship to politics and change has often been used by its detractors to discredit it.[38]

It remains unclear how much this shift in feminist theory has contributed to political uncertainty and to depoliticization, or even whether it may have led to the end of the second wave of the women's movement. After the fact it has become evident that feminist debates dominated by poststructural or postmodern theories were distant from or indifferent to the material and economic problems of most women—not only but especially those women from the former East Germany—and the issue has become the subject of heated debates.[39] Due to their different interests and history the women's movements in the East and West were unable to come together during the frantic period of unification and find common political ground or will to power. Only in regard to paragraph 218 of the German penal code, concerning the criminalization of abortion, were women able to intervene in the unification treaty to gain a postponement. The ultimate result, achieved in 1996, was problematic, as it made a woman's choice dependent on a mandatory doctor's consultation.

Just how difficult it was to avoid the dramatic possibility of having the GDR join the FRG as laid out in Article 23 of the Basic Law, rather than to address the question of unification via a referendum and a new constitution per Article 146, became evident with the failure of the constitutional initiatives of 1990, which called for debate and a new social contract in a reunited Germany. The Committee for a Democratically Constituted Federation of German States, founded in June of 1990, was a product of the civic movement in both East and West. After public debate, the committee presented a draft of a constitution, and saw its ratification as a "unique opportunity" to unite these two societies after forty years of division—not only in legal terms, but also as equals who would begin to shape the present and the future together in a sovereign act. A "constitution from below" was to serve as "the engine of unification."[40]

Feminists from East and West also participated in this debate in a number of ways. The group "Women for a New Constitution" published a "Women's Manifesto" in Frankfurt's St. Paul's Church in 1990, based on the bill of rights and the most important state principles of the Basic Law. The manifesto was expressly formulated as a gendered contract. These small steps to lay the foundations of a new constitution were a concrete attempt to translate the experiences and political utopias of a united German gender-equitable society into a rights-based language.[41] In the end, however, the all-German constitutional movement could only achieve a clarification of Article 3 in paragraph II of the Basic Law, which stated "that men and women have equal rights," by a "United Constitutional Commission of the Federation and the States" called into existence in 1992. According to the new article, "the state shall promote the actual implementation of equal rights for women and men and take steps to eliminate disadvantages that now exist."

Processes of Adaptation

After the fact it is evident that the constitutional debates were quite timely, as they anticipated later legal developments. Alternative draft constitutions like the feminist Frankfurt draft, as well as Article 6 of the Basic Law, which guaranteed the state's protection of marriage and the family, generated lively discussions. The Basic Law of the FRG and its institutional support of marriage and family had its roots in the past, specifically in the family law of the Civil Code of 1900, which formed a pillar of the traditional gender order. This conception of marriage upheld the so-called "housewife marriage" (which saw women's main responsibilities as household work and the raising of children) until the 1977 reform of marriage and family law. This appeared at odds with the claims for gender equality as had been laid out in Article 3 of the Basic Law since 1949. The stereotype of the male breadwinner fending off "developments hostile or destructive to families" served for decades as the main bastion against the policy of working mothers and "collective child-rearing" supported in the GDR.[42] The ideal is still maintained to this day by conservatives and Christian Democrats who support taxes and insurance privileges that favor marriage. In the name of the so-called free democratic order, family policy in West Germany always used GDR's women's policies as a foil to defend traditional values and outdated gender roles.

Current empirical evidence highlights the long-lasting way in which these different social policies and legal frameworks in East and West have shaped the self-conceptions and attitudes of mothers. A comparative German-German study carried out at the end of the 1990s on the occupations of mothers with infant children in the cities of Leipzig and Frankfurt am Main had the following results: East German women accepted as a given that their work would not harm their children; West German mothers felt they had to defend themselves against the notion that they were so-called *Rabenmütter,* or bad mothers who neglected their children for egotistical reasons.[43]

In the meantime, however, those alternative and feminist constitutional revisions to marriage and family (which were rejected with such vehemence at the time) have been anchored in legislation and judicial decisions, thus becoming the law of the land. The July 1998 reform of the law on parent(s) and children can be seen as a turning point in a new conceptualization of the family. Granting children born outside of wedlock equal status and establishing the custodial duties of unmarried fathers created a new understanding of family via legal means. A variety of changes have resulted in a cultural revolution with regard to traditional West German family law and the conception of family: an expanded notion of the family that includes all forms of expression, in which men and women can raise children or take care of old or sick people without having to be married; the irrelevance of marriage to alimony and custodial duties; the legal recognition of same-sex partnerships in January of 2001.[44] Having recognized the variety of life choices open to individuals, the law has on the one hand merely followed social changes that have already occurred, especially from the 1970s on in East Germany, with its high numbers of children born out of wedlock, single working mothers, and high divorce rates.[45]

West Germany's modernization gap with regard to family policy was no longer tenable in the face of European developments and within the integration process of the European Union. The FRG came under pressure to act in the face of numerous decisions of the European Court of Justice regarding the equality of women in the workforce, through the provisions of the 1997 Treaty of Amsterdam as well as European guidelines. But the fact that the paradigm shift with regard to the necessity for child care and educational facilities, the rights of fathers, and the economic independence of married couples could happen so seamlessly and without much notice by the broader populace is due in part to the fact the East German life choices and lifestyles promoted these developments and created a changed sense of normalcy. This is particularly apparent in the new alimony law, passed without much fanfare, which does not contemplate any claims for women caring for children over the age of three, a family policy that existed in the GDR that expected women to be responsible for their own so-called economic independence. This is problematic from a West German perspective, because larger structures, institutions, and social expectations still make it difficult, if not impossible, for women to be both workers and mothers.

Equality and Feminism Today

Even now, some twenty years after unification, differences persist between women in East and West regarding their life circumstances, incomes, job prospects, and private life choices. This includes higher numbers of working mothers in the East,[46] more children born out of wedlock or unmarried partners with children,[47] and rather different levels of child care availability.[48] After twenty years, these differences cannot simply be explained away by pointing to divergent social policies or infrastructures; rather, they are linked to differing understandings of gender arrangements, conceptions of mothers' roles, and ideas about what is best for children. In public opinion surveys carried out around the twentieth anniversary, people were asked whether or not they approved of unification; only 86 percent of West Germans approved, as compared to 91 percent of East Germans. Responses regarding East Germans' relationship to the Federal Republic are more varied: 66 percent do not want a return to the GDR but do not feel welcome in the FRG, 25 percent feel they are real citizens, and 10 percent would like a return to the GDR.[49] Without a doubt, the sensibilities of individuals in a united Germany are determined to a large degree by age and differing generational outlooks.[50] Shaped by the same challenges, young women's gender experiences in East and West are therefore also likely to get closer to each other.

In light of these changes, one has to ask if gender issues and gender politics are obsolete. Indeed, we are constantly reminded that girls and women have made huge strides in school performance, education, and professional training, and have in many ways even surpassed boys. A *Der Spiegel* article from 2007 was entitled "Alpha-Girls: How a New Generation of Women is Outpacing the Men."[51] Federal Minister of Family Affairs, Senior Citizens, Women and Youth Kristina Schröder is especially concerned about discrimination against young boys, because they are in her eyes at a disadvantage in an educational system of kindergartens and elementary schools dominated by women.[52] It is true that girls get better grades in high school and more than half (52.7 percent) of graduates are girls. However, in all career paths thereafter, starting with finishing university and on through obtaining post-graduate degrees or assuming positions of leadership in science, business, or politics, the numbers of women decline dramatically, so for example about 90 percent of all professorships are occupied by men.[53] Similar numbers are the rule for leading positions in politics, the media, and especially in business. Recently it was revealed that among the 200 leading businesses in Germany, 98 percent of the leadership positions were filled by men. Although changed perceptions and targeted policies have made real strides in the area of equality, this evidence of discrimination points to the enduring structural barriers that put women in a position of having to choose between work and family, thus being left with no choice at all.

The continuing wage gap between men and women is a fundamental stumbling block in this regard: in Germany the average wage discrepancy among all workers in 2005 was 22 percent, while in all EU countries the average was "merely" 15 percent.[54] Even the number of working women in Germany (which exceeded the EU target of 60 percent, with increased numbers of women in the workforce in the West outweighing a severe reduction in the East) obscures the fact that it reflects a dramatic rise in part-time, marginal, and precarious work, which means that the overall amount of women's work has actually not risen at all. Furthermore, this type of work is not sustainable and therefore does not represent economic autonomy or independence. It is simply not enough that some women, because of their better qualifications, have been able to pursue business or political careers (and this also only because they can delegate the care of their children and homes to low-paid women).[55] United Germany is still miles away from feminist goals of removing gendered hierarchies in the workplace; achieving equality in personal services such as education, nursing, and care for others; and enabling equal access to and participation in the public sphere. This holds true for women from both the East and the West.

Do we therefore need a "new feminism" yet again? The question has been raised in various media outlets at the turn of the century. Countless newspaper articles, books, and issues have repeated just as many clichés about the "old," obsolete feminism, with its hatred of men and its lamentations and myths of victimhood, as they have demanded a "new feminism" that would not need any of the old baggage. Successful women share following message: women today are strong, career oriented, and pleasure seeking, able "to make their way in a society like ours with energy, discipline, self-confidence and courage."[56] The news of its passing has always been part of the history of feminism, signified by the picture of "waves," doldrums, and a general lassitude. But the neoliberal spirit of the age—one that rewards performance and maintains the myth that everyone is the shaper of his or her own destiny—has left younger women facing serious contradictions. Yet they articulate their concerns in a different manner than did their predecessors. Current debates focus on completely novel feminist projects, alternative lifestyles, and cultural practices that have feminist motivations.[57] Well aware of the problems of gender difference and familiar with the language of the women's movement, young women today are once again struggling to defend themselves against stereotypes about femininity, working to overcome structural barriers that now appear in the guise of "glass ceilings," and striving to address issues of violence in sexual relations. These attempts and discourses are taking place on an international level. Well-connected via the internet, young women today are trying out new forms of civic action and cultural practices, particularly with regard to a new counterculture, especially in the art and music scenes.[58]

Campaigns advocating the slogan that "women's rights are human rights" have enabled the formation of new international networks which have been identified as "Third Wave Feminism" since the World Women's Conference held in Beijing in 1995.[59] The roots of this movement can be found in the World Women's Conferences, organized by the United Nations since 1975. These conferences have enabled women from the "Third World" to find a platform independent of Western feminism where they can build alliances. They have also empowered women to act in their own localities and regions. But it is impossible to subsume these activities under a *single* social movement, precisely because the initiatives and interventions are so varied and represent so many different interests and groups (and differences among women). In turn, however, the very plurality of these movements represents their strengths and future challenges. A young author put it in pragmatic terms: "Feminism is not an abstract concept, but experienced daily reality that permeates all areas of life."[60] Older or professional feminists either wonder skeptically whether "third-wave feminist confessionals read as apolitical manifestations of the expressive individualism that characterizes our predominantly liberal culture" or hope that the seeds of past struggles and findings may yet come to fruition some day.[61]

Even if young women today cannot really recognize the differences between East and West German lifestyles and utopias and are closer together than they are apart, we must recognize that a new women's movement is, like its predecessor, only possible if its agenda and concerns have transnational significance. Furthermore, new feminists should not simply take the path blazed by their predecessors and blindly accept their understanding of emancipation. Criticism of and distance from the status quo are some of the central tenets of feminism, fought for with great pathos by generations of feminists; another is an openness to new ideas and strategies.[62] Practically, this means that it is not enough to come to terms with existing inequalities or national sensibilities merely to make ends meet or to get ahead. A retreat like that would be—to quote Hannah Arendt—"a loss of the world." Such a retreat would mean that we would chose not to use the gift of freedom to work together and to help others. "What is lost is the specific and mostly irreplaceable space that exists between people and their contemporaries."[63] A new political movement dedicated to achieving further gender equality must proceed from this stance of participation and public discourse. Next time—and here I agree with the skeptics of an exclusive feminism—the male sex must be engaged and motivated to participate.

Notes

1. Hans Magnus Enzensberger, *Deutschland, Deutschland unter anderm. Äußerungen zur Politik* (Frankfurt, 1967).
2. Dolf Sternberger, *Verfassungspatriotismus* (Frankfurt, 1990); Jürgen Habermas, *Faktizität und Geltung. Beiträge zur Diskurstheorie des Rechts und des demokratischen Rechtsstaates* (Frankfurt, 1992).
3. Ulla Wischermann, *Frauenbewegungen und Öffentlichkeiten um 1900. Netzwerke, Gegenöffentlichkeiten und Protestinszenierungen* (Frankfurt, 2003).
4. Sozialausschüsse der Christlich-Demokratischen Arbeitnehmerschaft, "Die sanfte Macht der Familie. Leitsätze, Entschließungen," edited by the 19. Bundestagung of the CDA (Mannheim, 1981).
5. It took until 2006 for a "General Antidiscrimination Law" (ADG) to be passed, under pressure of four EU Guidelines. The law forbids discrimination according to gender but also discrimination "due to reasons of race or ethnic identity, gender, religion or world view, disability, age, or sexual identity."
6. Clarissa Rudolph and Uta Schirmer, *Gestalten oder Verwalten? Kommunale Frauenpolitik zwischen Verrechtlichung, Modernisierung und Frauenbewegung* (Wiesbaden, 2004).
7. Silvia Kontos, "Von heute an gibt´s mein Programm"—Zum Verhältnis von Partizipation und Autonomie in der Politik der neuen Frauenbewegung, in *Forschungsjournal Neue Soziale Bewegungen,* special issue 1989, 52–65; Ursula Beer and Hildegard Rode, "Kontroverse Politikstrategien der Frauenbewegung: Institutionelle Einbindung versus Autonomie," final report of a research project, Bielefeld, 1986.
8. Alberto Melucci, "Soziale Bewegungen in komplexen Gesellschaften," in Ansgar Klein, Hans-Josef Legrand, and Thomas Leif, eds., *Neue soziale Bewegungen. Impulse, Bilanzen und Perspektiven* (Opladen, 1999), 114–130.
9. Konrad H. Jarausch, *The Rush to German Unity* (New York, 1994).
10. Brigitte Young, *Triumph of the Fatherland: German Unification and the Marginalization of Women* (Ann Arbor, 1999).

11. Rita Süßmuth and Helga Schubert, *Bezahlen die Frauen die Wiedervereinigung?* (Munich, 1992), 44.
12. The comparison revealed that when entering the West German pension system, East German women would receive higher pensions from their continued employment than would West German women, a result that was not to be made public in light of the reigning ideology of the single-breadwinner family.
13. Bundesministerium für Frauen und Jugend, *Frauen im mittleren Alter. Lebenslagen der Geburtskohorten von 1935 bis 1950 in den alten und neuen Bundesländern* (Stuttgart, 1993).
14. Susan Faludi, *Backlash: The Undeclared War Against American Women* (New York, 1991).
15. *IG-Metall-Kongress* (Berlin, 1991).
16. Anne Hampele-Ulrich, *Der Unabhängige Frauenverband. Ein frauenpolitisches Experiment im deutschen Vereinigungsprozess* (Berlin, 2000), 20f.
17. The total fertility rate was 1.45 in West Germany and 1.56 in East Germany, where it sank dramatically after 1995 to 1.22. In the European context, united Germany is at 1.32 today, which is at the lower end of the scale compared to France, which has a rate of 2.00, and Sweden, which has a rate of 1.85. Heribert Engstler, Sonja Menning, *Die Familie im Spiegel der amtlichen Statistik* (Berlin, 2003), 71; Steffen Kröhnert and Reiner Klingholz, *Emanzipation oder Kindergeld?* (Berlin, 2008).
18. Kaufmann, Franz Xaver, *Schrumpfende Gesellschaft* (Frankfurt, 2005); Steffen Kröhnert and Reiner Klingholz, "Geschlechterrollen und Kinderwunsch," in *Dokumente. Zeitschrift für den deutsch-französischen Dialog,* 61 (2005), no. 5, 21–32; Ute Gerhard, Trudie Knijn, and Anja Weckwert, eds., *Working Mothers in Europe: A Comparison of Policies and Practices* (Cheltenham, 2005).
19. Goesta Esping-Andersen, *The Three Worlds of Welfare Capitalism* (Cambridge, 1990); idem, *The Incomplete Revolution: Adapting to Women's New Roles* (Cambridge, 2009).
20. Clara Zetkin, "Für die Befreiung der Frau!" in *Ausgewählte Reden und Schriften* (Berlin, 1957), 3–11.
21. Ute Gerhard, "Die staatlich institutionalisierte 'Lösung' der Frauenfrage. Zur Geschichte der Geschlechterverhältnisse in der DDR," in Hartmut Kaelble, Jürgen Kocka, and Helmut Zwahr, eds., *Sozialgeschichte der DDR* (Stuttgart, 1994), 383–403; Karin Hildebrandt, "Historischer Exkurs zur Frauenpolitik der SED," in Bergit Bütow and Heidi Stecker, eds., *EigenArtige Ostfrauen. Frauenemanzipation in der DDR und den neuen Bundesländern* (Bielefeld, 1994), 12–31.
22. Herta Kuhrig and Wulfram Speigner, *Wie emanzipiert sind die Frauen in der DDR? Beruf-Bildung-Familie* (Cologne, 1979), 22.
23. Silke Bothfeld, Ute Klammer, Christina Klenner, Simone Leiber, Anke Thiel, and Astrid Ziegler, *WSI FrauenDatenReport* (Berlin, 2005), 116–117.
24. Gunnar Winkler, ed., *Frauenreport '90* (Berlin, 1990), 79.
25. Bundesministerium für Frauen und Jugend, *Frauen im mittleren Alter. Lebenslagen der Geburtskohorten von 1935 bis 1950 in den alten und neuen Bundesländern* (Stuttgart, 1993), 103.
26. Bothfeld et al., *FrauenDatenReport,* 174f.
27. Barbara Einhorn, *Cinderella goes to Market: Citizenship, Gender and Women's Movements in East Central Europe* (London, 1993), 6.
28. Anita Grandke, "Festigung der Gleichberechtigung und Förderung bewusster Elternschaft," in *Neue Justiz,* 314 (1972), no. 11, 220.
29. Gislinde Schwarz and Christine Zenner, eds., *Wir wollen mehr als ein 'Vaterland'* (Reinbek, 1990), 18.
30. Cordula Kahlau, *Aufbruch! Frauenbewegung in der DDR. Dokumentation* (Munich, 1990), 28–30.
31. Eva Schäfer, "Die fröhliche Revolution der Frauen. Frauenbewegung in Ost und West," and Irene Dölling, "Frauenforschung mit Fragezeichen? Perspektiven einer feministischen Wissenschaft," in *Wir wollen mehr als ein 'Vaterland',* 17–55.

32. Dölling, "Frauenforschung," 47.
33. Hildegard M. Nickel, "Zur Lage der Frauen in der früheren DDR," in *Bezahlen die Frauen die Wiedervereinigung?*, 147–156; Hanna Behrend, "Frauenemanzipation made in GDR," in *EigenArtige Ostfrauen*, 32–49.
34. Annette Simon, "Vor den Vätern sterben die Söhne? Die Achtundsechziger der DDR," in idem and Jan Faktor, eds., *Fremd im eigenen Land?* (Gießen, 2000), 7–25.
35. Anette Simon, *'Bleiben will ich, wo ich nie gewesen'. Versuch über ostdeutsche Identitäten* (Gießen, 2009), 73.
36. Rita Casale, "Die Vierzigjährigen entdecken den Feminismus. Anmerkungen zur Epistemologisierung politischer Theorien," *Feministische Studien*, 26 (2008), 197–207; Gudrun- Axeli Knapp, "Give Sex, Gender and Sexuality More of a Society. Zur Standortbestimmung feministischer Theorie," ibid., 208–219.
37. Judith Butler, *Gender Trouble: Feminism and the Subversion of Identity* (New York, 1990).
38. Eveline Kilian, "Ein folgenreicher Paradigmenwechsel: 20 Jahre Judith Butler," in Freiburger GeschlechterStudien, ed., *Feminisms Revisited* (Freiburg, 2010), 95–108.
39. Rita Casale, Ute Gerhard and Ulla Wischermann, eds., *Feministische Studien—Neuer Feminismus?* (Stuttgart, 2008).
40. Kuratorium für einen demokratisch verfassten Bund Deutscher Länder, *Vom Grundgesetz zur Deutschen Verfassung. Verfassungsentwurf und Denkschrift* (Berlin, 1991), 12f.; Bernd Guggenberger, Ulrich K. Preuß, and Wolfgang Ullmann, eds., *Eine Verfassung für Deutschland. Manifest, Text, Plädoyer* (Munich, 1991).
41. Special issue of Feministische Studien, *Frauen für eine neue Verfassung* (Weinheim, 1991).
42. Bundestags-Drucksache, *Bericht der Bundesregierung über die Situation der Frauen in Beruf, Familie und Gesellschaft* (Bonn, 1966); Ute Gerhard, "Frauenleitbilder und Etappen bundesrepublikanischer Frauenpolitik," in Hg., Mechthild Veil, Karin Prinz, and Ute Gerhard, eds., *Am modernen Frauenleben vorbei. Verliererinnen und Gewinnerinnen der Rentenreform 1992* (Berlin, 1992), 17–41.
43. Isolde Ludwig, Vanessa Schlevogt, Ute Klammer, and Ute Gerhard, *Managerinnen des Alltags. Strategien erwerbstätiger Mütter in Ost- und Westdeutschland* (Berlin, 2002).
44. Bundesministerium für Familie, Senioren, Frauen und Jugend, *Siebter Familienbericht. Familien zwischen Flexibilität und Verlässlichkeit. Perspektiven für eine lebenslaufbezogene Familienpolitik* (Berlin, 2006), Deutscher Bundestag Drucksache 16/1360.
45. For details on the changing patterns of European life choices see Anton Kuijsten, "Variation and Change in the Forms of Private Life in the 1980s," in Franz-Xaver Kaufmann, Anton Kuijsten, Hans-Joachim Schulze, and Klaus Peter Strohmeier, eds., *Family Life and Family Policies in Europe: Problems and Issues in Comparative Perspective* (Oxford, 2002), 19–68. With regard to any trends that could weaken the position of marriage as an institution—higher divorce rates, extramarital fertility, high numbers of single mothers—the GDR consistently has, together with Sweden, had the highest figures.
46. The working rate of mothers with children younger than three years old was 29 percent in the West as opposed to 44 percent in the East in 2004. But these numbers say little about the parameters of mothers' work. In East Germany, women with infants are generally more likely to be in full-time positions—every fourth woman is, in contrast to approximately every tenth in the West. Bothfeld et al., *FrauenDatenReport*, 174f.
47. Nonmarried partnerships with children in 2000: 23.3 percent in the West; 48.7 percent in the East (Engstler and Menning 2003, 46); the numbers of children born out of wedlock are similar: in 2003 these were about 55 percent in the East and 15 percent in the West. These lifestyles, in particular the high numbers of single mothers (84 percent) have become accepted and have grown in the West by 10 percent since 1996. Engstler and Menning, *Die Familie*, 46; Bothfeld et al., *FrauenDatenReport*, 48f.

48. According to a survey carried out by the Federal Statistical Office, in 2002 in the West there were spaces in day care facilities for only 3 percent of children under the age of three, while in East Germany there were spaces for 37 percent. The relatively good numbers of facilities for children between four and six are limited by the fact that in West Germany only 24 percent offer day-long care, while in the East 98 percent do. Christine Henry-Huthmacher, *Kinderbetreuung in Deutschland—Ein Überblick* (Sankt Augustin, 2005), 4.
49. *Frankfurter Rundschau,* 2/3 October 2010.
50. Thomas Ahbe and Rainer Gries, "Gesellschaftsgeschichte als Generationengeschichte," in Annegret Schüle and idem, eds., *Die DDR aus generationsgeschichtlicher Perspektive. Eine Inventur* (Leipzig, 2006), 475–571.
51. *Der Spiegel,* no. 4, 2007.
52. Interview in *Die Zeit,* 4 October 2010.
53. Bothfeld et.al., *FrauenDatenReport,* 89–93.
54. Jutta Allmendinger, Kathrin Leuze, and Jonna M. Blanck, "50 Jahre Geschlechtergerechtigkeit und Arbeitsmarkt," *Aus Politik und Zeitgeschichte,* no. 24–25, 2008, 18–25.
55. Claudia Gather, Birgit Geissler, and Maria S. Rerrich, eds., *Weltmarkt Privathaushalt. Bezahlte Hausarbeit im globalen Wandel* (Münster, 2002).
56. Thea Dorn, *Die neue F-Klasse. Wie die Zukunft von Frauen gemacht wird* (Munich, 2006).
57. Solveig Bergman, "Der neue Feminismus in den nordischen Ländern: Eine Herausforderung für den Staatsfeminismus," *Feministische Studien* 26 (2008), 187–196; Alek Ommert, "'Feminists We're Calling You. Please Report to the Front Desk….' Ladyfeste als Queer-feministische Praxis," ibid., 230–238.
58. Anette Baldauf and Katharina Weingartner, *Lips, Tits, Hits, Power? Popkultur und Feminismus* (Vienna, 1998); Meredith Haaf, Susanne Klingner, and Barbara Streidl, *Wir Alpha-Mädchen. Warum Feminismus das Leben schöner macht* (Hamburg, 2008).
59. Amrita Basu, ed., *Women's Movements in Global Perspective: The Challenges of Local Feminism* (Oxford, 1995); Rebecca Cook, *Human Rights of Women: National and International Perspectives* (Philadelphia, 1994).
60. Sonja Eismann, ed., *Hot Topic. Popfeminismus heute* (Mainz, 2008), 12.
61. R. Claire Snyder, "What is Third Wave Feminism? A New Directions Essay," *SIGNS* 34 (2008), 175–196.
62. Ute Gerhard, "Daughters of the Women's Movement: Generation Conflict and Social Change," in Carmen Leccardi and Elisabetta Ruspini, eds., *A New Youth? Young People, Generations and Family Life* (Aldershot, 2006), 187–200.
63. Hannah Arendt, *Von der Menschlichkeit in finsteren Zeiten* (Munich, 1996), 7.

Chapter Eight

Women's Movements in East Germany

Are We in Europe Yet?

Ingrid Miethe

Twenty years after reunification, we don't hear much about the women's movement in East Germany. The bitter disputes that dominated the period after 1989 seem to be history. Does that mean there are no differences anymore? Have conditions converged to the point that unified German sisterhood is a reality? Or has the East German side simply accepted that it "lost," and learned to keep quiet about its "deviation" from the generally established West German norm? The answer, as I will show in this chapter, is somewhere in between. The dominance of the West German side in a merger process as one-sided as German unification can hardly be denied. At the same time, however, we can show that other developments, such as the unification of Europe and the advent of a new generation, fueled contrary tendencies, and that the process varied from one region to another. This chapter will first sketch the development of the independent women's movement in the GDR before 1989, since a knowledge of its autonomous roots is necessary to understand why it was so difficult for women in Eastern and Western Germany to converge after 1989. Next, I will outline four different phases in the changing relations between the East and West German women's movements.

The Independent Women's Movement During Unification

In contrast to other Eastern European countries, there were informal women's groups in the German Democratic Republic that considered themselves part of an independent women's movement, i.e., one separate from

Notes for this chapter begin on page 168.

state-sanctioned organizations, at least since the beginning of the 1980s.[1] The question whether the term "women's movement" is appropriate for the GDR in the period before 1989 remains subject to debate in view of the low number of women who were active and the lack of publicity in the Western democratic sense, but more important than these issues is the fact that the movement defined itself as such. Moreover, this definition is justified by a degree of networking and semipublic communication among women that was considerable by socialist standards.

Because in state socialism it was difficult to find spaces in which the government did not claim access, the term "independent women's movement" signifies the attempt to create such a space in the first place. The state-organized women's association called Democratic Women's League of Germany (DFD), which had some 1.4 million members, claimed exclusive status as the official women's organization in the GDR. The DFD remained almost completely isolated from new and critical discussions, and when the independent women's movement developed in the 1980s, the DFD was used and played off against the new informal women's groups by the SED government.[2]

By organizing largely under the roof of the Protestant Church, the independent women's groups took advantage of the only form of publicity found outside the sphere of state institutions. The "Women for Peace" groups, founded in 1982, were the first major mobilizations of women that attained a certain public visibility. These groups formed in response to a government plan to include women in compulsory military service. The petition against the new draft law is said to have been signed by some 200 women,[3] an extremely high number by East German standards.

The potential numbers of the women's groups in the 1980s, many of which existed only ad hoc, can only be roughly estimated. Although only seven women's groups are documented in the files of the State Security service,[4] Samira Kenawi has identified some 100 women's groups.[5] The national networking meetings were attended by 60 to 300 women.[6]

The existence of such groups was a condition for the mobilization of women that occurred in autumn of 1989.[7] 1989 was the year in which the socialist state system finally collapsed with the opening of the border to West Germany in November. When a Round Table was organized among government and dissident groups as an interim quasi-governmental body, the Independent Women's Association (UFV) was formed in order to take part in it and to try to influence the formation of a postsocialist society and the impending German unification. The UFV united existing and newly created women's initiatives and individuals from various social spheres. In this transitional period preceding the first postsocialist elections of March 1990, the Independent Women's Association was the only nationally known women's political organization.[8]

The issues raised by the independent women's movement in the GDR were determined by the specific situation in that country. East German women addressed issues that were ignored and stigmatized by the state, such as women and peace, anti-militaristic child rearing and nonideologized child care, feminism, lesbianism, domestic violence, etc. Many of the demands that motivated a feminist mobilization in West Germany, such as the demand for a liberalization of abortion policy, were fulfilled in the GDR by state policy. While abortion was criminal in West Germany, for example, first-trimester abortion had been legal in the GDR since 1972. Abortion, like contraception, was also financed by public health insurance. Thus it is no surprise that the East German feminist civil rights movement in the fall of 1989 did not share the West German women's movement's vital concern with paragraph 218, the abortion law.[9] Furthermore, women's employment and the compatibility of motherhood and career were givens in feminist discourse in East Germany: most women in the GDR were mothers, and continued to work after bearing children. East German women and mothers took paid employment for granted. At the time the GDR was dissolved, 78.1 percent of all women were employed.[10] The combination of work and motherhood was made possible in the GDR by a nearly universal provision of child-care facilities and by supportive social policies.[11] Although conventional role divisions existed in the GDR as well as in the West, women earned less than men, and the structure of the working world was gendered,[12] the experience of employment and the resulting financial independence from men had a lasting influence on the attitudes of East German women.

In Western Germany on the other hand, middle-class women in particular, in spite of all feminist criticism, often lived under the classic male-breadwinner model. East German women, who founded their identities solidly on the two pillars of motherhood and employment, tended to view that model with rejection and irritation.[13]

Thus German unification brought together women who had been socialized in very different systems, and who had consequently developed different notions of feminism and of women's role in society. Although the East German system largely adapted to West German conditions (which mainly involved dismantling rights that women had taken for granted) within a very short time, and hence the realities of women's lives in East and West became more similar, the differences did not disappear automatically. Thus in spite of the significantly less favorable labor market in the East, East German women continue to have higher employment rates than West German women. According to a study of demographic developments by the Max Planck Institute in Rostock, 50 percent of East German mothers between the ages of eighteen and forty-five were employed full-time in 2007, compared with 18 percent of the corresponding West German group. Feminist political positions also continue to differ from those in West Germany, although they are now more differentiated within Eastern Germany.[14]

Different experiences of socialization in the time before 1989 were not the only factor that contributed to the continuing alienation of East and West: East German and West German women's lives were also different after 1989. The process of German unification was not egalitarian. Rather, it demanded a one-sided adaptation of the East to Western conditions, and was characterized by many mechanisms of dominance. East German women did not necessarily see West German feminists as critical of the West German system. Often enough Western feminists were regarded as representatives of the dominant order, which was another source of conflict.[15]

Looking back to the development after 1989, we can discern four different phases in the development of the relationship between Eastern and Western German women's movements since 1989, each characterized by different treatment of East-West issues at the individual, academic, and public levels. In keeping with the emphasis of my own research, I will focus closely on the academic sphere. Because women's movements are now strongly concentrated in this institutionalized framework, the academic focus represents a certain current within these movements.[16] Since East-West issues were primarily in the public spotlight during the time immediately after 1989, the academic discourse cannot always be separated from the debates from and about East and West that have taken place in the media and on the political stage. A certain overlap of the public and academic levels in the descriptions of the individual phases that follow is therefore unavoidable, and symptomatic of the process itself.

First Phase: Expectations of Equality Give Way to Experiences of Difference

The first phase, which was characterized by a relatively rapid and open interaction between East and West Germany, lasted from late 1989 until about 1993. The expectations of the time were expressed by Willy Brandt's slogan: "What belongs together shall now grow together." This expectation was not only shared by a majority of the population in East and West Germany, but the sentiment was adopted with particular zeal by the women's movement. Was it not inevitable that women's solidarity would transcend the borders of political systems and add its sisterly support to the assumption of brotherly closeness between the two German states?

Expectations were great on both sides, and so were the disappointments, as the actual people encountered often did not live up to them. This is not surprising. One reason for the disappointment lay in the fact that, although the notion of a shared language suggested a common culture, the vast majority of the population on either side knew little about the other Germany. Moreover, people in East and West Germany grew up in countries that sported "a self-image which not only excluded the self-image of the other, but also desperately required the enemy concept of the other in order to stabilize and support its own ideology."[17] The first East-West women's conferences were held shortly after the GDR had ceased to exist, yet instead of celebrating nationwide sisterhood, the women attendees merely brought to light the significant differences between Eastern and Western feminist women, and their difficulties in understanding one another.

Catchwords about "strange" or "unequal" "sisters" or "stepsisters" circulated.[18] Women's East-West political conferences started out with efforts to reach understanding after all, and often ended—in spite of good intentions on both sides—more or less in an exchange of accusations about Western "know-it-alls" and Eastern "complainers." The expectations of equality thus turned to experiences of difference.

The positions presented in this chapter form a summary of the research results of various empirical studies.[19] However, it should not be forgotten that there are social groups in both the East German and the West German society who would not totally agree with the opinions presented in this paper. The opposite positions presented actually form a rather dominant and influential discourse, though, within the respective Eastern or Western society. The dispute between Eastern and Western feminists arose over issues such as the ones outlined below.

Motherhood

Eastern feminists, who were generally mothers, felt that the compatibility of career and family was a central issue. But for West German feminists who generally had no children and in many cases had consciously chosen not to have any in order to pursue a professional career, it was not an important issue.

Men

While many Eastern feminists often advocated cooperating with men to advance feminist interests, Western feminists regarded the idea with extreme skepticism or even disapproval.

Employment

East German women valued paid labor and financial independence from their husbands, because it offered as an essential, if not the most important, prerequisite for their own emancipation, and kept a focus on the notion throughout the process of transformation. In contrast, the West German feminist movement for a long time marginalized the question.

Abortion Rights

To Western feminists the right to abortion formed one of the central issues that in West Germany helped initiate the women's movement and provided an identification with a cause, while in the GDR and most other former socialist countries, the right to abortion had long been a fact and therefore no longer an issue for feminist discussions.

The State

Whereas Eastern feminists held the opinion that the state had a responsibility to address women's issues, Western feminists tended to take the position that women's issues needed to be addressed from the grassroots level, some of them even refusing to accept state funding.

Theory

Western feminists attached crucial importance to symbolic power, such as that of gendered language, and to the formulation of feminist theory. For Eastern feminists, such discussions carried negative connotations, and were considered no better than ideology and dogmatism.

Private-Public Distinction

Western feminism focused on the definition of the private sphere as a place of violence and moved it to the political stage. In contrast, women in socialist societies cherished the private sphere as protection from public, i.e., the state's, authority (even though violence at home was known there, too), since a Western democratic public had not existed in their environment. Western feminist concepts that were normally based on an interaction between a private and a public sphere, which are indicative of Western democratic societies, therefore were repeatedly rejected as difficult to adopt by Eastern European feminists.

Dominance

For a long time, Western feminists understood their society as patriarchal and assumed that the key dividing line was that between men and women. Eastern feminists on the other hand felt that the dominance of West over East was often more crucial than—or at least equivalent to—the dominance of one sex by the other. Thus Western women, much to their disappointment, were not primarily seen as women, but as representatives of dominant West German society.

This last issue in particular overshadowed many East-West debates, and continued to do so in the following years.[20] East German women's repeated attempts to address the unequal distribution of power between East and West were only reluctantly acknowledged by West German women, if at all. Since at the time there were hardly any scholarly studies available, the discussions in this phase took place on a very personal level, based on subjective experiences and biographies.[21]

Second Phase: The Research Boom and "Western" Dominance

The principal characteristic of the second phase was an enormous boom in research on topics concerning East Germany.[22] Although this effort began immediately after 1989, its results were not outwardly visible until about 1994/95, due to the time required to conduct research and publish results. New empirical studies prompted a certain tendency toward scholarly objectivity in the discussions, since the participants were now able to refer to concrete findings rather than only to personal opinions and states of mind.

However, this phase also saw an increasing displacement of East German academics, both male and female.[23] East German researchers were forced out of higher education en masse from 1992 on. At universities in East Berlin, for example, 60 percent of all East German academic staff had been replaced by West Germans by the end of 1992. This replacement of the elite took place in very different ways in the various disciplines and departments, and was without a doubt necessary to some extent in order to remove old SED cadres. Indeed, the process was initially welcomed by many East Germans for this reason.[24]

It soon became apparent, however, that the displacement was not being used to integrate politically unobjectionable East Germans into the new elite, but rather—especially in the social sciences—to establish an exclusive West German dominance. East German men were subjected to this process of displacement just as East German women were. As a result, it is not surprising that Eastern women academics were initially reluctant to perceive this process as having a gendered structure. Nor is it surprising that the few West German women involved were viewed by East Germans as acting in much the same way as their male colleagues.[25]

The result of this process of displacement is apparent in a representative study on the elite replacement in Germany, which found that the proportion of East Germans among the academic elite in united Germany had fallen to 7 percent by 1995.[26] Compared with the proportions of the East and West German populations, this means that East Germans have one-third the chance of advancing to elite academic positions of West Germans.[27] Moreover, this structural problem is always linked with the question of who has authority to define the terms of discourse in a united Germany: this power increasingly shifted away from Easterners during this time period.

Although both sides were still engaged in the discourse, "the East" often acted from a defensive position, not least because Western concepts and ideas were applied to the East with relatively little thought. "The West" increasingly became the unquestioned norm; "the East" became the deviation from the norm, and required interpretation. Thus a so-called "Culture of Dominance" developed in Germany between the Eastern and the Western part of the country through the inequality in the media.[28] The media discourse can be seen as contributing nothing to an objective comparison of Eastern and Western experiences. Rather, with a "highly selective use of facts, [it] serves to reinforce West German identities."[29]

This culture of dominance is also evident in the one-sided orientation of research. Thus, German reunification was not at all taken as an opportunity to examine and question both Western *and* Eastern premises and assumptions, much less their interdependencies.[30] Rather, the object of new research was simply "the East."

The problem of West German dominance in the discourses between East and West German women was, however, not reduced to academia. In East Germany, women's projects abounded in the period of the early to the mid 1990s, becoming one of the most popular types of project.[31] The women's movement, like any popular movement, is difficult to put into numbers. Rucht and his group estimate that the number of women's projects increased from about 28 groups in 1989 to some 123 groups in 1993 in the four East German cities that they investigated (Berlin, Leipzig, Halle, and Dresden).[32] The largest feminist protagonist, the UFV, founded in 1989, lost its central role in the movement and became just one project of many.[33] The women's initiatives that were formed from the early 1990s on took on topics that were central to the West German debate, for example violence against women, self-help initiatives, health, child rearing, and women's history as well as feminism. Despite discussing similar topics, the East German projects always also addressed specifics. For example, the question of the compatibility of having a family and working or the various options for re-entering working life have until today taken more space than more general topics in the discussion among East German women, and women's projects themselves often contain opportunities for paid work.

Women's initiatives and projects obtained a significant proportion of their resources through job creation measures in Eastern Germany, which were funded by the government as a means to combat the rapidly rising unemployment following the introduction of the market economy. The fact that they formed a segment of the job market therefore characterizes the structures of the women's projects in Eastern Germany to a much greater extent than in Western Germany. Many women earned their living participating in such projects as long as the public funds were available (until about 1994). At the same time many women's institutes and projects in Western Germany were closed, creating a situation of competition for scarce resources, which, understandably, did not further a closer association between Eastern and Western feminists.[34]

In summary, this phase was marked by a new tendency toward objectivity in dialogue between East and West thanks to the ability to draw on empirical studies. At the same time the dominance of the West German side was institutionalized, and so made manifest. The encompassing and diverse women's projects that developed in this period led on the one hand to feminist concerns being discussed more widely in public and to a stronger institutionalization of the East German women's movement. On the other hand, the competition between women's projects in the East and in the West grew since public means continued to shrink.

Third Phase: Mutual Withdrawal and Partial Integration

The third phase, characterized by stagnating public and academic interest in East-West issues due to "globalization," can be dated between 1997 and 2002. This silence was to some extent predictable, since—in the academic context, for example, and primarily in the humanities and social sciences—East German women had been reduced to such small numbers that many conferences and seminars were overwhelmingly Western, and East German objections were quite unlikely.

In contrast, the range of feminist projects grew comparatively more diverse. On the one hand there were many projects that had been initiated by West German women; on the other hand a number of East German projects had been established independently, too. Increasingly, women's initiatives, projects, and publications avoided the simple label of "Western" or "Eastern," since their personnel and range of concerns included both. This applies most of all to East Berlin, where the mixture was the strongest due to the proximity to West Berlin. Most often, however, women from the Western side of the city worked in women's projects of women's houses in East Berlin. Only in exceptional cases was there an opposite movement of East German women to the Western side.[35] Especially within Berlin, then an increasing process of integration may be determined. In practice, though, that meant an adjustment of the East to West German conditions—which is nothing unusual since today daily life in East Germany is determined by West German ways. A debate about the movement's own East German past and an independent Eastern female identity have become exceptions to the rule.

When looking at the structure of the projects that have been established in this period in all of Germany, it becomes clear that the differences between the East and the West were gradually diluted with respect to the quantitative existence of women's projects. Moreover, one can determine a north-south divide in East as well as in West Germany in the sense that women's projects are scarcer in the conservative, family-oriented Länder where the Christian Democratic Party is governing than in the Länder ruled by the Social Democrats. The farther south we go, the fewer women's projects we find. The Eastern states conform to this pattern as well.[36] The figures support the statement that Eastern Germans are neither more nor less feminist than Western Germans. But, since East Germany constitutes only 20 percent of the total population of unified Germany, the East German projects are always in the minority compared with West German projects. This means that East German women will always be a minority in national German discussions, both quantitatively and structurally.

At the same time, however, it was hard to overlook the fact that the East-West discourse itself had reached an impasse. The arguments and positions were clear, and no real progress toward reconciliation had been made. Equally hard to overlook was a certain ritualization of the victim's role on the Eastern side.

Although it had been absolutely necessary for Easterners in the first phase of the encounter with the West to refer to their own life histories and disappointments—simply in order to understand the extent of their differences—they could have assumed some awareness of this situation by the mid 1990s at the latest. East Germans' continuing reference to their biographical involvement became increasingly unproductive. In this situation Western women had almost no chance of getting it right in the eyes of East German women: if they tried to address East German interests, they were accused of interference and exercising dominance; if they withdrew, they were accused of ignoring East German problems. The discourse between Eastern and Western women had gradually come to a dead end. It was deadlocked, and yielded few new insights. Women in East and West became increasingly aware that instead of homogeneity, the common goal must be a conscious and productive way of dealing with their differences. However, both sides were at a loss in imagining how that might be achieved. As a result, both sides increasingly withdrew inward.

Of course there continued to be working contacts and personal friendships across East and West, and these may even have grown in numbers, but they were also characterized by a certain caution. The potential faux pas were well known and carefully sidestepped. However, women also avoided addressing differences that arose. Even this silence, though, was "unequally distributed," as Esther Hoffmann pointed out.[37] In the West, it did "not remotely reach the existential format" that it did in the East.

Such a retreat can be prerequisite for a very productive process. However, this requires that this phase serves to reassure one's own attitudes in order to renew the process of approaching a discourse with the other side on the basis of the existing distribution of power. If the silence endures and the East-West issue is simply filed away, this will mean, especially for the subordinate East German side, that their concerns will continue to be excluded from the unified German agenda for discussions, while the West German side can move on to determine their own agenda.

Sabine Hark's recent book, which claims to constitute a "history of discourse of feminism," confirms the fear of exclusion mentioned above.[38] In it, she points out that German feminist theory—which automatically implies *West German* feminist theory—has after 1989 to a large extent been influenced by Judith Butler's book "Gender Trouble." There is no mention of any influence of the East-West dialogue of attitudes and discourse, nor the East German–West German or the Eastern European–Western European ones. The intercultural discourse (e.g., between black women and white women) also does not feature in Hark's account as having had any major impact on German feminist theory. Her book therefore contributes mainly to canonizing a rather biased, although probably still dominant, West German feminist theoretical discourse that ignores its own hegemony over groups that are discriminated against. Turning away from the East German–West German confrontations slowly made room for viewing the wider European perspective, an aspect which has long been neglected in the German discourse.

Fourth Phase: Change in the West and Increasing Convergence

As the new millennium began, we can see that the old West Germany began to change increasingly, creating fertile ground for a gradual convergence. This is because the unified Germany's processes of transformation had now reached the old West Germany itself— although in a slower and less massive form—and are changing the status quo there as well. Furthermore, two other complex processes are also influential with regard to women's political issues. They can be summed up as the unification of Europe and the advent of the next generation.

The integration of Europe has brought with it a number of changes with regard to women's political issues. First, the Scandinavian countries in particular, which probably have the most advanced equal-opportunity policies in Europe, have weighed in. The regression of women's social standards that was feared by many Scandinavian feminists has not occurred to date. Instead, approaches such as gender mainstreaming have been adopted in European politics.[39] According to Silke Roth, this approach comes much closer to the positions of East German women's movements, which are less skeptical of state regulation in political issues affecting women and have traditionally taken stronger positions on gender integration than many Western feminists.[40] Thus the gender mainstreaming approach has strengthened East German feminists' positions.

The introduction of state benefits for parents, which is also based on a Scandinavian model, is a parallel development. It is not mentioned today in the public discussion of this measure that a very similar policy existed in the GDR, although the benefit there was paid only to mothers, not to fathers. But East German women remember it very well, and thus see the new development as—however belatedly—confirming and amplifying their own experience.

Another such development is the current increased priority put on providing child care in West Germany. The broader provision is connected with an ideological reinterpretation of child care: it is now represented as an important "educational opportunity" for young children, and not merely as "infant care." This constitutes a reframing for West Germany, where kindergarten had always had a more-or-less shabby reputation, and had been assumed to be inferior to child care at home. And last, but not least, more importance is given to discussions of the compatibility of motherhood and career than was just a few years ago. Employment was the most important issue for East German women. Only if I am financially independent from men—which in general I can only be if I am employed, according to the East German position—am I free to think about feminism.

At the same time, with the progressive eastward enlargement of the EU, the membership now encompasses other formerly socialist countries, including Hungary, Poland, and the Czech Republic. Although the process of their integration in the EU is hierarchically structured, like the unification of East and West Germany, it nonetheless alleviates the minority position of East German women.[41] East German feminists and those in Eastern European countries share a common experiential background that has shaped their political positions on women's issues. Thus in the broader European context, East German feminists are not as strongly relegated to a minority position as in Germany alone.

From a European point of view, it becomes apparent that many positions that were termed "East German" in the East-West discussion, such as the desirability of the compatibility of family and career or the responsibility of the state to address women's issues for example, are not specifically "Eastern" at all, but are held in other Western European countries as well, such as Sweden.[42] At the same time, many of the positions that had previously inflamed the debate between Eastern and Western German women appear on the European scale as merely West *German* characteristics, and not typical of "Western" feminism as a whole.

One example of the changing feminist values in a European context is the compatibility of family and career. In spite of an undeniably high rate of unemployment among East German women, East-West comparisons show again and again that East German women continue to place a high value on their working life.[43] Yet the ability to pursue an occupation is tied to the availability of child care, which is neither sufficiently provided in West Germany nor compatible with the West German notion of motherhood. This discrepancy between Eastern and Western women in the past has been repeatedly discussed as an East-West German difference. Yet in the European context we see that the East German concept of combining motherhood and a career, supported by publicly organized child care, is not at all a uniquely East German position, but also favored by women elsewhere in Western Europe, including in France[44] and the Scandinavian countries.[45]

Thus the broadening of narrow East and West German horizons in the European context gradually dissolves unproductive dichotomies and bolsters the position of East German women by reducing West German dominance. This makes it more likely that the two sides will be able to resume the discourse on a more equal footing.

The arrival of a new generation is probably the strongest influence in the current development of the East German women's movements. Since 1989, another age cohort of East Germans has grown up. This means a new generation of East German feminist academics has taken its place, relatively unobtrusively at first, a generation which had undergone most or all of its academic socialization in a united Germany. Women of this generation, for whom the end of the GDR was an opportunity, are perfectly familiar with the Western (and often international) discourse and do not consider themselves outsiders like their older East German colleagues do.[46]

Hence these younger women are less susceptible to assumptions of a more "advanced West," and less biographically vulnerable. This generation, quite familiar with Western standards, is at the same time able to look back on East German socialization and experience, and so contributes not only a new self-confidence, but also a new vantage point to the debate. Indeed, the dichotomy of "East" and "West" is gradually dissolving, not least due to the coming of age of a generation, socialized in a united Germany, which remembers East or West Germany only as part of their childhood, and who sometimes have difficulty identifying themselves with one or the other.[47] As women's studies have shown, the deconstruction of categories can pave the way for new discussions and perspectives that can carry the dialogue forward.

A new generation of women is taking its place in the West as well, women who no longer share the combative impetus of their grandmothers and mothers in the women's movement. Their socialization was quite different from that of earlier genrations, and they take for granted the access to areas that their predecessors had to fight for. Thus the differences that can be identified between women in East and West in attitudes toward the women's movement or feminist positions are much smaller in this generation. Differences on political and feminist issues are often felt to be much stronger between the generations than between East and West.

Conclusion

In a sense, it was simply hard luck for the East German women's movement that it was confronted with West Germany's particular feminism and feminists. Because the old West German policy on women was particularly conservative, it is little wonder that forms of feminism developed there that were especially radical in their arguments. If in 1990 East Germany had had to unify with France or one of the Scandinavian countries, for example, there would probably have been fewer points of friction with regard to fundamental positions on women's political issues and on feminism. West German positions were to a high degree West *German*, and not typical of for Western feminism as a whole.

The discussion of what feminism is in the first place, from a global perspective, has also been neglected for too long. Today such a debate can include East German and Eastern European positions only from a historic perspective, since the developments after 1989 have not—in East Germany at least—allowed an independent feminist discourse to develop. In the current discourse, East German development is summarily dealt with under the rubric "the West and the rest."[48]

Louise Otto-Peters, a protagonist of the bourgeois women's movement in nineteenth-century Germany, once said, "The history of every age, and of our age in particular, has taught us that those who forget to think of their rights are themselves forgotten."[49] Accordingly, it will remain the responsibility of East German women in the current discourse to point out specifically Eastern positions and experiences where they seem appropriate. The new generation of women in East Germany has a right at least to know its own roots. Whether these women cultivate them, or whether they find other foundations stronger today, is for them to decide. They have a right to their own history—but no duty to continue it.

Notes

1. Samira Kenawi, *Frauengruppen in der DDR der 80er Jahre. Eine Dokumentation* (Berlin, 1995).
2. Anne Hampele, "'Arbeite mit, plane mit, regiere mit'—Zur politischen Partizipation von Frauen in der DDR," in Gisela Helwig and Hildegard Maria Nickel, eds., *Frauen in Deutschland 1945–1992* (Bonn, 1993), 281–320.
3. Irana Kukutz, "Die Bewegung 'Frauen für den Frieden' als Teil der unabhängigen Friedensbewegung der DDR," in Deutscher Bundestag, ed., *Materialien zur Enquete-Kommission "Aufarbeitung von Geschichte und Folgen der SED-Diktatur in Deutschland,"* (Frankfurt, 1995), 1285–1408.
4. The State Security service only counted the Women for Peace groups, since feminist groups per se were not classified as antagonistic to the socialist state.
5. Kenawi, *Frauengruppen.*
6. Anne Hampele, "Der Unabhängige Frauenverband. Organisationslaufbahn eines frauenpolitischen Experiments im deutsch-deutschen Vereinigungsprozeß (Fallstudie)," Dissertation (Berlin, 1995), 423.
7. Myra Marx Ferree, "'The Time of Chaos was the Best': Feminist Mobilization and Demobilization in East Germany," *Gender and Society* 8 (1994), 601f.
8. Anne Hampele-Ulrich, "Der Unabhängige Frauenverband. Ein frauenpolitisches Experiment im deutschen Vereinigungsprozess," *Berliner Debatte Initial,* 2000.
9. Ferree, "Feminist Mobilization."
10. Hildegard Marie Nickel, "'Mitgestalterinnen des Sozialismus'—Frauenarbeit in der DDR," in *Frauen in Deutschland 1945–1992,* 233–256.
11. Myra Marx Ferree, "The Rise and Fall of 'Mommy Politics': Feminism and Unification in (East) Germany," *Feminist Studies* 19 (1993), 89–115.
12. Nickel, "Mitgestalterinnen des Sozialismus," 233–256.
13. Myra Marx Ferree, "Was heißt Feminismus? Frauenfragen, Frauenbewegungen und feministische Identität von Frauen in den neuen Bundesländern," in Christiane Lemke,

Virginia Penrose, and Ute Ruppert, eds., *Frauenbewegung und Frauenpolitik in Osteuropa* (Frankfurt, 1996), 115.

14. Katja M. Guenther, *Making their Place: Feminism after Socialism in Eastern Germany* (Stanford, 2010).
15. Ingrid Miethe, "Women's Movements in Unified Germany: Experiences and Expectations of East German Women," in *Feminist Movements in a Globalization World: German and American Perspectives*, ed. Silke Roth and Sara Lennox (Washington, 2002), 43–59; idem, "Dominanz und Differenz. Verständigungsprozess zwischen feministischen Akteurinnen aus Ost- und Westdeutschland," in Eva Schäfer, Ina Dietzsch, Petra Drauschke, Iris Peinl, and Virginia Penrose, eds., *Irritation Ostdeutschland. Geschlechterverhältnisse in Deutschland seit der Wende* (Münster, 2005).
16. Sabine Hark, *Dissidente Partizipation. Eine Diskursgeschichte des Feminismus* (Frankfurt, 2005).
17. Christine Kulke, Heidi Kopp-Degethoff, and Ulrike Ramming, eds., *Wider das schlichte Vergessen. Der deutsch-deutsche Einigungsprozess. Frauen im Dialog* (Berlin, 1992), 8.
18. Katrin Rohnstock, ed., *Stiefschwestern. Was Ost-Frauen und West-Frauen voneinander denken* (Frankfurt, 1994); Dorothy Rosenberg, "Stepsisters. On the Difficulties of German-German Feminist Cooperation," in Fred Casmir, ed., *Communication in Eastern Europe. The Role of History, Culture and Media in Contemporary Conflicts* (Mahwah, 1995), 81–109.
19. Ulrike Helwerth and Gislinde Schwarz, *Von Muttis und Emanzen. Feministinnen in Ost- und Westdeutschland* (Frankfurt, 1995); Myra Marx Ferree, "Patriarchies and Feminisms: The Two Women's Movements of Post-unification Germany," *Social Politics* 2 (1995), 10–24; Virginia Penrose, *Orientierungsmuster des Karriereverhaltens deutscher Politikerinnen. Ein Ost-West-Vergleich* (Bielefeld, 1993); Christina Schenk and Christiane Schindler, "Frauenbewegung in Ostdeutschland—Innenansichten," in Eva Maleck-Lewy and Virginia Penrose, eds., *Gefährtinnen der Macht. Politische Partizipation von Frauen im vereinigten Deutschland—eine Zwischenbilanz* (Berlin, 1995), 183–203; Ingrid Miethe, *Frauen in der DDR-Opposition: Lebens- und kollektivgeschichtliche Verläufe in einer Frauenfriedensgruppe* (Opladen, 1999); idem, "From the 'Mother of Revolution' to 'Father of Unification'—Concepts of Politics among Women Activists Following German Unification," *Social Politics* 6 (1999), 1–22; Peggy Watson, "Politics, Policy and Identity: EU Eastern Enlargement and East-West Differences," *Journal of European Policy* 7 (2000), 369–384; Anne Hampele-Ulrich and Ingrid Miethe, "Preference for Informal Democracy—The East(ern) German case," in Helena Flam, ed., *Pink, Purple, Green. Women's Religious, Environmental and Gay/ Lesbian Movements in Central Europe Today* (Boulder, 2001), 23–32.
20. Miethe, "Women's Movements" and "Dominanz und Differenz."
21. Ute Gerhard and Ingrid Miethe, "Debatten und Missverständnisse unter Feministinnen aus Ost- und Westdeutschland in der Nachwendezeit—ein nachholender Dialog," in Ingrid Miethe, Claudia Kajatin, and Jana Pohl, eds., *Geschlechterkonstruktionen in Ost und West. Biografische Perspektiven* (Münster, 2004), 325–344.
22. Hendrik Berth and Elmar Brähler, *Zehn Jahre Deutsche Einheit. Eine Bibliographie* (Berlin, 2000); Karin Aleksander, *Frauen und Geschlechtverhältnisse in der DDR und in den neuen Bundesländern. Bibliographie von DDR- und BRD-Publikationen ab 1989* (Berlin, 2005).
23. Helga Adler, "Gleichstellungspolitik. Ein nachgeordnetes Problem im Umstrukturierungsprozess ostdeutscher Hochschulen?" in Sabine Lang and Birgit Sauer, eds., *Wissenschaft als Arbeit—Arbeit als Wissenschaft* (Frankfurt, 1997), 67–74.

24 Konrad H. Jarausch, Matthias Middell and Anette Vogt, *Sozialistisches Experiment und Erneuerung in der Demokratie,. Die Humboldt-Universität zu Berlin 1945 – 2010* (Berlin, 2012).

25. Gisela Petruschka, "Ost- und Westwissenschaftlerinnen im kritischen Vergleich," *Utopie Kreativ* 43 (1994), 33f. Cf. Stefan Bollinger, Ulrich van der Heyden, and Mario Keßler,

eds., *Ausgrenzung oder Integration? Ostdeutsche Sozialwissenschaftler zwischen Isolierung und Selbstbehauptung* (Berlin, 2004).

26. Anneliese Bürklin, "Ost-West-Kontakte der eher (noch) seltenen Art. Feministische Denkweisen als Klammer und als Überlebenshilfe," *Beiträge zur feministischen Theorie und Praxis* 23 (2000), 67.
27. Miethe, "Women's Movements," 53.
28. Birgit Rommelspacher, *Dominanzkultur. Texte zu Fremdheit und Macht* (Berlin, 1995); Miethe, "Women's Movements."
29. Thomas Ahbe, *Die Ost-Diskurse als Strukturen der Nobilitierung und Marginalisierung von Wissen. Eine Diskursanalyse zur Konstruktion der Ostdeutschen in den Westdeutschen Medien-Diskursen 1989/90 und 1995* (Berlin, 2009), 110.
30. Braun (2000).
31. Dieter Rucht, Barbara Blattert, and Dieter Rink, *Soziale Bewegungen auf dem Weg zur Institutionalisierung? Zum Strukturwandel alternativer Gruppen in beiden Teilen Deutschlands* (Frankfurt, 1997), 84.
32. Ibid., 82.
33. Hampele, "Der Unabhängige Frauenverband."
34. Hampele-Ulrich and Miethe, "Preference for Informal Democracy," 29ff.
35. Ibid., 28.
36. Miethe, "Women's Movements," 48ff.; Guenther, *Making their Place.*
37. Esther Hoffmann, "'Wenn zwei das Gleiche lesen'. Eine Rezeptionsanalyse," in Ludwig-Uhland-Institut für Empirische Kulturwissenschaft, ed., *Spiegelbilder. Was Ost- und Westdeutsche übereinander erzählen* (Tübingen, 1995), 51.
38. Hark, *Dissidente Partizipation.*
39. Gender mainstreaming means the "(re)organization, improvement, development in all policies at all levels and at all stages by the actors normally involved in policy making" and "openly taking into account at the planning stage their possible effect on the respective situation of men and women." Commission of the European Union, 2000:5.
40. Silke Roth, "Sisterhood and Solidarity? Organizing for Gender Issues and Women's Equality in the European Union," Paper presented at the LSE Gender, Citizenship and Participation Conference, 23–24 March 2005.
41. Watson, "Politics, Policy and Identity."
42. Zenia Hellgren and Barbara Hobson, *Gender and Ethnic Minority Claims in Swedish and EU Frames: Sites of Multilevel Political Opportunities and Boundary Making* (New York, 2008).
43. Statistisches Bundesamt, ed., *Datenreport 2004. Zahlen und Fakten über die Bundesrepublik Deutschland* (Berlin, 2004), 503.
44. Beatrice Durand, "Geschlechterdenken und –politik im postfeministischen Frankreich," in Ingrid Miethe and Silke Roth, eds., *Europas Töchter. Traditionen, Erwartungen und Strategien von Frauenbewegungen in Europa* (Opladen, 2003), 101–118.
45. Solveig Bergmann, " Feminismus und Frauenpolitik in Finnland," in: *Europas Töchter,* 149–182.
46. Horst Strenger, "'Deshalb müssen wir uns fremd blieben.' Fremdheitserfahrungen ostdeutscher Wissenschaftler," in Herfried Winkler, ed., *Herausforderungen durch das Fremde* (Berlin, 1998).
47. Jana Simon, Frank Rothe, and Andrasch Wiethe, eds., *Das Buch der Unterschiede. Warum die Einheit keine ist* (Berlin, 2000).
48. Helma Lutz and Norbert Wenning, eds., *Unterschiedlich verschieden. Differenzen in der Erziehungswissenschaft* (Opladen, 2001), 20.
49. Louise Otto-Peters, "Adresse eines Mädchens," in Renate Möhrmann, ed., *Frauenemanzipation im deutschen Vormärz: Texte und Dokumente* (Stuttgart, 1978), 199–202.

Chapter Nine

Feminist Encounters

Germany, the EU, and Beyond

Myra Marx Ferree

While all the postunification reflections in this volume need contextualization in German history, European politics, and Western culture, the encounters among women and women's movements in and after unification demand an even wider framework, that of global feminist politics and gender change. Everywhere in the world—not only in Germany, Europe, or even that nebulous space, Western society—the status and consciousness of women has been undergoing transformation. Political interventions into gender relations by social movements, transnational advocacy networks, and states are ubiquitous. Both nation-states and supranational bodies have increasingly recognized women as individual citizens with legitimate aspirations to personal self-determination and their fair share of social decision-making power.[1]

There is thus no way to consider the position of women in more-or-less unified Germany today without examining the global context of feminist politics. Especially since the 1995 Fourth UN World Conference on Women in Beijing, one can speak of a transnational feminist network that encompasses grassroots movements, more formalized NGOs, and government agencies as well as individual elected representatives, academic researchers, and multi-issue activists. Gender has been actively "mainstreamed" by state policy at the urging of both the UN and EU.[2]

Notes for this chapter begin on page 178.

International Pressures

Much of the drive for achieving gender equality has thus shifted to the transnational level. Globally, feminists moved from outside positions in social movements to insider roles in both intergovernmental and nongovernmental organizations. Insider feminists brought both their expertise and networking power to bear to advance the project of gender mainstreaming and to lobby for specific measures advancing gender equality, a worldwide process that Alvarez called the "NGOization" of feminism.[3] The EU, as a new political entity just taking shape in this era, was particularly susceptible to the influence of women's organizing for two reasons. First, the EU sought democratic legitimacy for itself outside the national party systems of its members. The "proxy publics" of civil society networks—for which the European Women's Lobby is the model of early and effective mobilization—offered a nonelectoral mechanism for soliciting expert proposals and demonstrating popular support for what the European Commission would do.[4] Second, women's organizations and experts constructed quantitative and qualitative measures of gender equality on which the member states could compete for recognition and rewards. The EU had the power to press the states perceived as laggards, as West Germany had been, to achieve more, and the FRG could be made to feel that its own standing as a "leading state" in Europe was at stake in these well-publicized league tables and EU evaluations.[5]

In this context, the German commitment to gender equality was articulated in the 1992 reformulation of the nation's Basic Law, which no longer says merely that men and women have equal rights, but also that the state has an obligation to promote this equality through active effort. In addition, Angela Merkel's chancellorship carried significant symbolic value, putting an exclamation point on the dramatic increases (from under 10 percent to over 30 percent) of women in the Bundestag across all parties since the 1980s. There are gender equity efforts in academia, as universities seek to remedy an internationally low level of women in professorships, and some recent consideration of gender equality on corporate boards.[6] The reform of parental leave in 2006 was the most notable state shift, dismantling at least one key element of the institutionalized male-breadwinner family norm by making leaves shorter but better paid and reserving some of the time exclusively for fathers.[7]

Unification Effects

While gender relations in Germany thus shifted considerably over the past two decades, it is hard to attribute much of this change to the unification process, though there is also little reason to see the tensions and costs of unification as having been an obstacle. The real catalyst for change in gender policy and practice has come primarily from Germany's membership in the EU, which is more responsive to global gender norms than are its member states.[8] But as Ingrid Miethe notes, the GDR's gender policies were closer to the norms in the EU than to those of the FRG at unification, so this shift toward the EU standard makes gender politics one domain in which citizens in the East could actually see the West moving slowly in the direction they rightly could identify as theirs.

Certainly the progress made cannot be attributed to the emergence of a stronger, more unified feminist movement after the *Wende*. Indeed, as both Miethe and Ute Gerhard point out, the experience of unification was one of mutual disappointment and demobilization over time on both sides. Feminist hopes were initially high, but quickly dashed. In the East, the feminists hoped for a reformed socialism that would build on the accomplishments of the GDR but in a more participatory democratic and less gender-differentiating way. In the West, feminists looked eastward, where they expected to find already liberated recruits to their movement who could be easily mobilized. As the previous two essays explore, the encounter was more traumatic. Each side had illusions about itself and the other that the collision of two feminist movements in a single political space brought to the fore.[9]

The "mother-workers" of the GDR took the claims of freedom of choice in the FRG too literally, not recognizing how fundamentally lacking systems of support for combining work and family in the FRG still were and how important this lack was to any real freedom to choose. Feminists in the FRG were themselves struggling against the prevailing "wife-mother" model of the West German system (embedded in everything from school and store hours to pay and pension systems). Against this systematic marginalization, feminism in West Germany was largely practiced as a program of women-specific policies and projects to advance women's status. This model of autonomous feminist work for women seemed to feminists in the East to recapitulate the errors of the GDR in relying on a "mommy politics" of supporting women rather than offering a more fundamental challenge to gender inequality in both men's and women's lives. But the autonomous organizational approach was institutionalized as the template for what counted as "feminism" and thus (mis)guided the perceptions of West German media, parties, and movements.

Feminism in the GDR had been primarily practiced as embedded activism integrated either with democratic movements or the socialist state. For such activists, the new divisiveness of electoral politics posed a particular challenge. Spread among diverse Western parties (from the CDU to the Greens), the movement-based Eastern party (Bündnis 90) and the PDS, all of which made persuasive claims for feminist support, the "feminist vote" became invisible and thus was politically discounted. The measures on which women relied for employment, child care, and life planning collapsed around them. Local feminists did mobilize to stop as much damage as they could have, and their limited success partly explains why child-care centers remain much more available in the new federal states than in the old FRG.[10]

The one feminist umbrella organization that emerged in the East at the time of the *Wende* (the UFV) fell apart afterward because of its intentional internal diversity. On the one side, the dissident anti-institutional civic/cultural movement politics of some feminists produced deep hostility to the PDS, and on the other side, feminists with strong institutional ties in academia and local women's groups saw reform as most possible by working in and with the PDS, which was emerging as a representative of the claim that the GDR had made progress worth preserving on some issues.[11]

After the many disappointments of this moment of East-West encounter, painfully felt on all sides as these two essays still reveal, feminists on both sides turned away from movement-style politics. The insider politics that the EU and UN facilitated in the late 1990s did not require either grassroots movement–like mobilization or loyalty to any particular party, since it is more expert-driven than popularly based. Even today it is difficult to see any social movement that could be called all-German feminism. The women's movements have melted away from both sides of the former wall, replaced with gender political strategizing that engages German actors in EU and global networking.

Within the new Germany, there have been institutional convergences, but always from very different starting places. Reproductive rights are a good example, since the unification treaty itself was nearly derailed by the debate over abortion. Both men and women felt that the legal right to abortion in the first trimester, which the GDR had offered since 1972, had been exercised responsibly and they were loath to lose it. For women in the West, who had been shocked by the prosecutions of women and doctors for "legally unjustified" abortions in the Bavarian town of Memmingen in 1988, a legal reform was seen as essential so that judges would no longer have the last word about women's decisions. The resolution of the two legal frameworks in this particular case was deferred for the postunification parliament to decide. The tenuous compromise of the resultant law allowed "criminal but unprosecuted" abortions in the first trimester after "pro-life-oriented, but outcome open" counseling. This was a gain for the women in the West, although it was a step backward for women in the former GDR.

The expansion of "gender equality offices" in local, state, and national ministries and agencies also provided an institutional foothold for feminists in both new and old federal states. The understanding of what such offices should do, however, was sharply different since in the West, they were viewed as advocates for women, while in the East the feminists considered them as working toward gender equality, which was a concern for both women and men. This latter goal is closer to the "gender mainstreaming" mandate that the EU has placed upon member states to consider the implications of all policy for both women and men. Thus the perceived conflict now between gender mainstreaming and women's advocacy is more acute in the West—another instance of the convergence between EU goals and feminist hopes carried over from the GDR.

Finally, the family reforms that the grand coalition introduced in 2006 also began to move FRG gender policy more in the direction that the EU encouraged and that the GDR had made familiar. A real "baby year" of income-replacing parental leave replaced the three-year-long and badly paid "parental vacation" and was complemented by a funded commitment to the expansion of child-care places. This was an imitation of the rapidly diffusing "Swedish model," which had pioneered "daddy leave" (months of extra paid time if the father took some) as well as the flexibility of leave, a plan that made months off available to be taken anytime up to the child's eighth birthday, both of which were now officially encouraged by the EU. The EU also directed its members to increase women's labor force participation and to provide child care for all. While women raised in the West continue to be anxious about being labeled bad mothers (*Rabbenmütter*), and are thus less likely to take advantage of these provisions by working when their children are young, the return to a state policy of support for both women and men as workers—and now, for the first time, men as fathers too—was change in the direction that GDR feminists had sought.

Thus, in the end, the change that has emerged in German gender politics since unification was oriented more toward supporting GDR norms than anyone on either side ever expected. But it was not because the East had left an influential legacy of its own at the federal level.[12] Instead, the EU set in motion a variety of modernization projects—activation of women in the labor force, investments in early childhood, and gender mainstreaming—whose momentum was on the side of the working mothers of the GDR.[13] The downside for women of the dominance of the EU continues to be its focus on business competition and individual self sufficiency. Women are more likely to fall through the holes emerging in the national safety net, since women are still more likely to be caretakers for dependents (the elderly as well as children and the ill), more likely to earn too little in jobs that are too unstable, and more often poor, elderly, and victims of violence. The extent to which the EU embrace of both a neoliberal agenda of privatization and a feminist agenda of gender equality measures actually is consistent is currently a focus of feminist debate throughout Europe.[14]

The Intersectionality of Gender

The "East-West" encounter between German women with different experiences of freedom and repression, equality and domination, autonomy and solidarity is in some important ways a microcosm of the many encounters among women from diverse social locations. These differences have come to be theorized more generally as the *intersectionality* of gender, that is, the inability to disentangle gender relations from the other processes that generate social inequalities, such as class, race/ethnicity, age, and sexuality.[15] Intersectionality has informed studies of gender in at least three ways, across the main levels of social analysis: individual, interactional, and institutional.[16]

First, the concept of gender intersectionality directs attention to the incommensurable interactions of inequalities at the level of individual experience and biography. For example, although both Gerhard and Miethe stress differences in the meaning of unification by generation, the current and future East-West generational transitions carry different meaning for each of them, not only because of their initial position on opposite sides of the Wall, but because of their different generational location in relation to 1968 and 1989. Moreover, their concrete biographical situations—Gerhard as a renowned feminist scholar in Frankfurt, influenced by 1968, and Miethe as a peace activist and dissertation-writing student in Berlin in 1989—offered a different vantage point on the challenges of that moment of feminist encounter and continue to shape their reading of the changes since.

On the one hand, feminists in the West, like Gerhard, have long been using the EU's formal commitments to gender equality as a lever to challenge German gender policy. For example, the Bundestag's first prohibition of gender discrimination in hiring came in 1982 in the form of the "EU Conformity Law," which the European Court of Justice ruled inadequate, and the 2006 Equal Treatment Law was a late and grudging concession to an EU directive to all its member states. Gerhard's point of view highlights the transformations of social policy in Western women's family and work lives and the incorporation of feminism into conventional politics. Credit for these changes goes to the successful mobilization of feminist activists for which the opportunity structure provided by the EU is a valued tool.

On the other hand, feminists in the states of the former GDR, like Miethe, are relatively new to the mechanisms of EU policy making, but are pleased to recognize allies outside the relatively narrow scope of FRG party politics. From her perspective, the EU is useful primarily as a lever to change consciousness on both sides of the former wall. Making the experiences of gender relations in the "old" FRG more obviously exceptional even in the Western European context and bringing in new member-states who also share experiences with state socialism and regime transition that had been used to frame East German women as "different" are both important ways that the EU empowered women in the East.

At a second level, intersectionality is not just about the different social locations of gendered people but about the social forces acting upon them. Intersectionality as a theory points to the contexts in which multiple inequalities are being generated together, not merely colliding in particular locations in different configurations. Thus the process of unification was itself defined not merely by the dominance of West German political elites over the efficacious self-mobilization of dissident groups in the East, but also by the dominance of male elites in the West and their longer-term displacement of the participatory democratic ideals of the '68ers into institutionalized party politics. Both Miethe and Gerhard express a sense of lingering disappointment in how they were marginalized at the time. The idealistic political mobilizations in which they were engaged—Gerhard in organizing alternative visions of constitutional reform and Miethe in dissident peace politics—became sidelined by the juggernaut of party-led unification. While the way unification happened was not explicitly designed to exclude women or feminist ideas, both authors present a strong case for seeing that exclusion as intrinsic to the process as it actually occurred.

Finally, intersectionality offers a design for feminist practice, an argument that gender politics will only advance the interests of women collectively under certain conditions. As intersectionality emerged as theory, it also made a demand for reflexive practice on feminist organizers and organizations. Reflexivity is also characteristic of both essays in the way that feminist theorists suggest it should be.[17] Both Miethe and Gerhard address their efforts to make *visible* the divergent positions and interests among women rather than using gender to advance a totalizing view of women's essential similarity. Additionally, both are *choosing priorities* politically with an eye toward inclusive solidarity as a goal, intentionally seeking common ground against the background of these acknowledged differences. Finally, they assume the continued existence of *organizational variability* in the strategies and priorities that feminists embrace, not privileging either the autonomous women's movements that were once the harbingers of cultural change in the West or the reliance on state policy or gender-mixed political dissidence that mattered most in creating and upending the GDR gender regime.

The broader context to which both Gerhard and Miethe address themselves is therefore one in which intersectionality has become much more appreciated as a principle of feminist politics than it was twenty years ago. In this regard, no less that in the commonality of EU impact on German national gender policy and practices, the two varieties of feminism that they articulate have grown together while remaining distinct. Divided not only by their position in East or West initially but also by generation, Miethe and Gerhard still do not agree on what the process of unification brought for women. From a vantage point in which intersectionality is valued rather than decried, this is a gain in perspective and an opportunity to better represent the real variety of women's needs in feminist politics. Perhaps it is not a coincidence that Miethe harks back to the words of Louise Otto-Peters, a giant of the feminist movement in nineteenth-century Germany, whose works Gerhard previously edited. Otto-Peters articulated the intersection of class and gender politics as inclusive and mutually reinforcing claims for both economic justice and participatory democracy for women and men. Even though today there is no feminist movement on the streets in any part of Germany, feminist organizing continues in Germany, in the EU, and beyond.

Notes

1. Ann Towns, *Women and States: Norms and Hierarchies in International Society* (Cambridge, 2010).
2. Melissa Haussman and Birgit Sauer, *Gendering the State in the Age of Globalization: Women's Movements and State Feminism in Postindustrial Democracies* (New York, 2007).
3. For a good discussion of the emergence and relevance of the term, see Sonia Alvarez, "Advocating Feminism: The Latin American feminist NGO 'boom,'" *International Feminist Journal of Politics* 1 (1999), 181–209. On NGOization in Germany, see Sabine Lang, "The NGOization of Feminism," in *Transitions, Environments, Translations: Feminisms in International Politics*, eds. J.W. Scott, C. Kaplan, and D. Keates (New York, 1997), 101–120.
4. Sabine Lang, *NGOs, Civil Society and the Public Sphere* (Cambridge, 2012).
5. Anna van der Vleuten and Mieke Verloo, "Disappointing Pioneers and Surprising Laggards: Understanding Disparities Between Reputation and Performance," in *The Discursive Politics of Gender Equality: Stretching, Bending and Policy-making*, eds. Emanuela Lombardo, Petra Meier, and Mieke Verloo (London, 2009).
6. Myra Marx Ferree, "Gender Politics in the Berlin Republic: Issues of Identity and Institutional Change," *German Politics & Society* 28 (2010), 189–214.

7. Angelika von Wahl, "From Family to Reconciliation Policy: How the Grand Coalition Reforms the German Welfare State," *German Politics & Society* 26 (2008), 25–49.
8. Silke Roth, *Gender Politics in the Expanding European Union: Mobilization, Inclusion, Exclusion* (New York, 2008).
9. The analysis here recapitulates that more extensively developed in Myra Marx Ferree, "Patriarchies and Feminisms: The Two Women's Movements of Unified Germany," *Social Politics* 2 (1995), 10–24.
10. Both structural availability (311 public child-care places per 1,000 children aged 0–3 in the East and 19 per 1,000 in the West) and individual choices reflect the persistence of a different gender culture in the ex-GDR in the ensuing decade. See Karsten Hank and Michaela Kreyenfeld, "A Multilevel Analysis of Child Care and the Transition to Motherhood in Western Germany," *Journal of Marriage and Family* 65 (2003), no. 3.
11. Anne Hampele Ulrich, *Der Unabhängige Frauenverband: Ein frauenpolitisches Experiment im Deutschen Vereinigungsprozess* (Berlin, 2000).
12. There were and are influential legacies of GDR feminism at the local level, however. See Katja Guenther, *Places of Resistance: Feminism After Socialism in Eastern Germany* (Palo Alto, 2010).
13. Jane Jensen, "Writing Women Out, Folding Gender in: The European Union 'Modernizes' Social Policy," *Social Politics* 15 (2008), 131–153.
14. For the more optimistic view of the EU, see Sylvia Walby, *Globalization and Inequalities: Complexity and Contested Modernities* (London, 2009). For the more pessimistic perspective, see Jensen, "Writing Women Out" or Maria Stratigaki, "The Cooptation of Gender Concepts in EU policies: The Case of 'Reconciliation of Work and Family,'" *Social Politics* 11 (2004), 30–56.
15. Two important analyses of the origins and meaning of intersectionality are Leslie McCall, "The Complexity of Intersectionality," *Signs: Journal of Women in Culture and Society* 30 (2005), 1771–1800, and Ange-Marie Hancock, "When Multiplication Doesn't Equal Quick Addition: Examining Intersectionality as a Research Paradigm," *Perspectives on Politics* 5 (2007), 63–79.
16. For the elaboration of this typology see Hae Yeon Choo and Myra Marx Ferree, "Practicing Intersectionality in Sociological Research: A Critical Analysis of Inclusions, Interactions and Institutions in the Study of Inequalities," *Sociological Theory* 28 (2010), 29–49.
17. This typology is developed in Christina Ewig and Myra Marx Ferree, "Feminist Organizing: What's Old, What's New? History, Trends and Issues," *Oxford Handbook on Gender and Politics* (New York, 2011).

Part IV

Cultural Conflict

Chapter Ten

GDR Literature Beyond the GDR?

Klaus R. Scherpe

In October 1989, a few weeks before the fall of the Wall, the French sociologist Pierre Bourdieu gave a lecture in East Berlin about the changing roles of public intellectuals.[1] He presented the assembled comrades from the Academy of Sciences in the SED's Central Committee with his "reflexive sociology."[2] Bourdieu urged intellectuals to abandon their "positions from above or outside" and to apply their knowledge about how societies functioned to their own positions. The habitus and roles of a future-oriented avant-garde had not protected them from complicity with ruling political and economic powers, something Julien Benda had already asserted in his 1927 manifesto *La trahison des clercs.* Bourdieu's next lecture at the Humboldt University on October 25, 1989 received universal approval; by that point it did not require much courage to support it. In an interview after the *Wende,* Bourdieu called real existing socialism a "kind of official religion with corrupt priests," a characterization very different from Antonio Gramsci's Marxist conception of "hegemonic intellectuals."[3]

In his call for a renewed political engagement among the international intelligentsia Bourdieu did not expressly identify literary critics, whose power in the West had been relativized due to their position in the marketplace. Although intellectuals in the East, within the habitus of opposition and dissidence, could exert some influence as speakers for and on behalf of "the people," it was debatable whether a critique of power would not at the same time preserve existing power structures. Bourdieu's warning suggested that the hubris of intellectuals was based on their "king's role,"

Notes for this chapter begin on page 202.

and on the fact that their self-definition relied on a fundamental delusion ("the narcissistic mortification") about their own roles in relationship to "the people," whose representatives they purported to be.

One could argue that the now-famous Alexanderplatz mass demonstration on 4 November 1989, at which many of the "cultural workers" of the GDR spoke—among them Heiner Müller and Christa Wolf, who demanded a *literarisches Volksvermögen*—was in its exuberance already a swan song of the literary elite that had been granted such a leading role within the GDR system. In a *Spiegel* interview held not long thereafter, Stefan Heym voiced his bitter disappointment that the masses who had just been celebrating their longed-for freedom were now consumers flocking to the displays of Western retailers.[4] And Helga Königsdorf, in a melancholy look back at the "lovely beginning of the revolution," noted bitterly that the Alexanderplatz demonstrations were likely a theatrical experience, only "seeing oneself in the role of directors."[5]

Bourdieu's work is helpful in understanding the "literary landscape" of the GDR and the resurgence of post-*Wende* literature from the East because in his sociology of the intelligentsia, the opinions, morals, convictions, and avowals of authors, readers, and literary agents are not decisive. Rather, what matters are the "symbolic actions" that occur—the subsequent actions and behaviors, the "habitus" which is created through literary activity, as well as in the pursuit of recognition ("gaining of distinction").[6]

The German-German literary controversy after the *Wende* of 1989/90 with its Western accusations of subservience and its Eastern defensiveness about its conformist "literary society" has done little to explain how GDR authors served as intellectual spokespeople. Especially now, after the GDR's demise, the profile of its literary landscape has become rather more visible. Discussions about GDR identity in both East and West only really took off after the *Wende.* In the world of literature and its singular memory politics, that which remains is most significant. Some issues include: enduring an unendurable relationship to those in power (i.e., to the *Hauptverwaltung,* i.e. "main office," of the censorship bureaucracy, as it was called); justifying oneself or confessing (whether one was for something or against it); obsessing about one's role as an author. Christa Wolf, one of the leading lights of GDR literature, has made this self-reflection the subject of her work, even from the distance of her desk in the "city of angels."[7] After the demise of the GDR, the experienced, remembered, or imagined GDR past has become problematic for authors, whether they are representatives of the era, dissidents, or those who were younger and therefore indifferent. The number of autobiographical or quasi-autobiographical works that have appeared since the 1990s is a testament to the fact that looking back and beyond are still important; what has taken precedence is the *internal* task of finding and acknowledging oneself, rather than exploring the *external* role of the literary intellectual as a privileged representative of an entire system. The younger generation of authors finds it difficult to relate to this acknowledged or assumed role of spokesperson. In a united Germany, writers must, even if frequently lamented and criticized, find their own distinction in the literary marketplace.

Dismissal of the Heroes

The *Wende* of autumn 1989 has sometimes been compared to the "Zero Hour" of 1945. "Never before were there so many new beginnings"—at both points in time. Although the analogy is historically invalid, both periods do share a common theme. The West German author Alexander Kluge deemed the Zero Hour of 1945 "a temporarily open relationship to the past." "The Zero Hour momentarily suspends the relational principles of history. ... The cities are destroyed, but the horizon remains wide open."[8] We know now that the idea of a Zero Hour was a productive delusion, a historical fantasy promoted by intellectuals; it was as if history had taken a time-out and there was an "in-between time," a *kairos* of a historical moment between a ruined past and a future full of hope.

Similarly in the appeal *For Our Land* of November 1989, those literary intellectuals critical of the system hoped momentarily that they could create a new Germany, one that would cut across the continuities of GDR-Prussianism and the capitalism of Daimler-Benz land. "Fantastical repose, as if to decide about the whole future," was how Volker Braun put it: "On its heels/history turns around/decisive for a moment." Braun quotes these lines and adds: "That is precisely what we experienced: that history had made an about face and there was a brief moment when it was our own movement."[9] Common to both periods was a sense of rupture and a fascination with the single moment; the desire not just to reflect about history, but also to feel it and to make it. This was a moment of self-encouragement against the prevailing disillusionment of leading intellectuals, writers, and scholars.

Admittedly, those authors further from the system or entirely excluded from it experienced the fall of the Wall and the *Wende* differently. They were enthusiastic, but in private, not openly politically, and certainly not in favor of a renewed socialism: that was the hope of the leading representatives of GDR literature, and for West German authors like Günter Grass. "Our Christa has once again written the most beautiful preamble to the constitution,"[10] writes Thomas Brussig in his *Heroes Like Us,* a lively novel about the fall of the Wall in which Christa Wolf's spontaneously decides to work on a new GDR constitution. It mocks not just her as one of the leading representatives of GDR literature, but also those public intellectuals whose role as heroes, which they played either willingly or unwillingly in the GDR, suddenly came to an end: "How can we speak of it, in our halting speech, when they have held the exclusive rights to free speech … so that we can now know in no uncertain terms, what or whom we need to mourn when it comes to 1989?"[11] This shows how the generational conflict supersedes the political differences that seem less important to the younger generation. The polemic already presupposes the loss of stature that GDR literature hitherto enjoyed in the East and the West.

The intellectuals' politics that needed to be corrected appear with pregnant meaning as symbolic conflict. In 1992, the philosopher Hans-Peter Krüger, a former member of the Academy of Sciences, demanded in a collection of essays and personal reports from the GDR's last days that "the heroes be decommissioned," that we bid farewell to the "cultural workers" as the self-declared avant-garde of society who were also legitimized by the authorities. In this work he exposed the mental roadblocks and falsehoods that were at the root of the mistaken understanding of the avant-garde. Krüger described a visit to the Berlin Volksbühne at Rosa Luxemburg Square, where Heiner Müller's *The Mission: Memory of a Revolution* was premiering. The play centers on someone who abandons the role of hero, namely the French emissary Debuisson, sent to Jamaica to fulfill his revolutionary duty, while back in France the revolution had already been ended by the Directory. Debuisson refused to carry out his task. And Krüger, watching the play in Berlin, connected the scene to his own experiences: "It seemed to me that it revealed vulnerability—mine, yours, theirs, ours. It was as if I had been transformed from the figure of a revolutionary angel into a far-too-human dog, who has rolled over in submission in the face of a permanent state of war."[12]

Krüger speaks of the inevitable abandonment of a false, corrupted sense of the avant-garde prevalent among the GDR elite—"Why should I want the gift of prophecy," asks Christa Wolf presciently in her novel *Cassandra*—a work about the impossible duty to support social progress and follow the illusion of utopia which justified misdeeds in the present—this statement appears self-evident after the fact, and it has been repeated and radicalized by numerous former GDR intellectuals. For instance, Durs Grünbein noted that "Utopia is a hysterical category."[13] By abandoning the heroic mode, the role of victim should also be left behind, which in the post-*Wende* period has resulted in the figure of the *Jammerossi* among intellectuals. The Dresdner poet Thomas Rosenlöcher used "Eastern whining" as title for his ironic anecdotes about disgraceful observations by the "Know-it-all West Germans'" (*Besserwessis*) about GDR life.[14]

Heiner Müller has spoken of the need to carry out "post-heroic management." This kind of literary politics recognizes that intellectuals can no longer claim a "position from above or outside." In contrast to their claimed monopoly on possible solutions and criticisms, which frequently served to justify their positions of power, Müller noted in a conversation: "We don't have too many problems, but rather, we have too many solutions." This comment is directed at party intellectuals and the language of the Politbüro and similar institutions that had always viewed society in terms of training, educating, and planning. The problem, argues Müller, was that "one kept running into the fact that the actual confounding factor is man himself, and one cannot treat man *heroically* [my emphasis]. Man is not heroic; it goes against his nature to be heroic. ... Certain values that are still considered sacrosanct—those that concern the individual and personality—are already assumed as not given."[15]

This aptly summarizes the post-heroism of GDR intellectuals. Any heroic stance of literary intellectuals (as whole personalities in the Gramscian sense) was entirely illusory in the GDR, because they were always indebted to the party and the secret police. Post-*Wende* experiences have shown that this habitus, even as a self-reflexive gesture, no longer exists or has been weakened considerably, given the multifaceted and market-oriented nature of Western democracy. Müller, who spent many years crossing the border with a GDR identity card (without the right to emigrate), has reserved for himself in his negative dialectic the right to make his own mistakes, to forge his own inimitable way on the path of enlightenment. A confirmed and disillusioned cynic, he insists on participating in a kind of social reason that could no longer be the rationale of society. As a result, intellectuals, in a "post-heroic" position of self-reflection, must still carry out their public roles, even if they are left with "no answers."

Poetic *Tristesse*

Relatively soon after the *Wende*, gestures of "resignation" became common in GDR literature and scholarship, especially with regard to the image of the abdicating hero. Very few authors have carried on with the project of socialism in the years after "real existing socialism" had been radically exposed. Volker Braun is of note in this regard, often ridiculed in passing as "our last socialist." "The simple truth is not enough," proclaimed Braun in one of his early poems, when he did not tire of provoking the state and the party and continued to demand a socialist society with a human face. Post-*Wende*, Braun has shifted his focus and criticized capitalism and Western "colonizers"; this criticism has often been limited to observing the smugness of consumer culture and then making biting jokes, such as, "Socialism leaves, and Johnny Walker comes." Braun's most important and oft-cited post-*Wende* poem, "Property," ends with the following lines:

Hope lay across our path with gapping maw
You've got my property in your paws.
When can I say again "mine" and mean us all?[16]

The subject of this poem sees himself as someone or something left behind. But the poem renews old "heroic" demands for a total or unified society, something that was ever denied and never achieved. What "remains" for Volker Braun (unlike Christa Wolf's equally unremitting moral demand for a "subjective authenticity") is the dialectical construct with which the constant contradictions between individuals and society produce insight: "These are the pillars that allow for lofty, bold buildings. ..."[17]

In his *Dance of Death* cycle published in 2000 in the *Frankfurter Allgemeine Zeitung* after the news of his having won the Büchner Prize became public, Braun presented the virtues of socialism, one after the other (utopia, communism, people's property) to conjure up their apocalyptic fate. Even as he does this, he maintains the cathartic power of the revelation. A stroll through a neocapitalist Hall of Horrors may not offer a way out, but at least it suggests a manner of walking.

Braun's work is not simply a political attempt to renew the role of intellectuals as representatives or mouthpieces for the grand collective of "us." Rather, if we read his verses carefully, we can see that he constantly undermines seemingly clear concepts with stylistic irregularities. He speaks elsewhere of a "massacre of illusions," of a utopia that offers no comfort, no shelter in a time of troubles. It is clear that this author defends his position and carries his own vulnerability and inconsistency from text to text.

Recently he has changed tones yet again, switching to the well-proven populist tools of satire and farce. The great speech of reason seeks a new measure ("it seems that idiocy can be found on either side of any contradiction"); it is fragmented and considers the *Flickwerk*—thus the title of sixty "Pranks" in the bizarre lives of individuals composing the whole of society in places from Bochum to Venezuela, covering dismal low-wage jobs and the illegal sale of organs on the internet.[18] "The people turned in their *property* and were handed *freedom* in return," Braun wrote looking back on his poem from 1998 and again in 2009 in *Flickwerk*.[19] What should and must remain, Volker Braun has decided for himself and his readers as a literary measure against "shady business," is a critical form of dialectical reasoning that focuses on and criticizes the miserable material conditions of neocapitalism. He reinvokes proven literary forms familiar since the dialogues of the Enlightenment, whether it be Diderot and Lessing or

Hebbel and Brecht with their calendars for daily enlightenment. Similar to Brecht's *Geschichten vom Herrn Keuner,* Braun created his *Hinze-Kunze-Roman* for the GDR in which the master-servant dialogue reveals everything about society and what binds comrades together.

Braun continued in this vein with his picaresque novel *Machwerk* (*Botched*), a shift book in forty-nine chapters.[20] Engineer Flick has been laid off from the Lausitz mine and forced into early retirement. In the new economic landscape he comes off as the better loser; his antagonist is just a shadow of himself (which is part of the dialectic): his grandson, who will never amount to anything, a lazy, self-righteous good-for-nothing, who nonetheless still manages to be amazed at all his hardworking grandfather could achieve back in the GDR. Critics have asked whether this contrived story truly captures the new neoliberal organization of life and work from an Enlightenment perspective. Western (and thus united) German living conditions do not provide the kind of system opposition that has been at the heart of Braun's work as an enlightened literary critic in the GDR.

Uwe Kolbe, who regards himself as "a renegade," had left what he refers to as the "three-letter state" in 1987 and experienced the *Wende* in Austin, Texas, where he was a visiting writer. Both are exemplars of a younger generation of writers who present their lives in the GDR in the future perfect tense ("It will have been.") Their once-treasured aspirations to live "a true life in the wrong [system]" (forged from the sidelines of opposition) are now tattered and worn, as is the melancholy manner in which they nostalgically view real existing socialism as an "unlived life." As a destination, West Germany is often seen as potentially liberating, given its very mundane "normalcy" and the everyday possibilities of "democracy."[21] West Germany is liberating in the sense that it relieves authors of the constant demand to take a position either for or against something and to express opinions "in the interest of society."

In his essays and poems, Uwe Kolbe is clearly attempting to understand literature as an individual undertaking, whereby (with just the right touch) the author can allow everyday things, people, or landscapes to reveal their true sides and their real beauty. Kolbe views the past, in all its complexity and incomprehensibility, in the same manner, where nothing is ever achieved beyond "realizing one's own experiences." In *Renegatentermine,* his collection of essays from 1998, Kolbe bids his own personal farewell to socialist utopias and the associated demanding status of author: "Renegade appointment. Very small. Very small. Very banal. And beyond that, entirely apolitical. No discussions with political officers or military prosecutors, or with well-meaning friends. Nothing about the debilitating power of silence, or about the unknown doors that could be opened with careful calculation. Nothing about the responsibility of the author 'during the revolutionary period'; nothing about owing something to the GDR public. No. Not. Go ahead and throw that rock."[22]

Kolbe's farewell is a violent one, containing his anger about the debilitating power of silence (more powerful than keeping quiet about real persecution); the need to resist the temptation posed by "doors opened with careful calculation"—these are the major recurring themes of Kolbe's coming to terms with the GDR past. In the opening poem in the collection *Vineta* (1998), Kolbe writes:

This fear of words, this slight dread of
knowledge that means nothing....
Postwar then and now, remember?
I washed the windows and then decided
never to look out again....

I blessed the view with an averted turn of my head.
Remember, how we used to look out, and make predictions,
and we always said: "It will be as it is, and how
we laughed at ourselves, and our duty was a duty ..."[23]

This "slight dread of knowledge" mocks the grand phrases of the socialist utopia, and of the meaningless sense of duty that could only be defined in relational terms. The act of looking away, of not looking at all, is an unacceptable option. The poem has its own unmistakable sadness, without a trace of sentimentality; for Kolbe it is merely a "slight" tragedy. It is an assumed indifference in the face of the tautological phrase: "Our duty was a duty." Eventually, awaiting, anticipating, or expecting the arrival of the coming utopia became unbearable, meaningless, because what one had to think or feel was already determined. The "language of the collective lie" resulted in indifference and futility.

Kolbe's poems revealed the metaphoric ballast and the tempting simplicity of the dialectic, and made him wary of an oppositional language rich in contradictions that in the feints of negation sets its own rhetorical limits. It comes as no surprise therefore that after abandoning grand phrases and demands for a brighter future, Kolbe would turn to smaller gestures, to the rhetorical remnants of ideology that are to be found in *Vinetas Archives*.[24] In his collection *Vaterlandkanal: Ein Fahrtenbuch*, Kolbe takes the next step:

I've lost my country.
No nicer land in all the world,
of course.
It's only mountain remains standing
I can still see it in my mind.

We went there every Sunday.
Its name was the thimble.
I still have my fingers,
And bid farewell to all the rest.[25]

The "golden age of East German literature is over," proclaimed the disillusioned Suhrkamp author Durs Grünbein; "the oldest light in the firmament [Heiner Müller] has long since burnt out."[26] At the end, everyone felt lousy, "as sick as a dog." Grünbein also utilizes the dog metaphor to describe himself: out of the shell of the socialist personality that was shored up on all sides emerged the "modern variant of Pavlov's dog."[27] In 1995, Grünbein was the youngest author ever awarded the prestigious Büchner Prize of the Darmstadt Academy for Language and Literature. Since then he has continued to go his own way, and now primarily writes poetry, which cannot be "hermetic" enough, as he says, in order to distinguish it from the social duty of an "educational dictatorship." What writing is really about, claims Grünbein in elevated prose, is "to look for one's destiny and to achieve it, to be unique, one's own self, and to place one's unique experiences and sense of self on the map."[28]

Grünbein's rather prosaic conclusion that distinction in the literary marketplace can replace the once lofty (but now lost) status of poet and thinker in the GDR sells short his own remarkable productivity since the *Wende.* Commenting with insight on his development as a writer, Grünbein locates the origins of his "pyscho-poetics" in his determination "to overcome not only state boundaries and cement walls, but to transcend the limitations of time and space altogether. This can only be accomplished through poetry."[29] Although this sounds like the remnants of hopelessly outdated avant-gardism, Grünbein captures key moments quite convincingly, whether in regard to coming to terms with the East German past or standard complaints about Western consumerism. In the face of demands for "literature as an ideological service industry" and the oft-discussed "banality of permanence," one must reconstitute a resilient *poeta persona.* Unlike any other writer from the GDR, Grünbein has worked systematically from one publication to the next to transform himself into this *persona grata* of a literary intellectual. Literary critics admire him as a *poeta doctus,* as someone with a command of philology, philosophy, and the natural sciences, someone with a working knowledge of the treasures of *anthologia graeca* as well as the poetic *logos* of ancient Rome.

Grünbein followed up the *Schädelbasislektionen* (1993) with his *momento mori* collection *Die Teuren Toten* from 1994, a collection of thirty-three epigraphs in which the author develops his own idiosyncratic manner of dealing with the past. For Grünbein, a deliberate "poetics of sarcasm" serves as a kind of poetic filter to purify reality's intrusions. His subsequent collection of poems *Nach den Satiren* (1999), reminiscent of Juvenal, and his Seneca *Postscriptum* (2003) celebrate stoicism in the "name of extremes" as the greatest "standard of behavior" of the antique philosophers: "To stand above society was their highest goal."[30] Grünbein's penchant for the "life under glass" in archives and anatomical museums facilitates his cool aesthetic, which allows him to maintain a careful distance from the crush of experience. Grünbein is disciplined in interacting with the legacy of poetics and rhetoric, developing his poetics of knowledge that take scientific cultural language as its measure. This rigidity also results in a kind of exaggeration that the GDR's cultural experts responsible for the country's "classical tradition" would never have dreamt of.

In the end, Grünbein aims to revise his past experiences, as do almost all authors from the GDR—who strive to create a durable, defendable space for an alternative literary reality. The space is both real and imagined, like that created by the revered Friedrich Hölderlin, a place where literary existence can begin anew. Grünbein sees this reality as his "muse's palace": the city of Dresden, a source of poetic renewal for writers from Volker Braun to Uwe Tellkamp. For Grünbein's poetic sense of self, Dresden provides a constant warning about the continued "danger of losing one's place" because of its destruction in the Second World War; it is the "Ostrakon," a "code word for the descent through time,"[31] where the antique world can break through and save the poet's efforts:

> Awake I lie. Awake and the night
> Darkens what was light in me
> Until the end. This skin. . . .
> Around the hour, from ear to ear
> Wanders my breath, my feeble pulse,
> Exposed behind the wall. . . .
> Out there it's all too much for me.
> Even the compound eye of the smallest fly
> Exudes destruction.[32]

Short Story Ironies

In contrast to the idiosyncratic Durs Grünbein, most authors with a GDR past have sought to position themselves in the literary marketplace with a particular edge. One's own GDR past or prehistory is not always a part of the story, but it appears in the manner in which characters interact and conflicts arise, in the choice of literary forms, voice, or in the point of view. It is particularly remarkable that after poetry, shorter forms, especially the short story, have multiplied, often written with the American model in mind. Katja Lange-Müller, Kerstin Hensel, Ingo Schulze, and Kathrin Schmidt have excelled at this form, even though some of them have also proven their mettle with grander narratives. Crisis periods seem to call forth the form of the short story, which also holds true for the German post-1945 era.

With their focus on individual situations and experiences, short stories—oppositional voices or dissidents—offer a different moral than the GDR-era emphasis on the "social duty." This new voice is situated in the grayness of daily life and occupies itself with relationship issues and life choices, with the loss of work and career, with the challenges of new situations, and with the attempt to shape one's own life, to make one's own decisions and to decide what kind of person one can and will be in a new context. Critics have noted that these stories often have provincial or regional themes or contain echoes of "magical realism," as in Kerstin Hensel's *Spinnenhaus* from 2003, which offers some refuge from everyday problems.

Such everyday concerns, which have been chronicled by Katja Lange-Müller and Ingo Schulze (with his bestselling *Simple Stories*), reveal a different kind of "concern for oneself" than that found in the West German *Betroffenheitsliteratur*, where the individual's search for meaning often becomes a goal unto itself. When such stories engage in humor or grotesquery, when particular regions or subcultures take center stage, such as in Lange-Müller's bizarre novel *Die Letzten*—which recounts the end of the printing trade in East Berlin (and with it the end of preformulated phrases.)—one feels in the eccentric style of the narrative the intended decentering of the grand drama of history. Key themes such as emigration, the Stasi system, or censorship are ignored and then reappear in new guise in all-the-more-powerful fantastic scenes. In Lange-Müller's *Kasper Mauser*, when a young, gay African-German from Weimar living in an East Berlin commune receives his "Document of Dismissal from the Citizenship of the GDR," he cuts it up into pieces and burns it. He would insist on being a "non-person," which everyone is in this situation and would remain so: "Not a citizen of this state, not one of the other (German) country, not a citizen at all."[33]

Ingo Schulze has lovingly commented on this "selfless" behavior in his post-*Wende* story, *Tausend Geschichten sind nicht genug*, and has reflected on how difficult it is to come to terms with a new citizenship that is not one's own. It is not surprising that he chooses as his protagonist a writer and a dissident, who believes he can decide "as a priest of the word what was a lie and what was true." At the *Wende*, this author learns "how the unimaginable fall of the Wall had made his dreams pointless. Instead of being welcomed in the West as a celebrated dissident, he skulked over the border like millions of others."[34] Schulze deploys humor to show how very ordinary this historical event could be, allowing us to view human destinies up close. In this manner they become something worthy of note.

A few books written after the turn of the century that call themselves novels and are concerned with East and West German family history during the *Wende* reveal themselves, on closer inspection, to be collections of short stories, anecdotes, legends, and fables. One example is Ingo Schulze's novel *Neues Leben* (2005), an ambitious work that attempts to bring the epistolary novel of the eighteenth century to bear on contemporary history; another is Kathrin Schmidt's novel *Königs Kinder* (2002), which offers psychosociological insights from the bleak suburbs of new and old Berlin.

Wende Novels: Before And After

As with film, literature has found it difficult to withstand contemporary expectations that it will address key historical events like the fall of the Wall, attempted flight, the Stasi past, or emigration to the West in representative and poetic terms. The more significant novels from Kathrin Schmidt, Wolfgang Hilbig, Gert Neumann, and Reinhard Jirgl seem to avoid such demands from politicians, the media, and literary critics altogether. Kathrin Schmidt undermines reality with surreal constructions; Wolfgang Hilbig places subjectivity above all else and thus prohibits any simple interpretation; Reinhard Jirgl deconstructs both the GDR past and the FRG present with his own experimental language.

The theme of collaboration with the Stasi, brought to a broad public with the film *The Lives of Others* by the West German director Florian von Donnersmarck, is also the subject of Kathrin Schmidt's novel *Seebachs schwarze Katzen.* Schmidt participated in the Berlin 1990 Round Table, and her novel portrays the Stasi's role in garish terms—the perversity of personal entanglement serves as a metaphor for the monstrosity of social relations as a whole. Schmidt offers us a thriller with an antihero whose past catches up with him; a womanizing Stasi spy with the code name of Romeo who seduces his victims and then keeps them under surveillance. After the *Wende* and his "change in circumstances," his family finds out the truth about him. Schmidt approaches the precarious lives and relationships of her characters with deftness, choosing not to moralize about guilt, confession, or punishment, but instead focusing on the traumatic damage done to the victims: "Her paranoid schizophrenia emerged only in the years after the *Wende,* after the Stasi had ceased to exist. She suspected anyone she didn't know to be a spy and was convinced that people had just gone underground. It got so bad that she would crawl into bed, trembling with fear, and insist that they were just there, up in the tree outside of her window, waiting for her to lift her head."[35]

While Schmidt's novel traces traumatic experiences from the perspective of memory in semantically and grammatically correct prose, Wolfgang Hilbig's novel *Ich* moves beyond this in describing the relationship between an author-informant and the man he is spying on, a poet from the dissident scene in the Prenzlauer Berg district of Berlin. The very monstrosity of the act is expressed in an abstract listing of genitive endings that lead nowhere—in the "operative" language of the Stasi "classified documents."[36] Hilbig's novel is a relentless, penetrating view of literary intellectuals' betrayal, cast in the language of the Stasi, which critics dismissed as "unrealistic," since the plot does not match reality either topographically or biographically. We suspect that there are surprising similarities between the behaviors of both authors and spies. This does not refer to the actual discovery that two dissidents of the Prenzlauer scene were Stasi agents, but rather to the rhetorical deconstruction of the events themselves; the Stasi officer in charge of the case reads Beckett during his time off. The protagonist's voice reveals the absurdity of surveillance, on which the text itself relies for its existence. Hilbig exposes the formal logic of literary criticism in the GDR: "We always had to think the exact opposite of what the official position was. And then we had to formulate the opposite of that oppositional thought."[37]

As a result of the consequential observation of speech itself, Hilbig reveals the entire absurdity of the situation. The simulation theory of the French philosopher Jean Baudrillard (*The Agony of Power*), whose work is taken up with enthusiasm by the Prenzlauer Berg types, serves as the inspiration for a unique hyperrealism: "Security resulted from an infinite chain of consequences: to watch those in charge as they carried out their duties; to watch the watchers; to watch out for any thought on behalf of the watchers that might go against the norm with the knowledge that they themselves were being watched; ... to watch over dreams; ... to watch out that during sleep only the sleeper had fallen asleep, while the watcher continued to keep an eye open for its consequences."[38]

In Goya's satire *Sleep of Reason* the sleeper could still look forward to a hopeful awakening. But in Hilbig's text the constant act of watchfulness is present as virtual reality and there is no equivalent escape. With his awkward sentence constructions, Hilbig escalates to comical extremes, reporting on a social reality that only ever pretended to be real—the permanently dysfunctional GDR system.

Hilbig's autobiographical novel *Das Provisorium* (2000) revolves around his disappointing experiences as an author in West Germany starting in

1985, armed with an exit visa. Despite his contradictory and idiosyncratic encounters in the West, he created an identity for himself via his altered status as an author who had crossed over the GDR's boundaries. Looking back, he views the high regard that authors enjoyed in the GDR skeptically, as a rather dubious "indication of rank."[39] By obtaining an exit visa in the East, he had forced himself "to come to terms with those in power." Once in West Germany, he learned that his earlier "reason for living" as a writer was not of much use: en route from his original homeland of origin to what he considers a merely provisional way station, he experiences a fundamental crisis: "He slowly lost his grasp on reality.... He was shut out, and reality refused to recognize him; he was incapable of making any reference to reality at all.... Reality was hidden behind a wall, and he carried that wall with him at all times.... He couldn't get rid of the wall, he could only, if he really desired to change the situation, get rid of himself...."[40]

No wall, either a real one or the imaginary one "in our heads" stood in his way; rather, it was being cut off from his roots, from his sense of belonging, alone, that had given his writing any meaning. Hilbig's "temporary protagonist" takes little notice of the fall of the Wall. Like no other author, Hilbig conceives of the separation of the two German states both before and after the *Wende* as an existential and artistic crisis, thanks to his experiences living an authorial life caught between politics and the market.

Critics have sought to locate a kind of apocalyptic vision in the work of Hilbig and his contemporary Gert Neumann, as well in the fantastical works of Reinhard Jirgl. The act can be interpreted as a West German attempt to rescue the final poetics of "dissidents and professional victims," as Hilbig put it aptly at the first Leipzig book fair to occur after the *Wende*.[41] And yet (or precisely because of this), Hilbig and Neumann have been lauded in literary circles as models of a new literature of leave-taking and arrival. They are also celebrated as "real" GDR authors because both share proletarian origins or have worked in blue-collar jobs as toolmakers, heating specialists, locksmiths, or tractor operators and in the West are considered typical GDR "'workers' writers," a part they have adamantly refused to play.

Neumann has addressed the subject of ideologically infused language even more directly than Hilbig. As the son of the writer Margarete Neumann, a party loyalist, Neumann was able "to learn the language of power as my mother tongue." "This language ... was horrid. It had such absolute power that one could see the blood dripping from each sentence."[42] Neumann's criticism of the language of power, developed from firsthand experience, took form in his novel *Elf Uhr* (1977), which he wrote while working as a locksmith. Neumann radicalized his poetic language, inspired by his reading of deconstructionist thinkers like Michel Foucault, Roland Barthes, and Gilles Deleuze, hoping to find a resistance that he so desperately missed in the GDR and in his own personal relationships. Neumann created an aesthetic of opposition in his Dresden Poetry Lecture of 1998, which he directed at the speechless "consensus reality" of the GDR. After the *Wende* he fought against the "common German dictionary" based on the realities of the "media dictatorship."[43] Neumann shares with most other East German authors an absolute and emotional rejection of Western consumer and media culture.

Neumann entitled his poetic reflections *Verhaftet* to reference his own experiences at the hands of the Stasi and their measures against him and his family; using the term as a metaphor, he builds on his own life in the GDR and offers a response to East German complaints with the phrase "forty years of life wasted."[44] Neumann's attempt to create a poetic language beyond the constraints of power has its roots in the dissident scene of the Prenzlauer Berg. In a unified Germany, the movement must come to terms with the fact that there is no ruling power to oppose: literature is no longer "hostile" (or "blessed" with enemies) and thus is free from any ideological strictures or reactions.[45] The challenge is to create a literary language that does not define itself in purely negative terms, but instead embraces honesty and truthfulness and avoids the limitations set by existing power relations.

In his experimental text *Anschlag* (1999) Neumann writes, "explain resistance to me," echoing Ingeborg Bachmann's poem "Explain love to me." Neumann arranges a meeting between East and West, as two Germans make an outing to the ruins of Chorin Monastery, a German cultural monument. The East German author and his West German visitor walk along and develop a different sort of dialogue, the purpose of which is to find a language of understanding that can allow for things to be seen and interpreted in a new light. As the East German begins to share the story of his son's imprisonment with which the Stasi has blackmailed him, feelings of helplessness and guilt wash over him, along with the memory of how he fought against this at the time and the sense of how such memories block any real communication with his visitor from the West, functioning as a kind of "speech blockade." The Westerner in turn is without pity: "Oh please: you and your resistance! In the end it made no difference at all!" and simply cannot understand why his counterpart is suddenly affected by his feelings now, in the act of remembering and relating: "My utter devastation from having spoken of the past did, fortunately, slowly dissipate as we made our way silently along; under the power of sight, the healing power of which I hoped to find and had made a part of my goal in reaching the Chorin monastery."[46]

Another, nonfictional, conversational partner from the West, Martin Walser, who has been quite supportive of Neumann's literary experiment, recognizes the poetic power of resistance; he quotes Novalis in conjunction with Neumann's tale: "Novels arise out of the shortcomings of history."[47] A literary representation of history must by definition be more than a recounting of the past. Neumann ends the tale of his fictitious East-West encounter with a claim to possess the "right to recount."[48] Walser understands like few others that Neumann's *Anschlag* and other post-*Wende* works are often desperate attempts to gain recognition for post-GDR literature and to win a newfound appreciation for it. In Neumann's case, this lack of recognition may have more to do with his complicated, convoluted writing style and his self-reflexive, self-referential language than anything else.

This is also especially true for Reinhard Jirgl, who worked at the East Berlin Volksbühne as a lighting technician, and wrote before the *Wende* but was published only thereafter. Jirgl's prose, extreme in both form and content, is challenging, but after he received a number of literary prizes, including the Büchner Prize in 2010, his reputation was solidified. After Heiner Müller, who had been supportive of his work, Jirgl has emerged as the *furor teutonicus* of German contemporary literature. His formidable novels take on Germany's authoritarian past, in which the GDR's wretched state socialism and the "post-totalitarian mentality" of united Germany are only the last stations in a longer story of suffering. The pain encapsulated in the novel is "the only real thing," confesses one of the characters, "the most valuable thing left to me in the face of having to go on living."[49] Jirgl's text alienates readers with its "catastrophic" ironic sarcasm. Jirgl argues that the "style and approach of irony" cannot adequately capture the devastating nature of reality, just as text cannot adequately reproduce the nature of speech. Like Arno Schmidt before him, Jirgl confronts the reader with idiosyncratic spelling and phonetics, odd punctuation and formatting, and strange compound words, as if hoping to give the printed word a renewed ability to convey meaning.

Thus armed—without illusions but filled with the wildest images—Jirgl examines German destinies. In his novel *Abschied von den Feinden* (1995), Jirgl tells the East-West tale of two estranged brothers, and in the process takes a look back at the deceptive securities of GDR life and bids farewell to past social realities. Jirgl underscores the everyday brutality of human relationships that have found further expression after the *Wende* in attacks on foreigners or asylum-seekers. *Die atlantische Mauer* (2000) utilizes biographies of individuals from the GDR and FRG to denounce the idea that there can be such a thing as a clean break with the past. Any attempt to escape to the New World of the United States is doomed to failure: unlike those former GDR authors (Jürgen Kolbe, Ingo Schulze, Durs Grünbein, and Kerstin Hensel) who experienced a short-lived enthusiasm for the United States after the *Wende,* Jirgl has had no such illusions.

Although Wolfgang Hilbig and Gert Neumann were influenced in the 1980s by the posthumanist philosophy of poststructuralism, their deconstruction never came close to Jirgl's convulsively obscene language and his radical methods of exposure that leave the human subject without a glimmer of hope. Jirgl's novel *Abtrünnig* (2005) traces the history of two ruined lives, one of a former GDR border patrol guard and the other of a Western journalist who runs amok in an apocalyptic Berlin cityscape, where the dilapidated remnants of state socialism come together with the new venture capitalism to form a ruined backdrop. The book's table of contents lists in descending order "birthdays," "work days," and "death days," and chapter titles such as "People Streets Paranoia," or "Learning in Berlin. Sex = capitalism = machines" hint at the discursive mélange of social and emotional impoverishment. The characters are largely made up of their speech acts, which gives the story a forceful physical and psychological presence.

Jirgl's complex novels thrive on an evidentiary basis of the moment, an expressive devotion to that which is said or shown. The patient reader who follows Jirgl's printed characters will notice that the plot does follow a certain controlled logic. Although the stories expand beyond their discursive boundaries, they are linked genealogically, through the lives of family members over several generations with the disastrous course of German history playing its part in each individual's life.

This is particularly true for his most recent epic novel, *Die Stille* (2009), a family sage spanning 100 years of history, with more than 100 family photos. The literary public has been waiting so very anxiously for the novel of the *Wende* that can serve as a secular epic form, and Jirgl may have delivered it with this convoluted text—but his shattered story offers a shredded history that is shamefully ugly, a lesser counterpart. Jirgl's century-long family epic (modeled on Alfred Döblin's narratives) is a labyrinth of events, bodies, ailments, and relationships that history makes come together accidently. Georg Adam, the father figure, who is more of a housekeeper than the ancestor in this genealogical drama, approaches the past through the medium of photography. The images are destroyed in order to forget: "The exposure time was longer than the time we took to live the moment. But ... the paths point to having been walked."[50] Whether over- or underexposed, the ways have disappeared from the present, but not the fact of "their having been traveled," which remains as memory, as a construct of the historical past, which in theory has never gone away. Memory is captured through the plot and through displays; the former GDR appears at the end of the novel as a "stuffy vacuum," after it has robbed its citizens of their careers, their property, and their very lives; the unreality of the FRG present appears as a "genetic structure of money" that is only capable of producing human capital without any return on investment.[51]

Jirgl is not content to leave historical imagination to structures alone. Instead, he investigates the suffering and vulnerability of people who are forced into certain situations. This becomes clear in one of his descriptions: "Because understanding the True Limit means to understand how much you can endure.... But if people are forced across this line—well, what then? Then—."[52] These extremes are what interests Jirgl. His plot and characters are strained and eccentric. But nonetheless, he finds a way to regain the moral purpose of his tale even in the face of the complete collapse of his characters and despite total disillusionment. Jirgl's work, although unconditional and ruthless, concerns itself with "what remains"—to accept the "unwelcome legacy" of this "gray, dusty, sometimes even blood-smeared existence," to give "poetical justice" to the poor miserable creatures via the medium of literature.

During the past twenty years, authors have moved away from shorter forms and have started to historicize and universalize German-German relations. The modern novel has been, since Cervantes' *Don Quixote,* the universal form of "empirical literature" that can best present the totality of history and society in a real, possible world. Although we live in a postmodern world, we still see a demand for this kind of work, especially in times and places of war and crisis when historical knowledge and experiences require revision. During World War I, Alfred Döblin called the historical novel "an epic painting made for the short-sighted."[53] Historical novels can create broad perspectives when dealing with things close at hand and when the end of the story remains open and has not settled as "history." The literary quality of curiosity apparently combines with an interest in the past, an inspiration of collective memory appropriate for historians, which in the present can still feely roam as short-range recollection. When the literary critic Frederic Jameson speaks of a postmodern "nostalgia for the present,"[54] he is referring to the novelistic imagination that discovers the eternal desire for the past in the present, in an imagined world of a book or film, where the reader can discover him- or herself. Perhaps the wish for a literary portrayal of the German *Wende* can be called such a novel. But Reinhard Jirgl's *Die Stille* is not that book, since it lacks the potential for readers to positively identify with the plot or characters.

Uwe Tellkamp's massive epic *The Tower* might instead fit the bill, because its success seems to speak to the desires of readers. Tellkamp himself talks about the need to counter the "current fragmentation" with a comprehensive "view of the world" that would fit our times, being "archaic, because it is replete with the present."[55] This restorative gesture secured literary acclaim for this novel in united Germany. The novel deals with a middle-class family who are surviving in a Dresdner villa overlooking the Elbe River. The book won the German National Prize and the Literature Prize from the Konrad Adenauer Stiftung. The author uses various styles most skillfully, from the classical *Bildungsroman* to montage techniques, surreal intermezzos, parodies, and weighty reflections. Together they merge to form a large panorama around the tale of a small family. Like Theodor Fontane or Thomas Mann, this combination is best situated in a certain cultural milieu and in good conversations. The realities of real existing socialism—bureaucratic headaches, Stasi surveillance, compulsory service, censorship—these things are disturbances outside of the domestic world of music, Goethe, family togetherness, and anniversaries. Although threatening, politics are rendered harmless by a sense of humor.

Through his careful detail Tellkamp provides us from the beginning with a goal-driven narrative. Citing news flashes, from Brezhnev's death to the mass exodus of GDR citizens to Hungary and Czechoslovakia, he describes the end of the GDR in which the inhabitants of the Dresdner "Tower" had never really felt at home. Ambitiously phrased and laden with meaning, the book ends with a veritable Walpurgis Night during which the GDR regime is turned topsy-turvy, and the decks are cleared. With some hesitation (the more self-assured women are the first to leave), Tellkamp's "Tower" society joins the protesters on the street and at the Dresden station, where the trains filled with GDR citizens wanting to leave stopped on their way from Prague. Tellkamp's literary rendition of the slogan "We are the people" highlights the drama of events. He also captures the poetry of the extraordinary experience with fleeting impressions, such as the moment when a "cobblestone of white and black granite" is reflected on the "water-resistant shields" of the police.[56] This stylizing of an incidental observation is related to the surprising surfacing of a theme about the moral of standing and walking tall. "All the faces showed the fears of the past days, the sorrow and uncertainty, but also something new: a luster …; with still uncertain breath, but proud to know that it was possible to walk straight ahead, with one's head held high, to know what one wanted, and what not.[57]

The novel presents us with such a clear message and (as some critics would have it) it may not be far afield from the *laudatio* by Bernhard Vogel, who praised the book in 2009, on behalf of the Konrad Adenauer Stiftung, as a "document of the individual's freedom and dignity in the face of the repressive attempts of the GDR dictatorship."[58]

The future of GDR Literature

How to compensate the loss of the author's "king's role" in the GDR after the *Wende*, Tellkamp's successful book, which attempts to restore a middle-class literary perspective on the end of the GDR, is a most interesting example. This holds true even if such a question would have never occurred to the author himself. If we wanted to take a step further and speak about a post-GDR literature, of the ghostly paradox of a GDR literature without the GDR, then a variety of techniques and forms are come into view, which are now winning various degrees of "distinction" in the literary landscape of united Germany. Another question, which stems from the Cold War period, namely whether German literature has been permanently divided, has already long been answered—by the common presentation of authors on a bookshelf.

Even though they have very different subjects, the texts under consideration here give some indication of how the GDR and GDR literature will continue on in a unified German literary scene. We will not likely see a revival of the authors' claim to provide political truths— that may belong safely in the past—but rather a remarkable variety of literary production since the *Wende* that has captured the experiences of East German lives, such as coming to terms with new encounters, readings, discoveries, and contacts in a unified Germany squarely situated within the Western sphere of influence. But also of learning about other countries and cultures, from Eastern Europe to the United States and Latin America, which are becoming ever more important for what used to be considered national literature. There are indications that the former bubble that protected GDR literature will now open up for a future that will go far beyond German-German sensitivities. Perhaps Reinhard Jirgl's epigram for his negative chronicle of German history is meant to be understood along those lines. "This book is dedicated to the future."

Notes

For a longer German version of this essay see Klaus Scherpe, "DDR-Literaturnach der DDR?" *Cultura Tedesca* 42/43 (2012), 193–219.

1. This chapter draws on two earlier publications: "Die Demission der Helden. DDR-Literatur nach der DDR," in Fabrizio Cambi and Alessandro Fambrini, eds., *Zehn Jahre nachher. Poetische Identität und Geschichte in der deutschen Literatur nach der Vereinigung* (Trento, 2002), 11–28; "Die Wende von 1989. Moral, Ästhetik und Politik der

literarischen Intelligenz," in Klaus R. Scherpe, *Stadt Krieg Fremde. Literatur und Kultur nach den Katastrophen* (Tübingen, 2002), 289–313. Numerous conference proceedings and edited volumes address post-GDR literature, including Heinz Ludwig Arnold, ed., *DDR-Literatur der neunziger Jahre* (Munich, 2000); Roland Berbig, Birgit Dahlke, Michael Kämper-van den Boogaart, and Uwe Schoor, eds., *Zersammelt. Die inoffizielle Literaturszene der DDR nach 1990* (Berlin, 2000); Gerhard Fischer and David Roberts, eds., *Schreiben nach der Wende* (Tübingen, 2001); Peter Alheit, Kerstin Bast-Haider, and Petra Drauschke, eds., *Die zögernde Ankunft im Westen. Biographien und Mentalitäten in Ostdeutschland* (Frankfurt, 2004); Holger Helbig, ed., *Weiterschreiben. Zur DDR-Literatur nach dem Ende der DDR* (Berlin, 2007); Janine Ludwig and Mirjam Meuser, eds., *Literatur ohne Land. Schreibstrategien einer DDR-Literatur im vereinten Deutschland* (Freiburg, 2009); Patricia Herminghouse and Katharina Gerstenberger, eds., *German Literature in a New Century: Trends, Traditions, Transformations* (New York, 2008).

2. Pierre Bourdieu, *Die Intellektuellen und die Macht,* ed. Irene Dölling (Hamburg, 1991).
3. Pierre Bourdieu, "Revolutionen, Volk und intellektuelle Hybris," *Freibeuter* 49 (1991), 27–34.
4. Stefan Heym, "Aschermittwoch in der DDR," *Der Spiegel* 49 (1989).
5. Helga Königsdorf, *Aus dem Dilemma eine Chance machen* (Hamburg, 1991), 8.
6. Pierre Bourdieu, *Homo academicus* (Frankfurt, 1988); Gunter Gebauer and Christoph Wulf, eds., *Neue Perspektiven im Denken Pierre Bourdieus* (Frankfurt, 1993); Pierre Bourdieu, *Les règles e l'art* (Paris, 1992); idem, *Science de la science et réflexivité* (Paris, 2002).
7. Christa Wolf, *Die Stadt der Engel oder The Overcoat of Dr. Freud* (Frankfurt, 2010).
8. Alexander Kluge and Oskar Negt, *Geschichte und Eigensinn* (Frankfurt, 1981), 397.
9. Volker Braun, *Wir befinden uns soweit wohl. Wir sind erst einmal am Ende. Äußerungen* (Frankfurt,1998), 153.
10. Thomas Brussig, *Helden wie wir* (Berlin, 1995), 304.
11. Ibid., 311.
12. Hans-Peter Krüger, *Demission der Helden. Kritiken von innen 1983–1992* (Leipzig, 1992), 8.
13. Durs Grünbein, *Das erste Jahr. Berliner Aufzeichnungen* (Frankfurt, 2001), 44.
14. Thomas Rosenlöcher, *Ostgezeter. Beiträge zur Schimpfkultur* (Frankfurt, 1997).
15. Alexander Kluge and Heiner Müller, *Ich bin ein Landvermesser. Gespräche,* 2nd ed. (Berlin, 1996), 158.
16. Volker Braun, *Lustgarten Preußen. Ausgewählte Gedichte* (Frankfurt, 1996), 14.
17. Volker Braun, *Wir befinden uns soweit wohl. Wir sind erst einmal am Ende. Äußerungen* (Frankfurt, 1998), 34.
18. Volker Braun, *Flickwerk* (Frankfurt, 2009).
19. Ibid., 77.
20. Volker Braun, *Machwerk oder Das Schichtbuch des Flick von Lauchhammer* (Frankfurt, 2008).
21. Uwe Kolbe, *Renegatentermine. 30 Versuche, die eigene Erfahrung zu behaupten* (Frankfurt, 1998), 111.
22. Ibid., 216.
23. Uwe Kolbe, *Vineta* (Frankfurt, 1998), 11f.
24. Uwe Kolbe, *Vinetas Achive. Annäherung an Gründe* (Göttingen, 2011).
25. Uwe Kolbe, *Vaterlandkanal. Ein Fahrtenbuch* (Frankfurt, 1990), 7.
26. Durs Grünbein, *Das erste Jahr,* 26.
27. Durs Grünbein, *Galilei vermisst Dantes Hölle und bleibt an den Maßen hängen. Aufsätze 1989–1995* (Frankfurt, 1996), 48.
28. Durs Grünbein, *Vom Stellenwert der Worte. Frankfurter Poetikvorlesung 2009* (Berlin, 2010), 31f.

29. Ibid., 35.
30. Durs Grünbein, *Postskriptum: Seneca. Die Kürze des Lebens* (Frankfurt, 2004), 24.
31. Durs Grünbein: *Vom Stellenwert der Worte*, 41.
32. Ibid., 42.
33. Katja Lange-Müller, *Kasper Mauser—Die Feigheit vorm Freund* (Frankfurt, 1990), 63.
34. Ingo Schulze, *Tausend Geschichten sind nicht genug. Leipziger Poetikvorlesung 2007* (Frankfurt, 2008), 48.
35. Kathrin Schmidt, *Seebachs schwarze Katzen* (Munich, 2002), 180.
36. Wolfgang Hilbig, *Ich. Roman* (Frankfurt, 1993), 23.
37. Ibid., 77.
38. Ibid., 74.
39. Wolfgang Hilbig, *Das Provisorium* (Frankfurt, 2000), 54f.
40. Ibid., 35.
41. Ibid., 316.
42. Gert Neumann, *Anschlag* (Cologne, 1999), 95.
43. Gert Neumann, *Verhaftet. Dresdner Poetikvorlesung 1998* (Dresden, 1999), 9ff.
44. Ibid., 72.
45. Gert Neumann, *Anschlag*, 60.
46. Ibid., 212f.
47. Martin Walser, "Geist und Sinnlichkeit. Gert Neumanns deutsch-deutsches Gespräch," in Gert Neumann, *Verhaftet*, 93.
48. Gert Neumann, *Anschlag*, 258ff.
49. Reinhard Jirgl, *Die Stille* (Munich, 2009), 18.
50. Ibid., 496.
51. Ibid., 319.
52. Ibid., 456.
53. See Klaus R. Scherpe, "'Ein Kolossalgemälde für Kurzsichtige.' Das Andere der Geschichte in Alfred Döblins 'Wallenstein,'" in Hartmut Eggert, Ulrich Profitlich, and Klaus R. Scherpe, eds., *Geschichte als Literatur* (Stuttgart, 1990), 226–241.
54. Fredric Jameson, *Postmodernism, or The Cultural Logic of Late Capitalism* (Durham, 1991), 279–296.
55. Uwe Tellkamp, *Die Sandwirtschaft. Anmerkungen zu Schrift und Zeit* (Frankfurt, 2009), 154f.
56. Uwe Tellkamp, *Der Turm* (Frankfurt, 2008), 956.
57. Ibid., 966f.
58. http://www.kas.de/wf/de/71.6815/.

Chapter Eleven

Unity and Difference

Some Reflections on a Disparate Field

Frank Hörnigk

At the outset I must admit a certain reluctance to reflect anew on what has been an extremely unique and conflicted process of "culturally working through German unification," especially as these reflections come after more than twenty years and are being made in a public forum at that.[1] The reasons for this hesitation are complex, in that they relate both to past and present personal hopes and/or disappointments as well as cultural and political developments after 1990. The following remarks will focus largely on these concerns and, in so doing, consider the fundamental difficulties associated with arriving at a balanced judgment.

The fact that I have nonetheless accepted the offer to write a short piece on this subject from an "East German perspective" is due primarily to the intended *American* audience of this project and the hope it engenders that we can gain a broader space for theoretical reflection. In my opinion, this alone would be worth the effort if it could result in a more open and critical engagement with German politics. Backed by state power and possessing vast influence over public rhetoric, German political discourse has heretofore vigorously objected to any *real* alternatives to its own story of German reunification. Central to this image is the idea that the FRG possesses the sole right to interpret the culture and history of the former GDR, annexed as an "incorporated territory" after 1990, once the FRG had emerged as the "historic victor" in the struggle between socialism and capitalism. After this "incorporation" was secured, the Federal Republic could celebrate the amazing rebirth of its claim to legally represent both of the German postwar histories.

Notes for this chapter begin on page 212.

For this reason alone it is important to find a language based on equal regard for the other, that can resist the urge to repress a critical sense of the past. In the face of a uniform and polarizing (with few exceptions) media landscape, we must not succumb to the desire to receive information passively, or in "anticipatory agreement" to revive old class warfare slogans from the days when, in Heiner Müller's words "the enemy was still healthy."

We should therefore strive to contribute to an appropriate criticism of a thoroughly anachronistic rhetoric of power; a discourse based on simplistic polarized categories that when applied to social realities in and beyond Europe at the beginning of the twenty-first century have blocked progress instead of promoting it. Such a critical language would allow us to reflect on the ways in which we can think multiculturally about the inner unity of all conditions as well as those in one's own country.

For a possible way out of this dilemma, which appears, in the final analysis, to be determined largely by mental blocks formed by cultural differences and differing mentalities, I will draw on my experiences of more open forms of intellectual discourse. Over the past two decades, in numerous personal and academic encounters, I have learned to appreciate this more nuanced and differentiated approach, which is especially prominent in the United States. Included in this understanding is a sense of independence vis-à-vis the politics of one's own country as well as a certain skepticism regarding intellectual fashions coming from the outside, like from Germany. For example, beginning in the 1990s, only a few years after unification, the so-called German-German literary dispute gave rise to a painfully divisive and yet largely spurious theoretical debate centered on Christa Wolf's *What Remains?* The controversy, which can be seen as paradigmatic of the manner in which the legitimacy of East German history and culture has been called into question, was received in the United States with criticism and distance.

In April of 1990, Sander Gilman (then at Cornell) invited me to organize and participate in a lecture series to be held at several major universities along the East Coast. Included in our group were the writer Daniela Dahn, the pastor Friedrich Schorlemmer, and the filmmaker Thomas Heise, in addition to myself. This all happened just as the "romantic phase" of the so-called "peaceful revolution" in the GDR was coming to an end, just as reality was catching up with the revolutionaries. A more apt phrase to describe the period (at least from our perspective) might be "the short winter of anarchy." The brief intermission provided by the "roundtable" discussions and "the democracy of meetings," the citizens' movement—all this ended with the first free elections to the East German Parliament on 18 March 1990. The end of illusions came with the victory of the CDU under the leadership of the last prime minister of the GDR, Lothar de Maizière. What was once a possibility had been shrunk to a momentary state of emergency.

In lecture halls at Harvard, Brown, Amherst, and Cornell we spoke of the moments of discrediting the old power structures and of how it felt to experience freedom in those heady days. More than anything else, we emphasized our feelings of genuine happiness at being a part of the first successful political revolution in Germany, each of us in his or her own way, and the sense of being the real subjects of our own history, for the first time in our lives. All of us could sense our listeners' respect, as well as a reserve that was combined with much solidarity. The people who came to our lectures and stayed to talk with us had, at that moment, a much clearer understanding than we did about how the world of capital, into which we had just entered, functions. We were told repeatedly that in the future we would need to remember our own biographies and experiences and bring them to the foreground of our work.

Realizing the Cultural Divide

A month prior to the trip I had been named Dean of German Studies at Berlin's Humboldt University, where I was elected in a grassroots democracy, receiving the majority of votes from all members of the department, including students. At that point the stampede for newly freed up professorial positions had not yet begun, but it was clear to most of us (and to me) that we were, with our backgrounds and our membership status as the old elite, very close to the model of the "politicians of the transition" so aptly characterized by Hans Magnus Enzensberger in one of his excellent essays (Michael Gorbachev and Egon Krenz were two examples of the type). Enzensberger argued that the most important historical task for such figures, after they had done their part in helping to peacefully dismantle the old regime, would be to abolish themselves.

During the next few years most GDR academics were not even asked to perform such a task or to come to such a conclusion; rather, they were "phased out" (*abgewickelt*). Every member of the Academy of Science, every academic at a university or center for higher education, was evaluated in a process that did not promise equal opportunity. The resulting "cleansing" of elite positions was unprecedented, even when compared with the denazification policies in West Germany after 1945. The long-term effects of this process can still be seen today; scholars with a "GDR background" do not have the same chance for a position as scholars from the West, even after twenty years, and even if we take into consideration the different statistical size of the populations in East and West. An institutional pattern, based on the old FRG's values and ideas about what a future "republic of education" in Germany should look like, had already been set, certain to last across generations.

In 1990, when no one could see the consequences of such actions in all their clarity, the portents of what was to come were overlooked. From today's perspective, we can see that the signs were there all along. One of the very first such clues was a series of differentiations beginning in 1989 that were especially critical of artistic attitudes and modes of expression associated with the GDR. Such judgments were often linked to a fundamental realignment of previously held theoretical and poetological positions. Given the changed political situation, these criticisms were directed at the aesthetic values of GDR itself and questioned how criticism should function and by what measures the artistic intelligentsia (which has long since been celebrated in both East and West) would be judged. With the demise of the GDR, East German intellectuals had not only lost their original social status, but also their special appeal—above all from a Western perspective—namely to serve as an ever quotable, eternal voice of dissidence.

Still inspired by their former influence, and experiencing in the heat of the moment a wonderful sense of shared happiness, these critics (along with some Western activists) suffered from the illusion that the changes that were to occur after the fall of the Wall in the GDR (some spoke of and still speak today of a revolution) would lead to necessary and fundamental reforms in the FRG as well. This proved to be wishful thinking. Instead, the question concerning distinctions between the two systems was first debated as polarizing difference, and this in turn led to a stigmatizing of the entire history of the GDR. This was the moment when the distancing between all of GDR history and the FRG began; thereafter the GDR was further condemned and stigmatized by the FRG.

One example might shed light on this moment of inner separation shortly after the external walls had been toppled. It relates to a personally unsettling discussion (that was to have more persistent consequences) that occurred during the first GSA conference I attended in Buffalo in October 1990. I had been invited by the organizers to give a lecture about new developments in GDR literature after the fall of the Wall. Jost Hermand opened the panel with the prediction that this would likely be the last time such a large conference would deal in such a prominent fashion with the aesthetic and historic dimensions of a category that would soon no longer exist.

In my remarks I reminded audience members about a number of more recent critical articles about GDR literature in regard to their own society and attempted to move the discussion to a level beyond that relevant to the GDR alone. It seemed appropriate to consider the most important impulses within American German Studies and the broader reception of GDR literature, for instance to reflect on the cultural and critical potential of the works of such writers as Christa Wolf, Heiner Müller, and Volker Braun, and to bring my own observations to bear on the subject. Operating under the assumption that I would thus be able to convey the *Eigensinn* ("self-understanding") of the literary avant-garde that had grown out of the GDR and explore its further possibilities within a larger project of an international modern aesthetics, I was greeted with a great deal of skepticism. Wolfgang Emmerich (Bremen), who was at the time and who remains a close friend and colleague, indirectly but strongly questioned my views with his counterthesis regarding the *homo melancholicus*—which he considered to be the ideal type of the premodern, ideologically committed GDR artist. Volker Braun served as the model of this type; Emmerich compared him to the image of the artist sitting amidst the chaos of the world that had crumbled around him, staring at the ruins with his aesthetic convictions or tools left useless at his side, who would himself turn to stone. Albrecht Dürer's famous engraving *Melancholy* underscored Emmerich's point in a most convincing manner for those in the audience; it is a classic symbol of the tragic (or tragicomic?) fate of art, once in the service of politics. While I expressed my heartfelt respect for my colleague's insightful comments, I realized that I needed to face the difficult truths with which I was being confronted. Suddenly, I stood at the edge of an abyss that had opened up between us. After having spent so many years in seeming agreement about GDR literature and history, we were suddenly on two separate sides. The political status quo that had brought our lives and work together no longer existed.

Condemnations of GDR Literature

But that was just the beginning! Once the confrontation between East and West had been settled, with the GDR as the loser, we heard ever more radical criticisms of the historic failure of GDR art in general and GDR literature in particular, which went far beyond a critique that was academically balanced yet theoretically superior. These criticisms had an ideological bent, and they were framed around an enemy; "literature in the service of the state" and "ideological aesthetics" were two of the more popular phrases making the rounds in the daily newspapers. Given talk about its inevitable decline and demise, the next step was to assume that there never had been anything like GDR literature or art at all; what had been identi-

and grandchildren do. We can hope that the inner division of society, in which we still partially live, will also come to an end with us.

This author cannot and will not understand himself as representative of his own generation. He is not. It is always the idiosyncrasy of individual experiences that helps one write history. (Even being able to formulate such a sentence without reservation could only occur after 1990, and that good fortune he has not forgotten!) History will not repeat itself, but it can recover from a past experienced by a large group of people. These individuals, more than forty years after division, have lived through decades of another kind of inner division that continues to this day (in spite of political unification) and that hinders true equality and therefore ultimately denies *everyone* in society legal peace. Equality and justice do not begin (and therefore do not end, either) with the material equality of all people in society. This is (and must remain) an important constitutional goal. The fact that people living in the so-called "new" (or even worse, "young") states have experienced unequal material opportunities over the past twenty years does not fully explain why they can only see themselves as "second-class Germans." They feel this way because of the affront of the idea that their own pasts and their own cultural origin and present do not carry the same weight and are therefore not granted the same moral authority, despite all the claims and assertions that what is being denounced is the "communist system" and not the people who lived under it.

Those cultural experiences that relate to equal and just gains and losses in a historical process reach well beyond society's artistic or cultural forms of expression in the more narrow sense. Under all circumstances, we must think critically about this, simply because such values reflect the internal and external contradictions of society, as we have shown. But it is not enough to mention in passing those cultural achievements of public production: those that have been "worked through" and the entire constructed environment; the urbanity of the cities; the protection of natural resources; the availability of goods and services—all of these things belong to a communicative field of a broader concept of culture. If we consider the entirety of life circumstances in Eastern Germany, we can say that tremendous strides have been made in this cultural space after 1990. To recognize and appreciate that achievement is an imperative of intellectual and political honesty—and at the same time it raises important questions about the actual structural contradictions of society.

If we are to speak about how the unification experiences have been culturally processed in both German states after 1990 (without self-glorifying an autonomously desired morale of either Eastern or Western sensibilities), we must logically consider how, through their discursive mediation, communicative spaces define the intellectual-cultural sphere and structure of a society. If we wish to develop our open society further, we must be willing to continue criticizing its reality.

Notes

1. Since the following observations are more in the nature of a personal reflection than an academic article, the author has decided to dispense with endnotes.

Chapter Twelve

The Painful Exit from the Cold War

East German Writers and the Demise of the Reading Culture

Frank Trommler

Among literary scholars it has become a standard argument that the status of literature as part of high culture has precipitously declined in the late twentieth century. Scholarly discussions do not dwell much on this fact anymore. The relentless growth of electronic media as means of public and private communication provides ample evidence of it. Instead debates have moved toward the analysis of specific political and social transformations as likely contributors to this development, in particular the upheavals of 1989/91 that led to the collapse of the Soviet Empire and the end of the Cold War. As German writers both in the East and the West experienced the changes with strong emotions, the question has been raised: in what way did the reunification of the country affect the demise of their roles as mediators of the *Zeitgeist?*

In view of the enormous output of literary polemics, books, and pamphlets in the years of the *Wende,* it is almost counterintuitive to take up the argument about the diminishing role of literature in the public discourse in West and East Germany and, subsequently, in the reunified country. Though publishers could not help but promote essayistic treatises and polemic interventions more often than fictional accounts of the turmoil—because the latter did not easily emerge—they maintained the anticipation of a new German literature that would reflect the pains of unifying the country in moving narratives. Authors like Jurek Becker, who in *Amanda Herzlos* (1992) fictionalized the unification as a badly conceived wedding

Notes for this chapter begin on page 226.

of hardly compatible partners, and Ingo Schulze, who drew vivid portraits of East German journalists, doctors, nurses, and teachers, though not workers, in his "novel," *Simple Stories* (1998), whetted the public's appetite for a literary reckoning with the unexpected events that brought a troubled nation together (or not). And yet, already a decade later a consensus emerged that the supposed literary boom did not materialize, even with much goodwill on the part of newspaper feuilletons and reports from the reinvigorated Leipzig book fair. Consequently the anticipation of a reawakening of creative powers, now liberated from political straightjackets, gave way to assessments not just of the lack of literary prowess but also of the fact that the word of writers and intellectuals was increasingly discounted in public discourse.

If this decline was systemic, given the modernizing trends in the fields of communication and media technology, it should have been visible before 1989. In fact, it was, though scarcely, under the regime of the SED. In the West, the 1980s became the crucial decade for a twofold adjustment of the redefined and broadened concept of culture that had emerged in the 1960s when the dichotomies between high and mass cultures came under attack. The first was that the strong international dominance of American music, film, and media culture led to a wider acceptance of the commercial conditions of cultural production, including those of high culture, literature, and art. This development had already been anticipated in the 1930s by Walter Benjamin, who hoped to insert into the productive process an anti-capitalist incentive in the engagement of the working masses. Less prominently anticipated but even more powerful was the other adjustment of the broadened concept of culture that grew, under even stronger American influence in the area of international communication, from the digital revolution that transformed notions of space and time on a global scale. Communication technology reconstituted the relationships among economic, political, and cultural actors, absorbing functions and practices that traditionally had been considered to belong to the cultural realm. It represented a strong challenge to the literary writer and intellectual as a public voice that assumed responsibility for the affairs of the society as a whole—a remnant of the writers' universal mission that in Germany had almost been extinguished under National Socialism, yet regained strength in the cultural rebuilding of the postwar decades.

What Writers Gained and Lost

Until the fall of the Berlin Wall, East German authors and their works enjoyed much attention on both sides of the border. As suppliers to that

proudly labeled *Leseland DDR*, where reading books, literary works, still had a particular ring and provided entertainment and social information, writers were recognized as public, though censored, figures who knew about the limits of their influence yet could count on the acknowledgment of their voice. While the market society of the West generally did not easily bestow such a high status on writers, it supported this standing in applauding their projected critical mission under a communist dictatorship. The success of such authors as Christa Wolf or Ulrich Plenzdorf in the West arose to a considerable extent from a mixture of interest and respect; at the same time, they were still perennially thought of as voices from "over there" (*drüben*).

Western critics may not have bestowed a label of universalism on these writers in the East, but there was a distinct feeling that they fulfilled a function in the public discourse that seemed to have become rare in the short-term exposures of authors in the communication industry of the West. Their public recognition, on the one hand embattled by the Stasi and party cultural politics, on the other fortified by Western journalists and readers, helped build and maintain the idea that this state had a literature and that this literature was not subjugated to the market forces of the capitalist culture industry. Their literary works commanded an attention that seemed not to be based on the machinations of the market but rather on the value of their stories, their literary insights and political risk taking. When the state of the GDR collapsed, a discussion ensued about whether one could attach to this literature the attribute of a "pre-modern" modus operandi,[1] as Wolfgang Emmerich asserted, which would stress the notion of an enclave, claiming the Leseland as a kind of protected region, a *Schutzgebiet*. Hans-Peter Herrmann argued against such use of "modern" and "pre-modern" and stressed that the contradictions of culture in the West still fostered many insular and aura-laden constellations for writers amidst the prevailing trends toward consumerism, the cult of the media, and the impersonal.[2]

As much as this discussion illuminates the discrepancies between the forces of the communication machinery of the market economy and the promotion of the traditional accoutrements of literature, art, and culture, it misses the fact that this divergence was part of a larger political constellation. Only in the context of the Cold War can the prominence of writers and intellectuals in Europe at this time be fully grasped and the enormous emphasis on matters of culture and cultural policies be rationalized. If it had not been for the political stagnation of Cold War confrontations, culture and literature would not have been recognized as shaping forces on both sides of the Iron Curtain. This became most visible in the 1970s when the political stalemate between East and West allowed only a "cultural"

initiative to overcome the most flagrant injustices and when UNESCO's International Conference on Cultural Policy in Europe in Helsinki (1972) helped pave the way for the founding of the Conference on Security and Cooperation in Europe ("CSCE"). Hans Schwab-Felisch, an experienced observer of the postwar resurgence of Germany and Europe, summarized this turn to culture in the description of the meeting: "The Helsinki conference was characterized by an exceptional, almost otherworldly emphasis on culture, which was also a sign of the times. It was as if Europe had paused in shock to reflect on its role in modern history, in the face of the threats to the environment and civilization, which the world was beginning to notice. The call for 'culture' was heard on all sides."[3]

This elevation of cultural and literary exchanges created, of course, more problems in East than in West Germany. However, it also strengthened the focus on literature as a means of international bridge building, thereby hindering its absorption into the growing communication industry as well as its suppression by a censorship apparatus. It shielded writers and intellectuals from the extreme leveling effects of the media revolution not just in the East but also in the West, even allowing for first steps toward expressions of solidarity across the Iron Curtain in the 1980s. A breakthrough occurred in December 1981 when Stephan Hermlin, the renowned GDR writer, organized a writers' meeting, the Berliner Begegnung zur Friedensförderung, under the auspices of addressing the accelerating nuclear threat. Located in East Berlin, the writers' peace conference brought together such East and West German authors as Günter Grass, Franz Fühmann, Günter de Bruyn, Luise Rinser, Peter Härtling, Heiner Müller, and the Swiss novelist Adolf Muschg whose addresses about the devastating nuclear politics on both sides of the Wall were published in the West while the GDR officials eased their usual censorship by some degree. When the official representatives of the CSCE states met at a large cultural forum in Budapest in 1985, György Konrad, Hans Magnus Enzensberger, Susan Sontag, and others organized a well-publicized "antiforum." West and East German authors, among them Günter Grass and Hermann Kant, assured each other of their solidarity in opposition to the renewed escalation of the Cold War.

As the Helsinki accord helped stimulate literary life and dissention in all Eastern European countries, East German cultural institutions such as theaters, orchestras, publishing houses, and museums as well as individual artists and writers benefited richly from the attempts of their government to gain acceptance within this international framework. The inter-German cooperation was sealed in 1972 by the Basic Treaty between the Federal Republic and the German Democratic Republic. It became the basis for the long-planned cultural agreement between the two governments that

"legalized" various practices of cultural exchange that resulted from local and commercial initiatives. When the agreement finally became official in 1986, it had lost most of its provocative associations though it clearly did not eliminate the Wall as a cultural divide. At this time, however, it was also seen as evidence of the intensive cross-border exchange. Uwe Wittstock, a keen observer of East German culture, left no doubt about the extent to which East German culture was known in the Federal Republic when he commented on the agreement in 1986: "At least since the *Grundlagenvertrag*—and due to entirely other, sadder reasons, especially since Wolf Biermann's expatriation in 1976—the culture of the GDR has been rather well represented in the Federal Republic. Presently, however, there are far too few opportunities for our cultural life to present itself in the other Germany. The action plans that the agreement prescribes every second year will offer an exceptional chance in this regard."[4]

Concerning this presentation, East Germans were able to catch up after the fall of the Berlin Wall—*if* they were so inclined and not totally focused on the products of Western consumer culture. Their disregard for the agenda of an improved socialism that Christa Wolf, Heiner Müller, and other writers and intellectuals advocated at the mass rally on the Alexanderplatz in Berlin five days before the Wall fell on 9 November 1989, already signaled the limitations of the writers' hold on their audience (and the limits of intellectual politics in a moment of triumphant Western capitalism). The demise of the speaker role of the writers in the following months has long been seen as a sign of their disconnect from the population of the German Democratic Republic at large, but it was, at closer look, not inconsistent with the special role that had been bestowed on them both by the East German state and West German media, reflecting the controlled self-empowerment of the intelligentsia under the Helsinki conditions of the 1970s and 1980s. It was hardly surprising that those writers who most poignantly called on each other to propose a reform agenda turned against the politics of reunification that were promoted by Western parties and embraced by the Eastern population. Unlike their colleagues in Eastern Europe—especially those in Poland, Czechoslovakia, and Hungary, who had made use of the Helsinki conditions in their fight for national liberation and thus became symbols of the democratic self-liberation of their societies, best embodied by Vaclav Havel—East German writers tried to escape the trap of national wish-fulfillment, a predicament that some West German authors such as Günter Grass also shunned. Grass was most outspoken in his rejection of reunification, arguing that the crime of the Holocaust, committed in the name of all Germans, forfeited a reversal of that outgrowth of the Second World War, the division of Germany.

Much of the acrimonious debate among East and West German intellectuals in 1990/91 resulted from the attempt of West German critics to delegitimize their colleagues as symbols of literature being a moral force. Without the brutal reality of the Wall and in view of their rejection of the political and economic unification, GDR intellectuals lost the bonus of dissension within a totalitarian system that Western media had granted them for many years. "We all, meaning the West German critics, for years applied a bonus to GDR books," *Spiegel* editors stated in a discussion with Günter Grass in 1990. "We said to each other, literature over there originates under certain difficult conditions; the authors cannot say most things directly; they have to choose detours. We did not accuse anybody that he stayed in the GDR or that he left the GDR—it did not behoove us. But we yielded a bonus to literature. And we were careful when describing its effect since we did not want to harm its authors vis-à-vis the cultural functionaries." Upon which Günter Grass replied with some aggravation: "And this bonus that Christa Wolf claimed for herself, is now crossed out."[5]

Indeed, it was gone. Christa Wolf's book of 1989, *What Remains?*, in which she described her experience as a target of Stasi observation a decade before, became a bone of contention as it seemed to indicate that she claimed victim status despite her position as a much-honored writer in that state. It did not take long before numerous East German writers had to defend themselves against the accusation of having been Stasi informants.

It is hardly surprising that musicians, singers, and opera and theater directors received a much warmer welcome in the West in the years following the fall of the Wall. They had profited from the Helsinki accords concerning limited cultural exchanges—usually by having become known in the West through guest appearances—yet they had not, or had only rarely, been forced to articulate their aesthetic enterprise as a symbolic manifestation in the same language that state and party used. They were less affected by the fact that the unification and the prevailing estrangement between East and West Germans almost overnight became the target of a huge communication industry, easily converted into innumerable reports, stories, and visual narratives whose common denominator was easy accessibility and distribution. What could writers offer that reached beyond this publication machinery? A literary metaphor? An epic summary? Or were they restricted to defending themselves against Western critics who alleged that they were collaborating with the reigning powers? While musicians and performers slid into the larger arts and entertainment market of the 1990s, writers felt compelled to explain their plight as a legacy of a disappearing society that had been part of German history after Hitler.

Willingly or unwillingly they became exhibition objects for the demise of the writer's empowered role as a spokesperson for society.

And yet, the loss in professional standing also afflicted writers in the West. Although West German authors had a long-established grip on the publication market and knew how to approach new and more current topics such as the wars in Iraq and the Balkans, the Holocaust memorial in Berlin, or the growing concerns about the environment, they lost considerable sections of their audience. Beginning in the 1970s, long-term trends of elevating individual and milieu issues to core topics of literature increasingly overshadowed works that tried to deliver symbolic representations of larger social and political constellations.[6] And more importantly, the empowerment of the communications industry through the digitization and visualization of information began to drown out the literary voice as a particular cultural icon. When Günter Grass in 1995 published his attempt to catch the wide historical implications of the reunification in the 700-page novel *Ein weites Feld*, he ran into a wall of criticism the least of which was the comment that the old-fashioned technique of novel writing was inadequate to express the realities of the upheavals of 1989/90.

The Dismantling of Cold War Dividends

While literary scholars have produced an impressive array of studies about the impact of the dissolution of the German Democratic Republic on German literature and culture, they have rarely explored its dependence on the overriding dynamics of the Cold War in the field of culture. Due to this neglect of the larger framework, the whole complex of German-German reunification in this period, following the extended phase of internal antagonism, appears to outside observers as the latest—and hopefully last—culmination of a national exceptionalism which is as isolating when it is meant critically as when meant approvingly. As the Second World War had opened the gates for an unprecedented culture of propaganda, the Cold War presented the most influential framework for the dynamics and the sponsorship of culture in the second half of the twentieth century. It provides an important broader perspective to questions that are not adequately addressed through the analysis of purely national cultures or bilateral relations, for instance with the Soviet Union or the United States.

The key to the broader picture is the contradictions, not straightforward policies. The advancement of the communication culture tended to diminish the symbolic power of literature and culture in the increasingly interconnected world. At the same time a new emphasis on the importance of culture in the advanced societies gained momentum, even political power. This contradiction was a connection as well. The Cold War provided cultural and scientific incentives in a variety of ways. It sustained, even enhanced traditional patterns of cultural production and representation. This occurred not just within the Eastern bloc but also in the West and expressed itself in often lavish financing of cultural and scientific endeavors. It spanned the Atlantic and included such diverse phenomena as the huge expansion of the scientific establishment in the United States as well as the enterprises of the Ministry of German-German Affairs in Bonn and the whole support structure for maintaining Berlin as a cultural showpiece of the West. It also affected new concepts of cultural policies as part of the Social Democrats' 1970s reform agenda, which was propagated as a timely form of democratization of a society whose social petrification had been laid bare by the 1968 revolt.

What the Cold War assembled could not remain untouched once the Iron Curtain had come down. If the 1990s have been described as the decade of misery for East German writers and the whole cultural and academic establishment of their dissolved state, it is only a small, though distinct part of a worldwide process of dismantling the cultural buildup that had been sustained by, and, at the same time, had sustained, the Cold War. This is small consolation—and cannot account for the many injustices perpetrated on the East German intelligentsia by the West German intelligentsia—but needs to be kept in mind when tallying the devastating consequences of the crisis of public sponsorship for culture and science in the 1990s that left no scientific institute, no theater or orchestra, no cultural foundation untouched. What President George Bush lauded as a peace dividend had great potential for world politics and nuclear disarmament, but also meant the disassembling of a richly endowed sideshow of the Cold War confrontation. It brought liberation, it opened the window to unhindered international cultural exchange and creativity, yet it abolished most forms of privilege culture and literature outside of the capitalist market.

If one lists the reasons for the swift disappearance of the East German literary and cultural scene in the post-Wall world, the fast-spreading patterns of media business, bolstered both by entertainment offerings and communication advances, need to be counted as crucial forces against which no *Schutzgebiet* could endure. It is hardly surprising that the legacy of the GDR was conjured vividly in the realm of literature, which had proven to be the most privileged forum where a specific East German culture could be claimed, financed, and administered. And it is no less surprising that the new literary voices from this area that have captured the imagination of readers in the united country and beyond, most prominently Durs Grünbein, Ingo Schulze, and Uwe Tellkamp, belong to a younger generation that has learned to historicize the legacy of the GDR as part of a larger German culture. This development posed a dilemma to older writers who had became known through the state publication channels. Those who had grown in stature as authors for a broader audience faced a good chance that their specific politics mattered only somewhat. Authors such as Christoph Hein, Heiner Müller, Wolfgang Hilbich, and Monika Maron, to name just a few, succeeded by presenting a particular view from the East. However, numerous authors who had become relatively well known before 1989 fell from grace; aside from the threat of being associated with Stasi contacts, there was no soft landing in a crowded publications market that was rapidly losing customers.

The fact that many authors and playwrights of the GDR were quite well known in the West before the Wall came down might have inadvertently contributed to the rapid disappearance of a specific East German literary scene. Besides, numerous writers like Wolf Biermann, Sarah Kirsch, Jurek Becker, and Thomas Brasch already lived in the West.[7] New interest in their careers was only awakened by questions about the interactions with the Stasi. Curiosity about cultural life in the GDR, however, was more often found outside of German borders, where observers used the topic to gain access to the mysteries of German-German discord. Having constituted a neglected part of the Cold-War embrace of divided Germany especially in the United States, East Germany attracted fleeting interest as a model communist society in self-destruction, an accessible part of the Eastern bloc that officials and foundations included in their East European funding agendas up until 1994. Yet it was more of a sideshow in the early 1990s, whereas the strong competition between Western organizations and think tanks—which included George Soros' "Empire" in several East European countries, German political foundations, and American foundations as well as the State Department—developed with regard to Eastern Europe, retracing the desired yet stalled nation- and party-building opportunities of the Cold War. In the case of East Germany, culture, encompassing literature, film, visual arts, and music, including rock, once more was singled out and analyzed not just as an indicator of party politics but also as a medium of both restriction and self-liberation that never was fully contained.[8] In the long run, foreign assessments of the transformations caused by the unification moved their primary focus to two topics that framed the debates in the late twentieth century: nation and identity in their current state of reconstitution.[9]

Often these studies took off by pointing to the odd phenomenon that German intellectual elites only grudgingly accepted the reunification. Yet they noticed that West Germans, averse to reinstituting the concept of the nation with its dismal record in the German context, nevertheless took its assumption of a national culture as reference for their hegemonic discourse about the integration of East German culture into the new Federal Republic.[10] If there was a debate about the form of the emerging culture, it did not include much concern about the specific achievements with which East Germans had influenced the larger German culture. It did not help that East German intellectuals, except for Friedrich Schorlemmer, Richard Schröder, Wolf Biermann, and a few other critics, did not contribute new arguments to the public debate about the obligations of the German nation that was the subject of much national reflection in the 1990s: the nature and shape of the national monument that would commemorate the German perpetration of the killing of six million European Jews. While the East German state, under Soviet supervision, had engaged in a rigorous campaign to punish members of the National Socialist Party unless they were useful for communism, and eradicated any public display of "fascist" thinking, it had refrained from shouldering the international burden of atonement and compensation for the crimes of the Holocaust as part of its claim to be a German state after Hitler.[11] Writers had addressed, at times, the involvement of their heroes in the Nazi crimes but they had not been in a position to challenge the official insensitivity toward the fate of the Jews. When confronted with the need to raise their voice in the name of a national disaster, they understandably remained on the sidelines, addressing the difficulty of articulating their own calamity in the face of a resurgent attention on national identities.

When Uwe Wittstock opened an overview of contemporary German fiction in 1993 with the sentence: "The younger German literature has lost its audience," he meant West and East German authors.[12] What gave his comment bite was his way of discarding the often repeated reasons for the decline of literature, among them the increasing lack of reading time, the onslaught of new media, the need for utilitarian books, the decrease in the level of concentration required by new novels, the trend toward the trivial, in short, most of the factors mentioned above. He contested the inevitable role of these factors in the demise of the reading culture. Instead, he attributed much of the decline to the poor quality of contemporary German writers' prose, their tedious pursuit of modernist writing that came into fashion in the 1960s, and their lack of wit and entertainment. He claimed a need to expect something unusual from writers and not to cede the reasons for their diminishing prowess to the historical march of media technology. Wittstock displayed no illusion about the force of this march for which he quoted Hans Magnus Enzensberger's pessimistic assessment, yet he added concerning literature: "The dwindling rank as a social key medium does not inevitably have to result in dwindling popularity."[13] If literature has lost its overriding importance, Enzensberger concludes, it "is free but it can neither legitimate nor question the state of the whole; it can do anything but it does not matter anymore."[14] Be that as it may, replied Wittstock, writers should face the competition with the other media and create a literature that exhibits the manifold things that only literature can do.

Losing the Therapeutic Function

Looking at the painful exit of writers from the hazards and opportunities of the Cold War, one encounters many modes of indignation, anger, and resentment, none as powerful as the notion that the demise of East German literature and culture was part of the colonization of East Germany by West Germany. In the words of Günter Grass: "The East belongs to the West."[15] The argument entails the assertion that the events of 1989 saved the Federal Republic from rethinking and changing its raison d'être, enabling it to pursue its path to the much belabored normalcy, which now includes the new federal states of the East. Much has been said about the disappointing indifference of West Germans to a constructive rethinking of a new common national endeavor in the constitutional and economic realms. Less attention has been directed toward the discrepancies of the two-tier practice of hard-nosed business interventions that resulted in a cold-blooded takeover of the East German economy and, at the same time, the therapeutic handling of East Germany as a society that had been traumatized by totalitarianism and the Stasi and now needed to recover. Both practices, seemingly far apart as extreme tendencies under normal political circumstances, were well intertwined in their goal of keeping the transformations away from the routines of the Federal Republic. The patterns of the economic rationale had their origins in the successful economic system of the West and extended their reach according to the capitalist logic; the pattern of dealing with the legacy of a totalitarian system with its constant supervision of the individual had its origins in feelings of complicity in the Nazi regime, some guilty feelings about the fact that East Germans had borne the brunt of Soviet reparations claims, and a large measure of indifference. Whatever the exact motivation, the therapeutic modus operandi deserves particular consideration.

Foreign observers who had little insight into the workings of the Treuhandanstalt that dismantled the economy could get the impression that the whole process of reunification was a big therapeutic endeavor in which East Germans, ready to leave totalitarian structures behind and storm into the consumer society, had to be guided as new participants of a life of political, economic, and cultural freedom. For a short while, the therapeutic discourse indeed became the favorite shorthand in West Germany for what had, in the 1980s, already been cultivated with nonpolitical bridge building to the East German population.[16] The most influential use of this paradigm originated in the East, in the much debated, praised, and condemned treatise *Der Gefühlsstau* (1990) by Hans-Joachim Maaz, the renowned director of a therapeutic clinic in Halle. In his *Psychogramm,* Maaz diagnosed the GDR population as a patient. This allowed an unusually direct understanding of people's emotions and frustrations but also invoked the criticism that this kind of diagnosis of a large and diverse population as a patient led to inaccurate generalizations and conclusions. It found a witty echo in the similarly East German–based 2003 movie *Good Bye, Lenin!,* which has an elaborate plot that succeeds in shielding a "two hundred percent" communist mother, who lies in a coma when the Wall falls, from realizing that the GDR has ended when she awakens. With the actions of her son and his friend, the film conveys a GDR take on the therapeutic relief using GDR products, slogans, and visuals. The movie itself was seen as a kind of ironic therapy for wounded *Ossis.*

Most of these uses of the therapeutic paradigm provided only a short-term, vaguely political explanation. Very little pointed to a deeper understanding of those East Germans who had addressed the troubling incapacity of the new state to take care of emotional needs that had accumulated during the years of Stalinist suppression and the shocks of building and guarding the Berlin Wall. It was obvious that authors in East Germany had been intricately involved in addressing this incapacity while they had internalized the political agenda of anti-fascism, anti-capitalism, and the building of a new society. Whatever hopes writers and poets had expressed for the future of this republic, whatever moral and ideological agenda they had formulated for the new socialist community, they had found themselves, willingly or unwillingly, in a mediating position, trying to elucidate everyday reality and placing it in the ever-present context of the state and its claims, and to various extents observed and harassed by the true social worker of this state, the Stasi informant.

Despite the fact that Christa Wolf, Franz Fühmann, Günter de Bruyn, Volker Braun, Irmtraut Morgner, and the whole cohort of novelists and poets who accompanied the rise of the GDR in a more or less critical manner defined their role in aesthetic, biographical, ideological, or political terms, they embarked on a therapeutic function as they addressed people's aspirations and frustrations in a state without a free press, telling stories that resonated with a broad readership, even beyond its borders. At least until the early 1980s they enjoyed a higher standing whether they were celebrated as the voice of a socialist society or rebuffed, even arrested as its saboteurs. The concept of the therapeutic function symbolizes the loss of their semiofficial role when the GDR collapsed, but also the chasm between them and the younger generation that did not want to fulfill this function and instead moved to a seemingly freer existence in Prenzlauer Berg in Berlin in the 1980s. It was a precariously short period in which this cohort honed a new reading culture on the basis of their engagement as mediators. Their advancement as intellectuals in a socialist society contrasted sharply with the survival fights of an earlier generation of socialist intellectuals under fascist threat and Stalinist suppression, including writers such as Erich Weinert, Friedrich Wolf, Berta Lask, Willi Bredel, Bertolt Brecht, and Anna Seghers, who had shaped their profiles not as public mediators but rather as fighters for a cause.[17]

When Klaus Städtke asked the question, "Has the Literary Intelligentsia in the GDR Failed?" he did not reflect on this combative antagonism but rather invoked the strong German tradition of providing education and spiritual guidance to the reigning force as it had developed since the eighteenth century and was symbolized in classical Weimar and the small German states. Städtke pointed to the fact that East German writers, in their fight for a better society in which writers assumed a higher role, were indeed closer to Schiller and Hölderlin than to the concepts that dominated literary life outside of the closely locked GDR. If one used the term "to fail" against them, he concluded, one should indict this German tradition, more specifically the inherited "weakness of the German literary intelligentsia, to still conjure, in full view of the European modernization, the pre-modern image of the writer in order to stubbornly defend an inherited utopia and thereby—consciously or unconsciously—legitimize their own (symbolic) hegemonic claim, dating from the enlightenment."[18] According to Städtke, the verb "to fail" would not accurately reflect the situation, since it did not clearly mark the literary elites' coresponsibility for the helplessness of GDR society vis-à-vis the emerging national constellation and the vicissitudes of postmodern life. While the latter point does not fully convince (it rather *illustrates* the failure), the notion of the end of the authors' therapeutic function might show how much their fate was tied to the real processes of dismantling a state-based power apparatus that had drawn enormous energies from the Cold War. Writers of the Enlightenment or in Weimar were clearly not in a therapeutic role.

And yet, invoking a national tradition clarifies the potential and limits of the Cold War argument. When East German socialists revamped certain German traditions, they did not necessarily think of the Cold War but were ideologically shielded (and financially bolstered) by its competitive demands on culture. These demands seemed to have given a second life to those traditions which cannot be simply subsumed under the terms insularity and provincialism that have been the common denominator of post-Wall critiques. As the literary life transformed itself under the full onslaught of globalization and the communication industry in the 1990s, and as critics like Frank Schirrmacher ranted against *Gesinnungsästhetik* (the aesthetics of conviction) in both Germanies, the East German regions learned to accommodate specific cultural and literary traditions (especially in their regional forms) and invested substantial pride in their traditional support for the arts (*Kunstpflege*)[19] Many years later, as traditional cultural products like novels and plays gained or lost their importance in the media culture in unpredictable ways, having kept a cultural legacy is already a landmark achievement. As regionalism has continuously both warped and nurtured German culture, East German writers of this particular period have no less a chance to occupy a particular legacy. In the short run, it's regional. In the long run, it might be much more.

Notes

1. Wolfgang Emmerich, *Kleine Literaturgeschichte der DDR. Erweiterte Neuausgabe* (Leipzig, 1996), 456.
2. Hans-Peter Herrmann, "Der Platz auf der Seite des Siegers: Zur Auseinandersetzung westdeutscher Literaturwissenschaft mit der ostdeutschen Literatur," in *Baustelle Gegenwartsliteratur: Die neunziger Jahre,* ed. Andreas Erb (Opladen, 1998), 43.
3. Hans Schwab-Felisch, "Die Bedeutung der Kultur für die Politik wächst: Rückblick auf das Europäische Kulturforum in Budapest," in *Merkur* 40 (1986), 321; Frank Trommler, "Culture as an Arena of Transatlantic Conflict," in *The United States and Germany in the Era of the Cold War,* vol. 2: 1968–1990, ed. Detlef Junker (Cambridge, 2004), 258.
4. Uwe Wittstock, "Der dünne Draht nach drüben: Von Künstlern und Diplomaten. Zum Streit um das deutsch-deutsche Kulturbkommen," in *FAZ,* 26 February 1986.
5. Günter Grass, Hellmuth Karasek, Rolf Becker, "Nötige Kritik oder Hinrichtung?" SPIEGEL-Gespräch mit Günter Grass über die Debatte um Christa Wolf und die DDR-Literatur, in *"Es geht nicht um Christa Wolf:" Der Literaturstreit im vereinten Deutschland,* ed. Thomas Anz (Munich, 1991), 126.
6. Klaus-Michael Bogdal, "Klimawechsel: Eine kleine Meteorologie der Gegenwartsliteratur," in *Baustelle Gegenwartsliteratur,* 9–31.
7. Detlev Schöttker, "Mauerrisse: Kulturtransfer von Ost nach West," in *Merkur* 61 (2007), 1112–1121.
8. See the workshop series of the American Institute for Contemporary German Studies in Washington, DC, between 1997 and 2002, and its publications (www.aicgs.org/analysis/publications): *What Remains? East German Culture and the Postwar Public,* ed. Marc Silberman (1997); *Cultures in Conflict: Visual Arts in Eastern Germany since 1990,* ed. Marion F. Deshmukh (1998); *A Sound Legacy? Music and Politics in East Germany,* ed. Edward Larkey (2000); *Moving Images of East Germany: Past and Future of DEFA Film,* ed. Barton Byg and Bethany Moore (2002); *The Cultural After-Life of East Germany: New Transnational Perspectives,* ed. Leslie A. Adelson (2002).
9. As an example from the U.S., see *After Unity: Reconfiguring German Identities,* ed. Konrad H. Jarausch (Providence, 1997).

10. Stephen Brockmann, *Literature and German Unification* (Cambridge, 1999), 1–21.
11. Jeffrey Peck, "East Germany," in *The World Reacts to the Holocaust*, ed. David S. Wyman (Baltimore, 1996), 450. For the first summary of the East German shift in officially addressing the Holocaust, see Walter Schmidt, "Jüdisches Erbe deutscher Geschichte im Erbe- und Traditionsverständnis der DDR," *Zeitschrift für Geschichtswissenschaft* 37 (1989), 8.
12. Uwe Wittstock, "Ab in die Nische? Über neueste deutsche Literatur und was sie vom Publikum trennt," in *Neue Rundschau* 104 (1993), 45.
13. Ibid., 57.
14. Hans Magnus Enzensberger, *Mittelmaß und Wahn: Gesammelte Zerstreuungen* (Frankfurt, 1988), 55.
15. Günter Grass, "Die Steine des Sisyphos: Über das Verhältnis von Journalismus und Politik, die Geschwindigkeit der Zeitläufte und die Macht der Konzerne," in *Süddeutsche Zeitung*, 4 July 2011. For a vehement critique of this assessment see Daniela Dahn, *Wehe dem Sieger! Ohne Osten kein Westen* (Reinbek, 2009).
16. Frank Trommler, "German Intellectuals: Public Roles and the Rise of the Therapeutic," in *The Power of Intellectuals in Contemporary Germany*, ed. Michael Geyer (Chicago, 2001), 48.
17. Ibid., 36.
18. Klaus Städtke, "Zwischen staatlicher Förderung und Lesererwartung: Hat die literarische Intelligenz in der DDR versagt?" in *Neophilologus* 77 (1993), 465.
19. Wolfgang Thierse, *Zukunft Ost. Perspektiven für Ostdeutschland in der Mitte Europas* (Berlin, 2001), 70–73.

Part V

International Normalization

Chapter Thirteen

The "Normalization" of Humanitarian and Military Missions Abroad

Beate Neuss

On 2 August 1990 Iraq invaded Kuwait. When the United Nations asked to restore the country's sovereignty with military force and thirty-four countries, under the leadership of the United States, prepared to liberate Kuwait, in some windows in Germany white flags appeared. Protesters on the streets shouted: "No blood for oil." Today, more than twenty years later, nearly 7,000 German troops are engaged in missions worldwide. They have been participating in UN, NATO, and European military actions in regions like Afghanistan, the Balkans, and Africa, as well as off the coast of Somalia and Lebanon.

Shortly after the unification of Germany, few political actors would have foreseen German troops alongside their American, French, and British partners in combat missions outside the NATO area. Before 1990, German troops had been sent outside NATO more than a hundred times, but exclusively in humanitarian actions—fighting natural catastrophes, floods, hunger, fires, drought, and the like. German citizens got used to seeing the Bundeswehr as part of worldwide disaster relief. German soldiers in combat missions other than those involving the defense of NATO territory were beyond imagination for most people. As a consequence of the Third Reich, which had misused the military for large scale violations of human rights and brutal war crimes, the slogan "never again war" had become part of the collective value system. "Germans turned into zealous proponents of anti-militarism."[1] Opinion polls show that right after unification the majority of Germans would have preferred a status like Switzerland's, combining wealth with neutrality.

Notes for this chapter begin on page 248.

The first security challenge with a reach beyond NATO hit Germany even before unification: the Iraqi invasion of Kuwait on 2 August 1990. Although the government and population appreciated not having experienced an invasion by the Warsaw Pact members during the Cold War thanks to American and NATO deterrence, Germany decided against sending troops to Kuwait. Bonn argued it could not participate because of ongoing negotiations with the Eastern countries over conditions of unification and related questions. Instead, it continued its "checkbook diplomacy" and supported the UN mission financially and logistically.

Still, German unification and the end of the East-West confrontation marked the turning point of German security policy. The Federal Republic was no longer taken hostage by the bloc confrontation and finally, it was fully sovereign. Germany's room for maneuver had broadened considerably. Unification offered options for engagement with preference for nonmilitary instruments, multilateralism, and transfer of sovereignty—typical for the longstanding "culture of restraint."

In reflections about continuity and change since unification, security policy is widely seen as the break with an otherwise remarkable continuity in German foreign policy since 1949. But what does the "normalization" of military missions abroad actually mean? A Germany acting like France, Britain, Russia, or the U.S.—all states that have longstanding security obligations outside their regions and are used to unilateral military intervention? Has Germany taken its place in international relations as a "normal" regional power? When it was reluctant to join military missions like in Libya in 2011 was it due to a revolutionary "vision … that minimizes the role of power,"[2] was it because of *Realpolitik,* or was it just because of constraints in domestic politics? Germany's role after unification still puzzles observers: its new leverage, its political and economic power, still contrasts with its reluctance to make use of its military instruments.

Beverly Crawford sees German Foreign and Security as a "vision guiding policy" that "emphasizes multilateralism, integration, diplomacy and antimilitarism." Germany's "foreign policy Weltanschauung"[3] is based in the country's history and has survived unification and the years since. The constituent elements of German foreign policy that Crawford names are mostly overlapping with the criteria of Hanns Maull's theoretical approach of a "civilian power":[4] cooperative security, multilateralism as leading paradigm, the observance of international rules, and use of force as last resort. No doubt, this "vision" of civilian power was deeply ingrained in German politicians as useful strategy and as norm, or as its appropriate *raison d'état* during the country's decades as a "semi-sovereign power."[5] Indeed, these ideas still have normative power for German political decisions.

I consider the paradigm of "civilian power" appropriate for analyzing German foreign and security policy since 1949—*including* the past twenty years since unification. My thesis is that Germany came a long way from its refusal to participate in international missions to its participation even in combat missions. Although the change in the 1990s was substantial and revolutionary, it was reluctantly accepted by the public and large parts of the political and intellectual elite alike. In situations when "civilian power" values were contradicting each other, e.g., in Libya in 2011, Germany decided for an incoherent pacifist policy, motivated primarily by *Realpolitik* and domestic politics, not by a civilian power rationale. But Beverly Crawford and Maull point out that before and after unification Germany both adhered to and deviated from its "vision." Although debates in media and in politics asking Germany to act more "normal"—meaning in less restricted fashion—come up time and again, the overall concept of being a "civilian power" prevailed. Since 1990, this paradigm has been modified due to new challenges and outside expectations, but there is still no abandoning of it.

"Never Again Alone"

The decision for nonmilitary participation in the Gulf War by offering checkbook diplomacy[6] instead was still consistent with the "culture of restraint" that Germany had exercised since WWII. It was also in accord with the so called "security policy consensus"[7] of 1982: except for strictly humanitarian missions, the Bundeswehr would act only when there was a direct aggression against Germany and its allies; no troops would be stationed out-of-area.[8] The German constitution was interpreted accordingly although parts of the Christian Democratic Union and Christian Social Union (CDU/CSU) did not see these constitutional restraints.

The Gulf War challenged this attitude in two respects: first, the Iraquis' invasion of Kuwait was a clear breach of international law and the liberation was legitimized by the UN. Second, allied expectations of German participation were high, since Germany had been protected against Soviet invasion by the same states that were now deciding to defend Kuwait. Since the invasion took place during the negotiations for unification in the summer of 1990, the German government was completely absorbed by international and inter-German ramifications of that process and unsure which answer to give. On the one hand, there was still the fear among Eastern and Western neighbors that after unification Germany would become a Fourth Reich, militarily potent and seeking a dominant role. On the other hand, it was asked to send troops and act as a "normal" partner, notwithstanding its history. Chancellor Kohl was careful not to feed the anxiety of the USSR, Poland, and West European neighbors, including Margaret Thatcher of Great Britain.[9] Moreover the still-strong peace movement considered "only the negative aspects of military means …, not the fact that military force was sometimes the only way to stop a tyrant."[10] In East Germany, NATO was seen as an instrument of the enemy in the Cold War; neutrality was widely preferred. Participation in the liberation of Kuwait would have put additional strain on unification. Therefore financial contributions and logistical support was all Germany would agree to.

But Chancellor Kohl and CDU foreign policy expert Karl Lamers raised two interrelated questions. First: what about Germany's role as an NATO ally (*Bündnisfähigkeit*) when the organization was searching for a new role ("out-of-area or out-of business" as the German Secretary General of NATO Manfred Wörner had put it)? Second: what about its position as engine of integration toward a common European foreign and security policy (*Europafähigkeit*)?[11] The negotiations on the Treaty of Maastricht for a European Union only started in December 1990!

German politicians were aware that Germany's peculiar position as a semisovereign country located on the fault lines of the Cold War had come to an end and that the new geopolitical situation offered chances for a more influential role as a central power in Europe (*Zentralmacht*).[12] Any German government from 1990 on would have taken steps toward what is called "normalization" in piecemeal form. In the political sphere, debates in the Bundestag and interviews by some politicians tried to abandon thinking in Cold War terms by pointing out new challenges. But when the first steps toward military engagement had to be taken, the political elite preferred to transform the profoundly political questions of the constitutional restrictions on German military involvement into a legal issue. The question whether and how Germany would contribute to international security was finally forwarded to the Constitutional Court—a very German way of solving controversial political problems because it would pacify a deeply divided parliament and public.

The Balkan Wars served as a trigger for the change of Germany's identity as actor in international relations, because they were the first serious challenge to the country's self-image as a pacifist power. The conflict was right at its front door and hundred thousands of refugees were flooding into Germany. The European Community had considered it as a European task to maintain peace. When all negotiations failed, atrocities of the type Europe had not seen in more than forty-five years contributed to a change in public sentiment toward the military instrument. The 1995 humanitarian disaster of the massacre of 8,000 boys and men in Srebrenica under the "protection" of UN Blue Helmets played an important role for the

German debate as the development toward participation in the Kosovo war clearly shows.[13]

Back in 1991 the Kohl administration had vividly argued for the establishment of a protective zone in Slovenia and Croatia while refusing to contribute German soldiers. The government argued, like most members of parliament, that no German soldiers should go where they had been in WWII. But in a different theater Bonn tested reactions to deploying soldiers outside NATO. In May 1992 Germany participated for the first time actively with soldiers in an UN Blue Helmet mission in Cambodia (the UNTAC mission), although their participation was tentatively restricted to medical staff. Then within UN Operation Sharp Guard from 1992 to 1996 the Bundeswehr contributed three surveillance planes and two vessels to control the coast of Serbia and Montenegro. But the mandate only allowed the air force crews to "protect and help" Blue Helmets and allies. During UN Operation Deny Flight in 1994, German soldiers finally participated in integrated NATO crews in AWACS planes. This was seen by some politicians as the first combat mission with German soldiers out-of-area although the intelligence gained during the flights was not be used for air strikes. German contribution was justified to keep AWACS in the air, turning it into a question of *Bündnisfähigkeit.* The CDU/CSU considered a refusal to participate "a 'sabotage' of NATO which had to be prevented."[14] The motto "never again war" was changed into "never again alone"—the country did not want to be singled out as being unfit for alliances.

The fierce domestic debate about what was seen as German soldiers participating in combat ended in an appeal to the Constitutional Court. Besides the AWACS mission, two other UN operations were questioned: Sharp Guard and UNSOM in Somalia (involving logistical support for Indian Blue Helmets). The opposition party SPD filed a lawsuit, as did the FDP, the coalition partner of the CDU/CSU. The FDP was convinced that Bonn had to take responsibility for international security, but was not sure whether the action was in accordance with the constitution and so demanded clarification. The SPD and the Greens opposed German participation.

What does the constitution require? Article 24 allows participation within systems of collective security and in measures to secure "a peaceful and sustainable order in Europe and between the people of the world." Article 25 of the Basic Law puts international law before national law; Article 26 denies war of aggression; Article 87a simply talks about the role of the Bundeswehr in case of crises or defense, but not specifically about mandates by organizations of collective security and out-of-area missions.

In the summer of 1994 the Constitutional Court decided to let the AWACS missions proceed. The Court ruled that all missions were undertaken within the constitution and no change was needed:[15]

1) Article 24 allowed Germany not only membership in systems of collective security but the ability to take over tasks connected with that membership.
2) The Bundestag had to agree to a clearly defined mission by a simple majority.
3) The mission had to take place under the mandate of an organization of collective security, such as the UN, NATO, or later the EU.

Since then, military missions have had to be supported by the government as well as by the parliament. The Bundeswehr is now called a "parliamentary army," as no soldiers can be sent without the approval of the Bundestag or to a mission that is not precisely defined in terms of numbers and scope.[16] From then on, governments have acted on a firm legal basis, but with limited room for maneuver. The decision added a political restriction: all missions had to be legitimized by organizations of collective security and no mission could to be undertaken alone.

In 1995 Bonn eventually joined IFOR (Implementation Force) with 2,700 troops to secure the implementation of the Dayton Peace Agreement, provided that no German soldiers would be stationed in Bosnia. The mandate was characterized as strictly peacekeeping; the soldiers had only light arms. But soon thereafter in 1996 the Bundestag agreed to full participation in the Stabilization Force (SFOR). A broad consensus had developed within the coalition parties CDU/CSU and FDP and the opposition SPD and Greens, except for the postcommunist PDS, that the Bundeswehr should contribute to NATO missions on mandates of Chapter VII of the UN Charter to stabilize and protect peace in the Balkans. By then the genocide in Srebrenica had contributed to the insight that not all conflicts could be solved by soft power and diplomacy alone. The German population supported this stance by nearly two-thirds, but still opposed combat missions vehemently.[17]

Combat Mission in Kosovo

The civil war in Kosovo has to be seen according to Joschka Fischer as "a radical break with continuity"[18] concerning German participation in combat. In 1998 civil war had developed between Serbian forces and the Liberation Army of Kosovo (UCK). Albanians were fleeing Kosovo and a new humanitarian catastrophe was looming. Approximately 800,000 Albanians were forced from their homes in Kosovo during 1998/99. International attempts to mediate the conflict failed. During summer 1998, Chancellor Kohl had ruled out a German military contribution without a mandate of the UN, but it proved impossible to get Russian and Chinese consent in the Security Council.[19] The outgoing Kohl administration therefore decided in its last cabinet meeting, in agreement with the incoming SPD/Green government, to ask the Bundestag for air force capacities, explicitly excluding "boots on the ground" as long as there was no ceasefire. Joschka Fischer, foreign minister designate and leader of the Greens, knew that the coalition with the SPD would founder even before its start if his party failed to agree to military participation. The incoming chancellor Gerhard Schröder assured President Bill Clinton that Germany would participate, provided NATO agreed to a military mission.[20]

For the newly elected government of the SPD and the Greens it was an even greater problem than it had been for the CDU/FDP coalition to support a combat mission. Both parties looked back with reservation about or even opposition to the Bundeswehr and NATO. The Greens, who had never participated in a federal government before, strictly adhered to pacifism, while the SPD also had a strong pacifist wing. The decision could only be justified by the argument that one Srebinica was already too much, that military force to enforce peace was the last resort after negotiations with Milosevic had failed.[21]

For the government and the "Realo" wing of the Greens, another issue was of utmost importance: to prove to a skeptical U.S. administration and its NATO allies that Germany's new government was reliable, responsible, and not moving toward a German *Sonderweg*. The more assertive Schröder administration wanted Germany to be a "normal" state and a regional power; it became necessary not to isolate the country but to be a partner in dealing with decisions for Kosovo's and the Balkans' future. Members of and voters for the party could only be convinced by moral arguments. Fischer reversed the original contention that no German soldier could show up where the *Wehrmacht* had set his boots in WWII. Now German soldiers had to prevent atrocities because of German history. "Never again war" was transformed into "never again Auschwitz." With this phrase the leader of the Green Party legitimized sending German soldiers into a combat mission.[22]

The massacre of Srebenica in July 1995 had been the proof that the price of pacifism could be too high; it challenged and changed longstanding cultural beliefs and political positions on war and peace. Due to the humanitarian emergency and the deadlock in the UN Security Council, the Bundestag agreed with a large majority on participating on the basis of a NATO mandate.[23] Maull considers the German participation to have been part of an ongoing learning process and not a change of its principal norms: "[W]hile Germany tampered with a key ideal type norm when it took part in the NATO mission without (appropriate) UN Security Council mandate, policymakers still tried to uphold several other norms central to the civilian power concept."[24]

Mandating the air strikes by NATO instead of by the United Nations was fiercely debated. The authorization of a NATO-led peacekeeping force in Kosovo by Resolution 1244 of the UN Security Council was considered as a belated legitimization of the crackdown on Milosevic.[25] On 11 June 1999 an overwhelming majority of the Bundestag voted for the establishment of the multinational Kosovo Force (KFOR) to establish peace and security.[26] For the first time Bonn provided a large number of soldiers (8,500) on the ground and took over responsibility for one sector in Kosovo. More than another decade later there are still 1,500 armed German forces serving in KFOR, and civilian personnel are also involved in training the police in Kosovo and giving administrative assistance.

Certainly, this vote has to be seen as a major break in Germany's foreign policy, but restrictions on out-of-area engagement surfaced soon after. The following missions were heavily contested in parliament. Operation Essential Harvest aimed to disarm the conflict parties in Macedonia (FYROM) and to prevent the escalation of the conflict into a war. Amber Fox intended to improve the safety of international observers. Essential Harvest reacted to a call for help by the Macedonian president, but was not legitimated by UN Security Council. The German government argued for using military force to prevent escalation and human rights violations. The left was against "militarization" of German foreign policy and against preemptive actions as a matter of principle[27] and the conservatives were afraid of overstretching Germany's capacity.[28] All sides were wary about the new international role and responsibility of the country.[29] Finally Germany contributed 500 soldiers to NATO for Essential Harvest. Amber Fox was mandated by the UN. The Bundestag agreed to send 600 of the 1,000 deployed soldiers and Germany commanded the military mission.[30]

Ongoing Debate on Afghanistan

When on 12 September 2001 Chancellor Schröder declared "unrestricted solidarity" with the United States and supported the invocation of Article 5 of the NATO Treaty, he hit stormy waters. Schröder argued that NATO membership and the responsibility of a country of Germany's importance made participation inevitable.[31] Although on the streets and squares Germans showed great empathy with the victims of 9/11, military contribution for the War on Terror was something different. Gerhard Schröder had informed the Bundestag that no German combat troops would go into action; the air force would not bombard Afghanistan. To convince his coalition to support the deployment of soldiers for Operation Enduring Freedom (OEF) in the Bundestag, he had to connect the vote for participation in OEF with the question of confidence, risking the upcoming election if he did not obtain a majority.[32] Still, the SPD-Green coalition could not muster the necessary votes by its own majority (*Kanzlermehrheit*).[33] The Bundestag finally agreed on a maximum of 3,900 soldiers for OEF, most of them at sea in front of the African coast, in Central Asia, and providing further logistical support and medical aid, as well as 100 Special Forces (KSK) deployed in Afghanistan.[34]

Participation in International Security Assistance Force (ISAF) sent the message of securing peace and appeared to be different from military War on Terror, which seemed to be "a one-sided military approach to the problem of international terrorism."[35] Therefore it was easier to muster parliamentary support for ISAF. Germany contributed humanitarian support, five Provincial Reconstruction Teams in the north of Afghanistan and assistance for state building. Since then the mandate has been renewed annually. The deployment of KSK Forces in Afghanistan was not extended in 2008 but the German ISAF contribution was raised from 1,200 in 2001 to 4,590 in 2009. The operational range that originally included only Kunduz was broadened to Feyzabad and Mazar-e-Sharif.

Although the Taliban regime violated human rights, in the case of Afghanistan it was the argument of *Realpolitik* and *Bündnistreue* that counted. The government emphasized that Afghanistan was a hotbed for al-Qaida. Terror against the "West" was not only a permanent danger for the United States but for German security as well. Defense Minister Struck argued in 2004 that Germany is defended at the Hindu Kush.[36] An appeal to "never again Auschwitz" was not available, although human rights violations and the desire to end the Afghan civil war were important arguments in the discussion about the intervention. Since the Greens and much of the public rejected war as a means to solve conflicts, Foreign Minister Fischer hurried to give civil input and to host a UN conference on Afghanistan's future at Petersberg near Bonn. There, agreement on assistance for the reconstruction of Afghan political institutions and infrastructure was reached on 5 December 2001—the foundation of ISAF.

One could argue that until the fall of 2009, German military engagement in Afghanistan could be broadly described as a purely humanitarian intervention and development aid. It was pointed out that soldiers were building wells, bridges, roads, hospitals, and schools, especially for girls, an argument that counts with Greens and left wing SPD. The Bundeswehr supports more than 700 civil reconstruction projects. German military engagement is confirmed according to the concept and values of "civilian power." Restrictions for troops in action are numerous: OEF and ISAF may not operate together; German soldiers are not to be sent into combat to defeat the Taliban. Their task is securing a safe environment for civil Afghan structures. Chancellor Schröder's Minister of Defense Struck argued: "The Bundeswehr is the largest peace movement in the Federal Republic."[37] Merkel's defense minister Franz Josef Jung studiously avoided saying that German troops were at war.

In fall 2009 the approach toward combat missions changed and soldiers now fight back when attacked. The rising number of German casualties and the Kunduz affair when the Bundeswehr asked to bombard tank trucks, hijacked by Taliban, and about 120 civilians were killed,[38] caused a new debate leading to more openness. The decision of the German officer to risk the loss of civilian lives created more public awareness than the death of German soldiers. Realizing that the Afghanistan mission was more than reconstruction, public support for the contribution to ISAF reached its lowest level, with 60 percent against fighting the Taliban and 49 percent wanting to end the deployment.[39] Due to mismanagement of information on the Kunduz affair, Minister Jung had to leave office. His successor, Freiherr zu Guttenberg, took the opportunity for new openness in the debate on security policy. Within days of taking office in November 2009 he changed the wording, first talking about a "war-like situation" and later agreeing that his soldiers considered themselves to be at war. Chancellor Merkel endorsed his definition in December 2010 when she visited Kunduz. It is publicly debated whether fighting the Taliban, as opposed to just defending oneself, is necessary to secure reconstruction. Although support for the Afghanistan mission is low, people get used to bad news.

"No" to the Iraq War

Foreign Minister Fischer's visit to Washington, D.C. in the first days after 9/11 left him with troubling thoughts on whether President Bush intended to take the War on Terror to Iraq as well.[40] Fischer and Schröder saw no connection between Saddam Hussein and al-Qaida, no proof for the existence of weapons of mass destruction, and therefore no basis for regime change by military means consistent with international law.[41] Based on the difficult decision making concerning the missions in Macedonia and Afghanistan, they feared that parliament would not agree to participate in the Iraq invasion, no matter what kind of coalition government was in office. Even members of the CDU/CSU were against the Iraq intervention; the candidate for the chancellorship, Edmund Stoiber, argued tentatively against participating in Operation Iraqi Freedom.[42]

All prerequisites for joining the Iraq invasion were missing: the invasion was not legitimated by the UN, the EU, or NATO; proof of weapons of mass destructions was weak; and evidence of connections to al-Qaida was even more tenuous. In this respect the decision not to contribute was fully compatible with the self-image of a civilian power, and clearly in accord with the opinions of the majority of Germans. But Chancellor Gerhard Schröder's early "no" to any military action, as well as his refusal to participate even in case of a resolution of the UN Security Council, was not consistent with the usual strong backing of the UN.[43] It stood in sharp contrast to Germany's multilateral orientation for half a century, and was therefore not in line with this aspect of the tradition of "civilian power." A substantial part of Germany's identity as a multilateral power is nurtured by its role as a partner of the United States and as a loyal member of NATO, as well as a mediator in the EU between greater and smaller members, old and new ones. Therefore, the splitting up of the European Union over the Iraq invasion was not in line with its self-image as a broker of EU consent.

The complete breakdown of communication between the Chancellor and the White House was unheard of in post-war history. There is no doubt that Schröder's motivation for an open break with the U.S. government was also motivated by his election campaign. He correctly calculated the emotions of German voters: before the Iraq topic was part of the campaign, opinion polls did not give his coalition much hope for re-election. For the Greens a clear dissociation from the U.S. plans was a matter of survival as a party in parliament: before the Iraq case became public debate, the Greens did not reach the necessary quorum for re-election of 5 percent in opinion polls. "Iraq" successfully mobilized voters both for SPD and the Greens.[44] They won the elections, although by a small margin. Schröder and Fischer's successes in the elections of fall 2002 were to a large degree a result of the Chancellor's policy of strong opposition to U.S. intervention.[45]

Aside from domestic power politics, it was not realistic to expect German soldiers to be part of the "coalition of the willing." Since public opinion overwhelmingly considered military invasion illegitimate and military missions of the Bundeswehr needed the agreement of the parliament, there was no chance for a military contribution. Fischer's "I am not convinced!"[46] was shared by too many parliamentarians. In spite of the vehement public opposition and the icy atmosphere between Bush and Schröder, Germany tried to prove its loyalty to Washington with the usual logistical support and behind the scenes by tolerating CIA actions that violated human rights. In the Chancellor's refusal to accept a decision of the Security Council, Maull sees a clear infringement of the civilian power concept.[47] But the government's evaluation that an intervention violating international law was impossible was also consistent with Germany's principles and with other aspects of this concept.

Responsibility and Restraint

The grand coalition from 2005 to 2009 and the conservative-liberal coalition in place since then under Chancellor Angela Merkel restored the German-American relationship, but did not change the approach toward Iraq. Merkel stated that her government "can and wants to take responsibility" and she was determined to influence security policy in NATO and EU.[48] Merkel's policy is in line with characteristics of civilian power and at the same time is motivated by improving the transatlantic relationship in NATO and getting the EU's embryonic foreign and security policy off the ground.

When Chancellor Angela Merkel took over, the agreement of the coalition parties CDU/CSU and SPD on common goals in fall 2005 as well as the Ministry of Defense's 2006 whitepaper showed that a radical change concerning Bundeswehr missions was not to be expected.[49] As a substitute for developing a national security strategy, the whitepaper acknowledged the new challenges for national and international security. It argued for "effective multilateralism" and developed the approach of comprehensive security. Although reform in the Bundeswehr was supposed to make the military instrument more adequate for out-of-area missions and for the requirements of asymmetric war, the priorities clearly lay with civil crisis management, conflict prevention, and peace consolidation.[50]

To deploy troops has become even more difficult and regulated. While there had been no law to interpret and define the ruling of the Constitutional Court concerning military missions, the Schröder government had introduced a law, which the Bundestag approved in spring 2005, defining the rights of the parliament in sending soldiers into mission and in bringing them back if the situation worsened. Only for missions due to "imminent danger ahead" such as small fact-finding or rescue efforts, can the government ask for the parliament's consent later, or in advance by consulting the parliamentary whips and foreign affairs and defense committees only. In all other cases the scope, time, number, and tasks have to be defined precisely beforehand. Therefore, the type of mission has to be precisely defined.[51] In practice, this stipulation has often resulted in decoupling German soldiers from their Afghan partners and in withdrawing Germans from the AWACS mission that were not explicitly mentioned in the parliamentary mandate.[52]

Combat missions require difficult political decisions and are hampered by red tape. In spring 2006 the UN Security Council mandated a military mission to Congo to support UN Operation MONUC and to foster safe and democratic elections.[53] Germany had refused to send a European battle group, partly because the available forces consisted of Germans and only very few French soldiers. The government urged a more balanced and multilateral setup. Finally the council of the EU decided on a deployment of EUFOR RD CONGO, the first mission within the European Security and Defense Policy (ESDP). Germany contributed one-third of the contingent and insisted on a mandate restricted to civil and humanitarian aspects that allowed the use of weapons solely for self-defense. Thus, risks for German soldiers were minimized. The mission was not disputed in public, since it was in line with EU's Africa Strategy promoting rule of law and democracy as well as engagement with its own capabilities when necessary. As Germany was highly interested in a functioning ESDP, it hardly could stand aside when its first humanitarian intervention was enacted.

When the election process in Congo lagged behind schedule, the German government opposed an extension of the mandate, fearing for the necessary majority in Bundestag. Berlin risked letting the whole mission end in disaster because it left immediately after the final result was announced, a step that fortunately did not lead to fighting.[54] Due to the political expectations of EU members, the mission had been led by Germany. Foreign Minister Steinmeier and Chancellor Merkel hailed the mission as a success of the European security policy. Indeed, the UN-mandated European mission to prevent atrocities fitted well into Germany's self-image as a civilian power. But Berlin did not react automatically to outside expectations and still was reluctant to deploy troops; in 2007 it refused to take part in a European Union Force mission to Chad although its close partner France was expecting German participation.

From October 2006 on, the German navy nevertheless participated in the United Nations Interim Force with 2,500 soldiers off the coast of Lebanon. The decision-making process proves that the arguments cautioning against German participation in historically burdened contexts were still alive. Parliamentarians from all parties voted against any participation in the mission, although it was UN mandated, multilateral, and intended to prevent conflict. The mandate was set in direct relationship to the peace process in the Middle East and the negotiations of the quartet (EU, UN, the U.S., Russia).[55] Had it not been for Israel's (and Lebanon's) explicit request, Berlin would not have sent its vessels.[56] Foreign Minister Steinmeier and Chancellor Merkel alike looked for an engagement that would definitely avoid any confrontation between Israeli and German soldiers. Therefore, no missions on the ground were conceivable except support of reconstruction, training, and diplomatic help in reconciliation.[57] In both cases Germany hesitated, although the missions were mandated by the UN and the troops were not sent into fighting but in order to prevent it.

The Libyan Refusal

When in January 2011 upheaval started in the Arab world, European leaders were not prepared. EU members had aimed for reform within the framework of the European Neighborhood Policy that had in fact stabilized the ruling dictatorships. France and Italy were especially good friends with Mubarak and Gaddafi. The first was overthrown, the second started to fight against his people in February. While Germany had kept its distance from the dictator beforehand,[58] Paris switched sides within hours and asked for intervention. The first UN Security Council response, Resolution 1970, asked for tough sanctions and was approved by Berlin. From the beginning of the debate, Merkel and Foreign Minister Guido Westerwelle had shown their skepticism toward military actions in discussions as well as in public. Due to the "uncertain ending" of the mission, they announced that they would not participate in the mission, even with a positive vote in the Security Council.[59] In contrast to Afghanistan, Merkel saw no danger for Germany deriving from the Libyan situation.[60] The reasons she named in NATO and the EU against a deny flight zone established by UN Security Council Resolution 1973 were that the political orientation of the Arab opposition was not clear and neither were the goals of EU and NATO, the range and legitimacy of actions, the efficiency of civil protection, or the role of EU and NATO after the end of bombardment.[61]

Washington had been quite reluctant toward military engagement, but changed its mind when the Arab League asked for a deny flight zone in March. As in 2003, Berlin as a nonpermanent member of the UN Security Council abstained from the vote, together with China and Russia. A veto was out of question: "Never alone" is still one of the guiding principles.

The meaning of alliance loyalty was debated vehemently in Germany as well as in NATO. While two-thirds of the population applauded the German decision, some members of the government as well as of the parties in parliament were opposed. What *aspect* of alliance loyalty was the main question of politicians in CDU/CSU? The "Europeans" asked for close cooperation with Paris; the "Transatlanticists" for partnership with Washington.[62] What about the values of a civilian power?[63] The question was even more legitimate since in 2005 the UN had accepted Responsibility to Protect (R2P).[64] Values played a role: supporters of Resolution 1973 argued based on Srebrenica and R2P; those opposed based on the meager results in Afghanistan and the losses of life on all sides there.

Was Berlin's policy a repetition of Schröder's opposition to intervention in Iraq? Indeed, several ingredients suggested the "No" to participation in a possible UN decision due to upcoming elections ahead, siding with Russia against Washington. However, in obvious difference from Schröder, Merkel tried hard to minimize destructive elements for EU and the transatlantic alliance.

The German decision was driven by *Realpolitik*: the EU and NATO partners had no clear goals; time pressure from France, prompted by domestic factors, was immense; and a decision on immediate intervention seemed more important than thorough deliberation about the achievable results. Alliance loyalty made a veto impossible, but it did not mean following the partners blindfolded.[65] Voting for the resolution and not being militarily engaged was regarded as impossible for a NATO member of Germany's size and with the specialized weapons systems that might be needed.[66] Additionally, two-thirds of the population was against intervention. So, why further anger the electorate, especially when in federal states elections were ahead?[67] Merkel and Westerwelle knew that the Bundestag would hardly agree to a military mission in Libya. Instead, they preferred to prove their loyalty toward NATO by deploying AWACS for Afghanistan. However, there will be an additional price to pay in the Libyan case; substantial German contribution to reconstruction, development, and if necessary peacekeeping missions in Libya will certainly be imperative. Germany's influence in EU, NATO and the Arab world has not exactly improved as a result of its reticence.

Is Germany Still a "Civilian Power"?

Certainly Germany's approach to military intervention has changed dramatically since 1990. The simple numbers show the engagement: 270,000 German soldiers have been deployed in missions worldwide since 1994.[68] The range and scope have broadened from logistical and medical support to combat missions on other continents. However, all missions took place in a multilateral framework and were legitimated by a mandate of an organization of collective security, all by the UN with the exception of Kosovo and Essential Harvest (NATO). International law is seen by Germany as binding. For German politicians and the public alike it is out of the question to send troops on a national mission. "Never alone" and "effective multilateralism" are the explicit rules of conduct of the Federal Republic not only in the EU and NATO but as a principle of international relations. The military is not seen as an instrument to project power in spheres of interest.

Indeed, a discussion about what specific German interests are is still missing. Bundeswehr missions are hardly ever discussed from the perspective of national interest. The word is still a taboo with many Germans—in political elite as well as in the public. This is changing only very slowly. When Federal President Horst Köhler mentioned in an interview on his way back from Afghanistan in May 2010 that German interests might require participation in military action with partners to secure trade, media and political criticism became so fierce that he stepped down on 31 May 2010. He had made the point that a country of Germany's size and one of the largest trading nations might have to participate in multilateral missions to take care of its interests, e.g., free trading routes and preventing regional instability that would impair trade, jobs, and income.[69]

Whenever casualties happen, scandals such as losses of civilian lives or American special forces acting in the German sector in Afghanistan pop up, and the media and political actors are greatly agitated—for a short time. In public opinion the notion prevails that Afghanistan could be pacified without combat and casualties, and otherwise one should leave. Only since 2009 has Germany seen itself as engaged in warfare in Afghanistan. As a result, the debate about security interests falters before it gets seriously started. The public shies away from discussion; political actors do not try to force it on their constituency. Politicians sidestep discussions about the reasons for soldiers being sent to Afghanistan or anywhere else. They are afraid of a political debate spurred by the strength of pacifism, especially before elections. Only reluctantly did Defense Minister Struck discuss the impact of the Afghan situation for Germany and Europe, while its effect on Central Asia or Pakistan is a topic for political think tanks. Operation Enduring Freedom off the coast of Somalia is seen as a means to safeguard vessels containing relief for the Somalis, not for fighting terrorists or pirates. Open sea lanes themselves were hardly discussed as a legitimate goal, an amazing silence considering that Germany is one of the leading trade nations of the world.

On one hand, Germans are still not at ease with military missions abroad and a majority is strictly against combat missions, a pacifist pattern that is deeply rooted as a result of history. War is not seen as "politics with other means" but as a very last resort. On the other hand, UN-mandated multilateral humanitarian interventions are broadly accepted, as long as no fighting is involved. If they are questioned it is to determine whether they overstretch German capabilities and whether they are legitimate. Missions that might include combat are seen differently. The price of lives lost is debated intensively. Although public approval of the Bundeswehr as an institution is high, people prefer to see the troops employed in purely humanitarian missions. However, there is very little acknowledgment and respect for soldiers in missions. A memorial site for soldiers killed in action has existed in Berlin only since September 2009 and is well hidden on the back side of the Defense Ministry.

The paradox is obvious: the capability gap in the army has been deplored since the early 1990s with regard to equipment for asymmetric warfare and special armored vehicles for better protection of soldiers. But the contribution of the national budget to the military shrank to 1.2 percent, the lowest ratio among Germany's European neighbors.[70] There is no sign that any government will increase the budget for defense substantially anytime soon.

Germany therefore is still a "civilian power." It is still characterized by values and means specific to this theoretical approach. Going alone or deciding on combat action as quickly as France and Great Britain did in Libya would definitely be impossible. Masses of protesters would flood the streets. Chancellor Merkel and new Minister of Defense Thomas de Maizière soberly ask if a military action is well thought through and makes sense for Germany, the EU, and the region concerned. Additionally, Merkel takes into the account that the citizens and the parliament still abhor war and that no government can win with it, in contrast to the situation in other European countries and the U.S.

Is there "normalization"? Yes, Germans consider it normal to participate in humanitarian action. But, no, they do not want to have soldiers in combat missions. For the foreseeable future the German approach toward the military will be different from that of its partners. After Afghanistan the political elite will be even more reluctant to send soldiers into missions that might require combat and the public will be more skeptical concerning the results of asymmetric wars. A severe legal barrier is the institutionalization of the parliament's rights in decision making and the role of the Constitutional Court, which tends to set very narrow limits. Such restrictions also make German security policy different. The government's room for maneuver is even smaller because the opposition in parliament calls on the Constitutional Court when it suspects its rights might be ignored.[71] All this contributes to a security policy that is hardly predictable for Germany's partners. As long as Germany is searching for its international role, it is unlikely that there will be the political will and influence for a security policy as a normative power in Europe.[72]

Since 1990, German governments had avoided discussions about whether a draft army is appropriate for highly specialized missions in different parts of the world as opposed to Cold War attacks from the East. In August 2009, citing budget restrictions as a reason, Minister zu Guttenberg started a debate about ending conscription. He aimed to drastically reduce the number of soldiers (from 245,900 to 170,000) and to transform the army into a volunteer army. After strong protests in the beginning, the idea was broadly accepted, not because the Bundeswehr would be more suitable for international intervention, but because the draft system was seen as unjust, since only one-sixth of young men actually had to serve. The reform, starting in July 2011 under the guidance of Thomas de Maizière, will certainly change opinion toward the Bundeswehr, but it still will not make Germany trigger happy. The new doctrine sees up to 10,000 soldiers in missions at the same time, spread across two to six actions. "Prosperity demands responsibility," de Maizière said in May 2011 when he presented the new defense policy guidelines. And he added, when asked by the UN, that this may require military contributions, even when no German interests are challenged.[73] There was no protest—what a change compared to Köhler's remarks exactly a year earlier! Still, a German intervention force similar to the French, British, or American army is nowhere in sight. "Normalization" does not go as far as that.

Notes

1. Rainer Baumann and Gunther Hellmann, "Germany and the Use of Military Force: 'Total War', the 'Culture of Restraint' and the Quest for Normality," *German Politics* 10 (2001), 61.
2. Beverly Crawford, "The Normative Power of a Normal State," *German Politics and Society,* 28 (2010), 165.
3. Crawford, "Normative Power," 179.
4. Hanns Maull, "Zivilmacht: Die Konzeption und ihre sicherheitspolitische Relevanz," in Wolfgang Heydrich and Joachim Krause, eds., *Sicherheitspolitik Deutschlands. Neue Konstellationen, Risiken, Instrumente* (Baden-Baden, 1992), 771–786.
5. Peter Katzenstein, ed., *Tamed Power: Germany in Europe* (Ithaca, 1997).
6. Germany finally paid 18 billion DM to support the mission.
7. Alexander Siedschlag, *Die aktive Beteiligung Deutschlands an militärischen Aktionen zur Verwirklichung Kollektiver Sicherheit* (Frankfurt, 1995), 35.
8. Caroline Thomas and Randolph Nikutta, "Bundeswehr und Grundgesetz. Zur neuen Rolle der militärischen Intervention in der Außenpolitik," *Militärpolitik Dokumentation* 13 (1990), 72.
9. Andreas Rödder, *Deutschland Einig Vaterland* (Munich, 2009), 156; Siedschlag, *aktive Beteiligung,* 29.
10. Nina Philipp, "Civilian Power and War: the German Debate about Out-of-area Operations 1990–99," in Sebastian Harnisch and Hanns W. Maull, eds., *Germany as a Civilian Power* (Manchester 2001), 51.
11. Hendrik Schneider, *Die Außen- und Sicherheitspolitik der Großen Koalition (2005-2009)—Stringenz des Zivilmachtkonzepts?* (Grin-Verlag, 2010), 40.

12. Hans-Peter Schwarz, *Zentralmacht Europas. Deutschlands Rückkehr auf die Weltbühne* (Berlin, 1994).
13. Joschka Fischer, *Die rot-grünen Jahre. Deutsche Außenpolitik —vom Kosovo bis zum 11. September* (Cologne, 2007), 110.
14. Anja Dalgaard-Nielsen, *Germany, Pacifism, and Peace Enforcement* (Manchester, 2006), 56.
15. Bundesverfassungsgericht, *BverfGE* 90 (1994), 289.
16. Bundesministerium der Justiz, *Gesetz über die parlamentarische Beteiligung bei der Entscheidung über den Einsatz bewaffneter Streitkräfte im Ausland,* 18. März 2005, in http://www.gesetze-im-internet.de/parlbg/BJNR077500005.html.
17. Elisabeth Noelle-Neumann, "In der Nische," *FAZ,* 21 August 1996.
18. Fischer, *Die rot-grünen Jahre,* 84.
19. Ibid., 114.
20. Ibid., 109.
21. Ibid., 110.
22. Ibid., 185.
23. The votes were 500 yes, 63 no, and 18 abstaining, although some Greens, like Ludger Volmer, made strong points against involvement, arguing that it would set a precedent.
24. Maull, *Deutschland als Zivilmacht,* 7.
25. Enacted under Chapter VII of the UN Charter (enforceable).
26. 505 voted yes, 24 voted no, and 11 abstained.
27. Deutscher Bundestag, *Stenographischer Bericht,* 14. Wahlperiode, 184. Sitzung (29 August 2001), 18199, 18215, 18226.
28. Gunther Hellmann, "Jenseits von 'Normalisierung' und 'Militarisierung.' Zur Standortdebatte über die neue deutsche Außenpolitik," *APuZ,* No. 1–2 (1997), 24–33.
29. Joschka Fischer, *I am not convinced. Der Irak-Krieg und die rot-grünen Jahre* (Cologne, 2011), 426.
30. Schneider, *Die Außen- und Sicherheitspolitik,* 55–56.
31. Fischer, *I am not convinced,* 15.
32. Ibid., 58–61. The Chancellor had two votes over the necessary minimum. Parliamentarians of the Greens decided internally who would vote with the Chancellor to save the government.
33. Ibid., 60.
34. 336 voted yes, two more than were necessary.
35. Dalgaard-Nielsen, *Germany, Pacifism,* 87.
36. Peter Struck, "Unsere Sicherheit wird nicht nur, aber auch am Hindukusch verteidigt, wenn sich dort Bedrohungen für unser Land, wie im Falle international organisierter Terroristen, formieren," speech, 11 March 2004, http://www.bmvg.de/portal/a/bmvg/kcxml/04.
37. Ibid.
38. On 3–4 September 2009.
39. Opinion poll of the Sozialwissenschaftliches Institut der Bundeswehr in Strausberg, 17 February 2010, http://www.open-report.de/news/Deutsche+lehnen+Kampfeinsätze+in+Afghanistan+ab/40638.
40. Fischer, *I am not convinced,* 30, 78, 82.
41. Ibid., 141–152.
42. *Die ZEIT,* No. 14, 2003, http://www.zeit.de/2003/14/Stoiber/komplettansicht?print=true.
43. In 2003 Germany was a nonpermanent member of the UN Security Council.
44. Fischer, *I am not convinced,* 161.
45. Ibid., 146, 153.
46. Ibid., 212. Remarks to Secretary of Defense Rumsfeld at the Munich Security Conference in February 2003.

47. Maull (2003), 16.
48. Angela Merkel, "Deutsche Außen- und Sicherheitspolitik vor globalen Herausforderungen," 4 February 2006, http://www.securityconference.de/archive/konferenzen/rede.php?menu_2006=&menu_konferenzen_archiv=&menu_konferenzen=&sprache=de&id=170& (5-28-2011).
49. Coalition agreement, "Gemeinsam für Deutschland. Mit Mut und Menschlichkeit," 1 October 2005, http://www.cducsu.de/upload/koavertrag0509.pdf, 152–156.
50. Bundesministerium der Verteidigung, *Weißbuch 2006. Zur Sicherheitspolitik Deutschlands und zur Zukunft der Bundeswehr*, 23–25.
51. Deutscher Bundestag, *Gesetz über die parlamentarische Beteiligung des Bundestages bei der Entscheidung über den Einsatz bewaffneter Streitkräfte im Ausland (Parlamentsbeteiligungsgesetz)*, 18 March 2005, http://www.bundestag.de/dokumente/rechtsgrundlagen/parlamentsbeteiligung/index.html.
52. "Unzuverlässige Partner," *FAZnet*, 20 April 2011, http://www.faz.net/artikel/C30190/bundeswehreinsatz-unzuverlaessiger-partner-30334762.html.
53. UN Security Council Resolution 1671, 25 April 2006.
54. Denis M. Tull, "Die Führung und Beteiligung der Bundeswehr an EUFOR RD CONGO," in Stefan Mair, ed., *Auslandseinsätze der Bundeswehr. Leitfragen, Entscheidungsspielräume und Lehren* (SWP-Studie, 2007), 68–77, 73.
55. Schneider, *Die Außen- und Sicherheitspolitik*, 97.
56. "Warum sollen unsere Soldaten in den Libanon? Interview mit Angela Merkel," *Welt am Sonntag*, 20 August 2006; "Militärische Gewalt muss verhältnismäßig sein. Interview mit Frank-Walter Steinmeier," *Süddeutsche Zeitung*, 31 July 2006.
57. Muriel Asseburg, "Der Bundeswehreinsatz im Libanon. Die Maritime Task Force im Rahmen von 'UNIFIL plus',- two As in 2003, Berlin as non-s to this sentence are consistent with your intended meaning. " in *Auslandseinsätze*, 99–107.
58. Merkel had even skipped the EU-Africa Summit in December 2010 in Tripoli to avoid close contact with the dictator.
59. "Merkel lehnt deutschen Militäransatz in Libyen ab," *Saarbrücker Zeitung*, 16 March 2011.
60. *Focus online*, 13 March 2011, http://www.focus.de/politik/weitere-meldungen/politik-merkel-cdu-lehnt-militaereinsatz-in-libyen-ab_aid_609387.html.
61. Andreas Rinke, "Eingreifen oder nicht?" *Internationale Politik*, Juli–August, 2011. http://www.internationalepolitik.de/2011/06/09/eingreifen-oder-nicht/.
62. Volker Rühe, "Deutschland im Abseits," *FAZ*, 16 May 2011.
63. Wolfgang Ischinger, "Die Last der Verantwortung," Munich Security Conference, http://www.securityconference.de/Monthly-Mind-Detailansicht.67+M59436426018.0.html.
64. General Assembly: A/RES/60/1, 25 October 2005, 30. R2P demands protection of civilians by their government or by the international community.
65. Rinke, "Eingreifen oder nicht?" and interviews by the author.
66. Fischer, *I am not convinced*, 194, made the same argument when deliberating on how to vote if the Security Council were to decide on intervention in Iraq in 2003.
67. Baden-Württemberg, Rhineland-Palatinate, and Saxony-Anhalt had regional elections a few days after the decision on UN Security Council Resolution 1973, 17 February 2011.
68. *Das Parlament*, 23 August 2010, 1.
69. "Mehr Respekt für deutsche Soldaten," *Deutschlandfunk*, 22 May 2010, http://www.dradio.de/dkultur/sendungen/interview/1188780/.
70. In real figures the budget will be about the same until 2013 (31.2 billion € in 2009; 31.9 billion € in 2013). But the amount lags behind the 2 percent GDP that was agreed on in NATO and the EU for modernization. "NATO-Russia Compendium of Finance and Economic Data Relating to Defence," 20 December 2007, htttp.//www.nato.int/docu/pr/2007/p07-141.pdf.

71. In March 2011 the government did not ask parliament before ordering twenty soldiers to accompany a military rescue mission for German civilians from Libya.
72. Crawford, *The Normative Power*, 180.
73. Peter Blechschmidt, "Über den Hindukusch hinaus," *Süddeutsche online*, 18 May 2011, http://www.sueddeutsche.de/politik/auslandseinsaetze-der-bundeswehr-ueber-den-hindukusch-hinaus-1.1099173.

Chapter Fourteen

German Foreign Policy after 1990

Some Critical Remarks

Erhard Crome

The foreign policy of united Germany has a more than twenty-year history by now. Twice in the twentieth century Germans tried to conquer the continent or at least to control it. During the criminal Hitler regime no atrocity was too extreme for this goal. To thwart this, the efforts of nearly all other states and nations were required; what tipped the scales were the "outlying powers"—the Soviet Union and the U.S. After their victory against the German attempt at domination, they became entangled in a Cold War against each other, whose inner logic led to the dissipation of ever-greater portions of the gross domestic product. In the end, the Soviet Union's resources were used up. The real existing socialist system of rule and of society collapsed, and the USSR disintegrated.

In the heart of Europe a united Germany re-emerged, as if it had won the Cold War. This already had seemed to be the German dilemma at the beginning of the twentieth century, like that of the old German Empire up to the 1648 Peace of Westphalia: a Germany that is bigger and richer in resources than all European countries (apart from Russia); allegedly too big to simply fall into line in the normal pattern, but not big enough to really be able to dominate the other states and nations. It was not only British foreign policy analysts who worriedly wondered if, in view of a constellation that looked like that of the beginning of the twentieth century, Europe was condemned to repeat its history. Such worries have since proven groundless.

Notes for this chapter begin on page 265.

Nevertheless German diplomacy has gradually achieved a certain independence. The foundation of the Federal Republic's foreign policy, at least that of West Germany up to 1989, was always to avoid going it alone and to act in concert with or in the framework of international organizations, whether it was the European Union, NATO, or even the UN. Special importance was attached to "commitment to the West." After 9/11 German Chancellor Gerhard Schröder declared his "unconditional solidarity" with the United States. If there was a difference in the views of the U.S. and, say, France, federal German foreign policy determined which of the positions to support. Thus in 2003 the Schröder government refused German participation in the U.S.'s Iraq War, for which the Bush Administration was seeking a coalition of the "willing," while pointedly acting in agreement with France. Germany's abstention in the UN Security Council on Resolution 1973 (17 March 2011), which opened the way to the Western intervention in Libya, was the first case in which Germany agreed not with the U.S., France, or Great Britain, but with China, Russia, India, and Brazil—the emergent powers of the twenty-first century. On the level of symbolic politics, this was a signal to the former Western victorious powers and longtime allies in NATO and the European Union that Germany will only agree with them if it is in its own interest to do so. Or, in other words, since 2011 the policy in force is: Germany's perception of its interests in international politics is not a function derived from "alliance obligations" defined by others.

Historical Constellations

"German foreign policy remained centered on Europe following the example of Prussia," Hartmut Elsenhans remarked on Germany's diplomatic inclinations at the beginning of the twentieth century, "even if in the Wilhelmine period it strove to shift toward world politics."[1] But what was "the world as Will and Idea" and what was the actual policy and strategy? The Hungarian-born U.S. historian, John Lukacs, stressed that "the great wars and conflicts of the 20th century were not carried out between classes but between the nations of this world. Thus the two world wars were essentially, if not completely and exclusively, struggles led by the German nation against other nations, a consequence of Germany's rise to world-power status and of its claim to supremacy in Europe—by hindsight the last military and political attempt of a powerful European nation to achieve this goal."[2]

Since the end of the nineteenth century, large-scale industry, which, with the exception of the U.S., had nowhere else developed as quickly as in Germany, seemed to deliver the required means to an imperialist foreign policy.

However, "total war" was followed by total defeat. Germany was occupied by the victorious powers; from the zones of occupation arose a divided Germany according to the logic of the Cold War: the Federal Republic of Germany in the framework of NATO and the EU under the control of the U.S., Great Britain, and France, and the GDR in the framework of the Warsaw Pact and the Council for Mutual Economic Assistance (COMECOM) under the control of the Soviet Union. The change that occurred after 1945 in the West was captured by the historian Dan Diner in this way:

> The contrast between the essentially abstract exchange-based and informal Western expansion resting on world-market universalism, on the one hand, and the continental German imperial expansion with its violent expression, on the other, is not due to the mode of production. In both cases it is a matter of societies constituted capitalistically. At the same time, however, what is involved are two different 'civic cultures' ... two differently fashioned political forms within capitalism. From the point of view of its moral and historic significance, there is of course all the difference in the world. The Atlantic integration of the Federal Republic of Germany is accordingly not only an alliance-policy process. It also involves an integration, flanked by the world market, into another political culture, the culture of *civil society* as Western civilization.[3]

After the collapse of the communist system of rule this world market and cultural system was extended to Eastern Europe. After the end of the formal reign of communism the establishment of informal power structures were also placed on the agenda here.

Germany is and now remains a part of this Western cultural framework. However, with the advanced integration processes in the European Union, that cultural entity ceased to be identical with that economic entity. The Western culture essentially characterizes the globalized world of the twenty-first century, from which power and struggle for power and influence have not disappeared. But in comparison to the first half of the twentieth century, the conditions under which these conflicts are settled have been fundamentally and durably changed, and there are, in terms of the world economy and geopolitics, at least two poles within the structure of the West: the U.S. and Western Europe. They are tied to each other in a nexus of identity of interests on the one hand and a nexus of competition on the other.

At the same time, with the aspiring economies and powers, as they are articulated in the alliance of the BRICS countries—Brazil, Russia, India, China, and South Africa—new relevant actors have appeared on the international level, which are in fact in competition with the old power structures of the North Atlantic area. In this sense, today's actual world does not resemble, in terms of peace policy, that which most people had hoped for in 1989/90, but rather the world before 1914. Some time ago, the historian Timothy Garton Ash compared the current situation with the beginning of the twentieth century. At that time the context was the international system mainly shaped by Great Britain, which was being called into question mainly by the U.S. and German competitors. The twentieth century's two world wars were consequences of this, and in the end the U.S. emerged from these battles as victor. Today it is above all China and India that are questioning the system dominated by the U.S. The resulting competition and rivalry between countries exhibits, according to Ash, a series of parallels to the situation of a hundred years ago.[4] The vote in the UN Security Council on Resolution 1973 on Libya was a manifestation of this constellation.

After the Cold War

With the end of the bloc confrontation in Europe and Germany, the "German Question" returned to the historic agenda. According to Peter Bender, it always had two faces: "For the Germans this question always referred to German unity; for other Europeans it meant the German danger. Re-unification and European security stood in a conflicting relationship throughout the entire post-war period. The 1990 compromise tempered this antithesis to a point that was acceptable to all; the Germans were united and yet remained restrained."[5] This compromise had two basic features: the continued integration of Germany into NATO and the Two-Plus-Four Treaty.

In the turbulent winter months of 1990, the U.S. made it clear that it insisted on the continued existence of NATO, and this with the three main functions that had determined its strategy from the very beginning: to keep the U.S. inside (West) Europe, to keep the Russians out, and to keep the Germans under control. In Moscow, on 9 February 1990, the U.S. Secretary of State James Baker obtained Russian permission for the NATO membership of a united Germany. His argument to President Gorbachev and Foreign Minister Shevardnadze was: "Would you prefer to see a re-united Germany outside NATO and without the US Armed Forces, which means they might have their own nuclear weapons? Or do you prefer a re-united Germany that is tied to NATO resolutions …?"[6] In other words: if the Soviet Union was no longer in a position to participate in lasting and effective political control over the Germans, then the U.S. wanted to carry this out through NATO; this has remained a key factor of the U.S.'s European policy and of the German preference for NATO. The repeated statements of the then chancellor that the U.S. had a "permanent right of abode" in the "house of Europe,"[7] whatever that means, certainly have to be seen as repayment for the key supportive role of the U.S. in the process of German unification.

In U.S. understanding, the conclusion of the Two-Plus-Four Treaty was its own idea as well: negotiations about Germany only among the four allies of World War II and without German participation were not a possibility, Baker said in Moscow on 9 February 1990, and the CSCE was too cumbersome as a forum for negotiation.[8] Peter Bender calls the Two-Plus-Four Treaty—in connection with the integration of Germany in the EU and NATO—"the best solution for the German question, which was possible under the given circumstances."[9] In this respect, it is necessary to look at the stipulated provisions.

In Article 1 of the Treaty, the external borders of a united Germany were established as identical to those of the Federal Republic and the GDR, and Germany was to confirm its border with Poland in an internationally recognized treaty; it declared it had no territorial claims against other states and would not assert any in the future. With this a crucial point of tension of postwar history was finally eliminated. In Article 3, the governments of the FRG and the GDR reaffirmed their renunciation of the manufacture, possession, and control of nuclear, biological, and chemical weapons and declared that united Germany will abide by these commitments. France, Great Britain, the USSR, and the U.S. declare in Article 7 the termination of their "rights and responsibilities relating to Berlin and to Germany as a whole," with the consequence that "United Germany shall have accordingly full sovereignty over its internal and external affairs." With these clauses German interests in this matter were conclusively regulated.[10]

Article 2 points beyond, toward the maintenance of peace, and stipulates: "The Governments of the Federal Republic of Germany and the German Democratic Republic reaffirm their declarations that only peace will emanate from German soil. According to the constitution of the united Germany, acts tending to and undertaken with the intent to disturb the peaceful relations between nations, especially to prepare for aggressive war, are unconstitutional and a punishable offence." The governments of the FRG and the GDR "declare that the united Germany will never employ any of its weapons except in accordance with its constitution and the Charter of the United Nations."[11]

In this sense the Basic Law also states for the Federal Republic of Germany that the German people are "informed by the will to serve world peace as an equally entitled member of a united Europe" (Preamble). "The general rules of international law shall be an integral part of federal law. They shall take precedence over the laws and directly create rights and duties for the inhabitants of the federal territory" (Article 25). It is further stipulated that: "Acts tending to and undertaken with intent to disturb the peaceful relations between nations, especially to prepare for a war of aggression, shall be unconstitutional. They shall be made a criminal offense" (Article 26). The determination of a "state of defense" can be made when "the federal territory is under attack by armed force or imminently threatened with such an attack" (Article 115a).[12]

This legal situation, as it is anchored in the Two-Plus-Four Treaty and in the Basic Law, has consequences not only for government action regarding foreign and security policy decisions in Germany; it is at the same time the basis of sharp political controversies in every crisis situation. In the second Gulf War of 1990/91 the international legal status was clear: Iraq had, under Saddam Hussein, annexed Kuwait, whereupon the UN Security Council issued an ultimatum for a quick withdrawal of Iraqi troops and threatened the use of military force, which in the end would be applied by an international military coalition under the leadership of the U.S. The federal government at that time declared that Germany's position in terms of international law and national constitutional law forbade direct participation in the conduct of the war. Instead, it made a direct and indirect contribution to the Gulf War at a level of more than 18 billion DM. Subsequently, although nothing changed in material reality, the legal situation was reinterpreted with the participation of the Federal Constitutional Court, which legally justified foreign deployment of the Bundeswehr far beyond an immediate function of defense. At the same time, the strong reservations of the Bundestag were prescribed by law; in the end it is parliament that decides on military interventions, not the executive.

The opposition sharply attacked the German participation in the 1999 war against Yugoslavia, carried out by the Social Democratic–led Federal Government. But the strong argument of a constitutional violation by the government was rejected by the judges as well as by a majority of the German political class. In public argument, the government used strong, emotionally charged imagery, invoking for example "Auschwitz" in order to justify participation in the war, and spread, as came out later, false information (alleged concentration camps in Yugoslavia) in order to make its decision more plausible to the public. At the same time the government was anxious, at least after the fact, to get legitimation from the UN Security Council[13] in order to deflect the accusation of violation of international law and of the Constitution. It also turned the Two-Plus-Four Treaty, as far as possible, into a thing of the past, although it continues to be part of current international law.

Since that time Germany has participated in and still participates in diverse military interventions, from Afghanistan to the Horn of Africa to

Bosnia, Kosovo, and Macedonia. The barriers to military interventions, however, have up to now continued to be steeper than in other NATO countries, and these interventions themselves always produce sharp internal political confrontations.

Changed Strategy and Policy

At the beginning of the 1990s, the media and public opinion in Germany assumed that after German unification, and with the sovereignty allowed by the Two-Plus-Four Treaty, a "third, great foreign-policy debate" was necessary—this in itself expressed a point of view stressing the continuity with the old FRG. By this reckoning the first debate was the conflict in the old Federal Republic about Adenauer's integration with the West in the 1950s, and the second was the foreign policy debate involving Willy Brandt's *Ostpolitik* in the 1970s. But this big public discussion had not yet taken place; the participants in the debate were the foreign policy experts, while in the ministries the course had already been set for another policy. The central concepts with which public discourse in Germany was opened up in the direction of participation in military interventions were "normality," "responsibility," and "alliance loyalty." If Germany was now sovereign, then it ought to be able to have a "normal" foreign policy, to which even military intervention would belong. Since Germany is a big country with far-reaching, global trade and economic interests, so the thinking went, it would have also to assume larger responsibilities; in this reasoning, armed interventions were always justified as serving peace. "Alliance" always meant that never again would Germany undertake military actions alone.

The political scientist Hanns W. Maull already suggested in 1992 that Germany should act in the international arena as a "civilian power."[14] After this position was criticized as going against the rationale for NATO, Maull re-explained it theoretically in such a way that it could no longer be interpreted as peace oriented ("only deploying civic means"). Moreover, he used the "civilizing" concept of the sociologist Norbert Elias who had determined "that violent forms of deciding conflicts have been increasingly limited and pushed back during emergence of modern societies by the development of state monopolies on the use of force, by the institutionalization of alternative forms of settling conflicts and by the internalization of the prohibition on the use of force." This being so has permitted "the unfolding of the developmental potential of the social division of labor ... which is dependent on the predictability and non-violence of social relations." In this sense, Maull extended the civilizing concept beyond the boundaries of the nation-state to include the regional and global contexts and—with reference to Dieter Senghaas who had presented this concept as a "civilizational hexagon"—its acceptance as a foreign policy concept. Accordingly, "civil powers are ... states which feel themselves committed to the goal of a civilizing of politics," of a "civilizing of politics in general and of international relations in particular."[15] However, since the concept of "power" already contains a "right to shape reality," which includes the readiness to "realize one's own goals if necessary even against resistance," Maull also argued that "*Bundeswehr* participation in NATO military interventions in Kosovo" was "the continuation of established foreign-policy lines under different preconditions."[16]

The change in NATO's strategy and policy played a key role in this reconsideration. The Charter of Paris for a New Europe, the 21 November 1990 declaration of the heads of state and governments of the CSCE countries, was regarded as a document ending the Cold War and bloc confrontation. Peace, a democracy, and a market economy resting on human rights and basic freedoms were to form the common basis for the further development of Europe.[17] Since the Warsaw Pact had dissolved, it seemed obvious that NATO would likewise disappear. The opposite occurred. NATO was no longer to be only a military-political alliance for the defense of its members, from whoever their attackers might be, but was to exercise world-police functions, derived from a diffuse, nonspecific, analysis of threat.

The new course was set at the November 1991 NATO Summit in Rome, only several months after the disbanding of the Warsaw Pact. Instead of the big threat, now talk was of "instability and tension," an "environment of uncertainty and unpredictable challenges." The core of the approach was consistently the "transformation of the Alliance."[18] There was never any question of disbanding. This was then further developed in the declaration of the 1999 NATO Summit on the occasion of the fiftieth anniversary of the alliance's founding. By redefining the security policy environment the Western military pact justified its further existence. "In contrast to the predominant threat of the past, the risks to Allied security that remain are multi-faceted in nature and multi-directional ... which makes them hard to predict and assess" (Rome, paragraph 9). "Risks to Allied security are less likely to result from calculated aggression against the territory of the Allies, but rather from the adverse consequences of instabilities," from "the proliferation of weapons technologies in the area, including weapons of mass destruction and ballistic missiles," the presence of large nuclear arsenals that can be directed against NATO, or also from "disruption of the flow of vital resources and actions of terrorism and sabotage" (Rome, paragraphs 10–13). Regionally, NATO had already located the risks in Central and Eastern Europe, the CIS area, as well as in the southern Mediterranean and in the Middle East, but at the same time emphasized: "However, Alliance security must also take account of the global context" (Rome, paragraph 13, and, with the same wording, Washington, paragraph 24).[19] NATO's out-of-area orientation and with it the re-orientation to offensive tasks had already been established in 1991. The list of security risks has, however, been augmented: alongside the danger of "organized crime," (Washington, paragraph 20) "the uncontrolled movement of large numbers of people, particularly as a consequence of armed conflicts" was invoked (Washington, paragraph 20); thus NATO sees its security affected by movements of refugees. The first application case was the War in Yugoslavia.[20]

NATO after the Lisbon Summit

NATO remains the bracket that connects the U.S. and the EU, and from the point of view of its protagonists the lever for the realization of common interests and for avoiding deciding disputes in an openly military way. Although not stipulated in the 1949 NATO Treaty, with the 1999 Strategy Paper, enacted at the Washington Summit during the bombing of Belgrade, the alliance established a worldwide focus. During the 2009 NATO Summit in Strasbourg and Kehl, that Paper was declared insufficient and the need for a new rationale affirmed. Until November 2010 the draft was polished so that it could be voted on at the Lisbon Summit.

This Summit gave no answer that could be positively applied to the world situation unfolding at that moment. The main problems of our time are poverty, famine, diseases, child mortality, inadequate educational and health systems, climate change, and the destruction of the natural conditions of life and the extinction of species. None of these problems can be solved militarily. The failure of states, constantly cited as the cause of terrorism, migratory pressure, on Western countries and piracy, is as a rule the consequence of unresolved social and economic problems of the countries of the Global South, which have arisen under pressure of an unjust world economic order due to Western market power, the IMF, and the World Bank. To reverse this would require peaceful instruments and forces; political stability, good governance, and democracy cannot be established with tanks and guns. The consequences of the wars in Iraq and Afghanistan illustrate exactly this point. To this extent, the basic agreement in Lisbon to zealously continue the Afghan War is, despite the mention of nonbinding withdrawal dates, a fatal error, which will entail further suffering, sacrifice, and war crimes.

In addition, the Lisbon Summit took place shortly after the open outbreak of the biggest financial and world economic crisis since the Second World War, indeed since 1929. Gigantic "rescue packages" were straightaway prepared in order to save the banks and selected large companies in the U.S. and Western Europe. Its costs were deflected onto working people and the socially disadvantaged. Cuts in social spending, pension reductions, and dismantling of the health and education systems are the result. The crisis spread from the financial and economic spheres to become a crisis of state budgets, which resulted in a crisis of social cohesion. Against this background the continuation of a high level of armaments and military expenditures is particularly scandalous. Cuts in social services in Germany and the other NATO countries are the reverse side of the creation and maintenance of a worldwide war-fighting capacity.

For the U.S., after its defeat in the Iraq War and the collapse of the policy of a "unipolar world," the depletion of its domestic economic capacity is its biggest problem. The predominantly military orientation of the presidency of George W. Bush contemplated that the U.S. alone would determine the fate of the world and carry out its imperial interests. But a kind of tectonic shift of the world's economic weight is occurring from the North Atlantic area to Asia, mainly through the preeminent development of China. From the U.S. point of view this change is not to be dealt with by military means, as the price could be nuclear world war. Additionally, these same countries of the EU, who in the context of NATO sing the praises of the "Western community of values," owe their present economic upswing mainly to cooperation with China, and China remains the U.S.'s biggest creditor. Thus, NATO is not an instrument the West can use to deal with its weakening global economic possibilities.

During the Lisbon meeting much was said about "historic" significance. The Summit Declaration proclaimed that the new "Strategic Concept" would apply to the next decades.[21] The preface stated that NATO is committed "to the goal of creating the conditions for a world without nuclear weapons." This is different from the goal announced by U.S. President Barack Obama, as he took office, of a nuclear-free world; it is practically its retraction. It further asserted that "as long as there are nuclear weapons in the world, NATO will remain a nuclear Alliance." It appears that there is to be no increased multilateralization of access to nuclear weapons, but this formulation is somewhat ambiguous and contradicts the Nuclear Non-Proliferation Treaty. In other words: NATO's holding onto its nuclear weapons does not go in the direction of a reduction of world nuclear arms, but spurs it on further.

In describing NATO's security environment, the declaration speaks of "Euro-Atlantic integration" (paragraph 7). Integration, which is a "historic success of the policies of a robust defense." Do economic, social, and cultural factors, as well as mutual financial interlocking, play no role? The text goes on to claim that "the conventional threat cannot be ignored," since in "many regions and countries" there are attempts to create "modern military capabilities" (paragraph 8). Where this might be, who is doing this, what these attempts consist of—all this the summit participants still need to prove. Consistent with the saying "dangers lurk always and everywhere," they are only lumped vaguely together: proliferation of nuclear weapons (paragraph 9), terrorism (paragraph 10), "instability or conflict beyond NATO borders" (paragraph 11), "cyber attacks" (paragraph 12). What NATO as a highly armed military alliance should do in these areas remains completely nebulous. Further on, the declaration states that all countries "are increasingly reliant on the vital communication, transport and transit routes on which international trade, energy security and prosperity depend" (paragraph 13). This—in contrast to the somewhat self-absorbed view of the 1999 Strategy Paper—is the self-conception of NATO, which wants to look out for the economic interests of its member-states, even if this requires military deployment.

Territorial defense (paragraph 16) is once again defined as a goal and commitment as a throwback to the original founding context of NATO and against the background of the anti-Russian reflex in the new East European countries. Under the rubric of "deterrence," it is reaffirmed that NATO is to remain a nuclear alliance (paragraph 17) and that nuclear weapons will represent the "supreme guarantee of the security of the Allies" (paragraph 18). In the future it will be necessary to maintain "an appropriate mix of nuclear and conventional forces" (paragraph 19). On the subject of "crisis management," "a comprehensive political, civilian and military approach" is emphasized (paragraph 21), which up to now had already subordinated civic aid and conflict resolution to military logic, the consequence being warfare strategies. At the end there are vague references to arms control, disarmament, and nonproliferation, which, however, in view of the real developments of NATO, have a purely declarative alibi function. Finally, the EU is highlighted as an important partner in NATO's military cooperation (paragraph 32). This, however, says more about the EU post–Lisbon Treaty than it does about NATO.

The Need for Alternatives

A special feature of the Lisbon NATO Summit was the participation of then–Russian President Medvedev, which produced a special declaration of the NATO-Russia Council. After President Bush and NATO's plans to install anti-ballistic weapons in Eastern Europe, openly directed against Russia, there was a clear easing of tension. The Strategic Arms Reduction Treaty (START), which had been ratified in the meantime, contributed to this. Lisbon showed that Russia represents its own interests, which do not necessarily have to coincide with those of the West—but it does not want to settle these differences militarily. At the same time Russia logistically supports the Afghan War, because it fears an Islamist destabilization of Central Asia in the event of a "Taliban" victory, although this position has little prospect for success, as does the Afghan War as a whole. Thus Medvedev's participation in Lisbon was first of all a signal to the West on a symbolic level. What concretely follows is a matter for further observation and analysis.

This points to the fact that NATO cannot be the solution to security problems in Europe. There is no reasonable alternative to a system of mutual collective European security, which must be tied to disarmament, mutual incapacity to launch an attack, and the creation of zones in Europe and beyond that are free of nuclear and other weapons of mass destruction. NATO is not a help but an obstacle on this path, and the Lisbon Summit has widened this obstacle. The creation of a system of common collective security would be a possible answer.

The economic, political, and military developments in the world in the twenty-first century are quite dynamic, and will be compounded by increasing world problems such as climate change, species extinction, and the destruction of the natural bases of life, poverty, famine, diseases, child mortality, etc. In the long run there can be no peace without finding compromises, exercising tolerance, and implementing binding agreements. In searching for ways and mechanisms for this, great help can be found in what was thought about, worked out, and realized about preventing wars during the final phase of the East-West conflict. The concepts addressed at that time include "new thinking," "war and peace in the nuclear age," "capitalism's capacity for peace," "peaceful coexistence and positive peace," "the impossibility of winning a war conducted with nuclear weapons," "the concept of security and threat analyses," "common security," "arms limitation and disarmament," "system of collective security in Europe," "creation of zones free of nuclear weapons or weapons of mass destruction," "de-militarized security and an expanded concept of security," "structural incapacity to launch an attack," and "strategic sufficiency, that is reasonable defense capability, not offensive capabilities."

It follows, in summary, that the questions of war and peace after the end of the Cold War have lost none of their relevance, but rather have gained more importance. What is first involved in this is the question of conditions for world peace, which as a concept only has meaning as the antithesis of a world war. The tectonic shifts in the economic relations of power from the North Atlantic world to Asia have posed anew the question of world war and of the prerequisites for maintaining world peace. However, the situation of world peace, as we now experience it, is not a condition of global peace, but rather of a differentiated distribution of peaceful and belligerent or armed conflict situations in the world. The concept "world peace" relates to that of "world war" as its antonym. It intends "the absence of world war (and its improbability)," well understanding the reality "that qualitatively and quantitatively it is not war but peace in international relations which is preponderant," but that this is, however, "a peaceful order on a lower level, disturbed by sources of armed conflict, by local or regional breaches of the peace and the not excluded possibility of a collapse and shift to global war."[22]

Thus the questions of preempting conflict and war, the questions of the causes of conflict, of conflict prevention and civil conflict management and resolution, are also posed under new conditions. At the same time these conflicts are mostly not interstate clashes but arise from quasi–civil war situations, which frequently have as their points of departure poverty, famine, state failure, and the struggle for raw materials to benefit the industrialized countries as well as climate change and other global problems. In this respect, the contexts of peace and security as well as peace and development have to be approached from a fresh perspective.

The end of the Cold War did not lead to a secure peace and to less conflict. The hoped-for dominance of "the West" lasted only briefly. New competitors and challengers came to the fore. The preferred answer was war. But these wars (Iraq, Afghanistan, Libya) did not bring the anticipated success and moreover led the Western world into many crises. The West needs to adjust itself in the long term to a diverse world with challenges, conflicts, and confrontations. German foreign policy has up to now moved along old well-trodden paths, which do not correspond to the new requirements of the twenty-first century. The "normalizing" of German foreign policy after 1990 was overwhelmingly a return to old political patterns. Only a few highlights, like Germany's nonparticipation in the War in Libya, show that even under current conditions another policy is possible.

Finally, the old question is posed anew of how we want to live and survive in this world. There will be no dominance; all questions of whether China will take the place of the U.S. as superpower miss the root of the matter. The main tendency of international developments is to move toward a multipolar world. The question is whether this will be a "concert of powers," like the competing powers in Europe from 1815 to 1914, that stalk each other and conduct wars outside their immediate territories, which are also wars for competing zones of power and influence—or whether this multipolar world will be an international order of the "rule of law," as provided, ideally, by the UN Charter, and with the UN and the UN Security Council as the central institutions for securing the peace. Attention to and observance of international law must again become the guiding principle of foreign policy. It is the basis for the coexistence of countries and peoples. The elementary precept of law anchored in the UN Charter is peacekeeping. After the end of the Cold War it was trampled on, above all, by the West. Imperative in this is the sovereign equality of countries and the principle of noninterference in their internal affairs. On the other side, the countries are responsible for everything that arises from their territory (this also includes terrorist activities). If they cannot gain control over this themselves, international assistance can be given to them. But unrequested involvement can only be a final resort in the case of genocide, and only the UN Security Council can determine its existence. Human rights have a high value, but one's own interpretation bestows no right to intervention. The renewed strengthening of the role of the UN must proceed especially from the principle of peacekeeping.

As long as there are nation-states, there also must be a world constitution which binds these countries, with their interests and diverse social systems, to an international peace order that rests on international law. Such an order, as it is ideally outlined in the UN Charter—with all the inadequacies of realizing and enforcing international law and the shortcomings of the way the UN Security Council functions—must also work "in a world of devils," as Immanuel Kant noted in his treatise *On Eternal Peace.* The observance of sovereignty and sovereign equality of states, the prohibition of force and noninterference in internal affairs are the minimal preconditions. This holds also for the relation of states to other states. They should abstain from wanting to change others to conform to their own image. In view of its history, Germany has every reason to be particularly restrained.

Notes

1. Hartmut Elsenhans, "Reif für die Weltpolitik? Gedanken zur außenpolitischen Elite Deutschlands," *WeltTrends* 25 (1999/2000), 123.
2. John Lukacs, *Churchill und Hitler. Der Zweikampf,* (Stuttgart, 1993), 21–22.
3. Dan Diner, "Imperialismus, Universalismus, Hegemonie. Zum Verhältnis von Politik und Ökonomie in der Weltgesellschaft," in Iring Fetscher and Herfried Münkler, eds., *Politikwissenschaft. Begriffe—Analysen—Theorien. Ein Grundkurs* (Reinbek, 1985), 357.

4. See Timothy Garton Ash, "Müder Titan," *Süddeutsche Zeitung*, 20 August 2005.
5. Peter Bender, *Episode oder Epoche? Zur Geschichte des geteilten Deutschland* (Munich, 1996), 134.
6. Cited in Michael R. Beschloss and Strobe Talbott, *Auf höchster Ebene. Das Ende des Kalten Krieges und die Geheimdiplomatie der Supermächte 1989–1991* (Düsseldorf, 1993), 245.
7. For example, Helmut Kohl's speech at the Hebrew University in Jerusalem on 8 June 1995, http://www.helmut-kohl.de/index.php?menu_sel=17&menu_sel2=&menu_sel3=&menu_sel4=&msg=1596.
8. Ibid., 244f.
9. Bender, *Episode oder Epoche?* 134.
10. "Treaty on the Final Settlement with Respect to Germany September 12, 1990," http://usa.usembassy.de/etexts/2plusfour8994e.htm.
11. Ibid.
12. *Basic Law for the Federal Republic of Germany*, official translation at: https://www.btg-bestellservice.de/pdf/80201000.pdf.
13. For a more detailed account, see Erhard Crome, "In tempore belli," *WeltTrends* 23 (1999), 137–151.
14. Hanns W. Maull, "Zivilmacht Bundesrepublik Deutschland. Vierzehn Thesen für eine neue deutsche Außenpolitik," *Europa-Archiv* 23 (1992), 671f.
15. Hanns W. Maull, "Deutschland als Zivilmacht," in Siegmar Schmidt, Günther Hellmann and Reinhard Wolf eds., *Handbuch zur deutschen Außenpolitik* (Wiesbaden, 2007), 73f. The references are to: Norbert Elias, *Über den Prozeß der Zivilisation* (Frankfurt, 1976) and Dieter Senghaas, ed., *Frieden machen* (Frankfurt, 1997).
16. Maull, *Deutschland als Zivilmacht*, 74, 80.
17. "Charter of Paris," http://www.osce.org/mc/39516.
18. "The Alliance's New Strategic Concept agreed by the Heads of State and Government participating in the Meeting of the North Atlantic Council," 7–8 November 1991, http://www.nato.int/cps/en/SID-558F761F-05EF5A11/natolive/official_texts_23847.htm.
19. "The Alliance's Strategic Concept Approved by the Heads of State and Government participating in the meeting of the North Atlantic Council in Washington DC," 24 April 1999, http://www.nato.int/cps/en/natolive/official_texts_27433.htm?selectedLocale=en.
20. See also "Friedensmemorandum des Bundesausschusses Friedensratschlag 2000," http://www.uni-kassel.de/fb5/frieden/memorandum/NATO-Strategie.html.
21. "Lisbon Summit Declaration," 20 November 2010, http://www.nato.int/cps/en/natolive/official_texts_68828.htm; http://www.nato.int/strategic-concept/index.html.
22. Wolfgang Scheler," Fortschritt des Friedens in Idee und Wirklichkeit. Notwendigkeit und Möglichkeit in der heutigen Welt," http://www.sicherheitspolitik-dss.de/autoren/scheler/pasche32.htm.

Chapter Fifteen

"To Deploy or Not to Deploy"

The Erratic Evolution of German Foreign Policy since Unification

Andrew I. Port

"Germany has entered a new era of ambivalence and nationalist calculation," Roger Cohen, the former bureau chief of the *New York Times* in Berlin, fumed in an op-ed piece prompted by Germany's controversial decision in March 2011 to abstain from a United Nations Security Council vote to impose a no-fly zone over Libya.[1] Besides being unduly harsh and hyperbolic, his censure revealed a remarkably short memory, even for a journalist. After all, the press had leveled similar criticism at Germany less than a decade earlier following Gerhard Schröder's calculated unwillingness to participate in the "Coalition of the Willing's" 2003 invasion of Iraq.[2]

Many Germans themselves, not least ones in Chancellor Angela Merkel's own conservative party, nevertheless shared Cohen's outrage about the Federal Republic's vote—or lack thereof—at the UN. Former CDU Minister of Defense Volker Rühe spoke, for example, of "a major mistake of historic proportions." Those on the Left of the political spectrum tended to be more supportive, leading Joschka Fischer, former foreign minister under Schröder, to lament in the *Süddeutsche Zeitung*: "I can only feel shame for the failure of our government and—unfortunately!—also for those Red and Green leaders of the opposition, who initially even applauded this scandalous error." Along similar lines, his fellow Green politician Daniel Cohn-Bendit invoked "images of the Warsaw ghetto" to explain his support of the UN intervention to prevent a "bloodbath" in Benghazi, as well

Notes for this chapter begin on page 276.

as his criticism of those in his own party who supported the government's decision.[3]

In short, party membership and political affiliation were poor predictors of how politicians in the Federal Republic would react to what one Italian newspaper referred to as a German "Nyet à la Brezhnev."[4] But there seemed to be a consensus, even among those who supported the chancellor and her foreign minister, Guido Westerwelle of the liberal FDP, that their decision was motivated in no small part by *domestic* political considerations, above all the upcoming state elections scheduled for the week following the vote at the UN. After all, opinion surveys suggested just how unenthusiastic the overwhelming majority of ordinary citizens—already critical of German deployment in Afghanistan—felt about further military adventures abroad.[5] Similar considerations had clearly underlain Schröder's tactical announcement in August 2002 during the first ever nationally televised debate between chancellor candidates that Germany would not take part in an invasion of Iraq, even if it were sanctioned by the UN. While Schröder's gamble paid off, Merkel's did not and her party subsequently lost control of the government in Baden-Württemberg, which had been a CDU stronghold since the creation of the southwestern state in 1952.

Leaving aside the ludicrous suggestion that there was anything "nationalist" about Merkel and Westerwelle's decision, as well as the inherent contradiction in the suggestion that it was both "ambivalent" *and* "calculating," Cohen's remark does raise an interesting question: has German foreign policy entered a "new era"? Given Schröder's earlier démarche, the obvious response to this question would be that it has not. But there was a major difference. In 2002, the Federal Republic joined France in its refusal to go along with George W. Bush's Iraq policy; in 2011, it distanced itself from *all* of its major allies in Europe and across the Atlantic. Whether or not this marked a decisive break, as Cohen suggests, raises a more general question and one that Erhard Crome and Beate Neuss explicitly address in their essays: to what extent has German foreign policy changed since unification in 1990?

Contrasting Views

Focusing on the issue of troop deployment abroad, Crome and Neuss both argue that foreign policy has changed since unification. The 1990s, they argue, witnessed a gradual move *away* from a broad consensus on the part of the political elite and the broader population that German troops had no business abroad, *toward* a general acceptance, however ambivalent, of out-of-area military missions, at least ones involving some form of humanitarian assistance. To that extent, and as Neuss writes, military missions have become "normalized" over the past two decades, an evolution that marks, it would seem, a major break in German foreign policy going back to the late 1940s. But does it? Are there important elements of continuity as well? And if there was a sea change, what were some of the major reasons for that shift? Finally, does this policy affect compliance with the constitution of the Federal Republic?

Crome and Neuss respond very differently to this set of questions. While the former describes this evolution as a radical break—and an illegal one at that—the latter concedes that German foreign policy has changed a great deal since unification, but also places much emphasis on what she sees as significant lines of continuity. In fact, she argues that the same core values, and above all a belief in multilateralism, have continued to underlie that policy. This commitment to eschewing unilateral acts and working closely together with Germany's allies is part and parcel of the "culture of restraint" that continues to characterize German activity in the global arena as a "civilian power," an ethos, born of the country's traumatic experiences during the Second World War, that embodies Germany's renunciation of its tragic militarist past.[6]

Crome's main argument is that military and even humanitarian interventions are contrary not only to the Two-Plus-Four Treaty that cleared the path to unification in 1990, but also to the "spirit" of the constitution of the Federal Republic. But "spirit" is, of course, a notoriously slippery and subjective term. What, then, do the documents actually stipulate? On the one hand, they do not forbid the use of arms *if* the Federal Republic is under attack or facing imminent attack. Article 115 of the Basic Law clearly sets forth the conditions that constitute a so-called "state of defense" (*Verteidigungsfall*), while Article 25 permits Germany to enter a "system of mutual collective security." On the other hand, it *does* insist on the need to pursue peaceful policies and *does* forbid wars of aggression (Article 26). The Two-Plus-Four Treaty essentially reaffirmed the main elements of the existing "security policy consensus." That said, the potentially explosive issue of out-of-area missions, i.e., the deployment of German troops outside of NATO territory, remained open and thus subject to differing interpretation.

Over the course of the 1990s—and notwithstanding continuing opposition from the Left—the political elite and the general public as a whole moved away from rejecting the deployment of any German troops abroad whatsoever toward a resigned acceptance, at first, of troop deployment limited to humanitarian and/or peacekeeping missions, and then later, of outright military missions as well. To add some meat to the bones of this generalization: in 1991, the Federal Republic refused to participate in the first Gulf War, choosing to "pay instead of play." It also rejected at this time sending troops to former Yugoslavia, not least because of Germany's infamous role there during the first half of the 1940s. But less than a decade later in 1999, German soldiers had not only become an integral part of the so-called KFOR forces sent to Kosovo, but had also done so with the blessing of the Greens and the Social Democrats, who had brought a lawsuit to the Constitutional Court just a few years earlier in an effort to halt German participation in a humanitarian mission in Somalia.

Reasons for Deployment

How exactly did German foreign policy get from 1991 to its 1999 incarnation? And what were the major turning points of this evolution? As Neuss shows, it took place in a gradual, piecemeal fashion. The two previous essays identify at least three main factors driving this dramatic shift, though each deserves some qualification in terms of its explanatory power. The first was the way in which the end of the Cold War led to a fundamental change in perceptions of, as well as a more expansive definition of, perceived security threats; this was true both in terms of substance and provenance. To wit, global terrorism and the danger of "weapons of mass destruction" falling into "rogue" hands effectively replaced Communism and the Soviet Union as the mother of all bogeymen. In other words, perceived threats seemed to become more diffuse, especially in geographic terms.

A second major factor involved changing expectations on the part of Germany's allies, who now expected the Federal Republic to assume a much greater share of military responsibility. This put Germany in the unenviable position of being "damned if it did, damned if it didn't." That is to say, if it refused to send troops to out-of-area trouble spots, the country opened itself to censure for not shouldering its fair share of the global security burden. But if it demonstrated what could be interpreted as "too much" willingness, it ran the risk of awakening historically conditioned fears—especially among immediate neighbors such as Poland and France—about the possibility and danger of a resurgent Reich.

A third factor that played a significant role in reshaping the foreign policy of the Federal Republic involved the supposedly different *types* of crises that took place after unification, especially in Europe. With good reason, many considered the awful atrocities committed in the Balkans in the 1990s to have been the worst in Europe since 1945. It may be true, as Crome notes, that reports about "concentration camps" in the region were falsified or exaggerated. But Srebrenica was certainly not the product of an overactive imagination! In Neuss's memorable formulation, these crises go a long way in explaining how the maxim of German foreign policy morphed from "never again war" to "never again alone" to "never again Auschwitz"—the heavily weighted phrase invoked by Foreign Minister Fischer to justify German military participation in Kosovo.[7]

All of these factors certainly played a role, but they also deserve closer examination and qualification. Let us begin with the last point: the human rights violations that took place in the Balkans were undeniably egregious. But were they really the "worst" to have occurred since 1945? Besides, how does one even begin to measure such a claim? Subjective perceptions obviously play an important role here, and the very language used to describe what was transpiring in former Yugoslavia apparently brought to mind disturbing historical associations for many Germans (and non-Germans as well, of course). But that had been true as well for the reports used to describe the genocide taking place in Cambodia in the second half of the 1970s, to name only one prominent example. Of course, the Balkans hit much closer to home, both literally and figuratively. But that was even more true of the brutal acts of Soviet repression that took place periodically during the Cold War: 1953 in the GDR, 1956 in Hungary, and 1968 in Czechoslovakia. Were they any less egregious? It could be argued that they were because they lacked the "ethnic" dimension of the events that later transpired in former Yugoslavia. That is a debatable conclusion, of course. But there was, in all likelihood, a different and more obvious reason why no action was taken earlier: Soviet nuclear capability—an existential threat that became, for all intents and purposes, less of a pressing concern after unification. The point is that after the end of the Cold War, there were real possibilities for intervening militarily without the danger of nuclear annihilation or other violent repercussions on German territory. Besides, the very disappearance of the Soviet threat made it possible for the Germans to focus their attention to a much larger extent on developments outside of Europe. Those decisive changes were arguably more relevant in the context of Germany's changing foreign policy than the supposedly worsening character of human rights abuses across the globe.

Along similar lines, did the threat to the Federal Republic and the West really become more global in nature following unification? After all, the specter of communism had also been considered a *global* danger during the decade-long Cold War. And besides, the threat of global terrorism did not magically materialize after the abrupt end of that conflict—as a series of bombings in the 1980s of a French cultural center and a discothèque frequented by American soldiers in Berlin, as well as of the Radio Free Europe headquarters in Munich, made tragically clear. None of the three was directed against German nationals per se, but they were carried out by terrorist groups from the Middle East. Why, then, was greater pressure not placed on Germany earlier to assume its "fair" share of the security burden by deploying troops out-of-area? Why was German activity abroad prior to 1990 limited to mere technical and logistical support?[8]

It was, perhaps, simply a question of time: after all, the horrors and wounds of the Second World War continued to remain fresh. But did the Federal Republic really seem to be less of a threat to its allies in the 1990s than it did in the 1980s? Or in the 1960s and 1970s, for that matter? That seems doubtful. After all, the United States began to push for West German rearmament less than a decade after the defeat of the Third Reich. Though this was understandably a source of great concern to the French, who had been attacked by Germany no less than three times during the previous eight decades, the threat posed by its neighbor beyond the Rhine now seemed to pale in comparison to the alleged Soviet menace, especially after the latter acquired atomic capabilities and especially after the start of the Korean conflict in June 1950. That said, and despite the Cold War rhetoric of the period, one wonders if the fall of the Berlin Wall would have elicited the same type of unmitigated joy, untainted—for the most part—by fear, had it occurred, say, two decades *before* 1989.

What the foregoing suggests is that the most important factor leading to the shift in German foreign policy and especially the country's increasing willingness to deploy troops abroad was arguably a change in *perception*—not only on the part of the Federal Republic's friends and neighbors, but also on the part of the Germans themselves (to the extent that one can talk of "the" Germans, not least because of still significant political, regional, and class differences, as well as those between so-called *Ossis* and *Wessis*). One could argue that the Federal Republic and Germans as a whole have achieved a greater degree of self-confidence over the past two decades.[9] This is a highly impressionistic observation, of course, and almost impossible to measure with any degree of accuracy. It is not meant to accuse the Germans in a blanket fashion of resurgent nationalist bluster or crass triumphalism, of supercilious feelings of "we're somebody again" since 1989—though such sentiments naturally exist in some quarters, as they undoubtedly do in any country.

There were a number of causes for this growing self-assurance, but it should be emphasized that they all *predated* unification, at least in the West. These included pride in German economic success, in the achievements of the social welfare state, as well as in the very stability of the democratic order created after the nightmare of National Socialism, i.e., what Dolf Sternberger and later Jürgen Habermas memorably referred to as "constitutional patriotism." The surge in popular interest in the Holocaust that took place in the 1970s and 1980s was a double-edged sword in this respect: on the one hand, the crimes committed four decades earlier became an obsession of sorts and also a source of shame for many Germans, especially younger ones who were often reluctant to even identify themselves as Germans when traveling abroad or meeting foreigners. On the other hand (and despite worries by some German conservatives about what they considered to be a disturbing dearth of national pride), this very reckoning with the Holocaust was also *liberating*: it conceivably enabled younger Germans to acknowledge to themselves and to others the more positive achievements of the Federal Republic in a sober, non-chauvinistic, less self-conscious manner—without having to worry about accusations of being ugly nationalists trying to cover up their country's unsavory past.[10] It was this changing atmosphere that arguably made it possible for Gerhard Schröder to speak more openly and without embarrassment about German "national interests."

But there are other possible factors worth considering as well. In a recent study, Samuel Moyn argued that the concept of "human rights" was "discovered" in the 1970s as "the foundation of an international movement and a utopia of international law." It is the "last utopia," in fact, one constructed to serve as an alternative to all of the "prior universalistic schemes" that had more or less given up the ghost four decades ago.[11] Whatever one makes of this provocative thesis, it is true that humanitarian interventions are a relatively recent development that has become increasingly commonplace over the past two decades.[12] Does that mean that the foreign policy of the Federal Republic would have evolved in the way that it did after 1990 even in the absence of unification? This is doubtful, since such interventions were made possible, in no small part, by the demise of communism and the end of the East-West antagonism. In other words, the Federal Republic and the entire world community would likely have remained hemmed in by Cold War strictures, and it was only when they fell by the wayside that the game plan could change in the way that it subsequently did.

Whatever the reasons, there is no denying that the foreign policy of the Federal Republic has witnessed significant changes since unification. Military missions abroad were simply unimaginable before 1990. But there have also been other changes in substance and tone, all of which reflect the increased self-confidence alluded to earlier. One thinks of Foreign Minister Hans-Dietrich Genscher's unilateral recognition of Croatia and Slovenia during the Yugoslav crisis of the early 1990s, the Federal Republic's subsequent campaign for a permanent seat on the UN Security Council, Guido Westerwelle's brusque refusal at a press conference to comply with a provocative request by a BBC reporter to answer his question in English ("We are in Germany here."). Signs of German independence were neither entirely unprecedented before 1990, nor looked upon without suspicion: Willy Brandt's *Ostpolitik*, for example, aroused considerable concern in the West, where the name "Rapallo" could once again be heard in hushed tones in the corridors of power.[13]

As Beate Neuss rightly suggests, a process of "normalization"—however one defines this term—has indeed taken place. Military missions, at least those considered humanitarian in nature, now enjoy broad acceptance by the political elite as well as by the public, except for individuals on the more radical Left of the political spectrum. She makes another persuasive point as well: despite this decisive shift, the underlying core values of German foreign policy have remained essentially the same, namely, a belief in multilateralism and restraint. That is not to say that there are no exceptions to that rule, as the controversies over former Yugoslavia and, more recently, Libya make clear.

Erhard Crome nevertheless raises an important question: are these missions illegal? Do they run counter to the Basic Law and the Two-Plus-Four Treaty? The Constitutional Court apparently does not think so, and neither do the other signatories of the treaty that paved the path to unification. Crome claims as well that international law neither covers nor condones humanitarian interventions. There has indeed been much debate about this issue, but the UN Charter clearly permits the lawful use of force in at least two cases: as an act of individual or collective self-defense, and as a result of a mandate from the UN Security Council. Since the world stood aside during the atrocities that took place in Cambodia, Rwanda, and the Balkans—prime examples of the way in which large inter-state wars have gradually been displaced by violent internal conflicts involving state-sponsored mass murder—greater efforts have been undertaken to enforce the international Genocide Convention of 1948. This includes, for example, the R2P ("responsibility to protect") movement, which calls into question traditional claims about the inviolability of state sovereignty.[14] In short, Crome may be technically correct about the questionable legality of humanitarian interventions, but the issue is obviously still in flux.

A Lack of Predictability

The major shortcoming in German foreign policy since 1990 is not the purported illegality of its military and humanitarian missions abroad, but rather its erratic nature, at least from the perspective of outsiders. Sometimes the country "plays" (e.g., Kosovo and Afghanistan), sometimes it just pays (e.g., the first Gulf War), and sometimes it refuses to pay or play (e.g., the second Gulf War). Its decision about the Libyan no-fly zone in the winter of 2011 was especially confusing: Merkel and Westerwelle claimed that the government "completely shared" the goals of the resolution and that their abstention during the UN Security Council vote was not an indication of "neutrality." Yet, to mollify critics at home and abroad, they rapidly and concomitantly promised to participate in an upcoming AWACS mission in Afghanistan—though they were quick to emphasize that this was not intended as a form of "compensation" for the Libyan *jein*. Without passing undue judgment on the correctness of the German position, it must be said that the decision—not unlike Schröder's move during the buildup to the invasion of Iraq—smacked decidedly of populism motivated by short-term electoral considerations.

All of this makes it increasingly difficult, in short, for Germany's allies to know what to expect from the Federal Republic, especially since the criteria used to make a major foreign policy decision do not seem to be consistent. Given Germany's history over the past century, one can certainly appreciate, and applaud, its reticence when it comes to sending troops abroad. This general unwillingness to commit to hot spots where casualties might actually occur (such as southern Afghanistan) may be understandable, but it is not particularly practical; moreover, it only exacerbates the sense of uncertainty on the part of Germany's allies—who are not themselves, admittedly, entirely immune from pursuing equally erratic foreign policy agendas.

Crome and Neuss both indirectly suggest ways in which the Federal Republic might help avoid such erratic behavior in the future. As the former points out, Germany neglected to conduct a major public debate in the early 1990s about the future trajectory of its foreign policy. That was certainly understandable, because the country clearly had more pressing concerns at the time. It was self-absorbed with unification and the challenging process of "transformation" in its Eastern half. But the time is now undoubtedly ripe for such a public discussion. This was made abundantly clear by another controversy that took place less than a year before the vote on Libya. In May 2010, President Horst Köhler made the following comment during a radio interview: "In my estimation, though, we—including [German] society as a whole—are coming to the general understanding that, given this focus and corresponding dependency on exports, a country of our size needs to be aware that, where called for or in an emergency, military deployment, too, is necessary if we are to protect our interests, such as ensuring free trade routes or preventing regional instabilities that are also certain to have a negative impact on our ability to safeguard trade, jobs and income."[15]

The comment provoked an outpouring of criticism by those who accused the president of advocating an "unconstitutional" policy as well as "gunboat diplomacy." In a sign of pique, Köhler subsequently resigned his position. A more appropriate response from both sides would have been to start a difficult but necessary public debate about what constitute German "national interests." But, as Neuss suggests, there is still a great deal of reluctance to discuss this topic. The time is nevertheless ripe now for an open and sober discussion, one that eschews the habitual rhetoric and recriminations about some hidden agenda on the part of the Right to create a "Fourth Reich." After all, the Federal Republic *does* and *should* act in its own national interests, just like any other country. The weight of history has just compelled it more than others to justify its foreign policy choices by embedding them in a multilateral rhetoric. And that is something that has been true from the earliest days of the Federal Republic—from Konrad Adenauer's policy of Western integration to Willy Brandt's *Ostpolitik.*[16]

Notes

1. Roger Cohen, "France Flies, Germany Flops," *New York Times,* 16 April 2011.
2. Mark Lilla, "Ist die 'Umerziehung' zu weit gegangen? Amerikas Ideale und das deutsche Selbstverständnis," *Neue Zürcher Zeitung,* 5 April 2003.
3. See "Kritik an deutscher Libyen-Politik. 'Schwerer Fehler von historischer Dimension,'" *Spiegel-Online,* 26 March 2011; Joschka Fischer, "Deutsche Assenpolitk—eine Farce," *Süddeutsche Zeitung,* 22 March 2011; "Cohn-Bendit zu Libyen Debatte: 'Ich verstehe meine eigene Partei nicht,'" *Spiegel-Online,* 22 March 2011.
4. "NATO, lo strappo della Germania ritira la Marina dal Mediterraneo," *La Republicca,* 22 March 2011.
5. For a useful overview, see the working paper by Michael Paul, *Die Bundeswehr im Auslandseinsatz. Vom humanitären Impetus zur Aufstandsbekämpfung* (Berlin, 2010), 5–7.
6. The term "civilian power," coined by Hanns Maull, refers to a power that seeks to achieve foreign policy goals through nonmilitary forms of intervention as well as cooperation within supranational institutions. See Sebastian Harnisch and Hanns W. Maull, eds., *Germany as a Civilian Power? The Foreign Policy of the Berlin Republic* (Manchester, 2001).
7. There was a fourth factor as well, one that involved a major shakeup in the legal situation: over the course of the 1990s, the Federal Constitutional Court in Karlsruhe rendered, in a series of cases brought before it, a much broader reading of what constituted a legitimate *Verteidigungsfall.* It could be argued, however, that this last factor was more epiphenomenal in nature, i.e., an outcome brought about by the other major changes discussed in this essay.
8. For a good overview, see Peter Goebel, ed., *Von Kambodscha bis Kosovo. Auslandseinsätze der Bundeswehr* (Frankfurt, 2000).

9. See, for example, Gregor Schöllgen, *Der Auftritt. Deutschlands Rückkehr auf die Weltbühne* (Berlin, 2003), or Arnulf Baring, *Es lebe die Republik, es lebe Deutschland! Stationen demokratischer Erneuerung 1949–1999* (Stuttgart, 1999).
10. This was perhaps an important psychological reason for the great personal popularity that Daniel J. Goldhagen enjoyed among many young Germans after the appearance of his controversial book, *Hitler's Willing Executioners: Ordinary Germans and the Holocaust* (New York, 1996): by embracing his controversial claims, it enabled them to condemn—and at the same time personally distance themselves from—the crimes committed by an earlier generation of Germans. Making a similar point about the therapeutic value of such behavior three decades earlier, Hannah Arendt was unfairly dismissive of those young Germans who felt expiatory guilt for crimes they themselves had not committed. See Hannah Arendt, *Eichmann in Jerusalem: A Report on the Banality of Evil* (New York, 1994), 251. On the reaction to the Goldhagen controversy, see, for example, Geoff Eley, ed., *The Goldhagen Effect: History, Memory, Nazism—Facing the German Past* (Ann Arbor, 2000).
11. Samuel Moyn, *The Last Utopia: Human Rights in History* (Cambridge, 2010), 7.
12. For a provocative study which claims that humanitarian interventions did not begin with Jimmy Carter, Bill Clinton, or even Woodrow Wilson, but have a much older tradition going back to the nineteenth century, see Gary Bass, *Freedom's Battle: The Origins of Humanitarian Intervention* (New York, 2008).
13. In 1922, Germany and the Soviet Union signed a treaty at the Italian resort town Rapallo, whose name subsequently became "a catchword for sudden, shocking, and spectacular, as well as dangerous, agreements and forms of cooperation between Germany and Russia." See Peter Krüger, "A Rainy Day, April 16, 1922: The Rapallo Treaty and the Cloudy Perspective for German Foreign Policy," in Carole Fink, Axel Frohn, and Jürgen Heideking, eds., *Genoa, Rapallo, and European Reconstruction in 1922* (New York, 2002), 49. On the allergic reaction to Brandt's *Ostpolitik* in Washington, DC, see Robert Dallek, *Nixon and Kissinger: Partners in Power* (New York, 2007), 214–216.
14. Gareth Evans, *The Responsibility to Protect: Ending Mass Atrocity Crimes Once and For All* (Washington, 2008).
15. Interview with Horst Köhler, *Deutschlandradio Kultur*, 22 May 2010.
16. See Timothy Garton Ash, *In Europe's Name: Germany and the Divided Continent* (New York, 1993).

Contributors

Heinrich Bortfeldt is an East German historian who teaches at the University of Applied Sciences in Berlin (HTW). He specializes in contemporary German history and German-American relations. He is also the author of *Von der SED zur PDS. Wandlung zur Demokratie?* (1992) and of *Washington—Bonn—Berlin. Die USA und die deutsche Einheit* (1993). He continues to comment on the development of the post-Communists, now called The Left Party.

Erhard Crome is an East German political scientist, working as a senior research fellow on peace and security policy at the Rosa Luxemburg Foundation. He is a member of the editorial board of the journal *Berliner Debatte Initial* as well as of *Welt Trends,* a review of international politics. He has published widely on international politics, German foreign policy, and the history of the GDR. Most recently he has written on imperialism and war as well as the Western intervention in Libya.

Myra Marx Ferree is the Alice H. Cook Professor of Sociology and Director of the European Union Center of Excellence at the University of Wisconsin-Madison. She is the author of *Varieties of Feminism: German Gender Politics in Global Perspective* (Stanford, 2012), co-editor of *Global Feminism: Women's Transnational Activism, Organizations and Human Rights* (2006) and co-author of *Shaping Abortion Discourse: Democracy and the Public Sphere in Germany and the United States.* She is currently working on gender mainstreaming and the transformation of higher education in Germany and the U.S.

Ute Gerhard is professor emerita of sociology and Director of the Cornelia Goethe Center for Women's and Gender Studies at the University of Frankfurt/Main. Her many publications concern gender studies, women's movements and feminist theory, European social policy, and the history and sociology of law. She is the founder of *Feministische Studien* and co-editor of *L'Homme. Europäische Zeitschrift für Feministische Geschichtswissenschaft.* One of her recent publications is "Family Law and Gender Equality: Comparing Family Policies in Post-war Western Europe," in *Time Policies: Child Care and Primary Education in Post-war Europe* (2011).

Frank Hörnigk is an East German scholar of literature, retired from the Humboldt-Universität in Berlin. Due to his reformist views, it took until the end of the GDR for him to be appointed as Professor of German, but after unification he had to undergo several evaluations in order to be allowed to continue teaching until he became emeritus in 2008. His many publications concern German literature of the nineteenth and twentieth centuries. Most importantly, he has edited the works of the dramatist Heiner Müller (Suhrkamp Verlag) and of the writer Arnold Zweig (Aufbau Verlag).

Konrad H. Jarausch is Lurcy Professor of European Civilization at the University of North Carolina in Chapel Hill and Senior Fellow of the Zentrum für Zeithistorische Forschung in Potsdam. He has written or edited about forty books on topics such as the First and Second World Wars, students and professionals, GDR history, postwar history, and debates about historical methods and historiography. Some of his recent titles include *Reluctant Accomplice* (2011), "Contemporary History as Transatlantic Project. The German Problem 1960–2010," supplement 24 of *Historical Social Research,* and volume 3 of the *Geschichte der Humboldt Universität 1945–2000* (2012). He is currently writing a history of twentieth-century Europe from the perspective of "Taming Modernity?"

Rainer Land is an East German specialist in political economy, working at the Thünen Institut, which he cofounded in 2001. During the last years of the GDR he was one of the reform theorists at the Humboldt Universität. Subsequently he served as editor of the journal *Berliner Debatte Initial.* Currently he is interested in adapting Marxist theories to the problems caused by globalization, and his research has focused on the industrial implications of German unification. Since 2012 he has been directing a service company for innovative projects in renewable energy for rural areas.

Ingrid Miethe is professor of general education at the University of Gießen. She was born in East Germany but due to her dissident activity in the independent peace movement and the New Forum, she could only start her studies after the collapse of the GDR. She has written, for instance, on *Frauen in der DDR Opposition. Lebens- und kollektivgeschichtliche*

Verläufe in einer Frauenfriedensgruppe (1999). Her chief areas of research are social movements, gender and diversity, and questions of inequality in the educational system. She is also interested in the history of women's movements and the history of education in the German Democratic Republic.

Gero Neugebauer, is a retired political scientist of the Free University of Berlin. He has written numerous articles on GDR politics and the German party system and has published several books, among them *Politische Milieus in Deutschland* (2007). After German unification, his research interests have shifted to the German political parties, elections, and the history of German unification. Often cited in the media, he has been concerned with the problem of interpreting the impact of social change on the relationship between politics and society.

Beate Neuss is professor for international relations at the University of Technology Chemnitz (Saxony). She has written widely on issues of German foreign policy, transatlantic relations, and the development of the European Union. Her best-known book is *Geburtshelfer Europas? Die Rolle der Vereinigten Staaten im europäischen Integrationsprozess 1945–1958* (2000). She chaired the Advisory Board of the Federal Agency for Civic Education and has served as the Deputy Director of the Konrad Adenauer Foundation since 2001.

Andrew I. Port is associate professor of history at Wayne State University in Detroit. His research focuses on modern Germany and Europe, communism and state socialism, labor history, social protest, popular resistance under autocratic regimes, and comparative genocide. His acclaimed book, *Conflict and Stability in the German Democratic Republic,* has also appeared in German translation. His current research project looks at German reactions to genocide in other parts of the world since 1945.

Klaus R. Scherpe is professor of German literature and culture/media studies at the Humboldt University in Berlin. He has commented profusely on the social and political dimensions of literary developments from the Enlightenment to the present and been involved in the debates about East German writers. Some of his books include *Die rekonstruierte Moderne. Studien zur deutschen Literatur nach 1945* (1992) and *How German is it, and how American? Ironic replays in literature* (2005). He co-edited *Mit Deutschland um die Welt. Eine Kulturgeschichte des Fremden in der Kolonialzeit* (2004). He has also been the organizer of the Berlin Mosse-Lectures since 1997.

Wolfgang Seibel is professor of politics and public administration at the Universität Konstanz and adjunct professor at the Hertie School for Governance in Berlin. His research interests combine historical and contemporary issues such as the Holocaust in Western Europe, the development of NGOs, and the transformation of East German administration. His many books include *Theorieentwicklung in der Politikwissenschaft, eine Zwischenbilanz.* (1997), and *Verwaltete Illusionen. Die Privatisierung der DDR-Wirtschaft durch die Treuhandanstalt und ihre Nachfolger 1990-2000* (2005). Most recently he has published a monograph on the final solution in France (2010).

Frank Trommler is professor emeritus of German and Comparative Literature at the University of Pennsylvania. From 1995 to 2003 he was Director of the Humanities Program of the American Institute of Contemporary Studies in Washington, D.C. He wrote some of the earliest studies of East German literature in the 1970s. Among his books are *Sozialistische Literatur in Deutschland* (1976), *Die Kultur der Weimarer Republik* (1978), and *America and the Germans* (1985). He has commented widely on cultural politics in Germany, the impact of technology on culture, German-American cultural relations, and German Studies in the United States.

Helga A. Welsh is professor of political science at Wake Forest University. Her publications have focused on the history and politics of East Germany, German unification, transitional justice, and democratization processes in Central and Eastern Europe. She is the author of *Revolutionärer Wandel auf Befehl* (Munich 1989) and co-editor of *German Unification. Process and Outcomes* (Lanham 1994) and volumes IX and X of the web-based *German History in Documents and Images.* She is currently working on a study of the reform of German higher education.

Jonathan R. Zatlin is associate professor of history at Boston University. He has published on GDR topics such as the automobile industry, socialist consumer policy, the gendered distribution of work and the Stasi, popular discontent, racism in East Germany, and German unification. He is the author of *The Currency of Socialism: Money and Political Culture in East Germany* (2007) and co-editor of *Selling Modernity: German Advertising in the Twentieth Century* (2007). He is currently writing a short history of the GDR and a monograph on *Jews and Money, 1870–1990.*

Selected Bibliography

Aleksander, Karin. *Frauen und Geschlechterverhältnisse in der DDR und in den neuen Bundesländern. Bibliographie von DDR- und BRD-Publikationen ab 1989* (Berlin, 2005).

Anderson, Jeffrey J. and Eric Langenbacher, eds. *From the Bonn to the Berlin Republic: Germany at the Twentieth Anniversary of Unification* (New York, 2010).

Bahrman, Hannes and Christoph Links, eds. *Am Ziel vorbei. Die deutsche Einheit—eine Zwischenbilanz* (Berlin, 2005).

Beattie, Andrew. *Playing Politics with History: The Bundestag Inquiries into East Germany* (New York, 2008).

Berth, Hendrik and Elmar Brähler. *Zehn Jahre Deutsche Einheit. Eine Bibliographie* (Berlin, 2000).

Brockmann, Stephen. *Literature and German Unification* (Cambridge, 1999).

Bütow, Birgit and Heidi Stecker, eds. *EigenArtige Ostfrauen. Frauenemanzipation in der DDR und den neuen Bundesländern* (Bielefeld, 1994).

Caldwell Peter C. and Robert R. Shandley, eds. *German Unification: Expectations and Outcomes* (New York, 2011).

Cambi, Fabrizio and Alessandro Fambrini, eds. *Zehn Jahre nachher. Poetische Identität und Geschichte in der deutschen Literatur nach der Vereinigung* (Trento, 2002).

Dahn, Daniela. *Westwärts und nicht vergessen. Vom Unbehagen in der Einheit* (Berlin, 1996).

Dalgaard-Nielsen, Anja. *Germany, Pacifism, and Peace Enforcement* (Manchester, 2006).

Dennis, Mike and Eva Kolinsky, eds. *United and Divided: Germany Since 1990* (New York, 2004).

Diewald, Martin, Anne Goedicke, and Karl Ulrich Mayer, eds. *After the Fall of the Wall: Life Courses in the Transformation of East Germany* (Stanford, 2006).

Forschungsverbund Sozioökonomische Berichterstattung, ed. *Berichterstattung zur sozioökonomischen Entwicklung in Deutschland. Teilhabe im Umbruch. Zweiter Bericht* (Wiesbaden 2012).

Goebel, Peter, ed. *Von Kambodscha bis Kosovo. Auslandseinsätze der Bundeswehr* (Frankfurt, 2000).

Görtemaker, Manfred. *Die Berliner Republik. Wiedervereinigung und Neuorientierung* (Berlin, 2009).

Grosser, Dieter. *Das Wagnis der Währungs-, Wirtschafts- und Sozialunion. Politische Zwänge im Konflikt mit ökonomischen Regeln* (Stuttgart, 1998).

Guenther, Katja. *Places of Resistance: Feminism After Socialism in Eastern Germany* (Palo Alto, 2010).

Hamisch, Sebastian and Hanns Maull, eds. *Germany as a Civilian Power? The Foreign Policy of the Berlin Republic* (Manchester, 2001).

Hampele-Ulrich, Anne. *Der Unabhängige Frauenverband. Ein frauenpolitisches Experiment im deutschen Vereinigungsprozess* (Berlin, 2000).

Helbig, Holger, ed. *Weiterschreiben. Zur DDR-Literatur nach dem Ende der DDR* (Berlin, 2007).

Henke, Klaus-Dietmar, ed. *Die Mauer: Errichtung, Überwindung, Erinnerung* (Munich, 2011).

Herminghouse, Patricia and Katharina Gerstenberger, eds. *German Literature in a New Century: Trends, Traditions, Transformations* (New York, 2008).

Hufnagel, Rainer and Titus Simon, eds. *Problemfall Deutsche Einheit. Interdisziplinäre Betrachtungen zu gesamtdeutschen Fragen* (Wiesbaden, 2004).

Jarausch, Konrad H. *The Rush to German Unity* (New York, 1994).

Jarausch, Konrad H. and Volker Gransow, eds. *Uniting Germany: Documents and Debates, 1944–1993* (Providence, 1994).

Katzenstein, Peter, ed. *Tamed Power: Germany in Europe* (Ithaca, NY, 1997).

Kocka, Jürgen. *Die Vereinigungskrise. Zur Geschichte der Gegenwart* (Göttingen, 1995).

Kollmorgen, Raj, Frank Thomas Koch, and Hans-Liudger Dienel, eds. *Diskurse der deutschen Einheit. Kritik und Alternativen* (Wiesbaden, 2011).

Kowalczuk, Ilko-Sascha. *Endspiel. Die Revolution von 1989 in der DDR* (Munich, 2009).

Krause, Peter and Ilona Ostner, eds. *Leben in Ost- und Westdeutschland. Eine sozialwissenschaftliche Bilanz der deutschen Einheit 1990–2010* (Frankfurt, 2010).

Lange, Thomas and J.R. Shackleton. *The Political Economy of German Unification* (Providence, 1998).

Merkl, Wolfgang. *Systemtransformation. Eine Einführung in die Theorie und Empirie der Transformationsforschung*, 2nd ed. (Wiesbaden, 2010).

Miethe, Ingrid. *Frauen in der DDR-Opposition: Lebens- und kollektivgeschichtliche Verläufe in einer Frauenfriedensgruppe* (Opladen, 1999).

Neugebauer, Gero and Richard Stöss. *Die PDS. Geschichte, Organisation, Wähler, Konkurrenten* (Opladen, 1996).

Otte, Max. *A Rising Middle Power? German Foreign Policy in Transformation, 1989–1999* (New York, 2000).

Paqué, Karl-Heinz. *Die Bilanz—eine wirtschaftliche Analyse der deutschen Einheit* (Munich, 2009).

Plato, Alexander von. *Die Vereinigung Deutschlands—ein weltpolitisches Machtspiel. Bush, Kohl Gorbatschow und die geheimen Moskauer Protokolle* (Berlin, 2002).

Paul, Michael. *Die Bundeswehr im Auslandseinsatz. Vom humanitären Impetus zur Aufstandsbekämpfung* (Berlin, 2010).

Richter, Michael. *Die friedliche Revolution. Aufbruch zur Demokratie in Sachsen 1989–1990*, 2 vols. (Göttingen, 2009).

Rödder, Andreas. *Deutschland, einig Vaterland. Die Geschichte der Wiedervereinigung* (Munich, 2009).
Sabrow Martin and Irmgard Zündorf, eds. *Wohin treibt die DDR Erinnerung? Der Streit um eine Debatte* (Göttingen, 2007).
Scherpe, Klaus R. *Stadt Krieg Fremde. Literatur und Kultur nach den Katastrophen* (Tübingen, 2002).
Schluchter, Wolfgang and Peter E. Quint, eds. *Der Vereinigungsschock. Vergleichende Betrachtungen zehn Jahre danach* (Weilerwist, 2001).
Schroeder, Klaus. *Die veränderte Republik. Deutschland nach der Wiedervereinigung* (Munich, 2006).
Schröder, Richard. *Die wichtigsten Irrtümer über die deutsche Einheit* (Freiburg, 2007).
Schwarz, Hans-Peter. *Zentralmacht Europas. Deutschlands Rückkehr auf die Weltbühne* (Berlin, 1994).
Seibel, Wolfgang. *Verwaltete Illusionen. Die Privatisierung der DDR-Wirtschaft durch die Treuhandanstalt und ihre Nachfolger 1990–2000* (Frankfurt, 2005).
Silberman, Marc, ed. *What Remains? East German Culture and the Postwar Public* (Washington, DC, 1997).
Speirs, Ronald and John Breuilly, eds. *Germany's Two Unifications: Anticipations, Experiences, Responses* (New York, 2005).
Statistische Ämter der Länder, eds. *Von der Bevölkerung bis Wahlen—20 Jahre Deutsche Einheit in der Statistik* (Bad Ems, 2010).
Sutherland, Claire. *Soldered States: Nation-Building in Germany and Vietnam* (Manchester, 2010).
Timm, Angelika, ed. *20 Jahre deutsche Einheit. Ein Staat—zwei Identitäten?* (Tel Aviv, 2011).
Tuchscherer, Heike. *20 Jahre Vereinigtes Deutschland. Eine 'neue' oder 'erweiterte Bundesrepublik'?* (Baden-Baden, 2010).
Weidenfeld, Werner and Karl-Rudolf Korte, eds. *Handbuch zur deutschen Einheit, 1949-1989-1999* (Frankfurt, 1999).
Williams, John Alexander, ed. *Berlin Since the Wall's End: Shaping Society and Memory in the German Metropolis Since 1989* (Newcastle, 2008).
Winkler, Gunnar. *20 Jahre friedliche Revolution 1989 bis 2009. Die Sicht der Bürger der neuen Bundesländer. Auf Grundlage der empirischen Erhebungen* (Berlin, 2009).
Wirsching, Andreas. *Preis der Freiheit. Geschichte Europas in unserer Zeit* (Munich, 2011).
Wittek, Bernd. *Der Literaturstreit im sich vereinigenden Deutschland. Eine Analyse des Streits um Christa Wolf und die deutsch-deutsche Gegenwartsliteratur in Zeitungen und Zeitschriften von Juni 1990 bis Ende 1992* (Marburg, 1997).
Yoder, Jennifer A. *From East Germans to Germans? The New Postcommunist Elites* (Durham, 1999).
Young, Brigitte. *Triumph of the Fatherland: German Unification and the Marginalization of Women* (Ann Arbor, 1999).
Zatlin, Jonathan R. *The Currency of Socialism: Money and Political Culture in East Germany* (Cambridge, 2007).

Index

Y

Z